Social Trends

No. 35

2005 edition

Editors: Carol Summerfield

Baljit Gill

Office for National Statistics

palgrave
macmillan

First published 2005 by
PALGRAVE MACMILLAN
Houndmills, Basingstoke, Hampshire RG21 6XS and
175 Fifth Avenue, New York, NY 10010
Companies and representatives throughout the world.

PALGRAVE MACMILLAN is the global academic imprint of the Palgrave Macmillan division of St. Martin's Press, LLC and of Palgrave Macmillan Ltd. Macmillan® is a registered trademark in the United States, United Kingdom and other countries. Palgrave is a registered trademark in the European Union and other countries.

ISBN 1-4039-9070-0
ISSN 0306-7742

This book is printed on paper suitable for recycling and made from fully managed and sustained forest sources.

A catalogue record for this book is available from the British Library.

10 9 8 7 6 5 4 3 2 1
14 13 12 11 10 09 08 07 06 05

Printed and bound in Great Britain by Ashford Colour Press Ltd, Gosport.

A National Statistics publication

National Statistics are produced to high professional standards as set out in the National Statistics Code of Practice. They are produced free from political influence.

About the Office for National Statistics

The Office for National Statistics (ONS) is the government agency responsible for compiling, analysing and disseminating economic, social and demographic statistics about the United Kingdom. It also administers the statutory registration of births, marriages and deaths in England and Wales.

The Director of ONS is also the National Statistician and the Registrar General for England and Wales.

For enquiries about this publication, contact The Editor.
Tel: 020 7533 5778
E-mail: social.trends@ons.gov.uk

For general enquiries, contact the National Statistics Customer Contact Centre.
Tel: **0845 601 3034** (minicom: 01633 812399)
E-mail: info@statistics.gov.uk
Fax: 01633 652747
Post: Room D115, Government Buildings, Cardiff Road, Newport NP10 8XG

You can also find National Statistics on the Internet at
www.statistics.gov.uk

Contents

11: Environment

12: Transport

13: Lifestyles and social participation

List of figures and tables

Numbers in brackets refer to similar items appearing in *Social Trends 34.*

Overview: 35 years of social change

1: Population

2: Households and families

3: Education and training

4: Labour market

5: Income and wealth

6: Expenditure

7: Health

8: Social protection

9: Crime and justice

11: Environment

12: Transport

13: Lifestyles and social participation

List of contributors

Authors:	Lola Akinrodoye
	Lisa Almqvist
	Carl Bird
	Siân Bradford
	Simon Burtenshaw
	Jenny Church
	Craig Corbet
	Alessio Fiacco
	Lucy Fletcher
	Steve Howell
	Kylie Lovell
	Chris Randall
	Matthew Richardson
	Leicha Rickards
Production manager:	Mario Alemanno
Production team:	Sharon Adhikari
	Elizabeth Attree
	John Chrzczonowicz
	Joseph Goldstein
	Simon Huxstep
	Usuf Islam
	Kwabena Owusu-Agyemang
	Shiva Satkunam
	Steve Whyman

Acknowledgements

The Editors would like to thank all their colleagues in contributing Departments and other organisations for their generous support and helpful comments, without whom this edition of *Social Trends* would not be possible. Our thanks also go to the following for their help in the production process:

Reviewers:	Penny Babb
	Karin Bosveld
	Ben Bradford
	Hayley Butcher
	David Gardener
	Caroline Hall
	David Harper
	Caroline Lakin
	Nina Mill
	Camellia Raha
	Linda Zealey
Design and artwork:	Shain Bali
	Tony Castro
	Andy Leach
	James Twist
	Desk Top Publications
Publishing management:	Sini Dominy
	Paul Hyatt
Maps:	Pam Blunt
	Jeremy Brocklehurst
	Alistair Dent
	ONS Geography
Data:	SARD Core Table Unit

Introduction

This is the 35th edition of *Social Trends* – one of the flagship publications from the Office for National Statistics (ONS). It draws together statistics from a wide range of government departments and other organisations to paint a broad picture of our society today, and how it has been changing. In this edition we have included an overview chapter that highlights some of the major social changes over the 35 years since *Social Trends* was first published. One of *Social Trends'* most important sources of information is the General Household Survey (GHS). From this year, *Social Trends* has become the main means of reporting on the GHS data although GHS datasets will continue to be published via the National Statistics website as soon as they are available.

Social Trends is aimed at a wide audience: policy makers in the public and private sectors; service providers; people in local government; journalists and other commentators; academics and students; schools; and the general public.

The editorial team welcomes views on how *Social Trends* could be improved. Please write to the Editors at the address shown below with your comments or suggestions.

New material and sources

To preserve topicality, over half of the 296 tables and figures in the 13 chapters of *Social Trends 35* are new compared with the previous edition, and draw on the most up-to-date available data.

In all chapters the source of the data is given below each table and figure, and where this is a survey the name of the survey is also included. A list of contact telephone numbers, including the contact number for each chapter author and a list of useful website addresses, can be found on pages 183 to 190. A list of further reading is also given, beginning on page 191. Regional and other sub-national breakdowns of much of the information in *Social Trends* can be found in the ONS publication *Regional Trends*.

Definitions and terms

Symbols and conventions used in this publication can be found on page 199 and the Appendix gives definitions and general background information, particularly on administrative and legal structures and frameworks. Anyone seeking to understand the tables and figures in detail will find it helpful to read the corresponding entries in the Appendix, as well as the footnotes to the tables and figures. An index to this edition starts on page 216.

Availability on electronic media

Social Trends 35 is available electronically via the National Statistics website, www.statistics.gov.uk/socialtrends35. While *Social Trends* brings a range of statistics together in one place, it is only updated once a year. This year, for some of the key topics, there are links from the web version of *Social Trends* to topic-based summaries containing a key chart and short interpretative commentary. These will be updated as new data become available. By adding to these summaries over time, a continually updated version of the key topics in *Social Trends* will become available. A PDF file can also be found on the website, containing links to Excel spreadsheets giving the data for all tables, figures and maps.

Contact

Carol Summerfield

Baljit Gill

Social Analysis and Reporting Division
Office for National Statistics
Room: B5/04
1 Drummond Gate
London
SW1V 2QQ

Email: social.trends@ons.gov.uk

35 years of social change

By Len Cook and Jean Martin

Statistical reporting is at the heart of the work of the Office for National Statistics (ONS). Our role is to provide impartial and high quality statistical analyses and commentary on the state of the nation. We aim to provide statistical evidence to assist decision making and to ensure that citizens have the statistical information that they need to be able to make informed judgements about government, society and the economy. In this way ONS contributes to democratic debate and accountability.

Our reports aim to provide coherent and accessible pictures of UK society to help government, researchers and citizens to understand society and how it is changing. As one of our longest running and most prestigious publications, *Social Trends* plays a major part in contributing to the achievement of these aims. Its strength lies in bringing together statistics across themes and from different sources into a single annual report, with commentary that draws out the key points.

Social Trends has been the flagship social report of the UK statistical system since it was first published on 17 December 1970. It was produced in response to the growing need for economic progress to be measured, at least in part, in terms of social benefits. At the time it represented a major change in statistical publishing, banishing detailed footnotes to the back pages and presenting information about key changes taking place in society in simple tables and charts, accompanied by descriptive commentary. The first edition attracted enormous publicity and was on the list of Christmas reading recommended by the Sunday papers. The *Financial Times* described it as 'illuminating' and found that 'information is presented and processed … in such a way as to produce a picture that has not been regularly available before'.

Although the aim of *Social Trends* has changed little over time, the content has been developed. New data continually become available and areas of interest change, so each edition is looked at afresh. The first edition contained many gaps in information, particularly on social conditions such as environment, leisure and welfare services. This was because such information either had not been brought systematically together or the statistics had not been collected.

Overview

In 1970 the major government survey was the Family Expenditure Survey. It had been carried out on a continuous basis since 1957, and focused on expenditure and income information. The increasing interest in measuring the way policies affect individuals and families meant that it was at risk of being overloaded. So in October 1970 a new survey of around 15,000 households a year, the General Household Survey (GHS), was started. As the then Director of the Central Statistical Office (the precursor of ONS), Sir Claus Moser, said in his article on developments in social statistics in the first edition of *Social Trends*: 'This survey will provide a major new source of data on the social conditions of this country '.

Since then a range of other continuous and ad hoc surveys have been carried out and included within the pages of *Social Trends*. Nevertheless, the GHS has become one of its most important sources of information. So, from this year, while the GHS datasets continue to be published as soon as they are available, *Social Trends* has become the main means of reporting on the GHS data.

In this overview we highlight some of the main changes over the 35 years since *Social Trends* and the GHS first started. Later chapters provide more detail and cover a wider range of topic areas.

Economic context

Gross Domestic Product (GDP) is a commonly used measure of overall economic activity and the amount of wealth created by economic processes. By the end of the 19th century GDP in the United Kingdom (adjusted for inflation) rose to more than four times the level it was at the beginning of the century. This was well in excess of the growth rate in the previous three centuries. Between 1971 and 2004 the volume measure of GDP doubled (Figure A.1). Within this overall growth there were three periods of contraction of the economy. GDP fell in real terms in the mid-1970s, at the time of the OPEC oil crisis. Other falls occurred in the early 1980s and early 1990s. GDP grew at about 3 per cent in real terms in 2004 compared with annual average swings in the 1970s ranging from 7.1 per cent in 1973 to -1.4 per cent in 1974. UK GDP per head of population is well above the EU average; in 2002 the United Kingdom ranked sixth out of the 25 member states.

Household disposable income represents the amount that people in private households have available in their pockets to spend or save. Real household disposable income per head increased at a faster rate than GDP per head between 1971 and 2003: disposable income increased by one and a third over the period while GDP doubled (see Figure 5.1 in the Income and Wealth chapter).

Figure **A.1**

Gross domestic product in real terms[1]

United Kingdom
£ billion

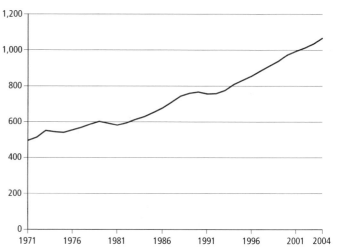

1 Chain linked volume measure of GDP.

Source: Office for National Statistics

The huge range of individual circumstances and the effect of things that influence them lead to the need to understand the social impact of economic change. Inequality remains a key feature of both the income and wealth distributions. Figure 5.13 in the Income and Wealth chapter illustrates how the distribution of real household disposable income has altered since 1971. During the early 1970s there was little change in the distribution, followed by a slight reduction in inequality between 1973 and 1979. However, in the 1980s there was a large increase in inequality that far outweighed the 1970s' decrease. This sharp increase ended in 1990 and the distribution was then stable in the early part of the decade. Since the mid-1990s incomes have grown at similar rates throughout the distribution. Some of the possible explanations for these changes are given on page 72 of Chapter 5.

Some social groups are more likely than others to be living on low incomes. The people most likely to live in families with low incomes include those in lone-parent families, the unemployed, children – particularly those in workless households, pensioners, and people from minority ethnic groups, particularly those of Pakistani or Bangladeshi origin. For some people this reflects their stage in the life cycle, for some their newness to the wealth creation processes of the United Kingdom, and for others it reflects their actual and perceived employability or living in places where work is difficult to find. For many, they are simply doing other things such as being educated, managing households, and caring for children, the aged or others who need care.

Wealth, which is defined on page 79, is more unevenly distributed than income though the wealth distribution became more equal over the 20th century. In 1911, it is estimated that the wealthiest 1 per cent of the population held around 70 per cent of UK wealth. This fell to 42 per cent in 1960. Using different methodology, in 2002 the wealthiest 1 per cent of the population held 23 per cent of marketable wealth (see Table 5.25). This was much the same proportion as in the late 1970s, though the proportion fell during the late 1970s/early 1980s to 18 per cent. Housing wealth is more evenly distributed than other forms of wealth such as savings and investments.

Demographic context

The United Kingdom has an expanding population. The number of births fell generally over the 20th century, but with significant fluctuations, mainly due to the effects of the two world wars when low numbers of births during the wars were followed by sharp increases immediately after (see Figure 1.8). There was a further peak in the mid-1960s due in part to the mid-1940s cohort reaching childbearing ages. These peaks in births are reflected in the peaks in the numbers of people in their late 30s and mid 50s in Figure A.2.

Figure **A.2**

Population: by sex and age, 2003

United Kingdom
Thousands

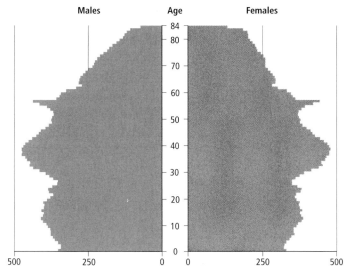

Source: Office for National Statistics

Since 1971 the population has increased by 3.6 million people, to 59.6 million in 2003. Growth has been faster in more recent years, with an annual growth rate of 0.3 per cent between 1991 and 2003. Long-term projections suggest that the population will continue to increase until around 2050, and will then start to fall. One reason for the increase is that there have

been more births than deaths, with the exception of the mid-1970s. The death rates for both males and females were lower in 2003 than 1971 (see Table 1.9). Meanwhile the birth rate has changed far less, with a small boom in births in the late 1980s and early 1990s, followed by a fall, and then remaining relatively stable from 2000.

This natural increase was the main driver of population growth until the mid-1990s. Thereafter, there has still been natural increase but net international migration into the United Kingdom has been an increasingly important factor (see Table 1.7), accounting for two thirds of population change since 1998. The United Kingdom is now a net importer rather than a net exporter of people. However, the proportion of the UK population born overseas is lower (8 per cent) than that of many other countries such as the United States (12 per cent), New Zealand and Canada (both 19 per cent) and Australia (22 per cent). Not all immigrants settle permanently in this country: almost half of all immigrants to the United Kingdom emigrate within five years of arrival (see Figure 1.14), while others leave after longer periods of time.

Waves of immigration from different parts of the world have helped shape the ethnic mix of the country. In the 1950s and 1960s many immigrants came from the Caribbean, followed in the late 1960s and early 1970s by immigrants from India, Pakistan and Bangladesh and in the past ten years, from Africa. Nevertheless, just over half (53 per cent) of the UK overseas born population is White, three fifths of whom were born elsewhere in Europe.

Marriage between members of different ethnic groups remains rare – only 2 per cent of all marriages – but varies considerably among different ethnic groups. Among Black Caribbeans, one quarter were married outside the Black ethnic group in 2001, whereas 6 per cent of married Indians, and 2 per cent of married Bangladeshis, had a non-Asian spouse. As the numbers of mixed-ethnicity marriages have increased so too have the numbers of children of mixed ethnicity, most of whom were born in the United Kingdom. In 2001, half of all people of mixed ethnicity were aged under 16 while only 3 per cent were aged 65 or over.

In the United Kingdom as a whole, the proportion of the population from a non-White ethnic minority is 8 per cent. However, ethnic diversity and minority ethnic communities are most common in London: 29 per cent of the population of London is from a minority ethnic group. This figure is much higher among young people – 41 per cent of those aged under 15.

The United Kingdom has an ageing population. The average (median) age was 38.4 years in 2003, compared with

34.1 years in 1971. This is primarily a result of fewer babies being born and people living longer, although migration can have a moderating effect since immigrants tend to be younger than the population as a whole and many leave again before reaching old age. The proportion of the UK population aged 65 and over has increased by nearly one quarter since 1971, to 16 per cent in 2003 (see Table 1.2).

While the population in Great Britain grew by 6 per cent between 1971 and 2003, the number of households increased much faster, by 32 per cent, due to the trend towards smaller household sizes. Family sizes have decreased but also more people live alone. In 1971, 18 per cent of households contained only one person but by 1991 this had risen to 27 per cent, with a small further rise to 29 per cent in 2004 (see Table 2.2). The rise has been most marked for people living alone who are under state pension age, from 6 per cent of all households in 1971 to 14 per cent in 2004. In addition, increasing rates of divorce and separation have led to more men in particular living alone. There has also been an increase in young adults living with their parents, but this trend has levelled off in recent years (see Table 2.7).

There has been a decrease in families of couples with dependent children and an increase in lone-parent families in Great Britain. The proportion of households comprising a lone parent and dependent children doubled from 3 to 7 per cent between 1971 and 2004. Nine out of ten lone-parent families are headed by the mother. Looking at the figures from the perspective of children, the proportion of dependent children living in lone-parent families more than tripled between 1972 and 2004 – to 24 per cent – while the proportion of children living in families headed by a couple decreased from 92 per cent to 77 per cent (see Table 2.4).

Marriage and childbearing have become less strongly associated over the last 35 years, with 41 per cent of births in the United Kingdom occurring outside marriage in 2003. However, much of the increase in births outside marriage has been to cohabiting couples rather than to single mothers.

Fertility rates fell rapidly throughout the latter part of the 1960s and the 1970s, stabilising in the 1980s. The 1990s saw fertility rates drift downwards, although fertility rates increased in 2003. Women have started childbearing at increasingly older ages – the fertility rates for women aged 30 to 34 overtook those for women aged 20 to 24 in 1992, and in 2003 were almost level with those for women aged 25 to 29 (see Table 2.14). The average age at which women have their first birth has increased, and women are having fewer children. In addition, more women are remaining childless. Around one in five women in England and Wales

currently reaching the end of their fertile life are childless, compared with one in ten women born in the mid-1940s.

Changing world of work

For the population as a whole, as life expectancy has increased, there has been a decrease in the proportion of life spent in paid work. Young people spend longer in education than their parents' generation and so are generally older when they start work. Increasing longevity means that more of life is spent in retirement. In addition, increasing numbers of people leave their main job before reaching state pension age (see Table 4.27), although some people do paid work during the early years of retirement.

The UK employment rate – the proportion of working-age people who are in employment – has not changed very much over the past 30 years or so, ranging from 68 to 76 per cent. But this overall picture conceals large and very different changes for men and women. The employment rate for men fell from 92 per cent in 1971 to 79 per cent in 2004 – though it reached a low of 75 per cent in 1993 – while the rate for women rose from 56 per cent to 70 per cent (Figure A.3). Thus the gap between men's and women's employment rates has decreased by a factor of nearly four, from 35 to 9 percentage points.

Figure **A.3**

Employment rates:[1] by sex

United Kingdom
Percentages

1 At spring each year. Males aged 16 to 64, females aged 16 to 59. The percentage of the population that is in employment. Data are seasonally adjusted and have been adjusted in line with population estimates published in autumn 2004. See Appendix, Part 4: LFS reweighting, and Historical LFS-consistent time series.

Source: Labour Force Survey, Office for National Statistics

The increase in women's economic activity since the 1970s has mainly been associated with an increase in part-time working, although there has been a smaller rise in full-time working as well. Women are still far more likely than men to work part time. This reflects their greater role in childcare and, as a consequence, their lower earnings.

It has long been the case that the majority of women either stop work, or switch to part-time work, when they have children, returning to work or moving from part-time to full-time work as their children get older. However, the effect of children on women's work has lessened since the 1970s. When the youngest child is still under 11, mothers are more likely to work part than full time. Once the youngest is of secondary school age, the rates for full- and part-time working are similar, and full-time work becomes the dominant pattern once all children are 16 or over. Women with pre-school children are the least likely to be working, although there has been an increase in both full- and part-time working among these women.

This general pattern differs somewhat between women who are married or cohabiting and those without partners. Lone mothers are less likely to be working than those with partners, whatever age their children (see Table 4.3).

Unemployment has fluctuated over the years since the early 1970s, reflecting changes in the economic cycle, and in 2004 was lower than at any time since the late 1970s. Unemployment was at its highest during much of the 1980s, peaking in 1984, and then again in 1993 (see Figure 4.17); in both periods men were more likely to be unemployed than women as male-dominated industries were more affected by recession.

There have also been changes in the sorts of jobs people do. The decline of manufacturing has led to fewer people – men in particular – working in skilled manual occupations. In 2004, only 18 per cent of men worked in manufacturing industries compared with 28 per cent in 1984 (see Table 4.12). On the other hand, the rise of the service sector has provided many opportunities for part-time work, particularly for women.

Changing lifestyles

Over the last 35 years, a growing population and a move towards smaller households has contributed to a higher demand for housing. The damage caused to the nation's housing stock during the Second World War made the provision of new housing a post-war priority. Housebuilding peaked in 1968 when 426,000 dwellings were completed in the United Kingdom, 47 per cent by the social sector – primarily local authorities (see Figure 10.3). In 2003/04 there were 190,000 completions, of which 10 per cent were by the social sector, predominantly housing associations.

The post-war housebuilding boom led to a shift in UK tenure patterns – private renting fell and renting from local authorities and owner-occupation increased. The rise in owner-occupation has continued: the number of owner-occupied dwellings in the United Kingdom increased by 88 per cent from 9.6 million in 1971 to 18.1 million in 2003. On the other hand, the number of social sector dwellings fell by 13 per cent, to 5.1 million in 2003. The number of privately rented dwellings fell to a low point in 1989, then recovered slightly following deregulation of new lettings and the recession in the owner-occupied market. In 2003 there were more than twice as many owner-occupied dwellings as rented dwellings (see Figure 10.5).

People in Great Britain now travel further than 35 years ago and the increase in car usage is a key feature of this change. The switch from public to private transport began in the 1950s, with cars, vans and taxis accounting for over half of passenger kilometres for the first time in 1961 (see Table 12.1). In 2003, 85 per cent of all passenger kilometres were by car. However, the rapid rates of growth in car travel, particularly in the 1960s and 1980s, were replaced by more gradual growth from 1989. The total distance travelled by car rose by nearly 5 per cent a year in the early 1980s, compared with an annual average increase of 1 per cent between 1991 and 2003.

The number of licensed cars on Britain's roads has increased steadily, more than doubling between 1971 and 2003 (see Table 12.9). The proportion of households with regular use of a car also increased. In 1971, 52 per cent of households had a car; by 2002 this had risen to 74 per cent (see Figure 12.10). The proportion of households with only one car has been stable at around 45 per cent, while the proportion with two or more almost quadrupled over the period, from 8 to 29 per cent. Increased car ownership is one of the factors behind the declining proportion of children who walk to school, down from 61 per cent in 1992/94 to 53 per cent in 2003 for 5 to 10 year olds.

The increase in air travel is another key transport trend over the last 35 years. Almost nine in ten of the 177 million terminal passengers at UK civil airports in 2003 were travelling internationally. The overall number of passengers at UK airports in 2003 was almost six times the number in 1971, though passenger numbers fell in the recession years of 1974, 1981, and 1991 (the year of the Gulf War), before continuing upward. There was also a marked flattening of the trend in 2001 – the year of the foot and mouth disease epidemic and September 11. Numbers resumed their steep rise in 2002 and 2003 and demand is projected to continue growing well into this century.

Rapid technological change has also transformed life and contributed to the explosion in global communications.

In 1971 children were still using slide rules at school in the United Kingdom. Nowadays computers are commonplace in UK homes, as well as in schools and the workplace. Access to the Internet means that people can communicate with those on the other side of the world at the touch of a button.

During the 1970s the proportion of households with a telephone doubled – from 35 per cent in 1970 to 72 per cent in 1980 (Table A.4). The first call in the world on a portable cell phone was made in 1973, though mobile phone ownership in the United Kingdom only took off in the 1990s. By 2002/03, 94 per cent of households had a telephone and 70 per cent had a mobile phone.

Table A.4

Households with selected durable goods[1]

United Kingdom				Percentages
	Telephone	Mobile phone	Home computer	Internet access
1970	35	..	..	..
1975	52	..	..	..
1980	72	..	..	..
1985	81	..	13	..
1990	87	..	17	..
1996/97	93	16	27	..
1998/99	95	27	33	10
2000/01	93	47	44	32
2002/03	94	70	55	45

1 Data from 1998/99 are weighted.

Source: Family Expenditure Survey and Expenditure and Food Survey, Office for National Statistics

The first personal computer was released commercially towards the end of 1974. By 1985 only one in eight UK homes had a computer. This proportion doubled over the next 11 years to 27 per cent in 1996/97, and then doubled again in the next six years to 55 per cent in 2002/03. The World Wide Web was invented in 1989, but only one in ten UK homes had home access to the Internet in 1998/99. This proportion more than trebled over the next two years before increasing more slowly to 45 per cent in 2002/03.

One way of illustrating changes in lifestyles is to look at how spending patterns have changed. Over the last 35 years spending on the less essential items – including communication, spending abroad, and recreation and culture – has risen far more sharply than expenditure on items such as food, and housing, water and fuel (see Table 6.1). For example, UK household expenditure on food and non-alcoholic drink increased by 41 per cent between 1971 and 2003, after allowing for inflation, to £63 billion. On the other hand, household expenditure on recreation and culture was £84 billion in 2003, six times the amount in 1971, after allowing for inflation. UK tourists' expenditure abroad in 2003 was seven times higher than in 1971 after inflation, which to a certain extent reflects the increase in the number of visits abroad. These changes result from higher levels of disposable income.

The basket of goods and services used in calculating the retail prices index (see explanation on page 92) gives an insight into detailed changes in spending patterns as some items leave the basket each year to make way for others that have become more popular. In the 1970s, mushrooms, yoghurt and mortgage interest payments were added for the first time. The 1980s added CDs, CD players and condoms while personal computers, mobile phone charges and camcorders were added in the 1990s. On the other hand lard, bottled pale ale and vinyl records were in the basket in 1970 but have since been removed. In 2004, dishwasher tablets replaced dishwasher powder and fresh turkey steaks replaced whole frozen turkeys. In addition, the growth of online retailing was reflected in the inclusion of CDs purchased over the Internet.

Latest developments

When Edward Heath, then Prime Minister, launched that first edition of *Social Trends* in 1970, the expansion of the collection of social statistics to measure social change was in its infancy. Today, 35 years later, that system is well developed and many of the changes that have taken place in society can be quantified. Nevertheless, sources and data continue to develop to measure new phenomena, and are then reflected in the changing content of *Social Trends*.

There is still a high demand for *Social Trends* as a paper document. However, since 2000 it has been available free on the National Statistics website and has enjoyed the highest demand of any document there, averaging around 6,000 unique visitors a month. While the advantage of *Social Trends* is that it brings everything together in one place, the disadvantage is that it is only updated once a year. So this year, for some of the key topics, we have created links from the web version of *Social Trends* to topic-based summaries that are held in the 'UK at a Glance' area of the National Statistics website. These topic-based summaries contain a key chart and short interpretative commentary on a topic and are updated as new data become available. Over time we intend to add to these summaries so in this way, a continually updated version of the key topics in *Social Trends* will become available.

Population

- There are more people living in the United Kingdom than there have ever been – 59.6 million people in 2003. (Table 1.1)

- The United Kingdom has an ageing population. Between 1971 and 2003 the number of people aged 65 and over rose by 28 per cent while the number of under 16s fell by 18 per cent. (Figure 1.3)

- The Mixed ethnic group has the youngest age structure of all the main ethnic groups in Great Britain – 50 per cent were aged under 16 in 2001. (Table 1.5)

- There were 696,000 live births in the United Kingdom in 2003 – the largest single year change since 1979 and the highest number since 1999. (Figure 1.8)

- In 2003, Wales gained 15,000 people from net migration within the United Kingdom and Scotland gained 13,000 people. England experienced a net loss of 28,000 people. (Table 1.11)

- In 2003 an estimated 151,000 more people arrived to live in the United Kingdom for at least a year, than left to live elsewhere. (Page 14)

Chapter 1

The number of births and deaths, and the number of people entering and leaving the country, all affect the size, age and sex structure, and geography of the population. These changes in demographic patterns not only influence social structures, but also the demand for services. Information on the size and structure of the population by other factors, such as marital and partnership status, ethnicity, and employment status is also essential in understanding aspects of society, such as the labour market and household composition.

Population profile

There are more people living in the United Kingdom than there have ever been – 59.6 million people in 2003 (Table 1.1). This is 3.6 million more than in 1971. The populations of England, Wales and Northern Ireland all grew between 1971 and 2003, while the population of Scotland remained fairly stable. Population projections suggest that the UK population will reach 63.8 million by 2021. Longer-term projections suggest that the UK population will peak around 2050, at almost 67 million, and will then start to fall.

Around 105 boys are born each year for every 100 girls, but there are more females overall in the United Kingdom: 30.4 million females compared with 29.1 million males in 2003 (Table 1.2). By age 22 the numbers of men and women are very similar, with slightly more women than men in their early to mid 20s. This is primarily caused by differences in levels of net migration, although higher male mortality, particularly death rates from accidents and suicide, plays a part. Women outnumber men at every age from 29 onwards. For people in their late 50s and onwards, the difference between the sexes increases, as death rates are greater among men than women. This is most pronounced in the very elderly as women, on average, live longer than men. In 2003 there were over three times as many women as men aged 90 and over. Although this

difference is predominantly due to differences in old age and mortality, the Second World War has also had an impact on the number of men aged in their 80s.

The age structure of the population reflects past trends in births, deaths and international migration. The number of people in any age group within the population depends on how many people are born in a particular period and how long they survive. It is also affected by the numbers and ages of migrants moving to and from the country.

The population of the United Kingdom is ageing. There are increasing numbers of older people aged 65 and over and decreasing numbers of children under 16 (Figure 1.3). In 2003 there were 11.7 million children under 16 years in the United Kingdom, 18 per cent fewer than in 1971. This is projected to fall to 11.1 million in 2011, and then remain around this level to 2031. There were 9.5 million people aged 65 and over in the United Kingdom in 2003, a 28 per cent increase since 1971. Projections suggest that the number of people aged 65 and over will exceed the numbers aged under 16 from 2013.

Historically the ageing of the population was largely the result of the fall in fertility that began towards the end of the 19th century. Early in the 20th century lower infant mortality helped increase the number of people surviving into adulthood. In the last three decades of the 20th century population ageing has been partly due to both lower fertility and improving mortality at older ages.

The increase in the number of older people has policy implications, placing greater demands on health, social services and social security arrangements. As a response to this, the state pension age (currently 65 for men and 60 for women) will be increased between 2010 and 2020 to 65 for both sexes. However, it is worth noting that demographically defined age boundaries such as these, whatever ages are used, take no

Table **1.1**

Population[1] of the United Kingdom

Millions

	1971	1981	1991	2001	2003	2011	2021
United Kingdom	55.9	56.4	57.4	59.1	59.6	61.4	63.8
England	46.4	46.8	47.9	49.4	49.9	51.6	54.0
Wales	2.7	2.8	2.9	2.9	2.9	3.0	3.1
Scotland	5.2	5.2	5.1	5.1	5.1	5.0	5.0
Northern Ireland	1.5	1.5	1.6	1.7	1.7	1.8	1.8

1 Mid-year estimates for 1971 to 2003; 2003-based projections for 2011 and 2021. See Appendix, Part 1: Population estimates and projections.

Source: Office for National Statistics; Government Actuary's Department; General Register Office for Scotland; Northern Ireland Statistics and Research Agency

Table 1.2

Population:[1] by sex and age

United Kingdom   Percentages

	Under 16	16–24	25–34	35–44	45–54	55–64	65–74	75 and over	All ages (=100%) (millions)
Males									
1971	27	14	13	12	12	11	7	3	27.2
1981	23	15	15	12	11	11	8	4	27.4
1991	21	14	16	14	12	10	8	5	27.9
2001	21	11	15	15	13	11	8	6	28.8
2003	21	12	14	16	13	11	8	6	29.1
2011	19	12	13	14	14	12	9	7	30.2
2021	18	11	14	13	13	13	10	8	31.4
Females									
1971	24	13	12	11	12	12	10	6	28.8
1981	21	14	14	12	11	11	10	8	28.9
1991	19	13	15	13	11	10	9	9	29.5
2001	19	11	14	15	13	11	9	9	30.2
2003	19	11	13	15	13	11	9	9	30.4
2011	17	11	13	14	14	12	9	9	31.2
2021	17	10	13	12	13	13	11	11	32.4

1 Mid-year estimates for 1971 to 2003; 2003-based projections for 2011 and 2021. See Appendix, Part 1: Population estimates and projections.

Source: Office for National Statistics; Government Actuary's Department; General Register Office for Scotland; Northern Ireland Statistics and Research Agency

Figure 1.3

Under 16s and people aged 65 and over

United Kingdom
Millions

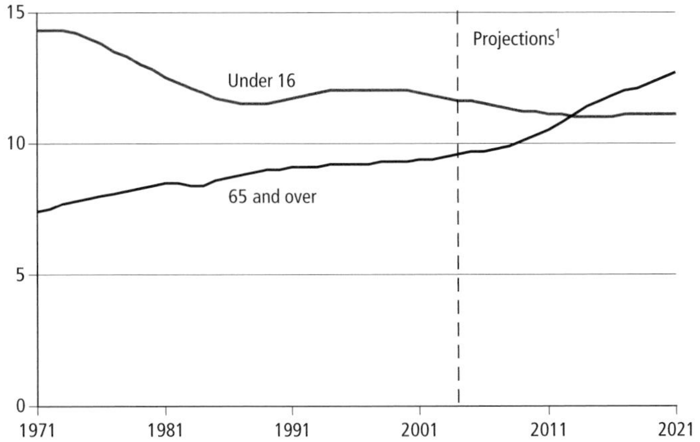

1 2003-based projections for 2004 to 2021.

Source: Office for National Statistics; Government Actuary's Department; General Register Office for Scotland; Northern Ireland Statistics and Research Agency

account of workforce participation rates and therefore do not represent real levels of economic dependence. In reality, full-time education ends, and retirement starts, at a range of ages.

The ageing population is a characteristic shared by other countries in the European Union (EU). The proportion of the UK population aged 65 and over increased by nearly a quarter between 1970 and 2003 compared with an increase of a third for the EU-25 as a whole. In 2003, 16 per cent of the UK population were aged 65 and over (Table 1.4 overleaf). This was the same as the EU average. Germany, Sweden, Belgium, Spain and Portugal had the largest proportions of people aged 65 and over in 2003, at 17 per cent. The largest increases between 1970 and 2003, of around 7 to 8 percentage points, were in Portugal and Spain. The proportion of people aged 65 and over in Ireland remained stable up to 2001, at 11 per cent, which was also the lowest percentage.

There has also been an ageing trend in the ten accession countries that joined the EU in May 2004. The proportions of people aged 65 and over in most of the accession countries were below the EU-25 average in 2003. Estonia and Latvia had the largest proportions of people aged 65 and over in 2003,

Table **1.4**

Population aged 65 and over: EU comparison

Percentages

	1970	1981	1991	2001	2003		1970	1981	1991	2001	2003
EU-15						**Accession countries**					
Italy	11	13	15	18	..	Estonia	12	12	12	15	16
Germany	13	15	15	17	17	Latvia	12	12	12	15	16
Sweden	14	16	18	17	17	Hungary	11	12	13	15	15
Belgium	13	14	15	17	17	Slovenia	10	10	11	14	15
Spain	9	11	14	17	17	Lithuania	10	10	11	14	15
Portugal	9	11	14	16	17	Czech Republic	12	12	13	14	14
Greece	11	13	14	17	..	Poland	8	9	10	12	13
France	13	14	14	16	16	Malta	..	..	..	12	..
United Kingdom[1]	13	15	16	16	16	Cyprus	..	..	..	11	12
Austria	14	15	15	15	15	Slovakia	9	10	10	11	12
Finland	9	12	13	15	15	EU-25 average	12	13	14	16	16
Denmark	12	14	16	15	15						
Luxembourg	12	14	13	14	14						
Netherlands	10	12	13	14	14						
Ireland	11	11	11	11	..						

1 Data for 2003 are taken from mid-year estimates.

Source: Eurostat

at 16 per cent, equal to the EU-25 average. The lowest proportions were in Cyprus and Slovakia, at 12 per cent. Projections suggest that the population of the EU will continue to age, although the rate of increase in the United Kingdom will be slower than in the EU overall.

In the 2001 Census, 4.6 million people (8 per cent of the UK population) described themselves as belonging to a minority ethnic group. The largest minority ethnic group was Indian, making up nearly 2 per cent of the UK population and nearly 23 per cent of the minority ethnic population. Pakistani, Mixed and Black Caribbean were the next largest groups, each making up around 1 per cent of the population.

In general, minority ethnic groups have a younger age structure than the White group (Table 1.5). In 2001 in Great Britain, the Mixed group had the youngest age structure, with 50 per cent aged under 16, compared with 19 per cent of the White group. After the White group, Black Caribbeans have the oldest age structure, with 20 per cent under 16, and 11 per cent aged 65 and over.

In the 1950s and 1960s, job opportunities led to the arrival of Caribbean immigrant workers, particularly men, while immigration from India, Pakistan and Bangladesh peaked in the

late 1960s and early 1970s. Much of the recent growth in the UK minority ethnic population has been through children born in the United Kingdom, as minority ethnic groups tend to have more children than White groups. Based on what is known so far, progressive ageing of the non-White group is anticipated in the future but this will depend on fertility levels, mortality rates and future net migration.

The minority ethnic population of the United Kingdom is concentrated in the large urban centres, particularly in London. Seventy eight per cent of Black Africans and 61 per cent of Black Caribbeans lived in London in 2001. More than half of the Bangladeshi group (54 per cent) also lived in London. Other minority ethnic groups were more dispersed. Only 19 per cent of Pakistanis resided in London, while 21 per cent lived in the West Midlands, 20 per cent in Yorkshire and the Humber, and 16 per cent in the North West.

In Great Britain the highest concentration of White Irish people was in London. Almost a third (32 per cent) of White Irish people lived in London where they made up 3 per cent of the population. Non-Whites made up 29 per cent of the population in London. After London, the second largest proportion was in the West Midlands (with 13 per cent of the non-White population), followed by the South East (8 per

Table **1.5**

Population: by ethnic group[1] and age, 2001

Great Britain   Percentages

	Under 16	16–64	65 and over	All people (=100%) (thousands)
White				
White British	20	63	17	50,366
White Irish	6	69	25	691
Other White	14	76	10	1,423
All White	19	64	17	52,481
Mixed	50	47	3	674
Asian or Asian British				
Indian	23	71	7	1,052
Pakistani	35	61	4	747
Bangladeshi	38	58	3	283
Other Asian	24	71	5	247
All Asian or Asian British	29	66	5	2,329
Black or Black British				
Black Caribbean	20	69	11	566
Black African	30	68	2	485
Other Black	38	59	3	97
All Black or Black British	26	68	6	1,148
Chinese	19	76	5	243
Other ethnic groups	19	78	3	229
All ethnic groups	20	64	16	57,104

1 See Appendix, Part 1: Classification of ethnic groups.

Source: Census 2001, Office for National Statistics; Census 2001, General Register Office for Scotland

cent), the North West (8 per cent), and Yorkshire and the Humber (7 per cent).

In 2002/03 in most ethnic groups in Great Britain, the majority of people described their national identity as either British, English, Scottish, or Welsh (Figure 1.6). This applied to almost all of the White British group, 88 per cent of people from the Mixed group, 81 per cent of the Black Caribbean group, and 75 per cent of the Other Black group. The Indian, Pakistani and Bangladeshi groups were similar to each other, with the proportions ranging from 75 per cent for Indians, to 80 per cent for Bangladeshis and 82 per cent for Pakistanis. People from the White British group were more likely to describe their national identity as English rather than British. Conversely, people from non-White groups were far more likely to identify themselves as British. The largest difference was in the

Figure **1.6**

Proportion who consider their identity to be British, English, Scottish or Welsh: by ethnic group, 2002/03

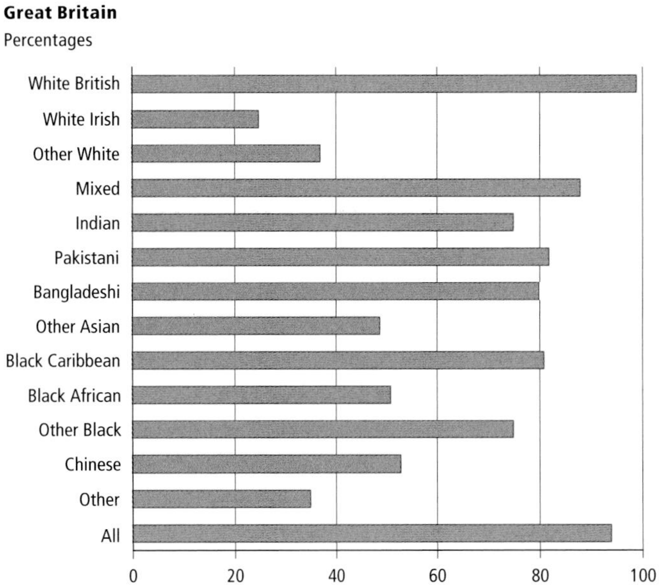

Great Britain
Percentages

Source: Annual local area Labour Force Survey, Office for National Statistics

Bangladeshi group, where 76 per cent said they were British, and only 4 per cent said they were English and 1 per cent said they were Scottish.

Population change

The rate of population change over time depends upon the net natural change – the difference between the numbers of births and deaths – and the net effect of people migrating to and from the country. Natural change is an important factor in population growth in the United Kingdom, although since the 1980s net migration has had an increased influence (Table 1.7 overleaf). Between 2001 and 2003 net migration accounted for over two thirds of the population change. Projections suggest that net migration will continue to account for over half of the change in population between 2003 and 2021.

There were 696,000 live births in the United Kingdom in 2003 (Figure 1.8 overleaf). This was the largest single year change since 1979 and highest number of births since 1999 although it is too early to say whether the long-term downward trend in fertility has been reversed. However, births in 2003 were 36 per cent fewer than in 1901 and 23 per cent fewer than in 1971. The two world wars had a major impact on births. There was a fall in the numbers of births during the First World War, followed by a post-war 'baby boom', with births peaking at 1.1 million in 1920. The numbers of births then decreased and remained low during the inter-war years and the Second World War.

Table **1.7**

Population change[1]

United Kingdom

Thousands

	Population at start of period	Live births	Deaths	Net natural change	Net migration & other	Overall change
				Annual averages		
1951–1961	50,287	839	593	246	6	252
1961–1971	52,807	962	638	324	-12	312
1971–1981	55,928	736	666	69	-27	42
1981–1991	56,357	757	655	103	5	108
1991–2001[1]	57,439	731	631	100	68	167
2001–2003[1]	59,113	672	603	69	151	220
2003–2011	59,554	689	588	101	130	231
2011–2021	61,401	698	585	113	130	243

1 Mid-year estimates for 1951–1961 to 2001–2003; 2003-based projections for 2003–2011 and 2011–2021. Population estimates for 1992 to 2002 were revised in light of the Local Authority Population Studies. See Appendix, Part 1: Population estimates and projections.

Source: Office for National Statistics; Government Actuary's Department; General Register Office for Scotland; Northern Ireland Statistics and Research Agency

Figure **1.8**

Births[1,2] and deaths[1]

United Kingdom

Millions

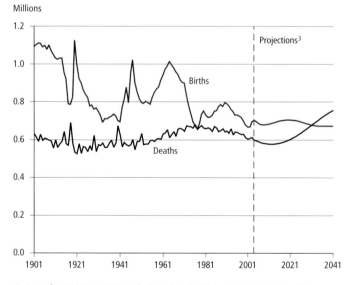

1 Data for 1901 to 1921 exclude Ireland which was constitutionally a part of the United Kingdom during this period.
2 Data from 1981 exclude the non-residents of Northern Ireland.
3 2003-based projections for 2004 to 2041.

Source: Office for National Statistics; Government Actuary's Department; General Register Office for Scotland; Northern Ireland Statistics and Research Agency

A second baby boom followed the Second World War, with a further, more sustained increase in fertility and consequent baby boom in the 1960s. In the mid-1970s the number of births fell to similar levels as the number of deaths. There was a mini boom in births in the late 1980s and early 1990s, the result of the larger cohorts of women born in the 1960s, before numbers began falling again. Projections suggest that the number of births will remain relatively constant over the next 40 or so years, ranging from around 670,000 to 710,000.

The number of deaths has fluctuated around the 600,000 level for most of the last century with 612,000 deaths registered in 2003. It is projected that the number of deaths will start to increase when the number of people born in the baby boom after the Second World War begin to reach advanced ages. The number of deaths is expected to exceed the number of births from around 2031.

Although the number of deaths each year over the last century remained relatively stable, death rates fell considerably due to an increasing population total (Table 1.9). Rising standards of living and developments in medical technology and practice help to explain the decline in death rates. Well over half of deaths at the beginning of the twentieth century occurred under age 45. By 2001, 96 per cent of deaths occurred at ages 45 and over. Infant mortality accounted for 25 per cent of deaths in 1901, but had fallen to 4 per cent of deaths by the middle of the last century and to less than 1 per cent in 2003. Between 1971 and 2003 the death rate for all males fell by 18

Table **1.9**

Deaths:[1] by sex and age

United Kingdom   Death rates per 1,000 in each age group

	Under 1[2]	1–15	16–34	35–54	55–64	65–74	75 and over	All ages	All deaths (thousands)
Males									
1971	20.2	0.5	1.0	4.8	20.4	51.1	131.4	12.1	329
1981	12.7	0.4	1.0	4.0	18.1	46.4	122.2	12.0	329
1991	8.3	0.3	0.9	3.1	14.2	38.7	111.2	11.3	314
2001	6.0	0.2	0.9	2.8	10.4	28.7	96.6	10.0	288
2003	5.7	0.2	0.9	2.7	9.9	27.0	95.6	9.9	289
2011	4.5	0.1	0.8	2.5	9.2	21.4	80.4	9.3	281
2021	3.9	0.1	0.8	2.3	7.8	19.5	71.2	9.7	306
Females									
1971	15.5	0.4	0.5	3.1	10.3	26.6	96.6	11.0	317
1981	9.5	0.3	0.4	2.5	9.8	24.7	90.2	11.4	329
1991	6.3	0.2	0.4	1.9	8.4	22.3	85.0	11.2	332
2001	5.0	0.1	0.4	1.8	6.4	17.9	81.6	10.4	316
2003	4.8	0.1	0.4	1.7	6.1	17.1	84.0	10.6	323
2011	4.3	0.1	0.3	1.7	6.0	13.6	73.5	9.5	297
2021	3.8	0.1	0.3	1.5	5.2	12.5	62.0	9.2	297

1 2003-based projections for 2011 and 2021.
2 Rate per 1,000 live births.

Source: Office for National Statistics; Government Actuary's Department; General Register Office for Scotland; Northern Ireland Statistics and Research Agency

per cent, while the death rate for all females fell by 4 per cent. Infant mortality rates also fell by around 70 per cent during this period.

Regional changes in the population within the United Kingdom are caused not just by births and deaths, but also by people relocating within the country supplemented by international migration. During the last century there was a net movement of people from the coal, shipbuilding and steel industry areas in the north of England, Scotland and Wales to the south of England and the Midlands, where many light industries and service industries are based.

Population change between 1993 and 2003 has produced changes in the geographical distribution of the UK population (Map 1.10). Over this period the largest population increases were in Banbridge in the southern region of Northern Ireland and Milton Keynes in South East England with rises of 17 per cent each, followed by Inner London-West with a 16 per cent rise. The biggest decline in population was in Eilean Siar in Scotland, where the population fell by 11 per cent.

Map **1.10**

Population change, mid-1993 to mid-2003[1]

United Kingdom

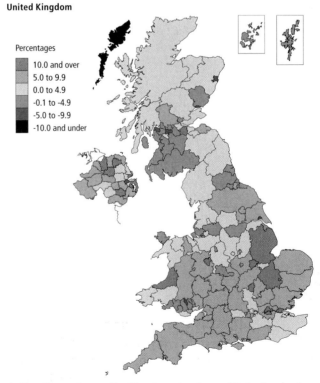

Percentages
- 10.0 and over
- 5.0 to 9.9
- 0.0 to 4.9
- -0.1 to -4.9
- -5.0 to -9.9
- -10.0 and under

1 Counties, unitary authorities, Inner London and Outer London in England, unitary authorities in Wales, council areas in Scotland and district council areas in Northern Ireland.

Source: Office for National Statistics; Statistical Directorate, Welsh Assembly Government; General Register Office for Scotland; Northern Ireland Statistics and Research Agency

Table **1.11**

Inter-regional movements[1] within the United Kingdom, 2003

Thousands

					Yorkshire									
											Origin			
	United Kingdom	England	North East	North West	& the Humber	East Midlands	West Midlands	East	London	South East	South West	Wales	Scotland	Northern Ireland
Destination														
United Kingdom	.	126	40	104	93	96	102	127	263	211	108	48	46	12
England	97	.	34	83	84	88	87	117	246	188	91	46	42	9
North East	42	36	.	6	9	3	3	3	5	5	2	1	4	1
North West	109	92	6	.	18	10	13	8	14	14	8	8	7	2
Yorkshire & the Humber	99	91	9	18	.	16	8	9	12	12	6	3	4	1
East Midlands	115	108	3	10	18	.	16	19	15	20	8	3	3	1
West Midlands	95	84	2	12	7	14	.	8	13	15	12	7	3	1
East	145	137	3	7	7	13	7	.	66	26	9	3	4	1
London	148	136	4	11	9	10	11	27	.	49	14	4	6	1
South East	220	205	4	11	9	13	13	28	95	.	32	7	7	2
South West	142	127	2	9	6	9	16	14	25	47	.	9	4	1
Wales	63	61	1	11	3	3	10	4	6	11	11	.	2	-
Scotland	60	56	4	8	6	4	4	6	8	10	5	2	.	2
Northern Ireland	12	9	-	2	1	1	1	1	2	1	1	-	2	.

1 Based on patients re-registering with NHS doctors in other parts of the United Kingdom. Moves where the origin and destination lie within the same region do not appear in the table. See Appendix, Part 1: Internal migration estimates.

Source: National Health Service Central Register; General Register Office for Scotland; Northern Ireland Statistics and Research Agency

In 2003 Wales gained 15,000 people from net migration within the United Kingdom and Scotland gained 13,000 people, while England experienced a net loss of 28,000 people (Table 1.11). Within the regions of England, the greatest net loss due to internal migration in 2003 occurred in London: 114,000 more people moved from the capital to other parts of the United Kingdom than moved into it. Of people leaving London for elsewhere in the United Kingdom, 36 per cent moved to the South East and 25 per cent to the East. The South West experienced the highest net gain (34,000 people), with 33 per cent moving in from the South East and a further 18 per cent moving from London.

Young adults are the most mobile age group. Many people in their 20s leave their home area to study or seek employment. In 2003 London experienced the largest net increase in people aged 16 to 24 due to migration within the United Kingdom (4,000) but experienced a net loss in all other age groups, especially those associated with young families: the under 16s and people aged 25 to 44. The West Midlands experienced the biggest net loss of 16 to 24 year olds (5,000).

Older people are the least mobile age group. Nevertheless, in 2003 the East and the South West of England experienced the largest net increases in people aged 65 years and over (3,000 people) and London experienced the largest net loss (12,000 people).

International migration

The pattern of people entering and leaving the United Kingdom has changed over the 20th century. There was a net loss due to international migration during the first four decades. However, since 1983 there has generally been net migration into the United Kingdom.

In 2003 an estimated 151,000 more people arrived to live in the United Kingdom for at least a year, than left to live elsewhere. The number of immigrants to the United Kingdom was 513,000, the same as in 2002. There were 362,000 emigrants in 2003, 3,000 more than in 2002. Net international immigration is projected to remain at a relatively high level over the next 25 years.

Figure **1.12**

Grants of settlement: by region of origin

United Kingdom
Thousands

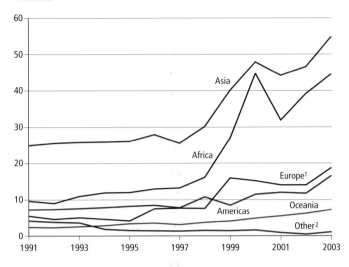

1 European Economic Area (EEA) nationals may apply for settlement, but are not obliged to do so. The figures do not represent the total number of Europeans eligible to stay indefinitely in the UK. Data on EEA nationals granted settlement have not been recorded since 1998.
2 Includes British Overseas citizens, those whose nationality was unknown and, up to 1993, acceptances where the nationality was not separately identified; from 1994 these nationalities have been included in the relevant geographical area.

Source: Home Office

Nationals of the European Economic Area (EU plus Iceland, Liechtenstein, and Norway) have the right to reside in the United Kingdom provided they are working or are able to support themselves financially. Nearly all other overseas nationals wishing to live permanently in the United Kingdom require Home Office acceptance for settlement. The number of people accepted for settlement in the United Kingdom increased by 26,000 to 144,000 between 2002 and 2003 (Figure 1.12). Thirty eight per cent of grants of settlement in 2003 were granted to Asian nationals, and a further 31 per cent to African nationals.

There are various reasons why people choose to move into or out of the United Kingdom. The most common reason for emigration in the period 1993 to 1997 was work-related (Table 1.13). The most common reason given by immigrants was 'other', which includes those looking for work, working holidaymakers, asylum seekers, people visiting friends and family, taking a long holiday or travelling for religious reasons. In the period 1998 to 2002, 'other' was the most common reason for both immigrants and emigrants.

Almost half of immigrants to the United Kingdom in the 1980s and 1990s emigrated again within five years of arrival, but there were variations by overseas country of birth (Figure 1.14 overleaf). This was in part due to the high rates of emigration among immigrants from the EU-15, North America, and Australia and New Zealand. More than five years after arrival in the United Kingdom, substantial numbers of immigrants continued to emigrate. Between 1982 and 2001, the number of immigrants born in the Indian subcontinent and emigrating from the United Kingdom after more than five years was 25,000; among those born in the Caribbean Commonwealth it was 15,000.

Table **1.13**

Average annual international migration:[1] by main reason for migration, 1993–1997 and 1998–2002

United Kingdom   Thousands

	1993–1997			1998–2002		
	Inflow	Outflow	Balance	Inflow	Outflow	Balance
Work related	59.2	85.3	-26.1	103.4	92.8	10.6
Accompany/join partner	72.3	64.0	8.2	77.2	51.1	26.0
Formal study	61.8	13.0	48.8	91.2	13.7	77.5
Other[2]	93.2	70.6	22.6	164.6	99.3	65.3
No reason stated	20.6	23.8	-3.2	27.7	49.2	-21.5
All reasons	307.1	256.7	50.4	464.0	306.0	158.0

1 See Appendix, Part 1: International migration estimates.
2 Includes those looking for work, working holidaymakers, asylum seekers, those visiting friends and family, taking a long holiday, or travelling for religious reasons.

Source: Office for National Statistics

Figure **1.14**

Cumulative proportion of overseas-born immigrants emigrating within 5 years of arrival in the UK in the 1980s and 1990s: by selected countries of birth

United Kingdom

Percentages

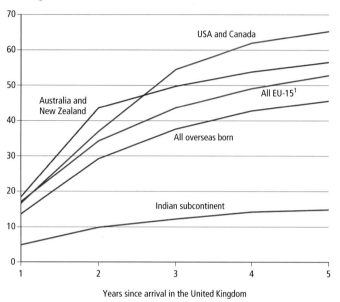

Years since arrival in the United Kingdom

1 Excluding Ireland.

Source: International Passenger Survey, Office for National Statistics

Table **1.15**

Asylum applications, including dependants: EU comparison, 2003

	Number of asylum seekers[1]	Asylum seekers per 1,000 population
Austria	32,400	3.9
Sweden	31,400	3.5
Luxembourg	1,600	3.1
Ireland	7,900	2.0
Belgium	19,300	1.9
France	62,000	1.0
United Kingdom	60,000	1.0
Denmark	4,600	0.8
Netherlands	13,400	0.8
Greece	8,200	0.7
Finland	3,200	0.6
Germany	50,600	0.6
Italy	13,500	0.2
Spain	5,900	0.1
Portugal	100	-
All applications to EU-15	313,900	0.8

1 Figures rounded to the nearest 100.

Source: Home Office

In 2003 the United Kingdom received 60,000 asylum applications including those relating to dependants (Table 1.15). This was 43,000 fewer than in 2002 – a fall of 42 per cent. This compares with a fall of 19 per cent for the rest of the EU-15. Luxembourg, France, Greece and Italy each recorded a rise in applications between 2002 and 2003; the remaining countries reported a decline. When the relative size of the countries' populations are taken into account, the United Kingdom ranked seventh in 2003, with a rate of 1.0 asylum seekers per 1,000 population. Austria had the highest rate at 3.9 per 1,000 population.

The nationalities of people claiming asylum in the United Kingdom vary with world events. Between 2002 and 2003 there was a decrease in asylum seekers from most countries in the world. The nationalities accounting for the most applications in 2003 were Somali, Iraqi, Chinese, Zimbabwean and Iranian.

European perspective

The United Kingdom is the third largest EU-25 member state in terms of population, after Germany and France. Table 1.16 shows how the United Kingdom compares with its European partners according to key demographic indicators such as fertility rates and life expectancy. In 2003 there were 5.3 infant deaths per 1,000 live births in the United Kingdom, the highest rate among the EU-15 countries. The rate was lowest in Sweden at 2.8 infant deaths per 1,000 live births. The Total Fertility Rate was fairly low throughout Europe compared with other parts of the world: Ireland had the highest rate in the EU-15 with 1.98 children per woman, and Greece, the lowest rate of 1.27 children per woman. Life expectancy at birth ranged from 77.9 years for males in Sweden and 83.7 years for females in Spain to 74.0 years for males in Portugal and 79.5 years for females in Denmark.

There was greater variability across the ten accession countries. In Latvia in 2003 there were 9.4 infant deaths per 1,000 live births, compared with 3.9 infant deaths per 1,000 live births in the Czech Republic. The highest Total Fertility Rate occurred in Malta with 1.41 children per woman and the lowest was 1.16 children per woman in Cyprus. Life expectancy at birth ranged from 76.1 years for males in Cyprus and 81.0 years for females in Cyprus and Malta, to 65.2 years for males in Estonia and 76.6 years for females in Hungary.

Table **1.16**

European demographic indicators, 2003

	Population (millions)	Infant mortality rate[1]	Total Fertility Rate[2]	Life expectancy at birth (years)			Population (millions)	Infant mortality rate[1]	Total Fertility Rate[2]	Life expectancy at birth (years)	
				Males	Females					Males	Females
EU-15						**Accession countries**					
Germany	82.5	4.2	1.34	75.5	81.3	Poland	38.2	7.0	1.24	70.5	78.9
France	59.6	3.9	1.89	75.8	82.9	Czech Republic	10.2	3.9	1.18	72.0	78.5
United Kingdom	59.6	5.3	1.71	76.2	80.5	Hungary[4]	10.1	7.3	1.30	68.3	76.6
Italy[3]	57.3	4.3	1.29	76.9	82.9	Slovakia[4]	5.4	7.9	1.17	69.9	77.8
Spain	41.6	3.2	1.29	77.2	83.7	Lithuania	3.5	6.7	1.25	66.3	77.7
Netherlands	16.2	4.8	1.75	76.1	80.8	Latvia	2.3	9.4	1.29	65.5	76.8
Greece[3]	11.0	4.8	1.27	75.4	80.7	Slovenia[4]	2.0	4.0	1.22	72.3	79.9
Portugal	10.4	4.0	..	74.0	80.5	Estonia[4]	1.4	6.8	1.35	65.2	77.0
Belgium[4]	10.4	4.3	1.61	75.6	81.7	Cyprus[5]	0.7	4.5	1.16	76.1	81.0
Sweden	8.9	2.8	1.71	77.9	82.4	Malta[4]	0.4	5.9	1.41	75.9	81.0
Austria	8.1	4.5	1.39	76.0	81.8						
Denmark	5.4	4.4	1.76	74.9	79.5						
Finland	5.2	3.1	1.76	75.1	81.8						
Ireland[4]	4.0	5.1	1.98	75.2	80.3						
Luxembourg[4]	0.4	4.9	1.63	74.9	81.5						

1 Per 1,000 live births.
2 Total Fertility Rate is the number of children that would be born to a woman if current patterns of fertility persisted throughout her childbearing life.
3 Population data are based on the latest population census.
4 Data are for 2002.
5 Life expectancy data are for 2001.

Source: Eurostat

Households and families

- The proportion of children living in lone-parent families in Great Britain tripled between 1972 and spring 2004, to 24 per cent. (Table 2.4)

- In 2003/04, one in six adults aged 16 and over lived alone in Great Britain. (Table 2.6)

- In spring 2004, 58 per cent of young men (aged 20 to 24), and 39 per cent of young women of the same age lived at home with their parents in England. (Table 2.7)

- There were 306,000 marriages in the United Kingdom in 2003. This was the second successive annual rise but was still 36 per cent below the 1972 peak. (Figure 2.8)

- The number of divorces in the United Kingdom rose for the third successive year in 2003, to 167,000, but was still 7 per cent below the 1993 peak. (Figure 2.8)

- In 2003 there were 4,800 adoptions in England and Wales, less than one quarter of the number in 1971. (Figure 2.23)

Chapter 2

Table 2.1

Households:[1] by size

Great Britain
Percentages

	1971	1981	1991	2001[2]	2004[2]
One person	18	22	27	29	29
Two people	32	32	34	35	35
Three people	19	17	16	16	16
Four people	17	18	16	14	14
Five people	8	7	5	5	5
Six or more people	6	4	2	2	2
All households (=100%) (millions)	18.6	20.2	22.4	23.8	24.1
Average household size (number of people)	2.9	2.7	2.5	2.4	2.4

1 See Appendix, Part 2: Households.
2 At spring. See Appendix, Part 4: LFS reweighting.

Source: Census, Labour Force Survey, Office for National Statistics

The types of households and families that people live in are becoming more diverse, reflecting changes in partnership formation and dissolution. People live in a variety of household types over their lifetime. They may leave their parental home, form partnerships, marry and have children. They may also experience separation and divorce, lone-parenthood, and the formation of new partnerships, leading to new households and second families. People may also spend more time living on their own, either before forming relationships, after a relationship has broken down, or after the death of a spouse.

Household composition

There were 24.1 million households in Great Britain in spring 2004 (Table 2.1). Although the population has been increasing, the number of households has increased faster due to the trend towards smaller household sizes. The population grew by 6 per cent between 1971 and 2003, while the number of households increased by 32 per cent. The average household size fell over this period from 2.9 to 2.4 people. More lone-parent families, smaller family sizes, and the increase in one-person households has driven this decrease. The rise in one-person households has levelled off in recent years. As a proportion of all households it

Table 2.2

Households:[1] by type of household and family

Great Britain
Percentages

	1971	1981	1991	2001[2]	2004[2]
One person					
Under state pension age	6	8	11	14	14
Over state pension age	12	14	16	15	15
One family households					
Couple[3]					
No children	27	26	28	29	29
1–2 dependent children[4]	26	25	20	19	18
3 or more dependent children[4]	9	6	5	4	4
Non-dependent children only	8	8	8	6	6
Lone parent[3]					
Dependent children[4]	3	5	6	7	7
Non-dependent children only	4	4	4	3	3
Two or more unrelated adults	4	5	3	3	3
Multi-family households	1	1	1	1	1
All households (=100%) (millions)	18.6	20.2	22.4	23.8	24.1

1 See Appendix, Part 2: Households, and Families.
2 At spring. See Appendix, Part 4: LFS reweighting.
3 Other individuals who were not family members may also be included.
4 May also include non-dependent children.

Source: Census, Labour Force Survey, Office for National Statistics

increased by 9 percentage points between 1971 and 1991, but only by a further 2 percentage points to 2004.

There has been a decrease in the proportion of households containing the traditional family unit – couple families with dependent children – and an increase in the proportion of lone-parent families (Table 2.2). The proportion of households in Great Britain comprising a couple with dependent children fell from over one third in 1971 to just over one fifth in 2004. Over the same period, the proportion comprising a lone-parent household with dependent children doubled, to 7 per cent of households in 2004.

While Table 2.2 shows that 57 per cent of households were headed by a couple in spring 2004, Table 2.3 is based on people. It shows that 70 per cent of people living in private households lived in couple family households in 2004. However, since 1971 the proportion of people living in the 'traditional' family household of a couple with dependent children has fallen from just over one half to under two fifths, while the proportion of people living in couple family households with no children has increased from almost one fifth to one quarter. One in eight people lived in a lone-parent household in spring 2004 – three times the proportion in 1971.

Table **2.3**

People in households:[1] by type of household and family

Great Britain   Percentages

	1971	1981	1991	2001[2]	2004[2]
One person	6	8	11	12	13
One family households					
Couple					
No children	19	20	23	25	25
Dependent children[3]	52	47	41	39	37
Non-dependent children only	10	10	11	8	8
Lone parent	4	6	10	12	12
Other households	9	9	4	4	4
All people in private households (=100%) (millions)	53.4	53.9	55.4	56.4	56.8
People not in private households (millions)	0.9	0.8	0.8	..	..
Total population (millions)[4]	54.4	54.8	56.2	57.4	58.1

1 See Appendix, Part 2: Households, and Families.
2 At spring. See Appendix, Part 4: LFS reweighting.
3 May also include non-dependent children.
4 Data for 1971 to 1991 are census enumerated. Data for 2001 are 2001 mid-year estimates. Data for 2004 are 2003 based projections.

Source: Census, Labour Force Survey, Office for National Statistics

Table **2.4**

Percentage of dependent children[1] living in different family types

Great Britain   Percentages

	1972	1981	1992[2]	2001[2]	2004[2]
Couple families					
1 child	16	18	17	17	17
2 children	35	41	38	37	37
3 or more children	41	29	27	24	23
Lone mother families					
1 child	2	3	5	6	7
2 children	2	4	6	8	9
3 or more children	2	3	5	6	6
Lone father families					
1 child	-	1	1	1	1
2 or more children	1	1	1	1	1
All children[3]	100	100	100	100	100

1 See Appendix, Part 2: Families.
2 At spring. See Appendix, Part 4: LFS reweighting.
3 Excludes cases where the dependent child is a family unit, for example, a foster child.

Source: General Household Survey, Census, Labour Force Survey, Office for National Statistics

Table 2.4 is based on children. It shows that since the early 1970s, there has been a fall in the percentage of dependent children living in families headed by a couple and an increase in those living in lone-parent families. In spring 2004, 76 per cent of children lived in a family unit headed by a couple. The proportion of children living in lone-parent families tripled between 1972 and spring 2004, to 24 per cent. Lone mothers head around nine out of ten lone-parent families.

There are differences in the types of households different ethnic groups live in. These partly reflect the different age structures of the groups. Three quarters (74 per cent) of Bangladeshi households contained at least one dependent child in 2001. This was the highest proportion for any ethnic group and was nearly three times that of White British households (28 per cent). Households headed by a Pakistani or Indian person were also more likely than non-Asian households to contain at least one dependent child – 66 per cent of Pakistani and 50 per cent of Indian households did so. White Irish households were least likely to contain dependent children (21 per cent).

In contrast, one-person or one-family households consisting only of pensioners were not very common among Asian households. The proportion of such pensioner-only households ranged from

Table **2.5**

Ethnic group:[1] by type of household, 2001

Great Britain

Percentages

	One person		One family and no others				Other households		
	Pensioner	Other	Pensioner only[2]	Married couple[3] families	Cohabiting couple[3] families	Lone parent families[3]	With dependent children	Other	All households
White British	15	15	9	37	8	9	2	4	100
White Irish	18	20	9	30	7	10	2	6	100
Other White	9	20	5	36	9	8	3	11	100
Mixed	5	25	2	25	11	18	5	8	100
Indian	4	12	3	53	2	8	10	8	100
Pakistani	3	9	1	51	2	11	16	7	100
Bangladeshi	2	7	1	54	2	11	17	6	100
Other Asian	4	15	2	48	3	9	9	10	100
Black Caribbean	10	28	3	19	7	23	5	5	100
Black African	3	27	1	24	6	20	9	10	100
Other Black	5	29	1	17	7	28	7	5	100
Chinese	4	23	2	41	4	8	5	12	100
Other ethnic group	3	21	1	44	5	10	5	11	100
All ethnic groups	14	16	9	37	8	10	2	4	100

1 Of household reference person.
2 Consisting only of people of pensionable age (males aged 65 and over and females aged 60 and over).
3 At least one partner or the lone parent is below pensionable age.

Source: Census, Office for National Statistics; Census, General Register Office for Scotland

2 per cent of Bangladeshi households to 27 per cent of White Irish households (Table 2.5). This reflects differences in the age structures of the ethnic groups and also the greater tendency for Asian pensioners to live with their extended family. For example, households containing more than one family (including unrelated adults) and with dependent children made up 17 per cent of Bangladeshi households but only 2 per cent of all households in Great Britain.

The highest proportions of married couples where at least one partner was under pension age, with or without children, were found in Asian households. Just over half of Bangladeshi, Indian and Pakistani households contained a married couple under pension age, compared with 37 per cent of White British households. Less than one fifth of both Black Caribbean and Other Black households contained a married couple under pension age, which were the lowest proportions of all the ethnic groups. Asian households were also the least likely to contain a cohabiting couple.

One of the most notable changes in household composition over the last three decades has been the increase in one-

person households. The proportion of such households in Great Britain increased from 18 per cent in 1971 to 29 per cent in 2004. In the mid-1980s and 1990s these households mainly comprised older women. This was a reflection of there being fewer men than women in older age groups and, in particular, the tendency for wives to outlive their husbands. In 2003/04, 60 per cent of women aged 75 and over were living alone, much the same proportion as in 1986/87 (Table 2.6). There has been an increasing tendency for people to live on their own at younger ages. The largest increases were among people aged 25 to 44 years – the proportions of men and women who lived alone both doubled between 1986/87 and 2003/04.

Another change in family structure and relationships has been the increase in the proportion of adults who live with their parents (Table 2.7). Some young people may be delaying leaving home because of economic necessity, such as difficulties entering the housing market. Others may simply choose to continue living with their parents. The later age at marriage may also be a factor.

Table **2.6**

People living alone: by sex and age

Great Britain   Percentages

	1986/87	1991/92	1996/97	2001/02[1]	2003/04[1]
Males					
16–24	4	4	5	7	6
25–44	7	9	11	17	15
45–64	8	9	10	15	14
65–74	17	18	21	19	19
75 and over	24	32	31	32	29
All aged 16 and over	9	11	12	16	15
Females					
16–24	3	3	3	3	3
25–44	4	5	6	6	8
45–64	13	13	12	14	15
65–74	38	37	39	35	34
75 and over	61	60	58	59	60
All aged 16 and over	16	16	16	17	17

1 Data from 2001/02 onwards are weighted to compensate for nonresponse and to match known population distributions.

Source: General Household Survey, Office for National Statistics

Young men were more likely than young women to live with their parents. In 2004, 58 per of men aged 20 to 24 did so compared with 39 per cent of women of the same age. Between 1991 and 2004 the proportion of men and women in this age group who were living with their parents increased by 7 to 8 percentage points.

Table **2.7**

Adults living with their parents: by sex and age

England   Percentages

	1991	2001[1]	2002[1]	2003[1]	2004[1]
Males					
20–24	50	56	55	55	58
25–29	19	23	20	22	24
30–34	9	9	9	9	10
Females					
20–24	32	38	39	38	39
25–29	9	12	11	11	12
30–34	5	3	3	4	4

1 At spring. See Appendix, Part 4: LFS reweighting.

Source: National Dwelling and Household Survey and Survey of English Housing, Office of the Deputy Prime Minister; Labour Force Survey, Office for National Statistics

Partnerships

The pattern of partnership formation has changed since the early 1970s but, despite the decrease in the overall numbers of people marrying, marriage is still the most common form of partnership for men and women. In 2003 around half of the UK population were married.

In 1950 there were 408,000 marriages in the United Kingdom (Figure 2.8). The number grew during the mid- to late-1960s to reach a peak of 480,000 in 1972. This growth was partly a result of the babies born in the post-war boom reaching marriageable ages and, at that time, people were marrying younger than in more recent years. The annual number of marriages then began to decline and in 2003 there were just over 306,000. This was the second successive annual rise.

The number of divorces taking place each year in Great Britain more than doubled between 1958 and 1969. After 1969 divorce was also permitted in Northern Ireland. By 1972 the number of divorces in the United Kingdom had doubled again. This latter increase was partly a 'one-off' effect of the *Divorce Reform Act 1969* in England and Wales, which came into effect in 1971. The Act introduced a single ground for divorce – irretrievable breakdown – which could be established by proving one or more certain facts: adultery; desertion;

Figure **2.8**

Marriages and divorces[1]

United Kingdom
Thousands

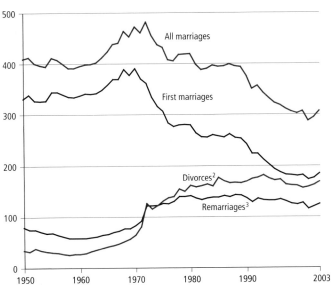

1 For both partners.
2 Includes annulments. Data for 1950 to 1970 for Great Britain only.
3 For one or both partners.

Source: Office for National Statistics; General Register Office for Scotland; Northern Ireland Statistics and Research Agency

separation either with or without consent; or unreasonable behaviour. Although there was a slight drop in the number of divorces in 1973, the number rose again in 1974 and peaked in 1993 at 180,000. The number of divorces then fell to 155,000 in 2000. In 2003 the number of divorces increased by 4 per cent to 167,000, from 161,000 in 2002. This was the third successive annual rise.

Following divorce, people often form new relationships and may remarry. Remarriages, for one or both partners, increased by a third between 1971 and 1972 after the introduction of the *Divorce Reform Act 1969,* and peaked at 141,000 in 1988. In 2003 there were just over 123,000 remarriages, accounting for two fifths of all marriages.

The age at which people get married for the first time has continued to increase. In 1971 the average age at first marriage was 25 for men and 23 for women in England and Wales and this increased to 31 for men and 29 for women in 2003. There has been a similar trend across Europe. Between 1971 and 2002, the average age at first marriage in the European Union (EU-25) increased from 26 to 30 for men and 23 to 27 for women. However there are differences between the EU-25 countries. In 2002 the country with the youngest newly-weds was Lithuania (26 for men and 24 for women) while Sweden had the oldest (33 for men and 30 for women). Traditionally women have married men who are older than themselves. The average age difference between partners in first marriages ranged from just under two years between partners in Ireland and in Portugal to just under four years in Greece.

Table 2.9

Age gap between males and females at marriage,[1] 1963 and 2001

England & Wales   Percentages

	1963	2001
Man younger	15	26
Man 0–5 years older	64	48
Man 6 years or more older	21	26
All marriages	100	100

1 All marriages in 1963 and 2001.

Source: Office for National Statistics

In England and Wales, the majority of women marry men older than themselves. However, an increasing proportion of women are marrying younger men. The proportion of couples where the husband was younger than the wife increased from 15 per cent for those who married in 1963 to 26 per cent for those

who married in 2001 (Table 2.9). Over the same period, the proportion of couples where the man was at most five years older than the woman fell from just under two thirds in 1963 to just under a half in 2001. The proportion of marriages where the man was more than five years older than the woman increased from 21 per cent in 1963 to 26 per cent in 2001.

Table 2.10

Non-married people[1] cohabiting: by sex

Great Britain   Percentages

	Males	Females
1986	11	13
1991/92	19	19
1996/97	22	22
2001/02[2]	25	28
2003/04[2]	25	27

1 Aged 16 to 59. Includes those who described themselves as separated but were, in a legal sense, still married.
2 Data from 2001/02 are weighted to compensate for nonresponse and to match known population distributions.

Source: General Household Survey, Office for National Statistics

The trend towards marrying later in life may, in part, be explained by the rise in cohabitation. The percentage of non-married men and women under the age of 60 cohabiting in Great Britain more than doubled between 1986 (the earliest year data are available on a consistent basis) and 2003/04, to 25 per cent and 27 per cent respectively (Table 2.10). The longest time series on cohabitation is for women aged 18 to 49. Between 1979 and 2003/04, the proportion of non-married women aged 18 to 49 who were cohabiting in Great Britain almost tripled from 11 per cent to 31 per cent.

Table 2.11

Non-married people[1] cohabiting: by marital status and sex, 2002–04[2]

Great Britain   Percentages

	Males	Females
Single	24	28
Widowed	14	7
Divorced	35	29
Separated	23	12

1 Aged 16 to 59. Includes those who described themselves as separated but were, in a legal sense, still married.
2 Data for 2002/03 and 2003/04 are combined.

Source: General Household Survey, Office for National Statistics

Higher proportions of divorced people cohabit compared with other marital status groups. Combined data for 2002/03 and 2003/04 show that 35 per cent of divorced men, and 29 per cent of divorced women, aged under 60 were cohabiting (Table 2.11). Cohabiting women aged under 60 were equally likely to be divorced or single, whereas men who cohabited were predominantly divorced. Among women aged 18 to 49, the proportion of single women who cohabited quadrupled from 8 per cent in 1979 to 33 per cent in 2003/04.

Changes in patterns of cohabitation, marriage and divorce have led to considerable changes in the family environment since the early 1970s. The number of children aged under 16 in England and Wales who experienced the divorce of their parents peaked at almost 176,000 in 1993 (Figure 2.12). This fell to 142,000 in 2000, and then increased each year up to 2003. Just over one fifth of children affected by divorce in 2003 were under five years old and nearly two thirds were aged ten or under.

Figure **2.12**

Children of divorced couples: by age of child

England & Wales
Thousands

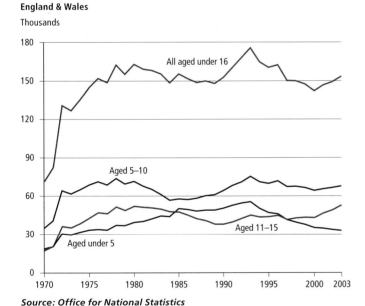

Source: Office for National Statistics

Children are living in an increasing variety of different family structures during their lives. Parents separating can result in lone-parent families, and new relationships can create stepfamilies. Children tend to stay with their mother following the break-up of a partnership. In 2003/04 the vast majority (83 per cent) of stepfamilies in Great Britain consisted of a stepfather and natural mother (Figure 2.13).

Figure **2.13**

Stepfamilies[1] with dependent children,[2] 2003/04

Great Britain
Percentages

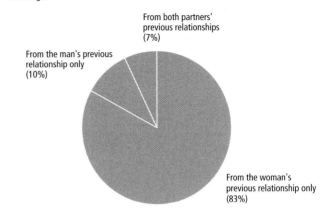

1 Family head aged 16 to 59.
2 Dependent children are persons under 16, or aged 16 to 18 and in full-time education, in the family unit, and living in the household.

Source: General Household Survey, Office for National Statistics

Family formation

Fertility patterns influence the size of households and families, and also affect the age structure of the population. Although there has been an overall downward trend in the fertility rate in the United Kingdom during the 20th century, from 115 live births per 1,000 women aged 15 to 44 at the start of the century to a rate of 57 per 1,000 at the end of the century, fertility has fluctuated with peaks after both world wars and in the 1960s. Fluctuations have continued in the 21st century with a record low in 2001, but an upturn in fertility in 2003.

Trends in fertility patterns vary by age. Fertility rates for women aged 30 and over increased from the 1980s while those for women aged under 30 declined (Table 2.14 overleaf). However, between 2001 and 2003 there was an increase in fertility rates for women in their 20s. Since 1992 the fertility rate for women aged 30 to 34 has exceeded the rate for women aged 20 to 24 and in 2003 was almost as high as the rate for women aged 25 to 29. Increased female participation in education and the labour market, and the greater choice and effectiveness of contraception, have encouraged the trend towards later childbearing and smaller families.

In 2003 the United Kingdom had a Total Fertility Rate of 1.7 children per 1,000 women, higher than the average for the EU-25 of 1.5 children per 1,000 women (Table 2.15 overleaf). The rate was lower in 2000 than in 1980 in most of the EU countries. The exceptions were Denmark, Finland, the Netherlands and Luxembourg. However, the rate increased in 12 of the countries between 2000 and 2003. In general

Table 2.14

Fertility rates: by age of mother at childbirth

United Kingdom   Live births per 1,000 women

	1971	1981	1991	2001	2003
Under 20[1]	50.0	28.3	32.9	27.9	26.6
20–24	154.4	106.8	88.9	68.0	70.1
25–29	154.6	130.4	119.9	91.5	95.9
30–34	79.4	69.5	86.5	88.0	94.5
35–39	34.3	22.4	32.0	41.3	45.9
40–44	9.2	5.0	5.3	8.2	9.1
General Fertility Rate[2]	84.3	62.1	63.6	54.5	56.3
Total Fertility Rate[3]	..	1.82	1.82	1.63	1.71
Total births (thousands)	901.6	730.7	792.3	669.1	695.6

1 Live births per 1,000 women aged 15 to 19.
2 Total live births per 1,000 women aged 15 to 44.
3 Number of children that would be born to a woman if current patterns of fertility persisted throughout her childbearing life.

Source: Office for National Statistics

the Total Fertility Rates were lower for the ten accession countries than the EU-15. The rates were lower in 2003 than in 1980 in all the accession countries.

Despite the overall trend towards later childbearing, the rate of girls aged under 20 in England and Wales becoming pregnant rose in the 1980s, but then fell slightly in the 1990s. There were 97,100 conceptions to girls aged under 20 in 2002 (Table 2.16). There were nearly 7,900 conceptions among girls under the age of 16 in 2002 which was 8 per cent of all conceptions to girls under 20. For women aged between 16 and 19, the proportion of conceptions resulting in maternities is higher than for younger girls. Almost two thirds of conceptions to 19 year olds resulted in a maternity, compared with over one half of conceptions to 16 year olds.

With the exception of the periods immediately after the two world wars, few births occurred outside marriage during the first 60 years of the 20th century. During the 1960s and 1970s such births became more common. In 2003 most children were born to married couples, but around 41 per cent of live births in the United Kingdom occurred outside marriage (Figure 2.17). Most of the increase in the number of births outside marriage has been due to an increase in the proportion of children born to cohabiting couples.

Table 2.15

Total Fertility Rate:[1] EU comparison

Number of children per woman

	1980	1990	2000	2003		1980	1990	2000	2003
EU-15					**Accession countries**				
Ireland	3.3	2.1	1.9	2.0	Cyprus	2.4	2.4	1.6	1.5
France	2.0	1.8	1.9	1.9	Malta	2.0	2.1	1.7	1.4
Denmark	1.6	1.7	1.8	1.8	Estonia	2.0	2.0	1.3	1.4
Finland	1.6	1.8	1.7	1.8	Hungary	1.9	1.9	1.3	1.3
Netherlands	1.6	1.6	1.7	1.8	Latvia	1.9	2.0	1.2	1.3
Sweden	1.7	2.1	1.5	1.7	Lithuania	2.0	2.0	1.4	1.3
United Kingdom	1.9	1.8	1.6	1.7	Poland	2.3	2.0	1.3	1.2
Luxembourg	1.5	1.6	1.8	1.6	Slovenia	2.1	1.5	1.3	1.2
Belgium	1.7	1.6	1.7	1.6	Czech Republic	2.1	1.9	1.1	1.2
Portugal	2.2	1.6	1.6	1.4	Slovakia	2.3	2.1	1.3	1.2
Austria	1.7	1.5	1.4	1.4	EU-25 average	1.9	1.6	1.5	1.5
Germany	1.6	1.5	1.4	1.3					
Spain	2.2	1.4	1.2	1.3					
Italy	1.6	1.3	1.2	1.3					
Greece	2.2	1.4	1.3	1.3					

1 Number of children that would be born to a woman if current patterns of fertility persisted throughout her childbearing life.

Source: Eurostat

Table 2.16

Teenage conceptions:[1] by age at conception and outcome, 2002

England & Wales

	Number of conceptions		Rates per 1,000 females[2]	
	Leading to maternities	Leading to abortions	Leading to maternities	Leading to abortions
Under 14	149	241	0.4	0.7
14	719	1,139	2.1	3.4
15	2,629	2,998	8.0	9.1
All aged under 16	3,497	4,378	3.5	4.4
16	7,283	6,192	22.4	19.1
17	12,162	8,439	37.3	25.9
18	16,314	9,596	51.6	30.3
19	19,084	10,162	61.1	32.5
All aged under 20	58,340	38,767	36.3	24.1

1 See Appendix, Part 2: Conceptions.
2 Rates for females aged under 14, under 16, and under 20 are based on the population of females aged 13, 13–15, and 15–19 respectively.

Source: Office for National Statistics

In most European countries there have been significant increases since 1980 in the proportions of births occurring outside marriage. However, there are large differences between countries. In 2003, over half of births in Sweden and Estonia occurred outside marriage (56 per cent in both countries) compared with only 4 per cent of births in both Greece and Cyprus.

The rate of multiple births in the United Kingdom increased from 12.8 per 1,000 of all maternities in 1993 to 14.8 per 1,000 of all maternities in 2003. The greater use of fertility treatment is an important factor. In 2003, twins were born at a rate of 14.7 per 1,000 maternities, while 0.2 per 1,000 maternities led to triplets or more (Table 2.18). Multi-birth rates are highest for women over the age of 35. Among women aged 35 to 39 years, twins accounted for 21.2 per 1,000 maternities, and triplets for 0.3 per 1,000 maternities. In comparison, for women aged under 20, the rates were 6.5 and 0.1 respectively. To decrease the likelihood of multiple births following fertility treatment, the Human Fertilisation and Embryology Authority revised its guidelines in 2004, restricting the number of eggs or embryos used at each IVF attempt, or similar treatment, from three to two.

Trends in abortion rates in England and Wales vary by age of woman (Figure 2.19 overleaf). Since 1969, following the introduction of the *Abortion Act 1967*, abortion rates have risen overall but particularly for women aged 16 to 34. In 2003 the

Figure 2.17

Births outside marriage as a percentage of all births

United Kingdom

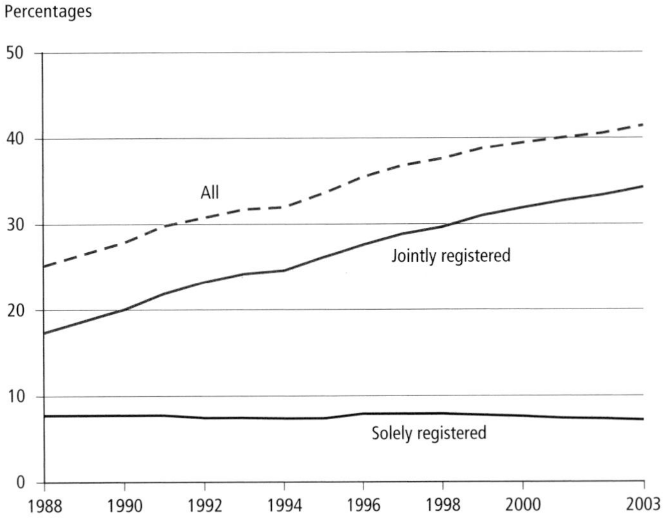

Percentages

Source: Office for National Statistics; General Register Office for Scotland; Northern Ireland Statistics and Research Agency

highest rate, of 31.2 per 1,000 women, occurred among 20 to 24 year olds. Girls under 16 and women aged 35 and over have far lower rates than women in other age groups. In 2003, the abortion rate for girls under 16 was 3.9 per 1,000 girls; for women aged 35 and over it was 6.8 per 1,000 women.

During the early 1990s the abortion rate among young women (aged 16 to 24) fell slightly, but then rose again – as it did for all age groups – between 1995 and 1996. This increase is thought to have been the result of a pill scare. In 1995 the Committee on Safety of Medicines warned that several brands of the contraceptive pill carried an increased risk of thrombosis.

Table 2.18

Maternities with multiple births: by age of mother at childbirth, 2003

United Kingdom   Rate per 1,000 maternities

	Maternities with twins only	Maternities with triplets and over
Under 20	6.5	0.1
20–24	9.1	0.1
25–29	13.0	0.2
30–34	17.6	0.2
35–39	21.2	0.3
40 and over	20.9	0.4
All	14.7	0.2

Source: Office for National Statistics; General Register Office for Scotland; Northern Ireland Statistics and Research Agency

Figure **2.19**

Abortion rates:[1] by age

England & Wales

Rates per 1,000 women

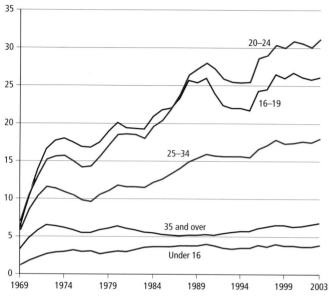

1 The rates for girls aged under 16 are based on the population of girls aged 13–15. The rates for women aged 35 and over are based on the population of women aged 35–44.

Source: Office for National Statistics; Department of Health

This warning is believed to have contributed to an increase in conceptions and a related increase in abortions in 1996, particularly among young women as they were more likely to have been using the pill. Following this pill scare the abortion rate did not fall back to the 1995 level but continued to rise for all age groups except the under 16s.

Table **2.20**

Average age of mother at childbirth[1]

England & Wales

Mean age (years)

	1971	1981	1991	2001	2003
All births					
All live births	26.2	26.8	27.7	29.2	29.4
All first births[2]	..	..	25.7	27.1	27.4
Births inside marriage					
All births	26.4	27.3	28.9	30.9	31.2
First births	24.0	25.4	27.5	29.6	29.9
Births outside marriage					
All births	23.8	23.5	24.8	26.7	26.9

1 Mean ages are not standardised and therefore take no account of the structure of the population by age, marital status or parity.
2 See Appendix, Part 2: True birth order.

Source: Office for National Statistics

Linked to the decline in fertility rates for younger women is the increase in the age of women at childbirth. In England and Wales the average age of married women giving birth for the first time has increased by nearly six years since 1971, to 29.9 in 2003 (Table 2.20). The average age of fathers at childbirth also rose, from 29.2 years in 1971 to 32.7 years in 2003 for births registered by both parents. Births outside marriage tend to take place at a younger age than those inside marriage. In 2003 women giving birth outside marriage were around four years younger than those giving birth inside marriage.

In the United Kingdom the average number of children per woman (family size) increased from 2.07 children for women born in 1920 (the first cohort for which data are available) to a peak of 2.46 children for women born in 1934 (Figure 2.21). This peak corresponds with the 1960s 'baby boom'. Family size declined for subsequent generations and is projected to decline to around 1.74 children for women born in the mid-1980s. Women born in 1955, and now at the end of their childbearing years, had an average of 2.03 children.

Figure **2.21**

Completed family size

United Kingdom

Average number of children per woman

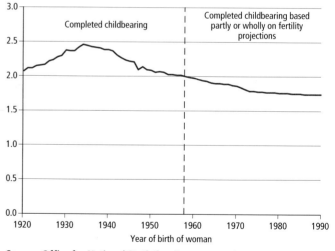

Source: Office for National Statistics; Government Actuary's Department

The decline in family size among women born in the mid-1930s onwards is the result both of fewer women having large families and more women remaining childless. In England and Wales, 31 per cent of women born in 1920 had given birth to three or more children by the end of their childbearing years. This increased to around 40 per cent of women born in the 1930s. It then dropped rapidly to a level of around 30 per cent, where it has remained for the 1945-born generation onwards.

Successive cohorts of women in England and Wales born since the Second World War have waited longer before starting a family. Thirty eight per cent of women born in 1948 were still childless at age 25; this increased to 65 per cent of women aged 25 born in 1978 (Figure 2.22).

Figure 2.22

Childless women at age 25, 35 and 45[1]: by year of birth

England & Wales
Percentages

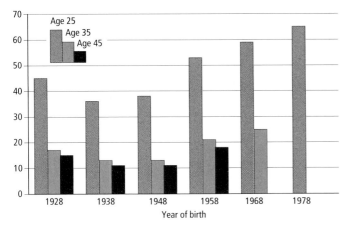

1 Includes births at ages over 45.

Source: Office for National Statistics

Figure 2.23

Adoption orders: by year of registration[1] and whether adopted child born within or outside marriage[2]

England & Wales
Thousands

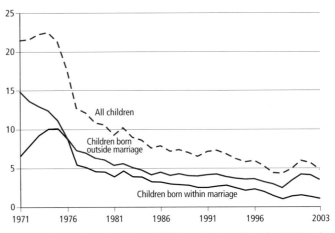

1 Year of entry into the Adopted Children Register. Data for 1990 and 2001 include cases where age of child was greater than 17 years.
2 Data for all children for 1985 to 1989 include cases where marital status was not stated. Where marital status for 1998 are missing they have been imputed.

Source: Office for National Statistics

Another way in which people may extend their families is through adoption. In 2003 there were 4,800 adoptions in England and Wales, with 47 per cent of adopted children aged between one and four years old (Figure 2.23). Increased use of contraception, new abortion laws and changed attitudes towards lone motherhood have meant that 16,700 fewer children were adopted in 2003 than in 1971. There was a rapid decline in the number of children available for adoption following the introduction of legal abortion in the *Abortion Act 1967* and after the implementation of the *Children Act 1975*. This latter act required courts dealing with adoption applications for children of divorced parents to dismiss applications for adoption where a legal custody order was in the child's best interests. Despite these changes, most of the children adopted since 1971 were born outside marriage: 72 per cent in 2003.

Education and training

- The proportion of three and four year olds enrolled in all schools in the United Kingdom tripled from 21 per cent in 1970/71 to 65 per cent in 2003/04. (Figure 3.1)

- The rate of permanent exclusion in England among Black Caribbean pupils has halved since 1997/98, to 37 for every 10,000 pupils of compulsory school age in 2002/03. This was still three times the rate for White pupils. (Figure 3.7)

- With the exception of mathematics and science at Key Stage 2, in 2004, girls outperformed boys in England in all subjects at Key Stages 1, 2 and 3; the greatest differences were for English. (Table 3.11)

- One in six people of working age in Great Britain held a degree or equivalent qualification in 2003/04. (Table 3.16)

- There were 189,000 support staff in classrooms in maintained schools in England in 2004, twice as many as in 1996. (Figure 3.22)

- Primary schools in England had one computer for every 7.5 pupils in 2004, three times as many as in 1994. (Figure 3.23)

Chapter 3

For increasing numbers of people, experience of education is no longer confined to compulsory schooling. Early learning and participation in pre-school education is seen as being important for building a foundation for future learning, and most people continue in full-time education beyond school-leaving age.

Qualifications attained at school are increasingly supplemented by further education and training to equip people with the skills required by a modern labour market.

Schools

There has been a major expansion in pre-school education over the last 30 or so years. The proportion of three and four year olds enrolled in all schools in the United Kingdom rose from 21 per cent in 1970/71 to 65 per cent in 2003/04 (Figure 3.1). This is due both to the expanding provision of places – there were over 3,400 state nursery schools in 2003/04, two and a half times the number in 1990/91 – and a fall in the three and four year old population in recent years. In 2003/04, 35 per cent of three and four year olds were enrolled in other non-school settings offering early education such as playgroups in the private and voluntary sectors, either instead of, or in addition to, their school place.

Figure **3.1**

Children under five[1] in schools as a percentage of all three and four year olds

United Kingdom
Percentages

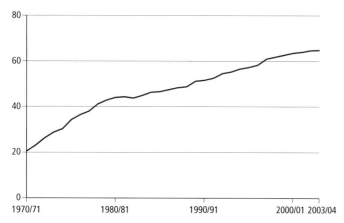

1 Pupils aged three and four at 31 December each year. See Appendix, Part 3: Stages of education.

Source: Department for Education and Skills; National Assembly for Wales; Scottish Executive; Northern Ireland Department of Education

The pattern of participation varies regionally. The proportion of three and four year olds in maintained nursery and primary schools is generally higher in the north of England and in Wales than in the south. In January 2004 around twice the proportion of three and four year olds attended maintained nursery and

primary schools in the North East (84 per cent) compared with the South East (41 per cent) and South West (43 per cent) of England. However, more children are enrolled with private and voluntary providers in the south than in other parts of the country.

The number of children of school age in the United Kingdom has fluctuated due to factors such as changes in the birth rate (see Chapter 1), and the raising of the school-leaving age in 1972. The declining birth rates during the late 1970s led to a fall in pupil numbers in the 1980s and early 1990s. Pupil numbers increased to 2000/01, but have declined since then, and are still below the peak level of the mid-1970s.

In 2003/04 there were around 34,600 schools in the United Kingdom, accommodating 10 million pupils (Table 3.2). Public sector schools (not including special schools) were attended by over 9 million, or 92 per cent of all pupils. Seven per cent of pupils attended one of the 2,500 non-maintained mainstream schools. These proportions have remained around this level since the 1970s. One per cent of pupils attended one of the 1,400 special schools in 2003/04, and there were over 400 pupil referral units (PRUs), catering for 13,000 pupils. PRUs provide suitable alternative education on a temporary basis for pupils who may not be able to attend a mainstream school.

Some pupils have special educational needs (SEN), that is, they have significantly greater difficulty in learning than other children of the same age, or have a disability that makes it difficult for them to use normal educational facilities. Approximately 1.4 million pupils with SEN were identified in England in January 2004. Eighteen per cent of pupils in maintained primary schools and 16 per cent in maintained secondary schools in England had SEN. These proportions varied by region and were highest in Inner London at 21 per cent in primary schools and 23 per cent in secondary schools (Figure 3.3). Yorkshire and the Humber (just under 17 per cent) and the South West (14 per cent) had the lowest proportions of pupils with SEN for primary and secondary level education respectively.

If an education authority or board believes that it should determine the education for a child with SEN, it must draw up a formal statement of those needs and the action it intends to take to meet them. Over 290,000 pupils in the United Kingdom had these statements (called a Record of Needs in Scotland) in 2003/04. In England, the number of pupils with statements of SEN increased from 195,000 in 1994 to peak at an estimated 258,000 in 2001. Numbers have since declined to around 248,000 in 2004. While the number of pupils with statements of SEN in special schools remained fairly constant in the ten years to 2004, the number of pupils with statements in mainstream maintained schools increased by 48 per cent, to 149,000 pupils.

Table **3.2**

School pupils:[1] by type of school[2]

United Kingdom   Thousands

	1970/71	1980/81	1990/91	2000/01	2002/03	2003/04[3]
Public sector schools						
Nursery	50	89	105	152	154	150
Primary	5,902	5,171	4,955	5,298	5,178	5,111
Secondary						
Comprehensive	1,313	3,730	2,925	3,340	3,434	3,455
Grammar	673	149	156	205	213	216
Modern	1,164	233	94	112	106	107
Other	403	434	298	260	242	235
All public sector schools	9,507	9,806	8,533	9,367	9,327	9,275
Non-maintained schools	621	619	613	626	644	654
Special schools	103	148	114	113	112	109
Pupil referral units	.	.	.	10	12	13
All schools	10,230	10,572	9,260	10,116	10,095	10,051

1 Headcounts.
2 See Appendix, Part 3: Stages of education, and Main categories of educational establishments.
3 Data for Wales refer to 2002/03.

Source: Department for Education and Skills; National Assembly for Wales; Scottish Executive; Northern Ireland Department of Education

For several years, reductions have been made in class sizes in the drive to improve standards, particularly in the size of primary classes. In 2003/04, the average class size in Great Britain was 25 pupils for Key Stage 1 (5 to 7 year olds)

Figure **3.3**

Pupils with Special Educational Needs (SEN):[1] by region, 2004[2]

England

Percentages

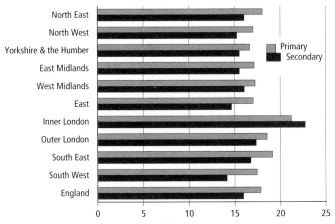

1 As a percentage of all pupils.
2 Data are at January.

Source: Department for Education and Skills

and 27 pupils for Key Stage 2 (7 to 11 year olds) (Table 3.4 overleaf). Key Stage 2 pupils were far more likely than Key Stage 1 pupils to be in classes of 31 or more pupils (21 per cent and 2 per cent, respectively). These proportions had fallen from 28 per cent and 4 per cent respectively in 2000/01. At least one in four Key Stage 2 classes in the East Midlands, South West and North West had 31 or more pupils in 2003/04, compared with around one in ten classes in London and even fewer in Northern Ireland. Average class size at Key Stages 3 and 4 (11 to 16 year olds) in England was around 22 pupils, despite secondary schools being larger than primary schools. This small average class size is in part because students choose different subjects in preparation for formal exams at the end of their compulsory secondary schooling.

In 2003, 37 per cent of adults in Great Britain thought that smaller class sizes would be the most useful way to improve primary education (Table 3.5 overleaf). Reducing class sizes was also seen as the best way of improving secondary education, though to a lesser extent (25 per cent). For both primary and secondary education, women were more likely than men to think smaller class sizes would be the most useful way of improving education, whereas men were more likely than women to feel that better quality teachers would be the most useful way of achieving this.

Table **3.4**

Class sizes in schools:[1] by region, 2003/04

	Key Stage 1[2]		Key Stage 2[2]		Key Stages 3 and 4	
	Average number in class	Percentage of classes with 31 or more pupils	Average number in class	Percentage of classes with 31 or more pupils	Average number in class	Percentage of classes with 31 or more pupils
Great Britain	25.4	1.9	26.9	20.8	..	..
England	25.8	1.9	27.3	21.9	21.8	8.3
North East	24.7	1.7	26.3	19.0	21.8	8.0
North West	25.4	1.9	27.2	25.5	21.7	9.2
Yorkshire & the Humber	25.6	2.6	27.3	23.7	21.9	8.2
East Midlands	25.1	2.6	27.6	27.2	21.9	8.1
West Midlands	25.8	1.9	27.3	20.9	21.8	9.0
East	25.7	2.3	27.4	21.2	21.7	7.5
London	27.0	1.5	27.2	11.0	21.9	6.3
South East	25.8	1.5	27.4	23.6	21.7	7.9
South West	25.8	1.9	27.3	27.0	22.2	10.7
Wales[3]	24.2	2.6	25.9	17.5	21.2	..
Scotland	23.1	1.1	24.7	13.7	..	..
Northern Ireland	22.8	1.2	23.8	6.8	..	..

1 Maintained schools only. Figures relate to all classes – not just those taught by one teacher. In Northern Ireland a class is defined as a group of pupils normally under the control of one teacher.
2 Pupils in composite classes which overlap Key Stage 1 and Key Stage 2 are not included. In Scotland primary P1–P3 is interpreted to be Key Stage 1 and P4–P7, Key Stage 2.
3 Data for Wales refer to 2002/03.

Source: Department for Education and Skills; National Assembly for Wales; Scottish Executive; Northern Ireland Department of Education

A reduction in class sizes was particularly favoured by respondents who were themselves parents: 41 per cent who lived with a child aged under 16 considered it the most useful improvement at primary level.

In England and Wales parents have the right to express a preference for a maintained school at all stages of their child's education. If their choice is not met, they may appeal against the decision to a panel made up of representatives that are independent of the school's governing body and the Local Education Authority (LEA) that maintains the school. Not all appeals are heard by an appeal panel, as parents may be offered places that become available either at the school they have appealed for, or at another suitable school, before their appeal can be heard. As parents may lodge multiple appeals, they may withdraw other appeals if an earlier one has been successful.

The rate of appeals lodged by parents in 2002/03 against non-admission to secondary schools in England was 99 per 1,000 new admissions. The rate of appeals against non-admission to primary schools was far lower – 25 per 1,000 new admissions.

The number of admissions appeals to secondary schools in England nearly tripled between 1993/94 and 2002/03. Around a third of appeals lodged to secondary schools and heard by appeal panels in England were decided in favour of the parents each year since 1993/94 (Figure 3.6). Although the number of admissions appeals both lodged to primary schools and heard by panels peaked in 1996/97, the numbers in 2002/03 were similar to those in 1993/94. However the success rate for decisions in the parents' favour declined from 51 per cent of appeals heard by appeal panels in 1993/94 to 33 per cent in 2002/03.

There has been growing awareness and concern over the number of children outside the education system. Some have been excluded from schools, while others truant. In 2002/03, 10,000 children in Great Britain were permanently excluded from schools. This was around 3 per cent lower than the previous year, and considerably lower than the peak year of 1996/97, when over 13,000 children were permanently excluded. The number of boys permanently excluded outnumbered girls by around four to one.

Table **3.5**

Attitudes to improving primary and secondary schools:[1] by sex, 2003

Great Britain   Percentages

	Primary			Secondary		
	Males	Females	All	Males	Females	All
Smaller class sizes	32	42	37	22	27	25
Better quality teachers	16	12	14	19	14	16
More resources for buildings, books and equipment	17	17	17	15	16	15
More training and preparation for jobs	..	..	..	12	14	13
More emphasis on developing the child's skills and interests	16	12	14	13	13	13
More links between parents and schools	11	10	10	7	8	7
More emphasis on exams and tests	1	1	1	4	3	4
Better leadership within individual schools	2	2	2	3	2	2
More information available about individual schools	2	1	2	1	1	1
Other	1	1	1	2	2	2
All[2]	100	100	100	100	100	100

1 Adults aged 18 and over were shown the above list and asked 'Which do you think would be the most useful one for improving the education of children in primary schools – aged (5–11/5–12) years?' and 'Which do you think would be the most useful one for improving the education of children in secondary schools – aged (11–18/12–18) years?'.
2 Includes those who responded 'Don't know' or did not answer.

Source: British Social Attitudes survey, National Centre for Social Research

Exclusion rates vary by ethnic group. In 2002/03 the highest rate of permanent exclusion in England was found among Black Caribbean pupils at 37 per 10,000 pupils, over 3 times the rate of both White pupils and Black African pupils (each at 12 per 10,000) and around 20 times the rate for Chinese pupils

(2 per 10,000), who were the least likely group to be excluded (Figure 3.7). The rate of exclusion for Black Caribbean pupils has, however, declined sharply since 1997/98 (76 per 10,000), while rates of exclusion for other ethnic groups have remained fairly stable.

Figure **3.6**

Appeals by parents against non-admission of their children to maintained schools decided in parents' favour[1]

England
Percentages

Figure **3.7**

Permanent exclusion rates:[1] by ethnic group, 2002/03

England
Rates per 10,000 pupils

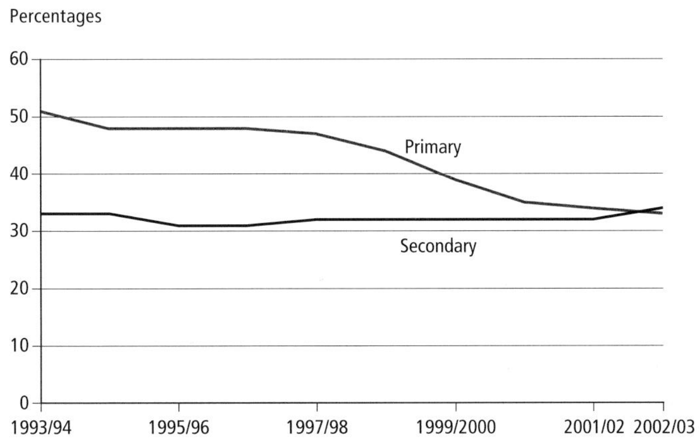

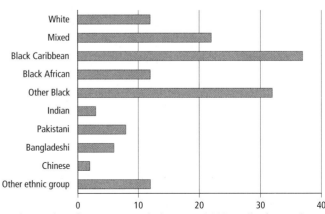

1 Number of appeals decided in favour of the parents expressed as a percentage of the number of appeals heard by panels.

Source: Department for Education and Skills

1 The number of permanent exclusions per 10,000 pupils of compulsory school age (headcount) in each ethnic group in primary, secondary and special schools (excluding dually registered pupils in special schools).

Source: Department for Education and Skills

Post-compulsory participation

Following compulsory education, at the age of 16 young people can choose to continue in full-time education, go into training or seek employment. However, not everyone working towards a qualification beyond the age of 16 will have worked their way continuously through the various levels of education. Just under half of working-age people who were studying towards a qualification in the United Kingdom in spring 2004 were aged 25 or over, and one fifth were aged 40 or over (Table 3.8). The age distribution varies according to the qualification being undertaken. Adults aged 25 and over comprised 20 per cent of people of working age studying towards a GCE A level or equivalent and 28 per cent of those studying towards a GCSE or equivalent. In contrast, 64 per cent of working-age people taking higher education qualifications below degree level, and 44 per cent of those studying at degree level or higher, were in this age group.

There were over 4.7 million students in further education in the United Kingdom in 2002/03, 59 per cent of whom were female (Table 3.9). There were almost four times as many female further education students in 2002/03 as in 1970/71, but only around twice as many male students.

There have also been substantial increases in the number of students in higher education over the last 30 or so years. In 2002/03 there were nearly 2.4 million students in higher education, 56 per cent of whom were female. There were six

and a half times as many female students in higher education in 2002/03 as in 1970/71, but only two and a half times as many male students.

Most further education students study part time and women are more likely than men to do so. Part-time study was also more common among those aged 30 and over, than those aged under 30. In 2002/03 one third of further education students were females aged 30 and over who studied part time. A smaller proportion of higher education students, than further education students, studied part time in 2002/03 (42 per cent compared with 78 per cent).

Young people in manual social classes are under-represented in higher education in Great Britain and the gap in participation rates between those from manual and non-manual classes has increased over the last 40 or so years (see Appendix, Part 3: Social class). Despite increasing from a participation rate of 4 per cent in 1960 to 19 per cent in 2001, participation in the manual social classes remains well below that of the non-manual classes. Participation rates for the non-manual social classes increased from 27 per cent to 50 per cent over the same period.

Destinations of UK and EU domiciled students who graduate in the United Kingdom with a first degree vary and include continuing in education as well as moving into employment. Around two thirds (63 per cent) of such full-time students whose destinations were known went into employment

Table 3.8

People working towards a qualification:[1] by age, 2004[2]

United Kingdom

Percentages

	Degree or higher or equivalent	Higher education[3]	GCE A level or equivalent	GCSE or equivalent	Other qualification[4]	All studying
16–19	15	17	71	66	12	33
20–24	41	20	9	6	13	20
25–29	13	12	4	5	13	10
30–39	17	25	8	11	27	18
40–49	10	19	6	8	22	13
50–59/64	4	8	3	5	14	7
All aged 16–59/64[5] (=100%) (millions)	1.9	0.5	1.4	0.9	1.7	6.4

1 For those working towards more than one qualification, the highest is recorded. See Appendix, Part 3: Qualifications.
2 At spring. Data are not seasonally adjusted and have been adjusted in line with population estimates published in spring 2003. See Appendix, Part 4: LFS reweighting.
3 Below degree level but including NVQ level 4.
4 Includes those who did not state which qualifications.
5 Males aged 16 to 64 and females aged 16 to 59.

Source: Labour Force Survey, Office for National Statistics

Table 3.9

Students in further and higher education:[1] by type of course and sex

United Kingdom   Thousands

	Males				Females			
	1970/71	1980/81	1990/91	2002/03	1970/71	1980/81	1990/91	2002/03
Further education								
Full-time	116	154	219	509	95	196	261	517
Part-time	891	697	768	1,424	630	624	986	2,278
All further education	1,007	851	987	1,933	725	820	1,247	2,795
Higher education								
Undergraduate								
Full-time	241	277	345	534	173	196	319	645
Part-time	127	176	193	261	19	71	148	430
Postgraduate								
Full-time	33	41	50	105	10	21	34	103
Part-time	15	32	50	135	3	13	36	160
All higher education[2]	416	526	638	1,036	205	301	537	1,339

1 Home and overseas students. See Appendix, Part 3: Stages of education.
2 Figures for 2002/03 include a small number of higher education students for whom details are not available by level.

Source: Department for Education and Skills; National Assembly for Wales; Scottish Executive; Northern Ireland Department for Employment and Learning; Higher Education Statistics Agency

Table 3.10

Destinations of first degree graduates:[1] by sex and occupation, 2003

United Kingdom   Percentages

	Males	Females	All
Managers and senior officials	12	8	9
Professional	28	23	25
Associate professional and technical	24	30	28
Administrative and secretarial	14	19	17
Skilled trades	2	-	1
Personal service	2	6	4
Sales and customer service	10	10	10
Process, plant and machine operatives	1	-	1
Elementary	6	3	5
All occupations	100	100	100

1 Occupations of UK domiciled full- and part-time first degree graduates in employment about six months after completion of their degree.

Source: Department for Education and Skills; Higher Education Statistics Agency

in 2003. The majority worked in the United Kingdom, a small proportion (3 per cent) went into employment overseas, around 1 in 12 (8 per cent) combined employment with further study and a further 1 in 6 (16 per cent) continued just to study. The proportion of full-time first degree graduates who were assumed to be unemployed fell from 11 per cent in 1991 to 7 per cent in 2003. This reflects the fall in unemployment in the population as a whole by around 1 million between 1991 and 2003 (see Figure 4.17).

Of those full- and part-time UK domiciled degree graduates, in 2003, whose destination after graduation was known to be employment, 28 per cent were employed in associate professional and technical occupations and 25 per cent were in professional occupations (Table 3.10). A higher proportion of female than male graduates gained posts in the associate professional and technical occupations, whereas a higher proportion of male than female graduates gained employment in managerial or professional occupations. Few first degree graduates were in skilled trades and process, plant and machine operation occupations.

Table **3.11**

Pupils reaching or exceeding expected standards:[1] by Key Stage and sex, 2004

England   Percentages

	Teacher assessment		Tests	
	Boys	Girls	Boys	Girls
Key Stage 1				
English				
Reading	81	89	81	89
Writing	78	88	76	87
Mathematics	88	91	89	92
Science	88	91	.	.
Key Stage 2				
English	69	80	72	83
Mathematics	75	76	74	74
Science	82	84	86	86
Key Stage 3				
English	62	77	64	77
Mathematics	72	76	72	74
Science	69	72	65	67

1 See Appendix, Part 3: The National Curriculum.

Source: Department for Education and Skills

Educational attainment

The Key Stages form part of the National Curriculum in England and Wales, more details of which can be found in Appendix, Part 3: The National Curriculum. Scotland and Northern Ireland have their own schemes. In 2004, the proportion of boys in England reaching the required standard for reading and writing at Key Stage 1 and English at Key Stages 2 and 3 was lower than that for girls (Table 3.11). The difference between the proportions of boys and girls reaching the expected level in tests and teacher assessments for mathematics and science was less pronounced.

The proportion of pupils achieving the expected level in English and science declined for both boys and girls between Key Stages 2 and 3 but for mathematics it only declined for boys. Sixty nine per cent of boys reached the expected standard in English teacher assessments at Key Stage 2 compared with 80 per cent of girls whereas at Key Stage 3 these proportions had fallen to 62 per cent and 77 per cent respectively. Similarly in science teacher assessments, 82 per cent of boys and 84 per cent of girls at Key Stage 2 reached the expected level, compared with 69 per cent and 72 per cent, respectively, at Key Stage 3.

In 2001 the Progress in International Reading Literacy Study (PIRLS) assessed the reading abilities of over 140,000 ten year old pupils in 35 countries. Pupils in both England and Scotland scored significantly above the standardised international average of 500 (Figure 3.12). English pupils ranked third among all the countries taking part, behind Sweden and the Netherlands (although only Swedish pupils did significantly better than the English). Boys in England had the third highest score (541) and girls had the second highest score (564). Scores in Scotland were 537 for girls and 519 for boys. In common with all participating countries, girls in England and Scotland performed significantly better than boys. Among the G8 countries (excluding Japan which did not take part), the difference in the mean scores of girls and boys was highest in England (22) and lowest in Italy (8). The average difference between boys and girls among all the participating countries was 20 points.

In England, Wales and Northern Ireland, pupils in their last year of compulsory education sit General Certificates of Secondary Education (GCSEs), while Standard Grades are taken in Scotland. In 2002/03, 53 per cent of pupils in the United Kingdom gained five or more GCSEs (or equivalent) at grades A* to C, compared with 46 per cent in 1995/96. These proportions rose for both sexes between 1995/96 and 2002/03 but girls continued to outperform boys. The gap between girls and boys in the proportion that achieved these high grades was around 10 percentage points throughout the period. In 2002/03, 59 per cent of girls gained five or more GCSEs at grades A* to C (or equivalent), compared with 48 per cent of boys.

Girls outperform boys in all the most common subjects that young people study at GCSE level (Table 3.13). Of the selected subjects shown, the biggest difference in the proportions of entrants achieving grades A* to C (20 percentage points) was in art and design for which 77 per cent of girls who entered for the exam achieved a high grade. The smallest difference (2 percentage points) was in mathematics: around half of boys and girls who took the exam achieved a grade A* to C. Even when more boys than girls entered for an exam, for example design and technology, a smaller proportion of boys than girls achieved a grade A* to C. This pattern was consistent across commonly studied subjects where male entrants outnumbered female entrants.

The General Certificate of Education Advanced level (GCE A level) is usually taken after GCSEs and a further two years of study in a school or further education institution, at around age 16 to 18, in England, Wales and Northern Ireland. In Scotland, Higher and Advanced Higher qualifications are usually taken at ages 17 and 18, as part of the National Qualifications framework.

Figure **3.12**

Mean score for reading achievement: by sex, G8 comparison,[1] 2001

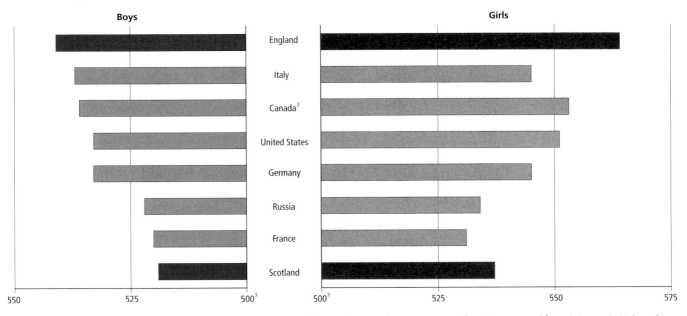

1 Fourth grade students in G8 countries, excluding Japan, which did not take part. The average age of students ranged from 9.8 years in Italy and
   Scotland to 10.5 years in Germany.
2 Ontario and Quebec only.
3 International average score for reading achievement.

Source: Progress in International Reading Literacy Study, National Foundation for Educational Research

Table **3.13**

GCSE or equivalent entries and achievements:[1] by selected subject and sex, 2002/03

United Kingdom   Percentages

	Number of entries (thousands)			Percentage of entrants achieving grade A*–C		
	Males	Females	All	Males	Females	All
Mathematics	371	362	733	51	53	52
English	348	347	696	54	69	62
English Literature[2]	269	287	555	58	73	66
Science Double Award	261	266	527	53	56	55
Design and Technology	252	215	467	47	63	54
French	171	194	365	43	59	52
Geography	137	107	245	59	66	62
History	119	119	237	61	68	64
Art and Design	96	132	228	58	77	69
Physical Education	93	46	139	58	62	60
German	66	71	138	49	62	56
Information Technology	70	47	117	57	64	60
Science Single Award	40	38	78	18	21	20

1 Some double counting may occur if a student enters for more than one subject within a subject category. Those in all schools who were 15 at the
   start of the academic year, 31 August 2002. Pupils in Year S4 in Scotland. See Appendix, Part 3: Qualifications.
2 Data are for England and Wales only.

Source: Department for Education and Skills; National Assembly for Wales; Scottish Executive; Northern Ireland Department of Education

There is a wide variety of subjects available, and there are differences in subject choice between males and females. In 2002/03, 76 per cent of school or further education students who entered for GCE A level (or equivalent) physics and 74 per cent of those entered for computer studies in the United Kingdom were male. Other male-dominated subjects included economics (69 per cent) and mathematics (60 per cent). In comparison, females made up around 70 per cent of those entered for religious studies, social studies, English literature, modern languages, and art and design (although data for English Literature are only for England and Wales). Furthermore, 94 per cent of entrants for home economics were female.

The proportion of pupils in the United Kingdom gaining two or more GCE A levels (or equivalent) increased from 19 per cent in 1992/93 to 39 per cent in 2002/03. The proportion of young women who achieved this increased from 20 per cent in 1992/93 to 43 per cent in 2002/03 (Figure 3.14). For young men the proportion increased from 18 per cent to 34 per cent over the same period. Thus the performance gap between the sexes widened to 9 percentage points, from just under 2 percentage points in 1992/93.

Figure **3.14**

Achievement of two or more GCE A levels[1] or equivalent: by sex

United Kingdom

Percentages

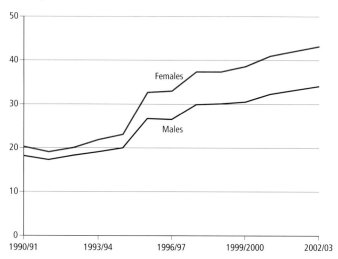

1 Two A levels are equivalent to three or more Highers. Data are for pupils in schools and further education institutions. Data prior to 1995/96, and for Wales and Northern Ireland in 2002/03, relate to schools only. Data for Scottish Qualifications from 2000/01 are not on the same basis as earlier years.

Source: Department for Education and Skills; National Assembly for Wales; Scottish Executive; Northern Ireland Department of Education

An alternative to the more traditional and academic GCE A levels (or equivalent) are National Vocational Qualifications (NVQs). Since their introduction in 1987, 4.4 million NVQs and

Scottish Vocational Qualifications (SVQs) had been awarded in the United Kingdom by September 2003. In 2002/03, 432,000 NVQs and SVQs were awarded, 6 per cent more than in the previous year. The majority were awarded at level 2, accounting for 57 per cent of all NVQ/SVQ awards (Table 3.15). Over one quarter of NVQs and SVQs were in areas providing goods and services such as catering and tourism. A further quarter were in areas providing business services such as management studies.

Table **3.15**

NVQ/SVQ awards:[1] by framework area and level, 2002/03

United Kingdom   Thousands

	Level				
	1	2	3	4 & 5	Total
Providing goods and services	33	69	16	..	118
Providing business services	4	58	32	11	106
Providing health, social and protective services	..	42	36	4	83
Constructing	3	30	14	..	47
Engineering	4	16	13	..	34
Manufacturing	5	20	1	..	26
Tending animals, plants and land	3	5	2	..	9
Other[2]	..	6	3	1	10
Total	52	247	116	18	432

1 Missing figures were each less than 1,000. See Appendix, Part 3: Qualifications.
2 Includes transporting, developing and extending skill and knowledge, extracting and providing natural resources, communicating and other not classified.

Source: Department for Education and Skills from the National Information System for Vocational Qualifications

In winter 2003/04, males in Great Britain were over one and a half times as likely as females to be qualified to at least GCE A level (or equivalent) standard (Table 3.16). The difference was less pronounced among those with at least a degree or equivalent: 18 per cent of working-age men, and 16 per cent of working-age women. This, however, is influenced by historic social effects: the proportion of men aged 50 to 64 with a degree or equivalent is one and a half times that of women aged 50 to 59. Among both working-age men and women, those aged 50 and over were the most likely to hold no qualifications, the proportion being more pronounced for women.

Large differences in qualification levels can be found between ethnic groups. Among men in Great Britain, Black Caribbeans and Bangladeshis were the least likely to have a degree in 2002–03 while Chinese, Indian, Black African and White Irish

Table **3.16**

Highest qualification held:[1] by sex and age, 2003/04[2]

Great Britain   Percentages

	Degree or equivalent	Higher education qualification[3]	GCE A level or equivalent	GCSE grades A*–C or equivalent	Other qualification	No qualification	All
Males							
16–19	..	..	28	42	11	17	100
20–24	14	6	38	22	12	7	100
25–29	29	8	23	17	14	8	100
30–39	22	9	25	19	15	9	100
40–49	20	9	30	15	13	12	100
50–64	17	9	32	10	13	20	100
All males	18	8	29	18	13	13	100
Females							
16–19	..	1	31	45	8	13	100
20–24	16	7	35	24	9	8	100
25–29	29	9	20	21	12	8	100
30–39	20	10	16	29	14	11	100
40–49	17	12	15	27	14	16	100
50–59	11	12	12	20	18	28	100
All females	16	10	18	27	14	15	100

1 Males aged 16 to 64, females aged 16 to 59.
2 At winter. Data are not seasonally adjusted and have been adjusted in line with population estimates published in spring 2003. See Appendix, Part 4: LFS reweighting.
3 Below degree level.

Source: Department for Education and Skills from the Labour Force Survey

men were most likely. Among women, the Bangladeshi and Pakistani groups were the least likely to have a degree while Chinese women were the most likely, followed by White Irish women and those in the White Other and Indian groups.

Adult training and learning

Learning throughout working life is becoming increasingly necessary because of the pace of change within the labour market, and many people receive training in the workplace. The National Employers Skills Survey found that in 2003, 59 per cent of employers in England had provided training over the past 12 months (see Appendix, Part 3: National Employers Skills Survey). Job-specific training was the most common form: 80 per cent of employers provided this kind of training. Where training was provided, 51 per cent of employers reported that at least some of the training was intended to lead to a formal qualification.

In spring 2004, 16 per cent of employees of working age in the United Kingdom had received some job-related training in the four weeks prior to interview in the Labour Force Survey, much

the same proportion as in each of the spring quarters since 1995. In general, greater proportions of women than men received job-related training, and the proportion was lower for older than for younger employees. Compared with other age groups men aged 16 to 17 (23 per cent) and women aged 18 to 24 (23 per cent) were the most likely to have received such training (Figure 3.17 overleaf). Job-related training was most common in professional, associate professional and technical, and personal service occupations. There are various education and training options available to young people who decide not to continue in full-time education, including a number of government-supported training initiatives. In England and Wales, Work Based Learning for Young People aims to ensure that all young people have access to post-compulsory education or training. Included within this initiative are Apprenticeships which provide structured learning programmes for young people aged 16 to 24, combining work-based training with off-the-job learning.

In November 2003 there were 290,000 young people on Work Based Learning schemes in England. Almost all participants in

Figure **3.17**

Employees receiving job-related training:[1] by age and sex, 2004[2]

United Kingdom

Percentages

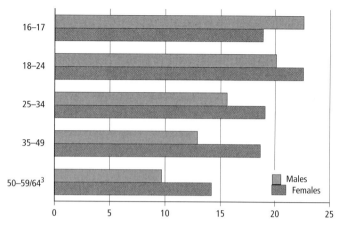

1 Employees (those in employment excluding the self-employed, unpaid family workers and those on government programmes) who received job-related training in the four weeks before interview.
2 At spring. Data are not seasonally adjusted and have been adjusted in line with population estimates published in spring 2003. See Appendix, Part 4: LFS reweighting.
3 Males aged 50 to 64, females aged 50 to 59.

Source: Department for Education and Skills from the Labour Force Survey

Figure **3.18**

Young people[1] in Work Based Learning:[2] by sex and selected area of learning, 2003

England

Percentages

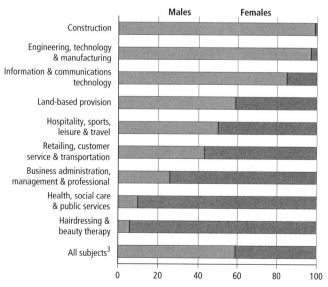

1 People aged 16 to 24. Data are at November.
2 Work Based Learning for young people comprises Advanced Apprenticeships at NVQ Level 3, Apprenticeships at NVQ Level 2, NVQ Learning, and Entry to Employment (E2E).
3 Includes science and mathematics, visual and performing arts and media, and people whose area of learning is not known.

Source: Learning and Skills Council; Department for Education and Skills

the areas of construction, and engineering, technology and manufacturing were men (Figure 3.18). In contrast, women greatly outnumbered men in hairdressing and beauty therapy and in health, social care and public services.

One initiative aimed at providing young people with basic skills are the Key Skills qualifications that were introduced in September 2000. These qualifications are available in England, Wales and Northern Ireland and are aimed at improving essential skills such as communication, application of number and information technology. The number of Key Skills qualifications achieved increased each year since their introduction, from 115,000 awarded in 2000/01 to 263,000 in 2002/03. Information technology accounted for 40 per cent of Key Skills qualifications in 2002/03, compared with 33 per cent two years earlier.

Many adults continue their education outside the work environment, either for enjoyment or to develop new skills. In November 2002, there were over 1.0 million enrolments on adult education courses provided by Local Education Authorities (LEAs) in England, nearly three quarters of which were by women. Enrolments on daytime classes increased from 504,000 in November 1992 to 580,000 in November 2002 (Figure 3.19). Over the same period evening and open distance learning course enrolments fell from 775,000 to 461,000. Since 2000, enrolments on daytime courses have outnumbered those for evening and open distance learning courses.

In November 2002 the majority of enrolments (660,000) were for courses that did not lead to any formal qualification, such as

Figure **3.19**

Enrolments on adult education courses:[1] by attendance mode

England

Thousands

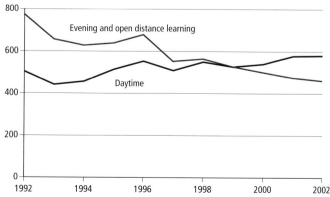

1 Adult education courses provided by Local Education Authorities. Data are at November each year and for 1992 to 1994 exclude contracted out provision. See Appendix, Part 3: Adult education.

Source: Department for Education and Skills

physical education, sports and fitness, or practical crafts. Enrolments on these courses have decreased by 29 per cent since 1992. Over one third of enrolments in 2002 (380,000) were for courses that usually lead to a qualification, an increase of 11 per cent since 1992. Fewer than one in ten of those who were enrolled on these courses were studying for GCSE, or GCE AS or A level qualifications compared with three in five who were studying for office and business, or other vocational courses.

Educational resources

Spending on education varies across the European Union (EU). The United Kingdom spent 5.5 per cent of gross domestic product (GDP) on education in 2001 (Table 3.20). This was the same as in 1995 and a slight increase (0.2 percentage points) compared with 2000. In 2001 the United Kingdom was ranked towards the middle of the EU-15 countries for such expenditure. Denmark spent the most on education as a proportion of GDP (7.1 per cent) and Greece the least (4.1 per cent).

In 2003/04, recurrent expenditure by central and local government on schools in England was an estimated

Table 3.20

Expenditure on education[1] as a percentage of GDP: EU comparison, 2001

Percentages

	Primary and secondary education[2]	Higher education	All levels[3]
Denmark	4.3	1.8	7.1
Sweden	4.3	1.7	6.5
Belgium	4.2	1.4	6.4
France	4.2	1.1	6.0
Portugal	4.2	1.1	5.9
Austria	3.9	1.2	5.8
Finland	3.7	1.7	5.8
United Kingdom	3.9	1.1	5.5
Germany	3.6	1.0	5.3
Italy	3.7	0.9	5.3
Spain	3.2	1.2	4.9
Netherlands	3.3	1.3	4.9
Ireland	3.1	1.3	4.5
Greece	2.7	1.1	4.1
Luxembourg	3.6	..	..

1 Public and private direct expenditure on institutions and public subsidies to students, eg for tuition fees and living costs.
2 Includes post-secondary non-higher education.
3 Includes expenditure for early childhood education and other miscellaneous expenditure.

Source: Organisation for Economic Co-operation and Development

£29.8 billion, 64 per cent of all education spending. This was an overall increase of 42 per cent in real terms since 1998/99, with spending on under fives, primary schools and secondary schools increasing by 71 per cent, 34 per cent and 35 per cent, respectively. Secondary schools accounted for the greatest percentage of expenditure (42 per cent in 2003/04), despite there being many more primary school pupils. In 2002/03 in LEA maintained schools in England, expenditure per full-time equivalent pupil at 2003/04 prices was £2,600 in primary schools and £3,320 in secondary schools.

In the 2003 British Social Attitudes survey, adults aged 18 and over in Great Britain were asked 'Which of these groups, if any, would be your highest priority for extra government spending on education?'. The six options were nursery or pre-school children, primary school children, secondary school children, less able children with special needs, students at colleges or universities, and none of these. The most popular choice overall was secondary school children: 31 per cent of men and 23 per cent of women said these school children should be the highest priority for extra government spending on education. The next most popular choice was less able children with special needs, although a higher proportion of women than men selected this group (29 per cent compared with 21 per cent). Primary school children were the priority for 21 per cent of people and students at colleges or universities were the priority for 15 per cent of people, while 10 per cent chose nursery or pre-school children.

The number of full-time qualified teachers in public sector mainstream schools in the United Kingdom decreased by around 53,000 between 1981/82 and 2002/03 to 440,000, although it has been rising since 1997/98 (Figure 3.21 overleaf). The number of full-time female teachers in these schools increased by 4 per cent to 306,000 over the 20 or so year period, while the number of male teachers fell by 33 per cent to 134,000. The majority of full-time teachers were women in both nursery and primary, and secondary schools. In nursery and primary schools 85 per cent of full-time teachers were female in 2002/03 whereas secondary schools were more balanced, with females comprising 55 per cent of full-time teachers. In 2002, 62 per cent of head teachers in maintained nursery and primary schools in England were female, compared with 32 per cent of head teachers in maintained secondary schools.

In 2003/04 there were 53 per cent more enrolments on teacher training courses in England and Wales than in 1990/91, although there were fluctuations in the number of enrolments during the 1990s. In 2003/04, over 36,000 students were enrolled on teacher training courses – just under 17,000 for primary education training and over 19,000 training for secondary education.

Figure **3.21**

Full-time teachers:[1] by sex and type of school

United Kingdom

Thousands

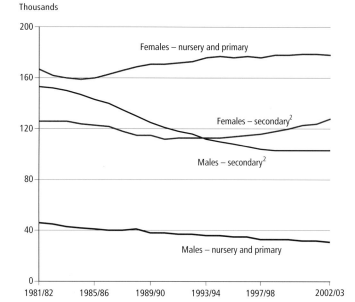

1 Qualified teachers only.
2 From 1993/94 data exclude sixth-form colleges in England and Wales which were reclassified as further education colleges on 1 April 1993.

Source: Department for Education and Skills; Scottish Executive; Northern Ireland Department of Education

Figure **3.22**

Support staff:[1] by type of school

England

Thousands

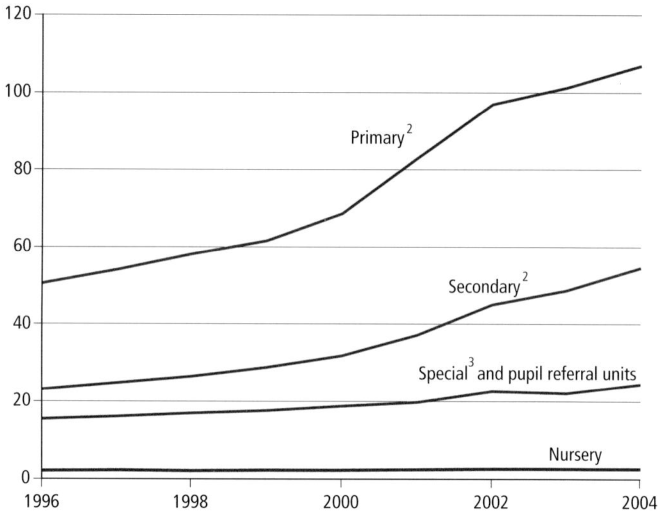

1 In maintained schools. Includes teaching assistants, technicians and other support staff but excludes administrative staff. Includes both full-time and the full-time equivalent of part-time support staff.
2 Includes middle schools as deemed.
3 Includes non-maintained special schools.

Source: Department for Education and Skills

An evaluation in 2002 of the impact of teaching assistants in primary schools found that teachers value their support and appreciate the benefits of having another adult in the classroom. The number of support staff in maintained schools in England who provide additional learning resources within the classroom more than doubled between 1996 and 2004, to nearly 189,000 (Figure 3.22). An increase in the number of support staff occurred in all types of school, but the largest percentage increase (136 per cent) was in secondary schools. However, most support staff are in primary schools, accounting for the placement of 57 per cent of these staff in 2004.

Computers have been widespread as resources for learning in schools since the 1980s. ICT (Information and Communications Technology) has been part of the National Curriculum since 1990, and ICT is used in teaching and learning across the subject areas of the National Curriculum. In 2003, after information technology, English lessons were the most likely to have a substantial use of computers at primary level. At secondary level, design and technology was the most likely to involve a substantial use of ICT, after information technology. Nearly all science lessons at both primary and secondary level had at least some use of computers.

The increase in the use of computers as an educational resource is reflected by the decrease in the average number of pupils per computer (used mainly for teaching and learning) in maintained

schools (Figure 3.23). In 1994 there was 1 computer for every 23 primary school pupils compared with 1 for every 8 pupils in 2004. In secondary schools, there was one computer for every ten pupils in 1994 compared with one for every five in 2004. Special schools had the lowest ratio in 2004: one computer for every three pupils.

Figure **3.23**

Average number of pupils per computer:[1] by type of school

England

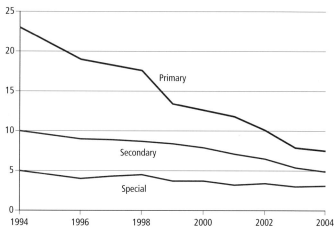

1 Computers used mainly for teaching and learning by pupils in maintained schools.

Source: Department for Education and Skills

Labour market

- Long-term sickness or disability was the most common reason given for economic inactivity by working-age men in spring 2004; for women the most common reason was looking after the family or home. (Table 4.5)

- The UK male working-age employment rate was 79 per cent in spring 2004, much the same proportion as in spring 1984; the female rate rose gradually over the period from 59 per cent to 70 per cent. (Figure 4.7)

- The proportion of UK male employee jobs in manufacturing fell by one third between 1984 and 2004, to 18 per cent; for females the proportion fell by more than half over the same period, to 7 per cent. (Table 4.12)

- In 2002-03, 23 per cent of Pakistani and 18 per cent of Chinese people in employment in Great Britain were self-employed. This compares with around one in ten White British people and fewer than one in ten Black people. (Figure 4.14)

- Almost half of male, and nearly one quarter of female, managers and senior officials in the United Kingdom usually worked over 45 hours a week in spring 2004. (Table 4.15)

- The proportion of UK male employees who were trade union members fell from 35 per cent in autumn 1995 to 29 per cent in autumn 2003. For women the proportion remained relatively stable over the period and was also 29 per cent in autumn 2003. (Figure 4.28)

Chapter 4

Most people spend a large part of their lives in the labour force, and so their experience of the world of work has an important impact on their lives and attitudes. The proportion of time people spend in the labour force has been falling. Young people are remaining longer in education and older people, due to the increase in longevity, are spending more years in retirement. More women than ever before are in paid employment, and employment in service industries continues to increase while employment in manufacturing continues to fall.

Labour Force Survey (LFS) data

Since October 2002, the Office for National Statistics (ONS) has published aggregate LFS estimates consistent with the population estimates derived from the 2001 Census. In March 2004, the ONS also published reweighted LFS microdata consistent with the post-2001 Census population estimates (published in February and March 2003). Since then the population estimates have been further revised as a result of methodological improvements and population studies. The aggregate LFS estimates continue to be adjusted to stay in line with the latest population estimates. They were most recently updated in October 2004. Analysis by the ONS has shown that the effect of the adjustments has a greater impact on levels data than on rates. Generally, revisions to rates are within sampling variability, while those for levels are not. This chapter uses the latest interim adjusted data where possible. However, where adjusted data are not available, only rates have been used. For more information, see Appendix, Part 4: LFS reweighting.

In December 2004 the ONS published a set of historical estimates of the headline measures of economic activity, economic inactivity, employment and unemployment covering the period 1971–91 which are fully consistent with post-1992 LFS data. This chapter uses these historical estimates where only headline data are reported (Figures 4.1, 4.7 and 4.17) but further breakdowns of the historical estimates are not yet available. For more information, see Appendix, Part 4: Historical LFS-consistent time series.

Economic activity

People are considered to be economically active, or in the labour force, if they are aged 16 and over and are either in work or actively looking for work. The proportion of working-age men in the United Kingdom who are economically active has fallen over the long term, while the proportion of women has increased (Figure 4.1). The male economic activity rate fell from 89 per cent in spring 1984, when the annual Labour Force Survey (LFS) began, to 84 per cent in spring 2004. The female economic activity rate, on the other hand, rose from 67 per cent in 1984 to 73 per cent in

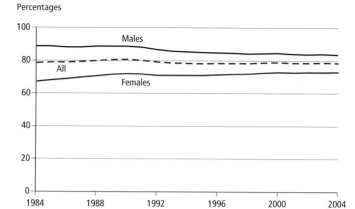

Figure 4.1

Economic activity rates:[1] by sex

United Kingdom

Percentages

1 At spring each year. Males aged 16 to 64, females aged 16 to 59. The percentage of the population that is in the labour force. Data are seasonally adjusted and have been adjusted in line with population estimates published in autumn 2004. See Appendix, Part 4: LFS reweighting, and Historical LFS-consistent time series.

Source: Labour Force Survey, Office for National Statistics

2004. The gap between economic activity rates for men and women has more than halved from 22 percentage points in 1984 to 10 percentage points in 2004. As the economically active include those who are unemployed (see Glossary at the end of the chapter), the rates are less likely to be affected by the economic cycle than employment rates.

In spring 2004 there were 28.4 million people in employment in the United Kingdom (Table 4.2). This is the highest number of people in employment in spring recorded by the LFS.

Comparing the labour market in spring 2004 with 15 years earlier, the number of people in employment has risen by 1.8 million, as more people are working, and fewer people are unemployed. Over a quarter (26 per cent) of employees were working part time in spring 2004 and the number was 27 per cent higher than in 1989. In spring 2004 around four in five part-time employees were women. However, more than two and a half times as many men as women were self-employed.

In the last 15 years the number of economically inactive people in the United Kingdom increased by 1.5 million. Men accounted for all of this increase as the number of inactive women was the same in spring 1989 as in spring 2004. Conversely women accounted for all of the increase in the number of economically active people over the period.

One of the main themes in this chapter is the increased participation of women in the labour market over the last two decades. However, the presence of a dependent child in the family still has a major effect on the economic activity of women of working age (Table 4.3). For both lone mothers and

Table **4.2**

Economic activity: by employment status and sex, 1989 and 2004[1]

United Kingdom   Millions

	1989			2004		
	Males	Females	All	Males	Females	All
Economically active						
In employment						
Full-time employees	11.6	6.0	17.5	11.4	6.8	18.1
Part-time employees	0.5	4.5	5.0	1.2	5.2	6.4
Self-employed	2.7	0.8	3.5	2.7	1.0	3.6
Others in employment[2]	0.3	0.2	0.5	0.1	0.1	0.2
All in employment	15.1	11.5	26.6	15.4	13.0	28.4
Unemployed[3]	1.2	0.9	2.1	0.8	0.6	1.4
All economically active	16.3	12.4	28.7	16.2	13.6	29.8
Economically inactive	5.2	10.8	16.0	6.7	10.8	17.5

1 At spring each year. People aged 16 and over. Data are seasonally adjusted and have been adjusted in line with population estimates published in
  autumn 2004. See Appendix, Part 4: LFS reweighting.
2 Those on government-supported training and employment programmes and, for 2004, also unpaid family workers.
3 See Appendix, Part 4: Unemployment.

Source: Labour Force Survey, Office for National Statistics

Table **4.3**

Economic activity status of women:[1] by marital status and age of youngest dependent child, 2004

United Kingdom   Percentages

	Age of youngest dependent child				No dependent children	All women[1]
	Under 5	5–10	11–15	16–18[2]		
Not married/cohabiting[3]						
Working full time	12	22	37	53	46	40
Working part time	21	34	29	19	21	23
Unemployed[4]	6	7	5	5	5	5
Economically inactive	61	37	29	23	28	32
All (=100%) (millions)	0.6	0.7	0.5	0.1	4.9	6.8
Married/cohabiting						
Working full time	20	27	38	43	52	40
Working part time	38	50	43	37	26	34
Unemployed[4]	2	2	2	2	2	2
Economically inactive	39	21	18	18	20	24
All (=100%) (millions)	2.2	1.7	1.2	0.4	5.3	10.8

1 At spring. Aged 16 to 59. Data are not seasonally adjusted and have been adjusted in line with population estimates published in spring 2003. See
  Appendix, Part 4: LFS reweighting.
2 Those in full-time education.
3 Includes single, widowed, separated or divorced.
4 See Appendix, Part 4: Unemployment.

Source: Labour Force Survey, Office for National Statistics

those with a partner, employment rates are lowest when they have a child under five. However, lone mothers with a pre-school child aged under five are less likely to be working than those who have a partner (33 per cent compared with 58 per cent in spring 2004). This differential decreases as the child gets older, so that for mothers whose youngest child is aged 16 to 18, 72 per cent of lone mothers worked, only 8 percentage points lower than for mothers with a partner.

Economic activity rates in the United Kingdom differ with age. In spring 2004, rates for men were highest for 25 to 34 and 35 to 49 year olds at 92 per cent for both groups, while for women they were highest for 35 to 49 year olds at 78 per cent. People over the state pension age (65 for men and 60 for women) can also be economically active, although the rates are low: 9 per cent for men aged 65 and over and 10 per cent for women aged 60 and over (see also Table 4.27). Of those under state pension age, young people aged 16 to 17 had the lowest economic activity rates.

Young people's labour market involvement is affected by whether or not they are in full-time education with economic activity rates being higher for those not in full-time education. In spring 2004, among those not in full-time education, young men (aged 16 to 24) were more likely than young women to be economically active – 91 per cent and 78 per cent, respectively (Table 4.4). Conversely, for those in full-time education, young women had higher economic activity rates than young men (50 per cent and 41 per cent, respectively).

Table 4.4

Economic activity status of young people:[1] by whether in full-time education, 2004[2]

United Kingdom   Percentages

	In full-time education		Not in full-time education		
	Males	Females	Males	Females	All
Economically active					
In employment	35	43	80	70	61
Unemployed	6	7	11	8	8
All economically active	41	50	91	78	70
Economically inactive	59	50	9	22	30
All (=100%) (millions)	1.3	1.3	2.1	2.1	6.8

1 Aged 16 to 24.
2 At spring. Data are seasonally adjusted and have been adjusted in line with population estimates published in autumn 2004. See Appendix, Part 4: LFS reweighting.

Source: Labour Force Survey, Office for National Statistics

Research using spring 2003 LFS data found that full-time and part-time students of working age have different reasons for their economic inactivity. As might be expected, 95 per cent of full-time students cited their studies as their main reason. Among part-time female students, looking after the family or home was the main reason for 42 per cent; only 27 per cent said they were inactive because they were a student. The reasons given by male part-time students differ to those for women: 37 per cent of men said it was because they were sick or disabled and 32 per cent gave being a student as their main reason.

Reasons for inactivity also vary by age. Long-term sickness or disability was the main reason for economic inactivity among working-age men, particularly for 35 to 49 year olds (60 per cent) (Table 4.5). Looking after the family or home was the most common reason for inactivity among working-age women: 45 per cent said this was their main reason for not seeking work but this rose to 72 per cent of 25 to 34 year olds.

In spring 2004 there were 7.8 million economically inactive people of working age in the United Kingdom, 60 per cent of whom were women. This compares with 7.3 million people in spring 1984, 73 per cent of whom were women. Over this period, there were different trends in economic inactivity for men and women. Inactivity rates for women declined from 33 per cent in spring 1984 to 27 per cent in spring 2004 while for men the inactivity rate increased from 11 per cent to 16 per cent.

One of the consequences of the increasing levels of employment in the United Kingdom is the rise in the number of working-age households that are work-rich – that is, households that include at least one person of working age and where all the people of working age are in employment. There were 10.7 million work-rich households in spring 2004, an increase of nearly 960,000 since spring 1997. Work-rich households as a proportion of all working-age households rose from 54 per cent in 1997 to 57 per cent in 2000 to 2004 (Figure 4.6). In spring 2004 around 16 per cent of working-age households were workless – that is, households where at least one person is of working age but no one is in employment.

The rate of worklessness for lone parent households with dependent children was 42 per cent in spring 2004. This was 1 percentage point lower than in the previous year and 8 percentage points below the rate in spring 1997. The rate of worklessness for couple households with dependent children was 5 per cent, unchanged from the previous year and 2 percentage points lower than in spring 1997.

Table **4.5**

Reasons for economic inactivity: by sex and age, 2004[1]

United Kingdom   Percentages

	16–24	25–34	35–49	50–59/64	All aged 16–59/64
Males					
Long-term sick or disabled	5	38	60	53	37
Looking after family or home	1	12	17	4	6
Student	84	25	4	-	30
Retired	0	0	-	31	13
Other	10	26	18	12	14
All males	100	100	100	100	100
Females					
Long-term sick or disabled	4	10	24	42	21
Looking after family or home	22	72	59	27	45
Student	64	8	4	1	19
Retired	0	0	-	15	4
Other	10	10	11	16	12
All females	100	100	100	100	100

1 At spring. Data are not seasonally adjusted and have been adjusted in line with population estimates published in spring 2003. See Appendix, Part 4: LFS reweighting.

Source: Labour Force Survey, Office for National Statistics

Figure **4.6**

Working-age households:[1] by household economic status

United Kingdom

Percentages

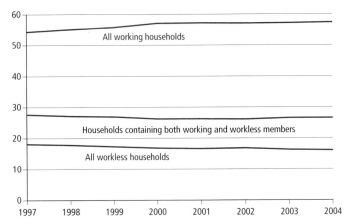

1 Percentages have been adjusted to include estimates for households with unknown economic activity and are for spring each year. Data are as a percentage of working-age households. A working-age household is a household that includes at least one female aged between 16 and 59 or a male aged between 16 and 64. Data are not seasonally adjusted and have been adjusted in line with population estimates published in spring 2003. See Appendix, Part 4: LFS reweighting.

Source: Labour Force Survey, Office for National Statistics

Employment

While the economic cycle has affected employment rates, the proportion of the working-age population in employment has risen slightly over the last 20 years and this has largely been driven by the increased participation of women.

Employment rates for men have risen from 78 per cent in spring 1984 to 79 per cent in spring 2004, with a peak in 1990 of 82 per cent, and a low in 1993 of 75 per cent following the recession of 1990 and 1991 (Figure 4.7 overleaf). For women, employment rates have generally risen gradually from 59 per cent in 1984 to 70 per cent in 2004. As with men the proportion of women in employment has followed the economic cycle, but for them such effects have generally been less marked. For example, between 1990 and 1993 the female employment rate fell less sharply than the male rate. However, since 1993 it has risen at virtually the same rate as the male rate. As with economic activity rates (see Figure 4.1) the difference between the employment rates of men and women has narrowed, from 19 percentage points in 1984 to 9 percentage points in 2004.

Employment rates are not uniform across the country. When considered by unitary authorities and metropolitan and shire counties, in 2003–04 some of the highest rates in the United Kingdom were in southern and central England and Scotland

Figure **4.7**

Employment rates:[1] by sex

United Kingdom

Percentages

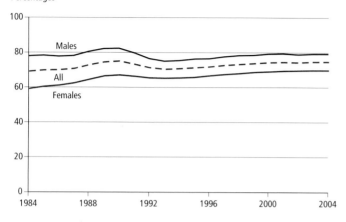

1 At spring each year. Males aged 16 to 64, females aged 16 to 59.
   The percentage of the population that is in employment. Data are
   seasonally adjusted and have been adjusted in line with population
   estimates published in autumn 2004. See Appendix, Part 4: LFS
   reweighting, and Historical LFS-consistent time series.

Source: Labour Force Survey, Office for National Statistics

Map **4.8**

Employment rates:[1] by area,[2] 2003–04[3]

United Kingdom

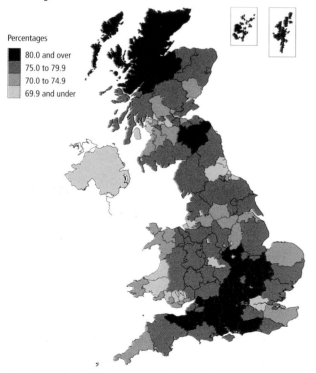

Percentages

- 80.0 and over
- 75.0 to 79.9
- 70.0 to 74.9
- 69.9 and under

1 Males aged 16 to 64, females aged 16 to 59. The percentage of the
   population that is in employment.
2 Counties and unitary authorities in England, unitary authorities in
   Wales and council areas in Scotland.
3 See Appendix, Part 4: Annual local area Labour Force Survey.

Source: Annual local area Labour Force Survey, Office for National
Statistics

with a number of areas having employment rates over 80 per cent (Map 4.8). The highest rates in the United Kingdom were in the Shetland Islands and Orkney Islands in Scotland and in Wokingham in England (83 per cent or more).

There were also variations in employment rates within areas. For example, the London Borough of Newham (52 per cent) had the lowest rate in the United Kingdom while the nearby borough of Havering had a much higher rate (80 per cent). Similarly Manchester was an inner city area with one of the lowest rates (60 per cent) but neighbouring Stockport had a far higher rate (80 per cent).

An alternative local area labour market indicator is jobs density. This is an indicator of labour demand and is defined as the total number of filled jobs in an area divided by the resident population of working age in that area (see Appendix, Part 4: Jobs densities for local areas). In 2002 there were just over 0.8 jobs per person of working age in the United Kingdom overall. The three local authorities with the highest jobs density were all in central London – City of London (57.4) where the resident population is very low, Westminster (4.3) and Camden (1.9). Chester-le-Street in the North East had the lowest density – fewer than 0.4 jobs per person of working age. Belfast (1.3), Aberdeen City (1.2) and Cardiff (1.0) were the areas with the highest jobs densities in Northern Ireland, Scotland and Wales, respectively. Large isolated rural areas, such as the highlands and islands of Scotland, tend to have relatively high jobs densities, as workers are less likely to travel outside the area.

In March 2000 the Lisbon European Council agreed an aim to achieve an overall European Union (EU) working-age employment rate of 70 per cent by 2010 and, for women, an employment rate of more than 60 per cent. The EU defines working age as people aged 15 to 64 so UK figures used in EU employment rate comparisons relate to people in this age group. In 2003 the overall employment rate in the enlarged EU was 63 per cent (Table 4.9). The United Kingdom had one of the highest employment rates after Denmark, the Netherlands and Sweden and was one of only four EU-25 countries with an employment rate above the 2010 target.

The average employment rate in the EU-25 was 71 per cent for males and 55 per cent for females – the United Kingdom had the fourth highest male rate and fifth highest female rate. The lowest employment rates for females were in the southern European countries of Greece, Italy and Malta. In contrast, the north European countries of Sweden, Denmark, the Netherlands and Finland had the highest rates. Among males the rates in 2003 varied from 57 per cent in Poland to 81 per cent in the Netherlands.

Table **4.9**

Employment rates:[1] by sex, EU comparison, 2003

Percentages

	Males	Females	All		Males	Females	All
EU-15				**Accession countries**			
Denmark	79.6	70.5	75.1	Cyprus	78.8	60.2	69.2
Netherlands	80.9	65.8	73.5	Czech Republic	73.1	56.3	64.7
Sweden	74.2	71.5	72.9	Estonia	67.2	59.0	62.9
United Kingdom	78.1	65.3	71.8	Slovenia	67.4	57.6	62.6
Austria	76.4	61.7	69.0	Latvia	66.1	57.9	61.8
Portugal	75.0	61.4	68.1	Lithuania	64.0	58.4	61.1
Finland	69.7	65.7	67.7	Slovakia	63.3	52.2	57.7
Ireland	75.0	55.8	65.4	Hungary	63.5	50.9	57.0
Germany	70.9	59.0	65.0	Malta	74.5	33.6	54.2
France	69.4	57.2	63.2	Poland	56.5	46.0	51.2
Luxembourg	73.3	52.0	62.7	EU-15 average	72.7	56.1	64.4
Spain	73.2	46.0	59.7	EU-25 average	70.9	55.1	63.0
Belgium	67.3	51.8	59.6				
Greece	72.4	43.8	57.8				
Italy	69.6	42.7	56.1				

1 People aged 15 to 64.

Source: Labour Force Survey, Eurostat

There is a range of factors underlying these comparisons: as well as economic cycle effects, which will vary across countries in a given year, they will also be affected by population structures and differing cultures, retirement ages and participation in post-compulsory full-time education across countries.

One of the factors that can affect employment rates is educational attainment: in the United Kingdom, for both sexes, employment rates increase generally with the level of qualifications (Table 4.10). In spring 2004, 90 per cent of men and 86 per cent of women who had a degree or the equivalent were in employment. This compares with 55 per cent of men and 44 per cent of women who did not have any qualifications. The difference in employment rates between men and women generally decreases as the level of qualification increases. For example, for those with a degree or equivalent there was a gap of 4 percentage points in employment rates between men and women, compared with 12 percentage points for those with qualifications at NVQ level 1 and below.

Table **4.10**

Employment rate:[1] by sex and highest qualification, 2004[2]

United Kingdom   Percentages

	Males	Females	All
Degree or equivalent	90	86	88
Higher education	87	84	85
GCE A level or equivalent	80	73	77
Trade apprenticeship	83	72	81
GCSE grades A* to C or equivalent	80	72	75
Qualifications at NVQ level 1 and below	77	65	71
Other qualifications – level unknown	79	65	73
No qualifications	55	44	49
All[3]	79	70	74

1 The percentage of the working-age population in employment. Males aged 16 to 64, females aged 16 to 59.
2 At spring. Data are not seasonally adjusted and have been adjusted in line with population estimates published in spring 2003. See Appendix, Part 4: LFS reweighting.
3 Includes those who did not state their highest qualification.

Source: Labour Force Survey, Office for National Statistics

Table 4.11

All in employment: by sex and occupation, 2004[1]

United Kingdom · Percentages

	Males	Females
Managers and senior officials	18	10
Professional	13	11
Associate professional and technical	13	14
Administrative and secretarial	5	22
Skilled trades	19	2
Personal service	2	14
Sales and customer service	5	12
Process, plant and machine operatives	12	2
Elementary	12	12
All occupations	100	100

1 At spring. People aged 16 and over. Data are not seasonally adjusted and have been adjusted in line with population estimates published in spring 2003. See Appendix, Part 4: LFS reweighting.

Source: Labour Force Survey, Office for National Statistics

Patterns of employment

The pattern of occupations followed by men and women is quite different (Table 4.11). In spring 2004 just over one fifth of women in employment were employed in administrative and secretarial work, while men were most likely to be employed in skilled trade occupations or as managers and senior officials. These occupations were among the ones least likely to be followed by women. Conversely women were more likely than men to be in employment in personal services and in sales and customer services. Only the professional, associate professional and technical, and the elementary occupations are almost equally likely to be followed by both men and women: between around one in seven and one in nine were employed in each of these occupations.

The UK economy experienced structural change in the post-war period, with a decline in the manufacturing sector and an increase in service industries. In 1984, 28 per cent of male employee jobs were in manufacturing but by 2004 this had fallen to 18 per cent (Table 4.12). The proportion of female employee jobs in the manufacturing sector also fell over the period, from 16 per cent to 7 per cent. The largest increase in both male and female employee jobs over the last 20 years has been in financial and business services, which accounted for about one in five of both male and female employee jobs in June 2004. Note that this table is based on jobs rather than people – one person may have more than one job, and jobs may vary in the number of hours' work they involve.

Table 4.12

Employee jobs:[1] by sex and industry

United Kingdom · Percentages

	Males			Females		
	1984	1994	2004	1984	1994	2004
Distribution, hotels, catering and repairs	18	20	23	26	26	26
Financial and business services	12	17	21	14	17	19
Manufacturing	28	24	18	16	11	7
Public administration, education and health	14	14	14	34	36	38
Transport and communication	10	10	8	2	2	3
Construction	8	7	8	2	2	1
Agriculture	2	2	1	1	1	1
Energy and water supply	4	2	1	1	-	-
Other community, social and personal services	3	4	5	5	5	6
All employee jobs (=100%) (millions)	12.3	11.3	13.3	10.2	11.7	12.9

1 Data are at June each year and are not seasonally adjusted.

Source: Short-term Turnover and Employment Survey, Office for National Statistics

Not all people in employment work as employees. In spring 2004, 3.6 million people were self-employed in the United Kingdom (see Table 4.2), accounting for 13 per cent of all those in employment. Self-employment is dominated by men – 73 per cent of self-employed people were men in spring 2004.

Men and women also vary considerably in the type of self-employed work they undertake. Almost one third of self-employed men work in the construction industry but very few women work in this sector (Figure 4.13). On the other hand, almost one quarter of self-employed women work in 'other services' – for example community, social and personal services – and over one fifth in public administration, education and health. Fewer than 1 in 12 self-employed men worked in each of these industries. The biggest changes over the ten years from 1994 were the increases in the proportions of both men and women in the banking, finance and insurance sector (by 4 and 5 percentage points respectively), and the falls in the distribution, hotels and restaurants sector, of 5 percentage points for men and 8 percentage points for women.

Figure **4.13**

Self-employment: by industry and sex, 2004[1]

United Kingdom
Percentages

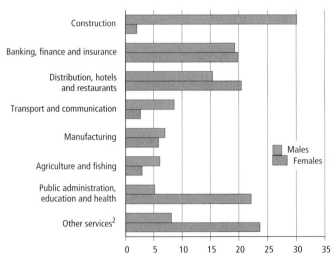

1 At spring. People aged 16 and over. Data are not seasonally adjusted and have been adjusted in line with population estimates published in autumn 2004. See Appendix, Part 4: LFS reweighting.
2 Community, social and personal services including sanitation, dry cleaning, personal care, and recreational, cultural and sporting activities.

Source: Labour Force Survey, Office for National Statistics

People in employment from Pakistani and Chinese groups are more likely to be self-employed than those in other ethnic groups (Figure 4.14). In 2002–03 over one fifth (23 per cent) of Pakistani and under one fifth (18 per cent) of Chinese people in employment in Great Britain were self-employed. This compared

Figure **4.14**

Self-employment:[1] by ethnic group, 2002–03[2]

Great Britain
Percentages

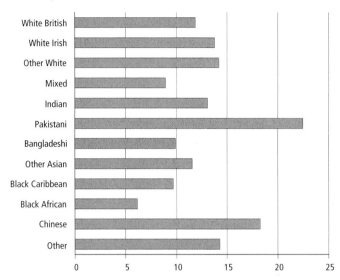

1 As a proportion of all in employment.
2 See Appendix, Part 4: Annual local area Labour Force Survey.

Source: Annual local area Labour Force Survey, Office for National Statistics

with around one in ten White British people and fewer than one in ten Black people.

Those most likely to be employed in professional occupations, either as employees or self-employed, were from the Indian, Chinese, White Irish, other non-British White and Other ethnic groups – between 16 and 18 per cent of those in employment in each of these groups were professionals. A relatively low proportion of White British people worked in professional occupations (11 per cent overall). The groups with the lowest rates of professionals were the Black groups, Bangladeshis and Pakistanis (less than 10 per cent each). There was a similar pattern across the ethnic groups for managers and senior officials.

There are larger ethnic differences between individual occupations. One in six Pakistani men in employment were cab drivers or chauffeurs in 2002–03, compared with 1 in 100 White British men. One in three Bangladeshi men were either cooks or waiters, compared with 1 in 100 White British men. On the other hand, the proportion of Indian men working as doctors, at 5 per cent, was almost ten times the rate for White British men. Among women in employment, around 1 in 10 Black African women and 1 in 12 White Irish women were nurses, compared with only 1 in 32 White British women. Indian women were seven times more likely than White British women to be working as sewing machinists, and four times more likely to be working as packers, bottlers, canners and fillers.

As well as their main full-time or part-time job some people also have second jobs. According to LFS estimates, 4 per cent of those in employment in the United Kingdom had a second job in spring 2004, a similar proportion to 20 years ago. The proportion was slightly higher for women (5 per cent), than men (3 per cent).

Table 4.2 shows that there were 6.4 million people working part time in the United Kingdom in spring 2004, of whom 5.2 million were women. However to distinguish only between full time and part time masks a variety of working patterns. The majority of men in employment (57 per cent) worked between 31 and 45 hours a week; the corresponding proportion for women was 46 per cent. About one in three men and one in ten women in employment usually worked more than 45 hours a week. These are usual weekly hours of work, including regular paid and unpaid overtime.

The length of the working week varies by occupation. Including routine overtime, 40 per cent of managers and senior officials worked over 45 hours a week – the occupational group most likely to work these long hours. Around half of male and almost one quarter of female managers and senior officials usually worked over 45 hours a week (Table 4.15). Women in professional occupations were the most likely women to work over 45 hours. Those who worked in sales and customer service, and elementary occupations, were the most likely to work less then 16 hours a week, and women were more likely than men to work these hours.

Government policy over recent years has stressed the importance of maintaining a healthy work-life balance. One factor seen as important is the availability of flexible working. Around one fifth of full-time, and one quarter of part-time, employees had some form of flexible working arrangement in spring 2004 (Table 4.16). Flexible working hours was the most common form of flexible working for full-time employees of both sexes. It was also the most common arrangement for men who worked part time, whereas term-time working was the most common arrangement for women who worked part time. In spring 2004 over two thirds of all term-time employees in the United Kingdom were either pre-school education workers, school teachers and support staff, post-compulsory education teachers, or other teaching assistants.

Regulations introduced across the United Kingdom in April 2003 give parents of children under six, or parents of disabled children under 18, the right to request a flexible work pattern: either a change to the hours they work; a change to the times when they are required to work; or the opportunity to work from home. Employers have a statutory duty to consider such applications seriously and may only refuse on business grounds. The ONS Omnibus Survey interviewed employees in Great Britain in 2003–04 and asked about their awareness of these laws. This varied by occupation – managers and senior officials were most likely to be aware (65 per cent) whereas process, plant and machine operatives were least likely to be aware (38 per cent).

Table **4.15**

Usual hours worked: by sex and occupation,[1] 2004[2]

United Kingdom

Percentages

	Males		Females	
	Less than 16 hours	Over 45 hours	Less than 16 hours	Over 45 hours
Managers and senior officials	2	48	5	23
Professional	3	33	8	27
Associate professional and technical	3	27	7	9
Administrative and secretarial	5	10	11	3
Skilled trades	1	33	10	11
Personal service	10	15	14	7
Sales and customer service	19	13	26	2
Process, plant and machine operatives	1	39	7	10
Elementary	11	21	39	4
All occupations	4	32	15	10

1 People aged 16 and over in employment. Time rounded to the nearest hour respondents worked on their main job.
2 At spring. Data are not seasonally adjusted and have been adjusted in line with population estimates published in spring 2003. See Appendix, Part 4: LFS reweighting.

Source: Labour Force Survey, Office for National Statistics

Table 4.16

Employees with flexible working patterns:[1] by sex, 2004[2]

United Kingdom   Percentages

	Males	Females	All employees
Full-time employees			
Flexible working hours	9.2	14.6	11.3
Annualised working hours	5.0	4.8	4.9
Four and a half day week	1.5	0.7	1.2
Term-time working	1.2	5.5	2.8
Nine day fortnight	0.3	0.3	0.3
Any flexible working pattern[3]	17.4	26.2	20.7
Part-time employees			
Flexible working hours	5.3	8.1	7.6
Annualised working hours	3.1	4.3	4.0
Term-time working	4.2	11.2	9.9
Job sharing	1.0	2.7	2.4
Any flexible working pattern[3]	15.0	27.0	24.7

1 Percentages are based on totals which exclude people who did not state whether or not they had a flexible working arrangement. Respondents could give more than one answer.
2 At spring. People aged 16 and over. Data are not seasonally adjusted and have been adjusted in line with population estimates published in spring 2003. See Appendix, Part 4: LFS reweighting.
3 Includes other categories of flexible working not separately identified.

Source: Labour Force Survey, Office for National Statistics

Unemployment

The number of unemployed people is linked to the economic cycle, albeit with a time lag. Broadly speaking, as the country experiences economic growth so the number of jobs grows and unemployment falls, though any mismatches between the skill needs of the new jobs and the skills of those available for work may slow this process. Conversely as the economy slows and goes into recession so unemployment tends to rise. The latest peak in unemployment occurred in 1993, when it reached nearly 3 million (Figure 4.17). The recession in the early 1990s had a much greater effect on unemployment among men than among women. In spring 2001 the number of unemployed people fell to 1.4 million. Unemployment then increased slightly before falling back to 1.4 million in spring 2004.

Figure 4.17 shows the last peak in UK unemployment was in 1993 and since then unemployment rates across all regions have generally fallen. London, the West Midlands and the North East had the highest unemployment rates in England in spring 2004 at 6.8 per cent, 5.6 per cent and 5.5 per cent respectively (Figure 4.18). The lowest rates were in the South West and South East at 3.3 per cent and 3.8 per cent.

Figure 4.17

Unemployment:[1] by sex

United Kingdom

Millions

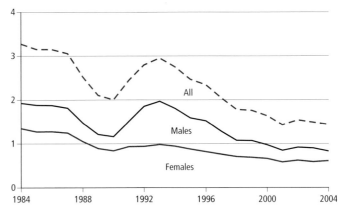

1 At spring each year. People aged 16 and over. Data are seasonally adjusted and have been adjusted in line with population estimates published in autumn 2004. See Appendix, Part 4: Unemployment, and LFS reweighting, and Historical LFS-consistent time series.

Source: Labour Force Survey, Office for National Statistics

The largest fall in unemployment rates in England between 1993 and 2004 was in the North East (6.9 percentage points) whereas the smallest fall was in the South East (4.5 percentage points).

Figure 4.18

Unemployment rates:[1] by region, 1993 and 2004[2]

Percentages

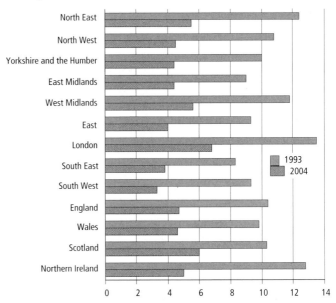

1 See Appendix, Part 4: Unemployment.
2 At spring each year. People aged 16 and over. Data are seasonally adjusted and have been adjusted in line with population estimates published in autumn 2004. See Appendix, Part 4: LFS reweighting.

Source: Labour Force Survey, Office for National Statistics

Of the constituent countries Scotland had the highest unemployment rate in 2004 whereas eleven years earlier the rate was highest in Northern Ireland. However unemployment rates in Northern Ireland fell by 7.8 percentage points between 1993 and 2004 – the largest fall in the United Kingdom over the period. Wales had the lowest rates of all four countries in both years.

In December 2003 the unemployment rate in the EU-15 was 8 per cent, ranging from 4 per cent in Luxembourg to 11 per cent in Spain (Table 4.19). Unemployment rates in the ten new member states ranged more widely than in the EU-15, from 5 per cent in Cyprus to 19 per cent in Poland, and seven of these accession states had rates higher than the EU-15 average. The United Kingdom had the sixth lowest unemployment rate of all the EU-25. The differences in rates between men and women were greatest in the southern European countries of Greece, Spain, Malta and Italy where rates for women were between 5 and 9 percentage points higher than for men. For most of the other EU countries, including the United Kingdom, the differences in rates were no more than 2 percentage points.

The unemployment rate in the United Kingdom is higher for young people than older people, and also higher for men than women. For 16 to 17 year old men, the unemployment rate was 25 per cent in spring 2004, compared with 18 per cent for young women. The lowest unemployment rates in spring 2004 were among men and women aged 50 and over, at 3.4 per cent for men and 2.2 per cent for women.

However, younger people are less likely than older people to have been unemployed for a long period. In spring 2004, 13 per cent of unemployed 18 to 24 year olds had been unemployed for over 12 months, compared with 33 per cent of those aged 50 and over. Since 1984, across all age groups, unemployed men have been more likely than unemployed women to have been out of work for over 12 months. As with the unemployment rates, the proportion of the unemployed who were unemployed for over 12 months reflects the economic cycle (Figure 4.20).

A rise in overall redundancy rates and job destruction may be indicative of economic slowdown and may lead to an increase in the unemployment rate. Rising redundancy rates in an industry may also indicate a decline in that industry. The redundancy rate is defined in the Glossary at the end of the chapter.

Table **4.19**

Unemployment rates:[1] by sex, EU comparison, 2003[2]

Percentages

	Males	Females	All		Males	Females	All
EU-15				**Accession countries**			
Luxembourg	2.9	5.4	3.9	Cyprus	4.2	5.2	4.7
Austria	4.0	4.5	4.2	Hungary	6.1	5.6	5.9
Netherlands	4.1	4.5	4.3	Slovenia	5.9	7.0	6.4
Ireland	4.8	4.2	4.6	Czech Republic	6.8	10.2	8.3
United Kingdom	5.3	4.2	4.8	Malta	7.1	12.1	8.6
Denmark	5.6	6.4	6.0	Estonia	9.6	9.6	9.6
Sweden	6.4	5.7	6.0	Latvia	10.3	10.7	10.5
Portugal	5.5	7.3	6.3	Lithuania	11.0	12.7	11.9
Belgium	8.1	8.7	8.3	Slovakia	16.2	16.9	16.6
Italy	6.6	11.4	8.5	Poland	18.5	19.9	19.1
Finland	9.1	8.8	9.0	EU-15 average	7.4	9.0	8.1
Greece	5.8	14.4	9.3				
France	8.7	10.6	9.6	EU-25 average	8.3	10	9.1
Germany	9.9	9.1	9.6				
Spain	8.2	15.6	11.2				

1 People aged 15 to 74, except for the United Kingdom and Spain where data refer to those aged 16 to 74.
2 Data are at December and are seasonally adjusted.

Source: Labour Force Survey, Eurostat

Figure **4.20**

Proportion of the unemployed[1] who were unemployed for over 12 months:[2] by sex

United Kingdom
Percentages

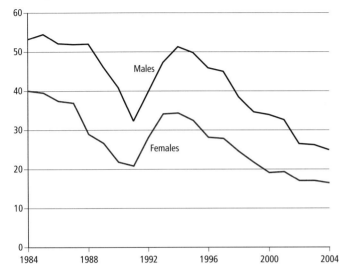

1 See Appendix, Part 4: Unemployment.
2 At spring each year. People aged 16 and over. Data are not seasonally adjusted and have been adjusted in line with population estimates published in autumn 2004. See Appendix, Part 4: LFS reweighting.

Source: Labour Force Survey, Office for National Statistics

Between 1995 and 1998 redundancy rates (at spring and not seasonally adjusted) in the United Kingdom fell from 8.3 redundancies per 1,000 employees to 7.3 per 1,000 employees but increased again to 7.8 per 1,000 employees in 1999. After a drop in spring 2000 and 2001 the redundancy rate peaked again in spring 2002 at 8.1 redundancies per 1,000 employees, after which it fell back to 5.9 per 1,000 in spring 2004 (Table 4.21). The fastest decline in redundancy rates between spring 2002 and spring 2004 was among young men (aged 16 to 24) where the rate fell by almost half. On the other hand, the redundancy rate for young women increased over the period. Men are more likely to be made redundant than women.

In spring 2004 the industrial sector with the highest redundancy rate was manufacturing, at 12.1 redundancies per 1,000 employees, followed by construction at 9.4 per 1,000. The rate for the services sector, which accounted for over half of the total number of redundancies, was 4.3 per 1,000 employees.

Working lives

People have different ways of finding work. Figure 4.22 (overleaf) shows that in spring 2004 men were most likely to have obtained their current job by hearing from someone who worked at their current workplace (32 per cent), whereas women were most likely to have obtained their job by replying to an advertisement (34 per cent). The methods people use to

Table **4.21**

Redundancy rates:[1] by sex and age

United Kingdom   Rate per 1,000 employees

	2000	2001	2002	2003	2004
Males					
16–24	12.6	12.8	12.2	8.0	6.7
25–49	8.2	7.2	9.2	7.8	7.0
50 and over	9.5	10.4	12.5	9.8	8.8
All males	9.2	8.7	10.4	8.3	7.4
Females					
16–24	6.2	7.1	4.3	5.6	5.2
25–49	5.2	5.0	5.8	4.2	3.8
50 and over	6.4	3.5	6.4	4.4	5.2
All females	5.6	5.0	5.7	4.5	4.4
All					
16–24	9.5	10.0	8.2	6.8	6.0
25–49	6.7	6.1	7.5	6.0	5.4
50 and over	8.0	7.1	9.5	7.2	7.1
All	7.4	6.9	8.1	6.4	5.9

1 The ratio of the number of redundancies in one quarter to the number of employees in the previous quarter, measured as redundancies per 1,000 employees. At spring. People aged 16 and over. Data are not seasonally adjusted and have been adjusted in line with population estimates published in spring 2003. See Appendix, Part 4: LFS reweighting.

Source: Labour Force Survey, Office for National Statistics

obtain their jobs also differ according to their occupations. Replying to an advertisement was the most common method for most occupational groups, but people employed in skilled trades, process, plant and machine operatives, and elementary occupations were most likely to have obtained their current job by hearing about it from a contact at their current workplace.

For unemployed 18 to 24 year olds who have claimed Jobseeker's Allowance continuously for six months, participation in the Government's New Deal for Young People scheme is mandatory. Initially there is a gateway period that includes intensive careers advice and guidance, and help with job search skills. The aim is to find unsubsidised jobs for as many people as possible. Those who do not find a job in the gateway stage move on to one of a number of options: subsidised employment; work experience with a voluntary organisation or on an environmental task force, both with training; or full-time education. For those reaching the end of their option without keeping or finding work, there is a follow-through period of support and further training if needed. There are also other New Deal programmes which cover different groups, including people with disabilities, the long-term unemployed, those aged over 50 and lone parents.

Figure **4.22**

Ways in which current job was obtained:[1] by sex, 2004[2]

United Kingdom

Percentages

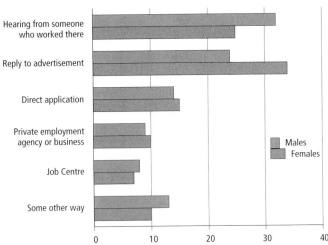

1 Employees or those on government schemes who have been with their current employer for three months or less. Males aged 16 to 64, females aged 16 to 59.
2 At spring. Data are not seasonally adjusted and have been adjusted in line with population estimates published in spring 2003. See Appendix, Part 4: LFS reweighting.

Source: Labour Force Survey, Office for National Statistics

In the 12 months up to the end of June 2004, there were 66,000 leavers to sustained (unsubsidised) employment from the New Deal for Young People programme in Great Britain and 28,000 from the New Deal 25plus programme (Figure 4.23). During the period January 1998 to June 2004, almost 419,000 (39 per cent) of those leaving the New Deal for Young People went into this type of employment. Among those aged 25 and over leaving the New Deal 25plus programme between July 1998 and June 2004, 129,000 (19 per cent) went into similar sustained (unsubsidised) employment.

Most people who want to move jobs do so because they are dissatisfied with aspects of their current job (Table 4.24). In spring 2004, 6 per cent of both male and female full-time employees in the United Kingdom were looking for a new job. For 28 per cent of these men and 22 per cent of the women, unsatisfactory pay in their current job was a trigger for looking for another one. Around 11 to 13 per cent of both men and women who were looking for a new job thought their present job may come to an end, and 6 to 9 per cent said they wanted shorter hours or that their journey to work was unsatisfactory.

Despite there being unemployed people looking for work and those already in employment looking to change work, employers can find some of their vacancies hard to fill. The National Employers Skills Survey 2003 found that the most common reason given by employers for their hard to fill vacancies was a

Figure **4.23**

New Deal[1] leavers entering sustained employment[2]

Great Britain

Thousands

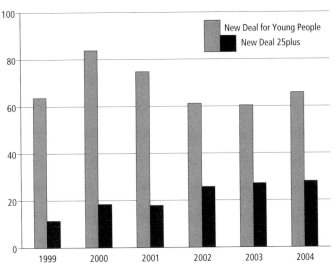

1 The New Deal for Young People programme (for those aged 18 to 24) started in January 1998 and the New Deal 25plus programme (for those aged 25 and over) began in July 1998. Data are for the 12 months to the end of June of each year.
2 Those who entered employment and remained off Jobseeker's Allowance for 13 weeks or more.

Source: Department for Work and Pensions

lack of skilled applicants (42 per cent of hard to fill vacancies). Other common reasons for being unable to fill vacancies included a lack of interest in the job (40 per cent) and, related to this, having too few applicants (37 per cent).

The number of employees in temporary work of some kind increased during the early 1990s from 1.2 million in spring 1992 to peak at almost 1.7 million in spring 1997 and has since declined to 1.4 million in spring 2004. Fixed period contracts accounted for almost half, about 670,000, of employees in temporary employment in spring 2004. In percentage terms, most types of temporary employment have seen some small fluctuation or small decline (Figure 4.25). The exception is agency temping which, as a proportion of all temporary work, increased from 7 per cent in 1992 to peak at 18 per cent in 2002 and has since fallen slightly to 16 per cent in spring 2004.

Around 30 per cent of employees who worked in a temporary job did so because they did not want a permanent one. This proportion was higher for women than men (33 per cent compared with 26 per cent). A slightly lower proportion of employees were in a temporary job because they could not find a permanent job (26 per cent).

Figure 4.26 indicates how long people stay in a job. In spring 2004, one in ten employees of working age had been in their current job less than six months, and a similar proportion had

Table 4.24

Reasons[1] full-time employees were looking for a new job: by sex and presence of dependent children, 2004[2]

United Kingdom   Percentages

	Males	Females		All females	All persons
		With dependent children	Without dependent children		
Pay unsatisfactory in present job	28	16	24	22	26
Present job may come to an end	11	10	15	13	12
In present job to fill time before finding another	10	3	8	6	8
Wants shorter hours than in present job	9	9	8	8	8
Journey unsatisfactory in present job	6	9	7	7	7
Other aspects of present job unsatisfactory	38	31	42	38	38
Percentage of full-time employees looking for a new job	6	6	6	6	6

1 Full-time employees who were looking for a new job. More than one reason could be given.
2 At spring. People aged 16 and over. Data are not seasonally adjusted and have been adjusted in line with population estimates published in spring 2003. See Appendix, Part 4: LFS reweighting.

Source: Labour Force Survey, Office for National Statistics

been in the same job for 20 years or more. Most people (80 per cent) had been in the job for a year or more and around one quarter (23 per cent) had been in their job between two to five years.

The proportion of people who had been with the same employer (or continuously self-employed) for less than two years can provide an indication of where job turnover is greatest or the workforce is youngest, as young people are likely to

change jobs more frequently than older workers. LFS data from winter 2002/03 show that around one third of those in employment had been continuously employed for less than two years. Half of all those employed in sales and customer service occupations had been with the same employer for less than two years. This contrasts with one fifth of managers and senior officials, the group most likely to have been continuously employed for two years or more.

Figure 4.25

Temporary employees:[1] by type of employment

United Kingdom
Percentages

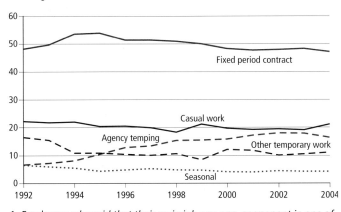

1 Employees who said that their main job was non-permanent in one of the ways shown. At spring each year. People aged 16 and over. Data are not seasonally adjusted and have been adjusted in line with population estimates published in autumn 2004. See Appendix, Part 4: LFS reweighting.

Source: Labour Force Survey, Office for National Statistics

Figure 4.26

Length of service of employees, 2004[1]

United Kingdom
Percentages

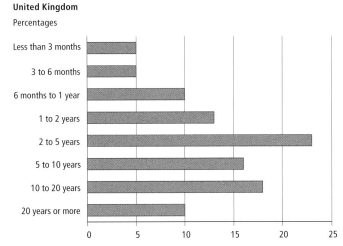

1 At spring. Males aged 16 to 64, females aged 16 to 59. Data are not seasonally adjusted and have been adjusted in line with population estimates published in spring 2003. See Appendix, Part 4: LFS reweighting.

Source: Labour Force Survey, Office for National Statistics

Some people in the United Kingdom withdraw from the labour market before state pension age (65 for men, 60 for women) while some continue to participate after it. In order to compare men and women, it is useful to consider them at the same distance from their respective state pension ages. In spring 2004 a higher proportion of men aged 55 to 64 than women aged 50 to 59 were full-time workers (55 per cent compared with 36 per cent) (Table 4.27). After state pension age the proportions of men and women who worked full time were more similar, though small. A higher proportion of women aged 50 to 59 than men aged 55 to 64 worked part time (31 per cent compared with 10 per cent). For those over their respective state pension ages, although the proportions who worked part time decreased substantially, a slightly higher proportion of women than men continued to do so (7 per cent compared with 5 per cent). Three out of ten men aged 55 to 64 and women aged 50 to 59 were economically inactive and this increased to nine out of ten for men and women who were over their state pension age.

Table **4.27**

Older workers: by employment status and sex,[1] 2004[2]

United Kingdom   Percentages

	Males		Females	
	55–64	65 and over	50–59	60 and over
Economically active				
In employment				
Full-time employees	42	1	33	2
Part-time employees	6	3	27	6
Full-time self-employed	13	2	3	-
Part-time self-employed	4	2	4	1
All in employment[3]	65	9	68	10
Unemployed[4]	3	-	2	-
All economically active	68	9	69	10
Economically inactive	32	91	31	90
All (=100%) (millions)	3.4	3.9	3.8	6.7

1 State pension age for men is currently 65 and for women, 60.
2 At spring. Data are not seasonally adjusted and have been adjusted in line with population estimates published in spring 2003. See Appendix, Part 4: LFS reweighting.
3 Includes those on government-supported training and employment programmes and unpaid family workers.
4 See Appendix, Part 4: Unemployment.

Source: Labour Force Survey, Office for National Statistics

Research commissioned by the Department for Work and Pensions in 2002 identified people who had retired before their state pension age and asked them to give reasons why (respondents could give more than one answer). Around half said ill health, and this was higher for men (53 per cent), than women (44 per cent). Nearly one quarter (23 per cent) mentioned wanting to enjoy life while still young and fit enough, while 18 per cent said they retired because they could afford to. A further 18 per cent had been made redundant and this proportion was higher among men (22 per cent) than women (14 per cent).

Industrial relations at work

In autumn 2003 there were 7.4 million trade union members (7.1 million of whom were employees) in the United Kingdom, a small increase since 2002. Union density (union membership as a proportion of all employees) has remained unchanged at 29 per cent between 2001 and 2003. For men, union density decreased from 35 per cent in 1995 to 29 per cent in 2003 whereas for women the density was also 29 per cent in 2003 having remained relatively stable over this period (Figure 4.28). Union density generally increases across the age groups – around one in three employees aged 35 to 49 or aged 50 and over were union members compared with around one in four of those aged 25 to 34 and around one in ten 16 to 24 year olds.

Union density for men was highest in personal service occupations (41 per cent) and for women it was highest in professional occupations (61 per cent). For both men and women, sales and customer service occupations had the lowest trade union membership. Large firms – those that employed at least 50 employees – had a density of 39 per cent compared with 19 per cent in smaller firms. Trade union membership was also much higher for public sector than private sector employees with densities of 59 per cent and 18 per cent respectively in autumn 2003.

Work-related issues such as labour disputes provide insight into the state of the labour market. The largest number of working days lost through stoppages in one year in the United Kingdom was during the General Strike in 1926 (just over 160 million working days). Further periods of high dispute occurred in 1972, 1979 and 1984. In 1972, a miners' strike accounted for 45 per cent of the 24 million days lost and a strike by the engineering workers in 1979 resulted in just over half of the 29 million days lost. Another miners' strike in 1984 was responsible for over 80 per cent of the 27 million days lost that year.

Figure **4.28**

Trade union membership of employees:[1] by sex

United Kingdom
Percentages

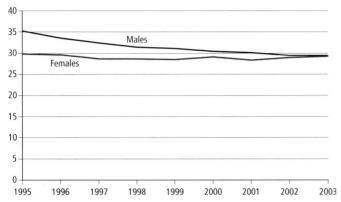

1 *Union membership (including staff associations) as a proportion of all employees. At autumn each year. People aged 16 and over. Data are not seasonally adjusted and have been adjusted in line with population estimates published in spring 2003. See Appendix, Part 4: LFS reweighting.*

Source: Labour Force Survey, Office for National Statistics

After the last major peak in 1984 the average number of working days lost per year fell sharply in the following two years. Since 1991 the number has only risen above 1 million twice – in 1996 and 2002 (Figure 4.29). In 2003 there were 0.5 million working days lost through labour disputes, the equivalent of 19 days lost per 1,000 employees. Wage disputes were the cause of 84 per cent of the working days lost in 2003.

Figure **4.29**

Labour disputes:[1] working days lost

United Kingdom
Millions

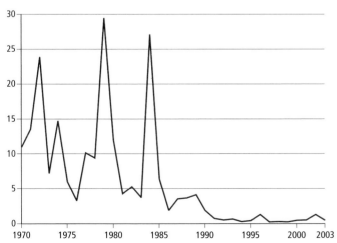

1 *See Appendix, Part 4: Labour disputes.*

Source: Office for National Statistics

Glossary

Employees (Labour Force Survey measure) – a measure, obtained from household surveys, of people aged 16 and over who regard themselves as paid employees. People with two or more jobs are counted only once.

Self-employed – a measure, obtained from household surveys, of people aged 16 and over who regard themselves as self-employed, that is, who in their main employment work on their own account, whether or not they have employees.

In employment – a measure, obtained from household surveys and censuses, of employees, self-employed people, participants in government employment and training programmes, and people doing unpaid family work.

Government employment and training programmes – a measure, obtained from household surveys, of those who said they were participants on Youth Training, Training for Work, Employment Action or Community Industry, or a programme organised by the Learning and Skills Council (LSC) in England, the National Council for Education and Training for Wales (ELWa), or Local Enterprise Companies in Scotland.

Unemployment – the measure based on International Labour Organisation (ILO) guidelines, and used in the Labour Force Survey, which counts as unemployed those aged 16 and over who are without a job, are available to start work in the next two weeks, who have been seeking a job in the last four weeks or are out of work and waiting to start a job already obtained in the next two weeks.

Economically active (or the labour force) – those aged 16 and over who are in employment or unemployed.

Unemployment rate – the percentage of the economically active who are unemployed.

Economically inactive – people who are neither in employment nor unemployment. For example, those looking after a home or retired, or those unable to work due to long-term sickness or disability.

Economic activity rate – the percentage of the population, for example in a given age group, which is economically active.

Working-age household – a household that includes at least one person of working age (16 to 64 for men and 16 to 59 for women).

Workless household – a household that includes at least one person of working age where no one aged 16 and over is in employment.

Redundancy rate – the ratio of the number of redundancies in one quarter to the number of employees in the previous quarter, measured as redundancies per 1,000 employees.

Income and wealth

- Between 2002 and 2003, UK real household disposable income per head rose by 1.8 per cent, compared with growth in GDP per head of 2.0 per cent. (Figure 5.1)

- The pre-tax income of pensioners in Great Britain rose by 26 per cent in real terms between 1994/95 and 2002/03, compared with an increase of 13 per cent in real average earnings. (Figure 5.4)

- In 2002/03, the 30 per cent of individuals at the top of the income distribution in Great Britain received over half of total disposable income. (Figure 5.14)

- Throughout the period 1984 to 2003, more than three quarters of adults in Great Britain considered that the gap between those with high incomes and those with low incomes was too large. (Table 5.15)

- The proportion of people living in households with income less than 60 per cent of contemporary median disposable income reached a peak of 21 per cent in 1992, since when it has fallen to 17 per cent in 2000/01 to 2002/03. (Figure 5.19)

- Wealth is very much less evenly distributed than income: in 2002 half the adult UK population owned only 6 per cent of total wealth. (Table 5.25)

Chapter 5

People's money income plays an important role in their social well-being, because it determines how much they have to spend on the goods and services that together make up their material standard of living. Household income depends on the level of activity within the economy as a whole each year – the national income – and on the way in which national income is distributed. Income represents a flow of money over a period of time, whereas wealth describes the ownership of assets, such as housing or pension rights, valued at a point in time.

Household income

Gross domestic product (GDP) is the most commonly used measure of overall economic activity. The total income generated is shared between individuals, companies and other organisations (for example in the form of profits retained for investment), and government (in the form of taxes on production). If GDP is growing in real terms (in other words, after taking out the effect of inflation) this means that the economy is expanding and there is more 'cake' available for distribution. Household disposable income per head represents the amount of this 'cake' that ends up in people's pockets – in other words it is the amount they have available to spend or save. Analysis of the trends in UK GDP may be found in the final section of this chapter.

Household income is derived not only directly from economic activity in the form of wages and salaries and self-employment income but also through transfers such as social security benefits. It is then subject to a number of deductions such as income tax, local taxes, and contributions towards pensions and national insurance. The amount of income remaining is referred to as household disposable income – the amount people actually have available to spend or save – and it is this measure that is commonly used to describe people's 'economic well-being'.

Household disposable income per head, adjusted for inflation, increased more than one and a third times between 1971 and 2003 (Figure 5.1). During the 1970s and early 1980s growth was somewhat erratic, and in some years there were small year on year falls, such as in 1974, 1976, 1977, 1981 and 1982. However, since then there has been growth each year, with the exception of 1996 when there was a very small fall. Over the period as a whole since 1971, growth in household disposable income per head has been stronger than that in GDP per head, indicating that there has been a small shift between the shares of households and organisations in GDP in favour of households. However, between 2002 and 2003 and between 2001 and 2002, real household disposable income per head grew by 0.2 percentage points less than GDP per head.

Figure **5.1**

Real household disposable income per head[1] and gross domestic product per head[2]

United Kingdom
Index (1971=100)

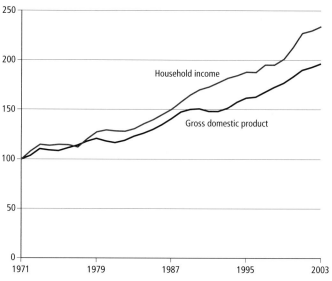

1 Adjusted to real terms using the expenditure deflator for the household sector. See Appendix, Part 5: Household sector.
2 Adjusted to real terms using the GDP deflator.

Source: Office for National Statistics

Despite strong growth in household disposable income since 1987, Table 5.2 shows that there has been considerable stability in its composition. Although there was a fall in the proportion derived from wages and salaries from 52 per cent in 1987 to 47 per cent in 1996, it has since risen to remain at around 50 per cent from 1999 onwards. In addition, the proportion of income derived from social benefits has remained at around 21 per cent over the last decade.

Taxes on income as a proportion of household income have also remained stable since 1987, at around 11 per cent, as have social contributions (that is, employees' national insurance contributions) at 8 per cent of household income. More information on taxes may be found in the Taxes section of this chapter.

The data in Figure 5.1 and Table 5.2 are derived from the UK national accounts (see Appendix, Part 5: Household sector). In the national accounts, households are combined with the non-profit making institutions such as universities, charities and clubs, and it is not at present possible to separate the two sectors. Non-profit making bodies receive income mainly in the form of property income (that is, investment income) and of other current receipts. Thus if it were possible to separate the two sectors, receipts of these two types of income by households alone would be lower than that shown in Table 5.2.

Table **5.2**

Composition of household income

United Kingdom   Percentages

	1987	1991	1996	2001	2002	2003
Source of income						
Wages and salaries[1]	52	50	47	49	50	49
Operating income[2]	11	11	12	12	13	13
Net property income	15	16	14	13	12	12
Social benefits[3]	19	19	21	21	21	21
Other current transfers[4]	3	4	5	4	5	5
Total household income						
(=100%) (£ billion at 2003 prices[5])	683	786	869	1,051	1,070	1,097
As a percentage of total household income						
Taxes on income	11	11	10	11	11	11
Social contributions[1]	9	8	8	8	8	8
Other current taxes	2	2	2	2	2	2
Other current transfers	2	3	4	3	3	3
Total household disposable income						
(=100%) (£ billion at 2003 prices[5])	462	538	605	727	737	753

1 Excludes employers' social contributions.
2 Includes self-employment income for sole traders and rental income.
3 Comprises pensions and benefits.
4 Mostly other government grants, but including transfers from abroad and non-profit making bodies.
5 Adjusted to 2003 prices using the expenditure deflator for the household sector.

Source: Office for National Statistics

The household sector includes people living in institutions such as nursing homes, as well as people living in private households. In most of the remainder of this chapter, the tables and charts are derived directly from surveys of households (such as the Family Resources Survey, the Expenditure and Food Survey, the European Community Household Panel Survey and the British Household Panel Survey) and surveys of businesses (such as the Annual Survey of Hours and Earnings). Data from these surveys cover the population living in households and some cover certain parts of the population living in institutions, but all exclude non-profit making institutions. They can be used to analyse the distribution of household income between different sub-groups of the population, such as pensioners and others.

Survey sources differ from the national accounts not only in their population coverage but also in the way that household income is defined. One of the main differences is that the national accounts include the value of national insurance and pension contributions made on behalf of employees by their employer as part of total household income, whereas survey sources do not. Also, receipts of investment income are usually expressed net of repayments of loans in the national

accounts. However, household income in Table 5.2 has been re-defined to exclude employers' social contributions and to include gross receipts of investment income. This means that the data are not comparable with those in national accounts publications, but they are more consistent with the definition of income used for most income surveys.

Survey sources are also subject to under-reporting and nonresponse bias. In the case of household income surveys, investment income is commonly underestimated, as is income from self-employment. All these factors mean that the survey data on income used in the rest of this chapter are not entirely consistent with the national accounts household sector data.

The main sources of household income identified in Table 5.2 differ considerably in their importance between different types of households. One of the major determinants is the extent to which household members are working. In families in the United Kingdom where at least one person was in full-time employment, wages and salaries in 2002/03 ranged from 85 per cent of income for couple households where one person was working full time, to 96 per cent where all adults

Table **5.3**

Sources of gross weekly income: by economic status of benefit unit,[1] 2002/03

United Kingdom

Percentages

	Wages & salaries	Self-employment	Investment income	Tax credits	Retirement pensions	Private pensions	Disability benefits	Other benefits	Other income	All income
Self-employed	20	71	2	1	1	3	-	2	2	100
Single or couple, all in full-time work	96	-	1	-	-	1	-	1	1	100
Couple, one in full-time work, one in part-time work	91	2	2	-	-	2	-	2	1	100
Couple, one in full-time work, one not working	85	-	2	1	1	4	2	3	2	100
One or more in part-time work	41	11	4	5	6	16	2	7	8	100
Head or spouse aged 60 or over	-	-	6	-	42	34	7	9	2	100
Head or spouse unemployed	-	-	3	2	-	6	5	73	11	100
Head or spouse sick or disabled	2	-	2	-	-	8	32	52	4	100
Other	3	-	4	1	-	12	1	45	35	100
All benefit units	65	9	2	1	6	7	2	6	3	100

1 Benefit units are allocated to the first category that applies. See Appendix, Part 8: Benefit units. Full-time work is defined as 31 hours or more.

Source: Family Resources Survey, Department for Work and Pensions

were working full time (Table 5.3). The state retirement pension formed 42 per cent of the income of families where the head or spouse was aged 60 or over and neither was working, followed by private pensions at 34 per cent. These families also derived a higher than average proportion of their income from investments. Unsurprisingly, families where the head or spouse was sick or disabled derived nearly a third of their income from disability benefits, though a further half came from other benefits. 'Other benefits' (in other words, excluding the state retirement pension and those for disability) – for example, income support – were the most important source of income for families where the head or spouse was unemployed, at 73 per cent.

Pensioners in Great Britain have experienced particularly strong income growth over the last eight years: their gross (pre-tax) income rose by 26 per cent in real terms between 1994/95 and 2002/03, compared with an increase of 13 per cent in real average earnings. Benefits, including the state retirement pension, were the most important component and rose by a fifth in real terms between 1994/95 and 2002/03 (Figure 5.4). However, the fastest growing sources of income were occupational pensions which grew by over a third in real terms; personal pensions which more than doubled, though still only a small minority of pensioners receive them; and earnings, which also increased by nearly a half, though again this type of income is concentrated among a small group of pensioners. It should be noted that changes in average income do not simply reflect

Figure **5.4**

Pensioners'[1] gross income: by source[2]

Great Britain

£ per week at 2002/03 prices[3]

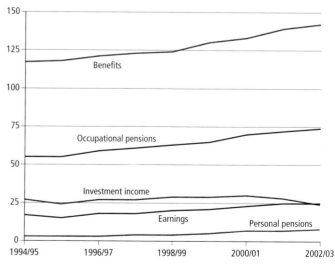

1 Pensioner units are either pensioner couples where the man is over 65, or single pensioners over state pension age (65 for men, 60 for women).
2 Excludes 'other income'.
3 Adjusted to 2002/03 prices using the retail prices index less local taxes.

Source: Pensioners' Income Series, Department for Work and Pensions

changes experienced by individual pensioners, but also reflect changes in the composition of the group, for example as new retirees with greater entitlement to occupational pensions join the group.

At the other end of the adult life cycle, students too have seen changes in the structure of their income caused mainly by changes in the way in which they are financed through public funds. Student loans were introduced in 1990 to replace the student maintenance grant, and take-up has risen from 28 per cent in 1990/91 to 81 per cent in 2003/04. Further changes were introduced by the *Teacher and Higher Education Act 1998*, in particular the introduction of means-tested grants towards tuition fees and support for living costs solely via loans that were to be partly income-assessed.

Overall, the average income of single childless students in England and Wales aged under 25 rose by 7 per cent in real terms between 1998/99 and 2002/03 (Table 5.5). Student financial support made up about half their total income in both years. However, in 1998/99 loans formed 30 per cent and mandatory grants formed 17 per cent of total income, whereas in 2002/03 loans (including hardship loans) formed 49 per cent of the total. Income from the student's family fell from 31 per cent to 24 per cent of total income. This arose partly because fewer students received any money from their families, and partly because those that did, received slightly less in real

terms in 2002/03 than in 1998/99. The reasons for these falls are not certain, though they may be related to the increased contribution that parents had to make to tuition fees. Income from paid work increased by 6 percentage points: 70 per cent of students worked at some point during the academic year 2002/03 compared with 64 per cent in 1998/99, and the number of hours worked during term-time increased.

Most of the information presented in this section so far has been in terms of household or family income, since these are generally considered to be the units across which resources are shared. Thus total household income can be taken as representing the (potential) standard of living of each of its members. The assumption of equal sharing of resources between each member of the household is very difficult to test. Using certain assumptions it is possible to use household survey data to derive estimates of the income accruing to individuals, but it is not possible to infer their living standards from these.

The results of such an exercise are shown in Figure 5.6, which compares the median net incomes of men and women by life stage. See Appendix, Part 5: Individual income for details of how these estimates were derived, and the analysing income

Table **5.5**

Composition of student[1] income

England & Wales		Percentages
	1998/99	2002/03
Student loans[2]	30	49
Mandatory awards[3]	17	.
Other sources of student support[4]	2	3
Paid work	14	20
Family	31	24
Social security benefits	-	-
Other	7	4
All income (=100%) (£ per student per academic year at 2002/03 prices[5])	5,154	5,513

1 Single, childless, full-time undergraduate students in higher education institutions in England and Wales aged under 25 at start of course.
2 Includes hardship loans and Access/Hardship scheme funds.
3 Grants for living costs.
4 Includes money from bursaries, charities, EU programmes and other organisations.
5 Adjusted to 2002/03 prices using the retail prices index, and average earnings index for paid work.

Source: Student Income and Expenditure Survey, Department for Education and Skills

Figure **5.6**

Median net individual income:[1] by life stage and sex, 2002/03

Great Britain

£ per week

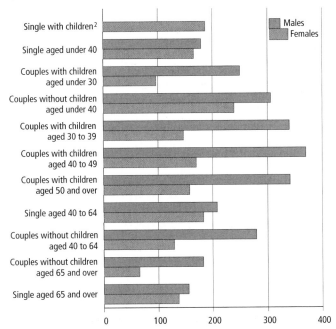

1 See Appendix, Part 5: Individual income.
2 No estimate available for single men with children.

Source: Individual Income, Department for Work and Pensions

distribution box below for an explanation of median. Note also that, as explained further in the Appendix, the term net income is used in place of disposable income because the term disposable income for this series has a different definition from elsewhere in this chapter.

On average, men's net incomes exceed those of women throughout the life cycle. Taken over all family types, in 2002/03 the median net income of women was 60 per cent of that of men in Great Britain. However, the gap was narrowest for single people and generally widened with age. The net income of women aged under 40 was 92 per cent of that of men, reducing to 88 per cent for those aged 40 and over. The gap for single people aged 65 and over contrasts with that of couples without children aged 65 and over, where the median net income of women was 36 per cent of that of men, the largest gap of all the family types in the chart. This arises as a result of historic factors leading to lower entitlements among wives for both state and occupational pensions while their husbands are alive, but higher incomes in their own right when they are widowed because of entitlements to widows' pensions. The second largest gap was for couple families aged under 30 with children: in these families the median net income of women was 38 per cent of that of men. This is a

result of the propensity of women to work part time or to leave the labour force entirely while bringing up young children. The gap then gradually closes for older couples with children, as women return to the labour market.

Earnings

Income from employment is the most important component of household income overall (see Table 5.2). When there is rapid earnings growth across the economy as a whole, this may indicate that the labour market is under-supplied with employees in the right numbers and with the right skills to meet the level of demand within the economy. In addition, a rapid rise may indicate that wage settlements are higher than the rate of economic growth can sustain and thus create inflationary pressures. Slower earnings growth may be a reflection of reduced demand within the economy and may give warning of a fall in GDP and an increase in unemployment. The relationship between earnings and prices is also of importance. If earnings rise faster than prices, this means that employees' pay is increasing faster than the prices they have to pay for goods and services and that therefore, all things being equal, their purchasing power will rise and they will feel 'better off'.

Between April 2002 and April 2003, the average gross weekly pay of full-time employees in Great Britain increased by 2.4 per cent to £476 compared with growth in prices as measured by the UK retail prices index (RPI) of 3.1 per cent, indicating a real terms fall in earnings. The level of weekly earnings below which the bottom 10 per cent of full-time employees on adult rates fell (or bottom decile point – see the analysing income distribution box to the left) increased in line with the RPI, at 3.2 per cent, whereas the top decile point failed to keep pace with inflation, growing at only 2.2 per cent (Figure 5.7). This is a reversal of the usual position: in most of the period shown in the chart the top decile point of the earnings distribution grew faster than the bottom decile point, indicating a widening in the dispersion of earnings. There have been some other exceptions in earlier years (1991, 1997, 1999 and 2000), but in all of those years the growth in the top decile point of the earnings distribution still outpaced inflation. The particularly high growth in earnings at the top decile point in 2001 is largely attributed to exceptional bonuses among senior managers and professionals, notably in the financial sector.

A wide variety of factors influences the level of earnings which an employee receives, such as their skills and experience, their occupation, the economic sector in which they work, the hours they work, and so on. The area of the United Kingdom in which they work and their gender may also have an impact. The remainder of this section explores some of these factors.

Analysing income distribution

Equivalisation – in analysing the distribution of income, household disposable income is usually adjusted to take account of the size and composition of the household. This is in recognition of the fact that, for example, to achieve the same standard of living a household of five would require a higher income than would a single person. This process is known as equivalisation (see Appendix, Part 5: Equivalisation scales).

Quintile and decile groups – the main method of analysing income distribution used in this chapter is to rank units (households, individuals or adults) by a given income measure, and then to divide the ranked units into groups of equal size. Groups containing 20 per cent of units are referred to as 'quintile groups' or 'fifths'. Thus the 'bottom quintile group' is the 20 per cent of units with the lowest incomes. Similarly, groups containing 10 per cent of units are referred to as 'decile groups' or tenths.

Percentiles – an alternative method also used in the chapter is to present the income level above or below which a certain proportion of units fall. Thus the ninetieth percentile is the income level above which only 10 per cent of units fall when ranked by a given income measure. The median is then the midpoint of the distribution above and below which 50 per cent of units fall.

Figure **5.7**

Annual growth in earnings at the top and bottom decile points[1] of full-time employees[2]

Great Britain

Percentages

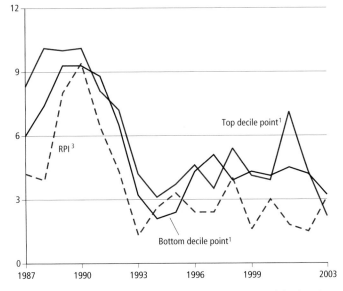

1 See Analysing income distribution box for explanation of decile points.
2 Earnings are of full-time employees on adult rates.
3 RPI data are for the United Kingdom.

Source: New Earnings Survey, Office for National Statistics

However, it should be borne in mind that they are all very much interlinked, and no attempt is made here to disentangle the effect that any single factor may have.

Government legislation may also have an effect on wages. The *Equal Pay Act 1970* and subsequent revisions, together with the *Sex Discrimination Act 1975*, established the principle of equal pay for work that can be established to be of equal value to that done by a member of the opposite sex, employed by the same employer, under common terms and conditions of employment. The impact of this legislation, together with other important factors such as the opening up of higher paid work to women, has been to narrow the differential between the hourly earnings of men and women (excluding overtime). There was a sharp narrowing of the gap in the mid-1970s, followed by a period of stability up to 1984 after which it began to narrow again, though more gradually than in the 1970s (Figure 5.8). In 1971, the hourly earnings of women working full time in Great Britain were 64 per cent of those of men, whereas in 2003 they had risen to 82 per cent. The ratio appears to have levelled out, having remained at 81 or 82 per cent since 1999. Because even those women who work full time tend not to work as many hours as men, the gap for weekly earnings is wider. In 2003, women working full time earned 75 per cent of the weekly earnings of men (including overtime).

Figure **5.8**

Hourly earnings sex differential[1]

Great Britain

Ratio

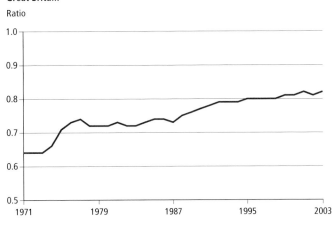

1 The ratio of women's to men's gross hourly earnings (excluding overtime) for full-time employees at April each year. Until 1982, women aged 18 and over, men aged 21 and over. From 1983 onwards for employees on adult rates whose pay for the survey period was not affected by absence.

Source: New Earnings Survey, Office for National Statistics

Although average weekly and hourly pay provide a useful comparison between the earnings of men and women, they do not necessarily indicate differences in rates of pay for comparable jobs. Such averages reflect the different employment characteristics of men and women, such as the proportions in different occupations and their length of time in jobs. The fact that women are more likely than men to be in non-manual occupations raises their overall average pay relative to that of men: the average hourly earnings of non-manual women is higher than that of men in manual work. However, among both manual and non-manual workers, women are concentrated in lower paid occupations which reduces their relative pay.

In 2004, the Office for National Statistics (ONS) replaced the New Earnings Survey (NES) by the Annual Survey of Hours and Earnings (ASHE) – see Appendix, Part 5: Earnings surveys for a summary of the differences between the two. The NES has been retained for long-run time series data in this edition of *Social Trends*, but for the remainder of this section which concentrates on snapshot information for 2004, the data source is ASHE.

Median gross weekly earnings for full-time employees in the United Kingdom in April 2004 were highest in a central band of England running roughly from Bristol in the west to Essex and Kent in the east (Map 5.9 overleaf). Within this geographic band, gross earnings were the highest in Bracknell Forest Unitary Authority at £579 per week, followed by Wokingham Unitary Authority at £572 per week and London

Map **5.9**

Median gross weekly earnings: by area,[1] April 2004
United Kingdom

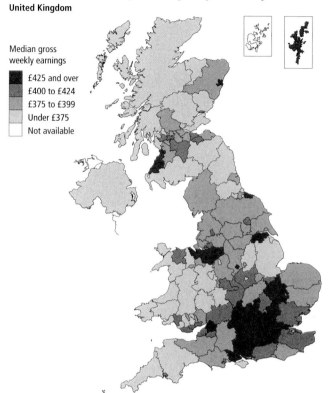

Median gross
weekly earnings

- ■ £425 and over
- ▨ £400 to £424
- ▨ £375 to £399
- ▨ Under £375
- □ Not available

1 Counties and unitary authorities in England, unitary authorities in Wales and council areas in Scotland.

Source: Annual Survey of Hours and Earnings, Office for National Statistics

at £541 per week. A number of isolated pockets of high earnings also exist elsewhere: for example, Redcar and Cleveland, and Derby Unitary Authorities. The lowest earnings were to be found in parts of Wales such as Powys, in the Bournemouth and Torbay Unitary Authorities, in Cornwall, and in parts of Scotland.

Wage rates vary between industrial sectors and according to occupation. In April 2004, directors and chief executives of major organisations, with median earnings of £1,791 per week, topped the earnings league for full-time employees in Great Britain (Table 5.10). Senior officials in national government, medical practitioners and aircraft pilots and flight engineers also had median weekly earnings exceeding £1,000. The lowest paid of all adult full-time employees were leisure and theme park attendants and floral arrangers and florists, with median earnings below £200 per week, only just over a tenth of the earnings of the highest paid occupational group.

For many employees, overtime and other additions can supplement basic weekly pay. Overtime accounted on average

Table **5.10**

Highest and lowest paid occupations, April 2004

Great Britain

£ per week

	Median gross weekly pay
Highest paid	
Directors and chief executives of major organisations	1,791
Senior officials in national government	1,168
Medical practitioners	1,168
Aircraft pilots and flight engineers	1,094
Financial managers and chartered secretaries	951
Solicitors and lawyers, judges and coroners	832
Police officers (inspectors and above)	825
Managers in mining and energy	819
IT strategy and planning professionals	797
Information and communication technology managers	795
Lowest paid	
Hairdressers, barbers	219
School mid-day assistants	218
Kitchen and catering assistants	216
Bar staff	213
Waiters, waitresses	206
Retail cashiers and check-out operators	204
Elementary personal services occupations[1]	204
Launderers, dry cleaners, pressers	204
Floral arrangers, florists	197
Leisure and theme park attendants	191

1 Not elsewhere classified.

Source: Annual Survey of Hours and Earnings, Office for National Statistics

for 12 per cent of median weekly earnings of adults working full time in the United Kingdom in April 2004, but it was a larger component of men's than women's pay: 13 per cent compared with 8 per cent.

Taxes

Table 5.2 showed that, in 2003, 11 per cent of household income was paid out in taxes on income and 8 per cent in social contributions. Every taxpayer is entitled to a personal allowance and those with income below this do not pay any tax. In 2004/05 the personal allowance is £4,745 for those aged under 65, with further allowances for people aged 65 and over. The income tax regime for 2004/05 includes three different rates of tax. Taxable income of up to £2,020 (that is, after the deduction of allowances and any other tax relief to which the individual may be entitled) is charged at 10 per cent.

Table **5.11**

Income tax payable: by annual income,[1] 2004/05[2]

United Kingdom

	Number of taxpayers (millions)	Total tax liability after tax reductions[3] (£ million)	Average rate of tax (percentages)	Average amount of tax (£)
£4,745–£4,999	0.3	4	*0.2*	12
£5,000–£7,499	3.1	435	*2.2*	142
£7,500–£9,999	3.5	1,700	*5.6*	486
£10,000–£14,999	6.2	7,750	*10.1*	1,250
£15,000–£19,999	5.0	11,500	*13.2*	2,300
£20,000–£29,999	6.0	22,700	*15.5*	3,790
£30,000–£49,999	4.1	27,300	*18.1*	6,730
£50,000–£99,999	1.4	23,800	*25.8*	17,200
£100,000 and over	0.4	31,800	*33.6*	73,300
All incomes	29.9	126,900	*18.2*	4,240

1 Total income of the individual for income tax purposes including earned and investment income. Figures relate to taxpayers only.
2 Projected estimates based upon the 2001–02 Survey of Personal Incomes, in line with the March 2004 Budget.
3 In this context tax reductions refer to allowances given at a fixed rate, for example the Married Couple Allowance.

Source: Inland Revenue

Taxable income above £2,020 and up to £31,400 is charged at 22 per cent, while income above this level is charged at 40 per cent. Special rates apply to savings and dividend income.

The Inland Revenue estimates that in 2004/05 there will be around 29.9 million taxpayers in the United Kingdom (Table 5.11). Because of the progressive nature of the income tax system, the amount of tax payable increases both in cash terms and as a proportion of income as income increases, averaging £142 per year for taxpayers with taxable incomes between £5,000 and £7,499 and £73,300 for those with incomes of £100,000 and above.

National insurance contributions are paid according to an individual's earnings rather than their total income, and for employees, payments are made both by the individual and by their employer. In 2004/05, employees with earnings up to £91 per week pay no contributions, and neither do their employers. Employees with earnings above £91 and up to £610 per week pay contributions equal to 11 per cent of their earnings, and those with earnings above £610 per week pay an additional 1 per cent. Employers pay contributions equal to 12.8 per cent of earnings for all those with earnings above £91 per week.

Figure **5.12**

Indirect taxes as a percentage of disposable income: by income grouping[1] of household, 2002/03

United Kingdom

Percentages

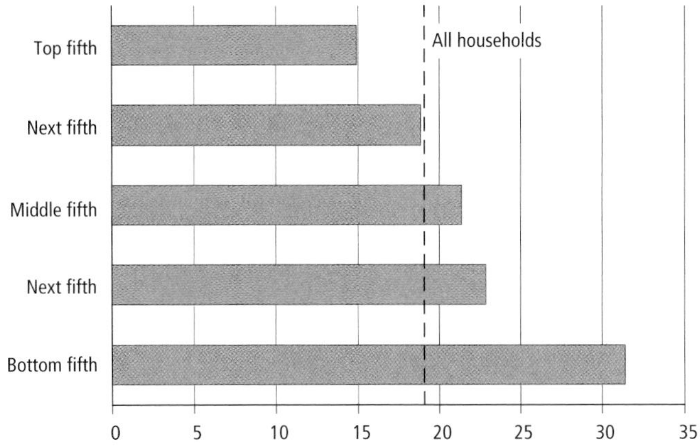

1 Equivalised disposable income has been used for ranking the households. See Appendix, Part 5: Equivalisation scales.

Source: Office for National Statistics

In addition to direct taxes such as income tax, households also pay indirect taxes through their expenditure. Indirect taxes include value added tax (VAT), customs duties and excise duties and are included in the prices of consumer goods and services. These taxes are specific to particular commodities: for example, in 2002/03, VAT was payable on most consumer goods at 17.5 per cent of their value, though not on most foods or on books and newspapers or on children's clothing and at a reduced rate on heating and lighting. Customs and excise duties on the other hand tend to vary by the volume rather than value of goods purchased.

Because high income households are more likely to devote a larger proportion of their income to investments or repaying loans, and low income households may be funding their expenditure through taking out loans or drawing down savings, the proportion of income paid in indirect taxes tends to be higher for those on low incomes than for those on high incomes. Figure 5.12 shows that in 2002/03, households in the top fifth of the income distribution were paying 15 per cent of their disposable income in indirect taxes, compared with 31 per cent for those in the bottom fifth of the distribution.

A further means of raising revenue from households is through local taxes, comprising council tax in Great Britain and domestic rates in Northern Ireland. These taxes are raised by local authorities to part-fund the services they provide. For both council tax and domestic rates, the amount payable by a household depends on the value of the property they occupy. However, for those on low incomes, assistance is available in the form of council tax benefits (rates rebates in Northern Ireland). In 2002/03, estimates from the Expenditure and Food Survey indicate that the average council tax/rates payable (excluding payments for water and sewerage) was £690 per household, after taking into account the relevant benefit payments. Net local council tax varied from £810 per year in the South East to £520 in Wales. Net domestic rates in Northern Ireland, which are based on a quite different valuation system, averaged £430, representing 1.8 per cent of gross income. Within Great Britain, council tax as a percentage of gross household income varied from 1.8 per cent in London to 2.9 per cent in Scotland.

Income distribution

The first two sections of this chapter demonstrated how the various components of income differ in importance for different household types and how the levels of earnings vary between individuals. The result is an uneven distribution of total income between households, though the inequality is reduced to some extent by the deduction of taxes and social contributions and their redistribution to households in the form of social security benefits and other payments from government. The analysis of income distribution is therefore usually based on household disposable income, that is total income less payments of income tax and social contributions.

In the analysis of Households Below Average Income carried out by the Department for Work and Pensions (DWP), on which most of the tables and figures in this and the next section are based, disposable income is presented both before and after the further deduction of housing costs. It can be argued that the costs of housing faced by different households at a given time may or may not reflect the true value of the housing that they actually enjoy. For example, the housing costs faced by someone renting a property from a private landlord may be much higher than they would have to pay for a local authority property of similar quality for which the rent may be set without reference to a market rent. Equally, a retired person living in a property that they own outright will enjoy the same level of housing as their younger neighbour in an identical property owned with a mortgage, though their housing costs will be very different. Thus estimates are presented on both bases to take into account variations in housing costs that do not correspond to comparable variations in the quality of housing. Neither is given pre-eminence over the other. For more details, see Appendix, Part 5: Households Below Average Income.

The shape of the income distribution and the extent of inequality have changed considerably over the last three decades. In Figure 5.13, the closer the percentiles are to the median line, the greater the equality within the distribution.

Figure **5.13**

Distribution of real[1] disposable household income[2]

United Kingdom/Great Britain[3]
£ per week at 2002/03 prices

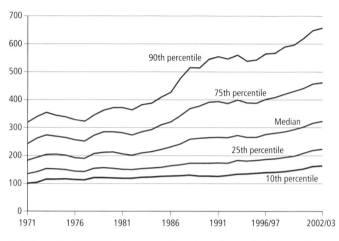

1 Adjusted to 2002/03 prices using the retail prices index less local taxes.
2 Equivalised household disposable income before deduction of housing costs. See Appendix, Part 5: Households Below Average Income, and Equivalisation scales.
3 Data from 1993/94 onwards are for financial years. Source of data changed in 1994/95, definition of income changed slightly and geographic coverage changed from United Kingdom to Great Britain.

Source: Institute for Fiscal Studies from Family Expenditure Survey, Office for National Statistics (1971 to 1993/94); Households Below Average Income, Department for Work and Pensions (1994/95 onwards)

During the early 1970s the distribution of disposable income among households seems to have been broadly stable. Between about 1973 and 1979 there was a gradual decrease in inequality, but this was reversed during the early 1980s and the extent of inequality in the distribution continued to grow throughout the 1980s. During the first half of the 1990s the income distribution appeared to be stable again, albeit at a much higher level of income dispersion than in the 1970s. It should be recalled that the early 1990s was a period of economic downturn when there was little real growth in incomes anywhere in the distribution. Between 1994/95 and 2002/03, income at the 90th and 10th percentiles and at the median all grew by over one fifth in real terms, though on some measures such as the Gini coefficient there appears to have been a further small increase in inequality.

The Institute for Fiscal Studies (IFS) has investigated some of the possible explanations for these changes in inequality, and in particular why the trends are different over the economic cycles of the 1980s and 1990s. They found that wage growth played a part: inequality tends to rise during periods of rapid wage growth because the poorest households are the most likely to contain non-working individuals. Growth in self-employment income and in unemployment were also found to be associated with periods of increased inequality. It would appear that demographic factors such as the growth in one

Figure **5.14**

Shares of total disposable income: by decile group,[1] 2002/03

Great Britain
Percentages

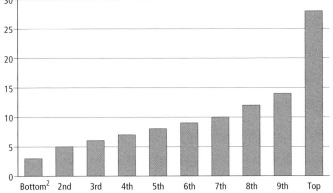

1 Equivalised household disposable income before deduction of housing costs has been used to rank individuals. See Appendix, Part 5: Households Below Average Income, and Equivalisation scales.
2 Estimate should be treated with caution as it is sensitive to data of uncertain reliability.

Source: Households Below Average Income, Department for Work and Pensions

person households make a relatively unimportant contribution compared with labour market changes. However, the IFS has found that changes in the tax and benefit system have an impact in accordance with what economic theory would suggest: the income tax cuts of the 1970s and late 1980s worked to increase income inequality while direct tax rises in the early 1980s and 1990s – together with the increases in means-tested benefits in the late 1990s – produced the opposite effect.

However, IFS research also indicates that the slight increase in inequality between 1996/97 and 2002/03 is very different in nature from that observed over the 1980s. During the 1980s the higher the income, the greater was income growth and

it was this that drove the increase in inequality. However, between 1996/97 and 2002/03, income growth was much more evenly spread across the whole of the income distribution, with exceptions only at the very top and bottom of the distribution. Changes at the very bottom of the distribution are difficult to disentangle from measurement error. However, there is evidence not only from these data, based on the Family Resources Survey (FRS), but also from data from tax returns, that there has indeed been much more rapid growth in the top 1 per cent of incomes than for the rest of the distribution. The reasons for this growth are not yet well understood, but possible explanations include changes in the nature of executive remuneration and the dynamic effects of the cut in top rates of tax over the 1980s on capital accumulation.

An alternative way of examining the degree of inequality is to calculate the shares of total disposable income received by equal sized groups of the population when ranked by their income. If income was evenly distributed each group would receive the same share. Figure 5.14 shows that this is far from the case: the top decile group (see analysing income distribution box earlier in this chapter) accounted for 28 per cent of total income in 2002/03; if there was complete equality each group would account for 10 per cent. In fact the bottom seven decile groups received nearly half of total income, with the other half going to the top three decile groups.

Figures 5.13 and 5.14 illustrate that the income distribution in Great Britain shows considerable inequality, and that the gap between the highest and lowest incomes has increased over the last three decades. The British Social Attitudes survey has measured attitudes towards these trends since 1984 (Table 5.15). Throughout the period, more than three quarters of adults surveyed considered that the gap between those with high incomes and those with low incomes was 'too large'. Between 1984 and 1995 this proportion rose from 75 to 87 per cent, and has since fallen back to 78 per cent in 2003.

Table **5.15**

Proportion who think that the gap between high and low income is 'too large':[1] by self-rated economic hardship

Great Britain   Percentages

	1984	1986	1991	1995	1998	2001	2002	2003
Living comfortably	68	70	71	80	80	74	77	74
Having difficulty managing	83	82	86	88	86	87	90	83
All adults aged 18 and over	75	78	79	87	81	80	82	78

1 Respondents were asked whether they thought 'the gap between those with high incomes and those with low incomes is too large, about right, or, too small'. Table shows percentage thinking it was too large.

Source: British Social Attitudes Survey, National Centre for Social Research

Table **5.16**

Distribution of equivalised disposable income:[1] by disability among family members, 2002/03

Great Britain

Percentages

	Bottom fifth	Next fifth	Middle fifth	Next fifth	Top fifth	All (=100%) (millions)
Before deduction of housing costs						
No disabled adults	18	18	20	22	23	42.0
One or more disabled adults	26	26	21	15	11	15.1
No disabled children	20	20	20	20	21	54.6
One or more disabled children	27	28	24	13	8	2.4
No disabled adults in family	23	26	26	16	9	1.5
One or more disabled adults in family	33	30	22	8	7	0.9
All individuals	20	20	20	20	20	57.0
After deduction of housing costs						
No disabled adults	18	18	20	21	23	42.0
One or more disabled adults	25	26	21	16	12	15.1
No disabled children	20	20	20	20	21	54.6
One or more disabled children	27	30	23	14	7	2.4
No disabled adults in family	22	30	23	16	9	1.5
One or more disabled adults in family	34	29	23	9	5	0.9
All individuals	20	20	20	20	20	57.0

1 Equivalised household disposable income, before and after deduction of housing costs, has been used for ranking the individuals into quintile groups. See Appendix Part 5: Households Below Average Income, and Equivalisation scales.

Source: Households Below Average Income, Department for Work and Pensions

As one might expect, people who themselves are having difficulty in coping on their current household income were more likely to feel that the gap between those on high and low income was too large than those who consider that they are living comfortably. Although these proportions fluctuate considerably from year to year, it seems that concern about inequality has generally been increasing among both groups.

There is a variety of factors that influence people's position in the income distribution, for example their labour market participation and the composition of the family in which they live. In 2002/03, people living in couple families without children both working full time had nearly twice the expected likelihood of being in the top quintile group, while those living in couple families where the head or spouse was unemployed had more than three times the risk of being in the bottom quintile group. Single parents also had a greater than average risk of being in the bottom quintile group. The presence of disabled people within the family is also a factor. Individuals living in families with one or more disabled children were less than half as likely to be in the top quintile group as those with none (Table 5.16). Conversely, they were more likely

to be in the bottom quintile group than those with none. A third of individuals living in families containing one or more disabled children and one or more disabled adults were in the bottom quintile group, and less than a tenth were in the top quintile group.

The DWP's Households Below Average Income analysis from which Figures 5.13, 5.14 and Table 5.16 are derived, provides an annual cross-sectional snapshot of the distribution of income based on the FRS. The British Household Panel Survey (BHPS) complements this by providing longitudinal information about how the incomes of a fixed sample of individuals change from year to year. This enables us to track how people move through the income distribution over time, and to identify the factors associated with changes in their position in the distribution.

Around 14 per cent of those adults in the top quintile group of net equivalised household income in 1991 remained in the same group throughout the period 1991 to 2002 (Table 5.17). A much lower proportion of people (6 per cent) remained in the bottom quintile group throughout the 12 year period. The majority of people (95 per cent) moved between quintile

Table **5.17**

Number of movements made by individuals within the income distribution[1] between 1991 and 2002

Great Britain   Percentages

	1991 income grouping					
	Bottom fifth	Next fifth	Middle fifth	Next fifth	Top fifth	All individuals
Number of movements between quintile groups						
None	6	1	1	1	14	5
One	4	4	4	6	6	5
Two	10	6	5	7	13	8
Three	11	13	10	14	9	11
Four	15	14	15	13	11	14
Five	13	16	17	16	14	15
Six	14	15	17	15	13	15
Seven	12	14	14	13	8	12
Eight	9	11	10	9	6	9
Nine	4	5	5	5	3	4
Ten	1	2	2	2	2	2
Moved every year	-	-	-	-	-	-
Total (all individuals)	100	100	100	100	100	100

1 Equivalised household disposable income before deduction of housing costs has been used for ranking the individuals. See Appendix Part 5: Households Below Average Income, and Equivalisation scales.

Source: Department for Work and Pensions from British Household Panel Survey, Institute for Social and Economic Research

groups at least once over the period, and about two thirds moved between three and seven times. There is more movement in and out of the three middle quintile groups, simply because it is possible to move out of these groups through either an increase or a decrease in income. Movement out of the top group generally only occurs if income falls – an individual will remain in the group however great an increase in income is experienced. The converse is true at the bottom of the distribution. Nevertheless, the table shows that there is considerable mobility within the income distribution.

As discussed earlier in this chapter, households initially receive income from various sources such as employment, occupational pensions, investments, and transfers from other households. The state intervenes both to raise taxes and national insurance contributions from individuals. It then redistributes the revenue thus raised in the form of cash benefits and in the provision of services that are free or provided at a subsidised price at the point of use. Some households will pay more in tax than they receive in benefits, while others will benefit more than they are taxed. Overall, this process results in a redistribution of income from households with higher incomes to those on lower incomes.

The average taxes paid and benefits received by each quintile group in 2002/03 are set out in Table 5.18 (overleaf). The distribution of 'original' income – before any state intervention – is highly unequal, with the average income of the top quintile group about 15 times greater than that of the bottom quintile group. Payment of cash benefits reduces this disparity so that the ratio of gross income in the top group compared with the bottom is 6 to 1, and deduction of direct and local taxes reduces the ratio further to around 5 to 1. Based on people's expenditure patterns it is then possible to calculate an estimated payment of indirect taxes such as VAT and excise duties, which are deducted to produce a measure of post-tax income. Finally, an estimate is made for the value of the benefit received from government expenditure on services such as education and health. (It is not possible to estimate the benefit to households of some items of government expenditure, for example defence and road-building.) Addition of these estimates gives a household's final income. The ratio of average final income in the top quintile group to that in the bottom quintile group is 4 to 1. In this analysis, around 58 per cent of general government expenditure is allocated to households in the form of benefits.

Table **5.18**

Redistribution of income through taxes and benefits,[1] 2002/03

United Kingdom

£ per year

	Quintile group of households[2]					All house-holds
	Bottom fifth	Next fifth	Middle fifth	Next fifth	Top fifth	
Average per household						
Wages and salaries	2,450	7,050	14,920	26,650	45,270	19,270
Imputed income from benefits in kind	10	30	110	360	1,110	320
Self-employment income	580	660	1,330	2,390	7,150	2,420
Occupational pensions, annuities	580	1,360	2,200	2,530	3,700	2,070
Investment income	240	360	550	910	2,840	980
Other income	170	150	220	250	250	210
Total original income	4,030	9,610	19,320	33,080	60,310	25,270
plus Benefits in cash						
Contributory	2,520	3,080	2,210	1,420	930	2,030
Non-contributory	3,120	2,930	2,030	1,080	460	1,930
Gross income	9,670	15,630	23,560	35,580	61,700	29,230
less Income tax[3] and NIC[4]	470	1,370	3,320	6,440	13,690	5,060
less Council tax /Northern Ireland rates[5] (net)	440	530	670	830	960	690
Disposable income	8,760	13,730	19,570	28,310	47,050	23,480
less Indirect taxes	2,750	3,140	4,180	5,340	6,990	4,480
Post-tax income	6,010	10,590	15,390	22,970	40,060	19,000
plus Benefits in kind						
Education	2,500	1,770	1,620	1,520	850	1,650
National Health Service	2,980	3,030	2,630	2,360	2,120	2,620
Housing subsidy	80	70	40	20	-	40
Travel subsidies	70	60	60	70	100	70
School meals and welfare milk	80	30	10	-	-	20
Final income	11,710	15,550	19,750	26,940	43,130	23,410

1 See Appendix, Part 5: Redistribution of income.
2 Equivalised disposable income has been used for ranking the households. See Appendix, Part 5: Equivalisation scales.
3 After tax relief at source on life assurance premiums.
4 Employees' national insurance contributions.
5 Council tax net of council tax benefits. Rates net of rebates in Northern Ireland.

Source: Office for National Statistics

Low incomes

Although being in the bottom quintile or decile group is one way in which to define low income, these definitions are not generally used because of their relative nature. It would mean that 20 or 10 per cent of the population would always be defined as poor. Other approaches generally involve fixing a threshold in monetary terms, below which a household is considered to be poor. This threshold may be calculated in variety of ways. In countries at a very low level of development it may be considered useful to cost the bare essentials to maintain human

life and use this as the yardstick against which to measure income. Although this 'basic needs' measure is of limited usefulness for a country such as the United Kingdom, a similar approach is illustrated in Table 5.23 which analyses hardship defined by not being able to afford to buy certain items.

However, the approach generally used is to fix an income threshold in terms of a fraction of population median income. This threshold may then be fixed in real terms for a number of years, or it may be calculated in respect of the distribution for each successive year. The Government's 'Opportunity for All'

(OfA) indicators use both approaches. The proportions of people living in households with incomes below various fractions of contemporary median income are monitored, referred to as those with relative low income. In addition, the proportions with incomes below various fractions of median income in 1996/97, known as those with absolute low income, are also monitored. A third OfA indicator measures the number of people with persistent low income, defined as being in a low income household in three out of the last four years. In addition, the Government has announced that to monitor progress against its child poverty target, it will add to these measures one that combines material deprivation and relative low income. Deprivation measures resonate well with the public perception of poverty, and it has also been established that there is a strong relationship between material deprivation and persistent low income. As time spent on low income increases, the severity of deprivation increases.

In this section, the low income threshold generally adopted is 60 per cent of contemporary equivalised median household disposable income before the deduction of housing costs. In 2002/03, this represented an income of £194 per week, just below the lowest quintile. Using this threshold, the IFS calculates that the proportion of the population living in low income households rose from 11 per cent in 1982 and 1983 to reach a peak of 21 per cent in 1992 (Figure 5.19). Official estimates made by DWP indicate that it has since fallen back to

17 per cent in each of the three years from 2000/01 to 2002/03. This pattern is also reflected in the proportion of people with incomes less than 50 per cent of the median. Note that from 1994/95 onwards these figures exclude Northern Ireland: however, the proportion of individuals living in low income households in Northern Ireland in 2002/03 was very similar to that in Great Britain.

Table 5.20 illustrates the likelihood of individuals in particular family types being in low income households. In 2002/03, people living in lone-parent families were nearly twice as likely as the population as a whole to be living in a low income household (income before deduction of housing costs), whereas people living in couple families without children were only half as likely than the population as a whole to be living in a low income household. The likelihood of living in a low income household has fallen since 1991–92 for all the family types shown, though the fall has been greatest for those living in a lone-parent family. The likelihood of living in a low income

Figure 5.19

Proportion of people whose income is below various fractions of median income[1]

United Kingdom/Great Britain[2]

Percentages

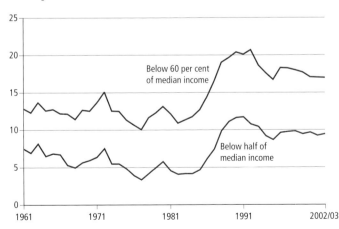

1 Equivalised contemporary household disposable income before deduction of housing costs. See Appendix, Part 5: Households Below Average Income, and Equivalisation scales.
2 Data from 1993/94 onwards are for financial years. Source of data changed in 1994/95, definition of income changed slightly and geographic coverage changed from United Kingdom to Great Britain.

Source: Institute for Fiscal Studies from Family Expenditure Survey, Office for National Statistics (1961 to 1993/94); Households Below Average Income, Department for Work and Pensions (1994/95 onwards)

Table 5.20

Individuals in households with incomes below 60 per cent of median disposable income:[1] by family type

United Kingdom/Great Britain[2]   Percentages

	1991–92	1996/97	2001/02	2002/03
Income before deduction of housing costs				
Pensioner couple	26	19	22	21
Single pensioner	23	23	22	21
Couple with children	20	19	16	15
Couple without children	9	9	9	9
Single with children	46	37	31	31
Single without children	22	16	16	17
All individuals	21	18	17	17
Income after deduction of housing costs				
Pensioner couple	25	22	22	23
Single pensioner	30	33	22	20
Couple with children	24	23	20	19
Couple without children	11	11	11	11
Single with children	59	62	53	51
Single without children	28	25	22	24
All individuals	25	25	22	22

1 Equivalised contemporary household disposable income before deduction of housing costs. See Appendix Part 5: Households Below Average Income, and Equivalisation scales.
2 Data for 1996/97 onwards are based on the Family Resources Survey that covers Great Britain only. Data for 1991–92 combined are for the United Kingdom, and are based on the Family Expenditure Survey.

Source: Households Below Average Income, Department for Work and Pensions

household is higher after housing costs have been deducted, because housing costs for low income households are large in relation to their income as a whole.

Children are disproportionately present in low income households: 21 per cent of children (2.6 million) were living in households with below 60 per cent of median income (before deduction of housing costs) in Great Britain in 2002/03. This proportion peaked at 27 per cent in 1991/92 and 1992/93, having risen from 12 per cent in 1979. A further 0.1 million children in Northern Ireland were living in low income households in 2002/03 (using the low income threshold for Great Britain). Children living in workless families or households have a much higher risk of low income than those in families with one or more adults in full-time work. Around half of children in workless lone-parent families and around seven in ten children in workless couple families in 2002/03 were living in households with below 60 per cent of median income (before deduction of housing costs). If housing costs are deducted, these proportions rise to around three quarters for children in both workless couple and lone parent families, for the reason explained in the previous paragraph. Other risk factors include being part of a large family, having one or more disabled adults in the family, and being in a family where the head of household comes from a minority ethnic group, particularly if of Pakistani or Bangladeshi origin.

The European Community Household Panel Survey allows us to compare the proportions of children living in low income families in each of 15 European Union (EU) member states (this excludes those that joined in 2004, for which data are not available). In 2001, 19 per cent of children in the EU-15 were living in households with income below 60 per cent of the EU-15 average (Figure 5.21). Finland, Denmark and Sweden had the lowest rates of child poverty, with 6, 7 and 7 per cent of children respectively living in low income households. At the other end of the scale, Portugal had the highest rate at 27 per cent. Using this data source, the proportion for the United Kingdom was 24 per cent. Note that UK data from this survey differ from the national data source used in the previous paragraph because of different methodologies used in the surveys, including the use of different income equivalisation scales.

For some people, for example students and those unemployed for only a brief period, the experience of low income may be a relatively transient one, whereas for others it may be a more or less permanent state through their lifetimes. The BHPS provides longitudinal data that allow income mobility and the persistence of low income to be analysed. Using the Government's OfA indicator for persistent low income, between 1999 and 2002 around 11 per cent of individuals in Great Britain experienced persistent low income and this figure has changed little since

Figure **5.21**

Children living in households with incomes[1] below 60 per cent of the median: EU comparison, 2001

Percentages

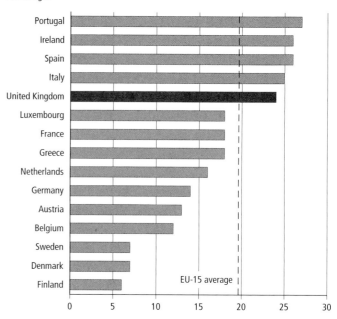

1 Equivalised disposable income in each country.

Source: Eurostat from European Community Household Panel and national sources for Denmark and Sweden

1991–94 (Table 5.22). Those living in workless households – at least in the first year of each four year period – were at most risk of persistent low income, though it appears that since 1991–94 there has been a reduction in this risk. Pensioner families were also at greater than average risk of persistent low income, whereas people in families where all adults were full-time employees had a very low risk throughout the period.

While low income is an important measure of poverty, it does not present the whole picture. Material deprivation measures provide a wider measure of people's living standards – put simply, the inability of families to afford to buy essential goods or to participate in leisure activities. The DWP's Families and Children Study analyses the affordability of 34 'deprivation items', covering four dimensions of material deprivation: food and meals; clothing and shoes; consumer durables; and leisure activities. For more details see Appendix, Part 5: Families and Children Study. The data were used to calculate the total number of all deprivation items a family would like but could not afford. Around one fifth of low income families with children could afford to buy all the deprivation items covered, but a further one fifth could not afford 11 or more of them (Table 5.23). Lone-parent families are more likely to experience material deprivation than couple families. The group experiencing the highest level of material deprivation of those shown in the table were lone-parent families with three or more children, more than a third of whom were unable to afford 11 or more items.

Table **5.22**

Risk of experiencing persistent low income: by economic status[1] of household

Great Britain   Percentages

	3 out of 4 years below 60 per cent of median income[2]		
	1991–94	1995–98	1999–2002
Fully employed	3	3	2
Partially employed	6	6	7
Workless	41	37	33
Pensioner	19	21	20
Self-employed	10	6	10
All individuals	12	11	11

1 Individuals are classified according to the economic status of the household in which they are living in the first year of the relevant period.
2 Equivalised contemporary household disposable income before deduction of housing costs. See Appendix Part 5: Households Below Average Income, and Equivalisation scales.

Source: Department for Work and Pensions from British Household Panel Survey, Institute of Social and Economic Research

Table **5.23**

Families with incomes below 60 per cent of median income:[1] by number of deprivation items[2] a family would like but cannot afford, and family type, 2002

Great Britain   Percentages

	None	1–2 items	3–5 items	6–10 items	11 or more items
Lone parent families					
1 or 2 children	12	17	22	28	22
3 or more children	7	8	21	30	35
Couple families with children					
1 or 2 children	38	21	17	13	11
3 or more children	24	14	18	25	19
All families with children	22	17	19	23	19

1 Equivalised household disposable income before deduction of housing costs. See Appendix, Part 5: Households Below Average Income, and Equivalisation scales.
2 For definition of deprivation items see Appendix, Part 5: Families and Children Study.

Source: Families and Children Study, Department for Work and Pensions

Wealth

Although the terms 'wealthy' and 'high income' are often used interchangeably, in fact they relate to quite distinct concepts. 'Income' represents a flow of resources over a period, received either in cash or in kind. 'Wealth' on the other hand describes the ownership of assets valued at a particular point in time. Wealth can be held in the form of financial assets, such as savings accounts or shares, which provide a flow of current income, or pension rights that provide entitlement to a future income flow. These types of asset form financial wealth. Ownership of non-financial wealth may also provide financial security even if it does not provide a current income flow: for example, ownership of a house or a work of art that could be sold to provide income if necessary. In this section the term 'wealth' includes both financial and non-financial assets. There is a further distinction sometimes made between marketable and non-marketable wealth. Marketable wealth comprises assets that can be sold and their value realised, whereas non-marketable wealth comprises mainly pension rights which often cannot be 'cashed in'. Wealth may be accumulated either by the acquisition of new assets, through saving or by inheritance, or by the increase in value of existing assets.

Aggregate data on the wealth of the UK household sector compiled in the ONS National Accounts indicate that of total assets of £6,500 billion in 2003, over 50 per cent was held in the form of non-financial assets, primarily housing (Table 5.24 overleaf). Even when account is taken of the loans outstanding on the purchase of housing, this form of wealth has shown strong growth between 1991 and 2003. This reflects the buoyant state of the housing market, as well as the continued growth in the number of owner-occupied dwellings.

The second most important element of household wealth is financial assets held in life assurance and pension funds, amounting to £1,620 billion in 2003. This element of household wealth grew strongly in real terms during the 1990s, as a result of increases in the contributions paid into occupational pension schemes as well as increased take-up of personal pensions. It fell by 11 per cent in real terms between 2001 and 2002, reflecting the fall in stock market values over this period, but recovered to its 2001 level in 2003. Occupational and private pensions are important determinants of where older people appear in the income distribution, and so one of the Government's OfA indicators is the proportion of working age people contributing to a non-state pension. In 2002/03 the FRS found that 44 per cent were doing so in Great Britain, with substantially more men (49 per cent) than women (39 per cent) making contributions.

Table **5.24**

Composition of the net wealth[1] of the household sector

United Kingdom

£ billion at 2003 prices[2]

	1991	1996	2001	2002	2003
Non-financial assets	1,938	1,694	2,631	3,119	3,424
Financial assets					
Life assurance and pension funds	814	1,211	1,627	1,447	1,620
Securities and shares	347	511	591	450	511
Currency and deposits	522	571	711	752	808
Other assets	109	116	131	131	137
Total assets	3,730	4,103	5,690	5,899	6,500
Financial liabilities					
Loans secured on dwellings	433	470	609	681	774
Other loans	116	109	173	190	198
Other liabilities	61	58	63	76	81
Total liabilities	610	637	845	946	1,053
Total net wealth	3,119	3,466	4,845	4,953	5,448

1 See Appendix, Part 5: Net wealth of the household sector.
2 Adjusted to 2003 prices using the expenditure deflator for the household sector.

Source: Office for National Statistics

Table **5.25**

Distribution of wealth[1]

United Kingdom

Percentages

	1991	1996	2000	2001	2002
Marketable wealth					
Percentage of wealth owned by:[2]					
Most wealthy 1%	17	20	23	22	23
Most wealthy 5%	35	40	44	42	43
Most wealthy 10%	47	52	56	54	56
Most wealthy 25%	71	74	75	72	74
Most wealthy 50%	92	93	95	94	94
Total marketable wealth (£ billion)	1,711	2,092	3,131	3,477	3,464
Marketable wealth less value of dwellings					
Percentage of wealth owned by:[2]					
Most wealthy 1%	29	26	33	34	35
Most wealthy 5%	51	49	59	58	62
Most wealthy 10%	64	63	73	72	75
Most wealthy 25%	80	81	89	88	88
Most wealthy 50%	93	94	98	98	98

1 See Appendix, Part 5: Distribution of personal wealth. Estimates for individual years should be treated with caution as they are affected by
  sampling error and the particular pattern of deaths in that year.
2 Adults aged 18 and over.

Source: Inland Revenue

Over the 20th century as a whole, the distribution of wealth became more equal. In 1911, it is estimated that the wealthiest 1 per cent of the population held around 70 per cent of UK wealth. By 1936–38, this proportion had fallen to 56 per cent, and it fell again after the Second World War to reach 42 per cent in 1960. Using different methodology from the historic data, during the 1970s and 1980s the share of the wealthiest 1 per cent of the population fell from around 22 per cent in the late 1970s to reach 17 to 18 per cent during the second half of the 1980s. Since then the distribution appears to have widened again, with proportions of 22 to 23 per cent recorded during the period 1997 to 2002 (Table 5.25).

However, even during the 1970s and 1980s when the distribution was at its most equal, these estimates indicate that wealth is very much less evenly distributed than income: half the population owned only 6 per cent of total wealth in 2002. To some extent this is because of life cycle effects: it usually takes time for people to build up assets during their working lives through savings and then draw them down during the years of retirement with the residue passing to others after their death. If the value of housing is omitted from the wealth estimates, the resulting distribution is even more concentrated at the top of the distribution, indicating that housing wealth is rather more evenly distributed than the remainder.

These wealth distribution estimates are based on inheritance and capital transfer taxes rather than direct measurement through sample surveys. As such they cover only marketable wealth and so some important elements such as pension rights are excluded. Although some surveys carry questions on some elements of wealth there is no comprehensive source of UK data on wealth, savings and debt.

This analysis of the aggregate data available on the distribution of wealth is borne out by information available from the FRS based on individuals' own estimates of their savings. In 2002/03, 33 per cent of households in the United Kingdom reported having no savings at all, whereas 13 per cent had savings of £20,000 or more (Table 5.26). Households headed by a Black/Black British or Asian/Asian British person are nearly twice as likely as households overall to have no savings. However, among Asian/Asian British households, those headed by someone of Indian origin are more likely to have savings than are those of Pakistani/Bangladeshi origin. Around half of all households headed by someone of Indian origin have no savings compared with three quarters of households headed by someone of Pakistani/Bangladeshi origin, though these estimates are subject to year on year volatility.

Table 5.27 overleaf explores the extent to which key life events influence people's saving behaviour, using data pooled from the BHPS over the period 1991 to 2000. All the events shown in the table were more likely to result in savers ceasing to save rather than non-savers starting to save. The event most closely associated with stopping saving was becoming unemployed, when 71 per cent of savers stopped doing so. Divorce or separation, having a first child and moving house were also strongly associated with stopping saving.

Table **5.26**

Household savings: by ethnic group of household reference person, 2002/03

United Kingdom   Percentages

	No savings	Less than £1,500	£1,500 but less than £10,000	£10,000 but less than £20,000	£20,000 or more	All households
White	32	21	26	9	13	100
Mixed	46	25	..	..	..	100
Asian or Asian British	60	15	16	5	5	100
Black or Black British	63	18	15	..	..	100
Chinese or Other ethnic group	50	18	19	..	..	100
All households	33	20	25	8	13	100

Source: Family Resources Survey, Department for Work and Pensions

Table **5.27**

Effect of selected life events on savings behaviour of people of working age, 1991–2000[1]

Great Britain   Percentages

	Percentage of non-savers starting to save after the event	Percentage of savers ceasing to save after the event
Divorce/separation	15	46
Marriage	25	29
Having a first child	23	41
Having a second or subsequent child	14	38
Becoming unemployed	8	71
Moving into employment from unemployment	29	38
Moving house	20	40
Becoming a carer for at least 20 hours per week	18	33

1 Data have been pooled for the period 1991 to 2000.

Source: Department for Work and Pensions from British Household Panel Survey, Institute for Social and Economic Research

Figure **5.28**

Annual growth in gross domestic product in real terms[1]

United Kingdom

Percentages

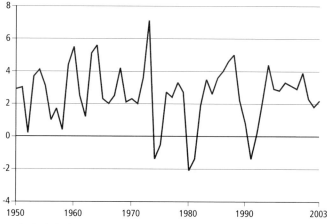

1 Chain-linked volume measure of GDP.

Source: Office for National Statistics

National income and expenditure

Gross domestic product (GDP) measures the level of income generated by economic activity in the United Kingdom in accordance with international conventions. Figure 5.1 at the beginning of this chapter showed that, when adjusted for inflation, the trend in GDP per head since 1971 has generally been one of steady growth. However, within this long-term trend the United Kingdom is nevertheless subject to cycles of weaker and stronger growth, usually referred to as the economic or business cycle.

The year on year growth rates for total GDP, adjusted to remove the effects of inflation, shown in Figure 5.28 suggest

Table **5.29**

Gross domestic product[1] per head: EU comparison

€ per head

	1991	1996	2002
Luxembourg	25,200	28,400	45,000
Ireland	12,200	16,600	28,400
Austria	18,500	20,700	26,000
Denmark	17,300	20,100	25,900
Netherlands	16,900	19,300	25,800
United Kingdom	15,000	17,900	25,000
Belgium	17,000	19,000	24,700
Sweden	17,200	18,800	24,300
Finland	15,700	16,900	24,000
France	16,700	18,300	23,900
Italy	16,500	18,400	23,100
Germany	17,200	18,900	23,000
Spain	12,500	14,100	20,000
Cyprus	..	13,500	17,600
Greece	10,800	11,500	16,500
Portugal	10,500	11,700	16,200
Slovenia	9,430	11,200	15,900
Malta	..	..	15,700
Czech Republic	..	11,500	14,300
Hungary	7,310	7,900	12,400
Slovakia	..	7,400	10,900
Estonia	..	5,700	9,700
Poland	..	6,800	9,700
Lithuania	7,460	5,700	9,000
Latvia	9,500	4,900	8,200

1 Gross domestic product at current market prices using current purchasing power standard and compiled on the basis of the European System of Accounts 1995.

Source: Eurostat

that the UK economy contracted in the mid-1970s, at the time of the OPEC oil crisis, and again in the early 1980s and early 1990s. However, growth has exceeded 4 per cent per year ten times in the post-war period, most recently in 1994. The long-term average annual growth rate was 2.5 per cent between 1950 and 2003. Growth between 2001 and 2002 fell to 1.8 per cent, the lowest rate since 1992, but between 2002 and 2003 it recovered to 2.2 per cent. In 2001, the base year for these figures, over two thirds of gross value added was from the services sector, compared with just over one fifth from the production sector. Agriculture accounted for about 1 per cent, and construction for about 6 per cent.

A comparison of GDP per head across the countries of the EU-25 in 2002 shows that Luxembourg, where the financial sector dominates the economy, had the highest level of economic activity (Table 5.29). This was nearly 60 per cent higher than Ireland, which had the second highest GDP per head. Nine out of the ten new member states that joined the EU in 2004 had GDP per head lower than each of the original EU-15: the exception was Cyprus, which had GDP per head higher than Greece or Portugal. Estonia, Poland, Lithuania and Latvia all had GDP per head less than half of the average for the 25 member states (€21,200). UK GDP per head was the sixth largest among the EU-25 member states, and was about a fifth higher than the EU-25 average.

To examine trends in GDP per head within the EU it is necessary to restrict the analysis to the EU-15 because data are unavailable for early years for the ten new members. The gap between Luxembourg and EU-15 grew during the 1990s: in 2002, Luxembourg's GDP per head was 94 per cent above the EU-15 average compared with 59 per cent in 1991. At the other end of the scale, Portugal and Greece both had GDP per head about 30 per cent below the EU-15 average in 2002, though in both countries it grew relative to the EU average during the 1990s. The most dramatic increase in GDP per head was for Ireland, which rose from 77 per cent of the EU-15 average in 1991 to 22 per cent above average in 2002, and from being thirteenth highest to being the second highest.

Government receives income which is then spent on the provision of goods and services such as health care and education, on servicing government debt, and on transfer payments such as social security benefits (Table 5.30). Although the way in which public expenditure is allocated to different purposes depends on government policy priorities, significant shifts in expenditure patterns tend only to be discernible over a relatively long time period. Over the last 16 years, by far the most important category of expenditure in the United Kingdom both in cash terms and as a percentage of total expenditure has been social protection – mainly social security benefits. Government expenditure on social protection

Table 5.30

Expenditure of general government in real terms:[1] by function

United Kingdom   £ billion at 2003 prices[1]

	1987	1991	1996	2000	2001	2002	2003
Social protection	115	129	153	159	166	169	177
Health	39	44	51	60	65	69	76
Education	36	38	42	46	49	55	56
Defence	36	36	27	29	28	28	31
Public order and safety	14	18	19	20	20	22	23
General public services	9	14	18	22	22	26	28
Housing and community amenities	13	12	8	5	6	7	8
Recreation, culture and religion	5	5	6	5	5	5	6
Other economic affairs and environmental protection[2]	29	30	30	30	35	35	41
Gross debt interest	34	26	33	28	24	22	22
All expenditure	326	352	387	404	423	438	467
Expenditure by local authorities (percentages)	25.8	25.6	24.3	25.0	25.3	25.3	25.3

1 Adjusted to 2003 prices using the GDP market prices deflator.
2 Includes expenditure on transport and communication, agriculture, forestry and fishing, mining, manufacture, construction, fuel and energy, and services.

Source: Office for National Statistics

rose by over 50 per cent in real terms between 1987 and 2003, and accounted for 38 per cent of expenditure in 2003 compared with 35 per cent in 1987. Expenditure on health nearly doubled in real terms between 1987 and 2003, while expenditure on education rose by about a half. Expenditure on defence fell during the 1990s but there was an increase between 2002 and 2003. Expenditure on housing and community amenities also fell during the 1990s but has since risen a little. The proportion of total expenditure accounted for by local authorities has remained around 25 per cent of general government expenditure over the last 16 years.

The United Kingdom, in common with most other developed economies, also allocates part of its public expenditure each year to the support of poorer countries and the elimination of world poverty. Concepts and definitions for the measurement of aid flows are agreed by the Development Assistance Committee (DAC) of the Organisation for Economic Co-operation and Development. Most donor countries are committed to a target set by the United Nations in 1970 of allocating 0.7 per cent of their Gross National Income (GNI) to official development assistance. (GNI comprises GDP plus income received from other countries – notably interest and dividends – less similar payments made to other countries.)

In 2003, none of the G7 countries met the United Nations target, and even France, which was the closest, still fell substantially short at 0.41 per cent (Figure 5.31). Scandinavian countries perform considerably better than the G7 in meeting the target: Denmark, Norway and Sweden all exceeded the target in 2003, as did Netherlands and Luxembourg. In 2003,

the UK proportion was 0.34 per cent compared with the DAC average of 0.25. It has remained at or above the DAC average since 1993.

Government expenditure also includes the contributions made by the United Kingdom to the EC budget. In 2003, figures published by the European Commission show that the United Kingdom contributed €10.0 billion (£7.0 billion) and had receipts amounting to €6.2 billion (£4.3 billion) (Table 5.32). Germany was the largest net contributor, with contributions exceeding receipts by €8.6 billion. The table shows that Belgium, Luxembourg, Ireland, Greece, Portugal and Spain were net recipients from the EC budget in 2003.

Of total EU expenditure in 2003, just under half was spent in support of agriculture in the form of Agricultural Guarantee. Although still substantial, this proportion has fallen by 13 percentage points since 1981 (when there were just ten member states), while structural operations expenditure has risen by 11 percentage points over this period. Structural operations aim to reduce regional disparities and thus to achieve a more even social and economic balance across the EU. The areas within the United Kingdom currently eligible for EU Structural Funds include Cornwall, West Wales and the Valleys, South Yorkshire and Merseyside.

Table **5.32**

Contributions to and receipts from the EC budget, 2003

€ billion

	Contributions	Receipts	Indicative net receipts[1]
Germany	19.2	10.6	-8.6
United Kingdom	10.0	6.2	-3.8
Netherlands	4.9	2.0	-2.9
France	15.2	13.4	-1.7
Italy	11.8	10.7	-1.1
Sweden	2.5	1.5	-1.0
Austria	1.9	1.6	-0.4
Denmark	1.8	1.5	-0.3
Finland	1.3	1.3	0.0
Belgium	3.5	4.2	0.7
Luxembourg	0.2	1.1	0.9
Ireland	1.1	2.7	1.6
Greece	1.5	4.9	3.3
Portugal	1.3	4.8	3.5
Spain	7.4	15.9	8.5

1 A minus sign indicates a net contributor to the EC budget.

Source: European Commission

Figure **5.31**

Official development assistance to developing countries as a percentage of donor country gross national income: G7 comparison, 2003

Percentages

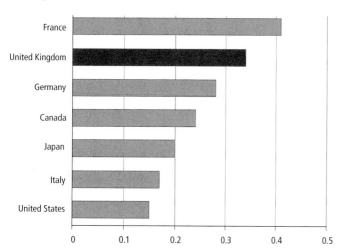

Source: Department for International Development

Expenditure

- Household spending on communications in the United Kingdom almost trebled in volume terms between 1991 and 2003. (Table 6.1)

- Between 1996 and 2003 the volume of UK total domestic expenditure on goods grew at twice the rate of expenditure on services, at 4.6 and 2.1 per cent per year respectively. (Figure 6.2)

- In 2002/03, 7 to 15 year old girls in the United Kingdom spent about 12 per cent more than boys of the same age. (Table 6.5)

- In 2003, 91 per cent of men and 90 per cent of women in Great Britain held at least one plastic card; this compares with 80 and 73 per cent respectively in 1993. (Table 6.9)

- UK consumer credit has continued to rise and in 2004 was over two and half times greater than in 1993, after taking account of inflation. (Figure 6.11)

- Of all the EU-15 countries, in June 2004 a UK resident would have found only Denmark, Ireland, Finland and Sweden more expensive than the United Kingdom. (Page 94)

Chapter 6

The types of goods and services people choose to spend their income on have changed considerably over the past 30 years. Such personal spending allows insights into both people and society – being an indication of a person's standard of living and material well being, as well as a reflection of changes in society, consumer preference, and the growth in choices available to the consumer.

Household and personal expenditure

Between 1971 and 2003, spending by households in the United Kingdom increased in terms of volume for all the broad categories of expenditure with the exception of alcohol (bought from off-licenses) and tobacco, which fell (Table 6.1). This may reflect the decline in smoking, which is described in the Health chapter (see Figure 7.12).

The greatest increases in spending since 1971 have been on the less essential items, and proportionally less is now spent on essential items, such as food, or housing, water and fuel.

This probably reflects higher levels of disposable income. There have been particularly sharp rises in household expenditure on communication, spending abroad, and recreation and culture. Spending on communication has almost trebled since 1991, which may reflect the increase in mobile phone ownership over the period.

The volume of total domestic spending on goods and services combined increased steadily within the United Kingdom over the past 30 years, at an average rate of 2.5 per cent a year, that is after allowing for the effects of inflation (Figure 6.2). However, there were years (1974, 1980, 1981 and 1991) when it fell, possibly as a result of general economic downturns. From 1996, spending on goods has grown at a faster rate than spending on services (by 4.6 per cent a year compared with 2.1 per cent).

Levels of expenditure vary among different groups in the population. In Table 6.3 average UK household expenditure is analysed by the National Statistics Socio-economic Classification

Table 6.1

Volume of household expenditure[1]

United Kingdom

Indices[1] (1971=100)

	1971	1981	1991	2001	2003	£ billion (current prices) 2003
Food and non-alcoholic drink	100	105	117	137	141	63.1
Alcohol and tobacco	100	99	92	88	91	27.3
Clothing and footwear	100	120	187	346	411	41.2
Housing, water and fuel	100	117	138	152	156	125.5
Household goods and services	100	117	160	262	267	39.1
Health	100	125	182	180	205	12.1
Transport	100	128	181	238	247	98.0
Communication	100	190	306	790	846	15.5
Recreation and culture	100	161	283	549	610	83.7
Education	100	160	199	253	232	9.6
Restaurants and hotels[2]	100	126	167	193	206	81.2
Miscellaneous goods and services	100	119	230	284	293	84.7
Total domestic household expenditure	100	121	166	220	232	681.1
of which goods	100	117	156	225	244	329.1
of which services	100	129	182	222	227	351.9
Less expenditure by foreign tourists, etc	100	152	187	210	211	-14.2
Household expenditure abroad	100	193	298	668	712	26.7
All household expenditure[3]	100	122	167	227	240	693.6

1 Chained volume measures. See Appendix, Part 6: Household expenditure. Classified to COICOP ESA95. See Appendix, Part 6: Classification of Individual Consumption by Purpose.
2 Includes purchases of alcoholic drink.
3 Includes expenditure by UK households in the United Kingdom and abroad.

Source: Office for National Statistics

Figure **6.2**

Volume of domestic household expenditure[1] on goods and services

United Kingdom

Indices (1971= 100)

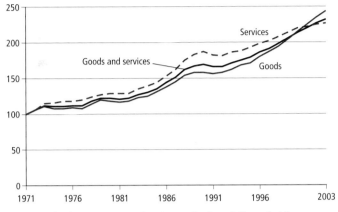

1 Chained volume measures. See Appendix, Part 6: Household expenditure.

Source: Office for National Statistics

(NS-SEC) of the household reference person. The detailed NS-SEC classification can be reduced to four broad classes: managerial and professional; intermediate; routine and manual; and never worked and long-term unemployed. Total expenditure in 2002/03 was highest for those households where the household reference person was in the managerial and professional group. Their expenditure was nearly double the spending of households in the never worked and long-term unemployed group. Indeed, the managerial and professional group had the highest level of spending on most expenditure categories. Spending on education by this group was similar to that of the never worked and long-term unemployed group (which included students) and was about two and a half times the average for all households (£13.20 per week compared with £5.20). Although households in the routine and manual group spent markedly less in total than those in the managerial and professional group, they spent more than any other group on alcohol and tobacco.

Table **6.3**

Household expenditure:[1] by socio-economic classification,[2] 2002/03

United Kingdom

£ per week

	Occupations			Never worked[3] and long-term unemployed	All households[4]
	Managerial and professional	Intermediate	Routine and manual		
Food and non-alcoholic drink	52.60	44.90	43.40	30.90	42.70
Alcohol and tobacco	13.50	11.60	13.80	9.00	11.40
Clothing and footwear	33.60	25.30	24.10	24.50	22.30
Housing, fuel and power[5]	47.00	39.40	38.30	67.20	36.90
Household goods and services	49.50	29.70	26.80	13.90	30.20
Health	7.30	4.50	3.10	2.00	4.80
Transport	98.40	72.10	57.70	37.80	59.20
Communication	13.80	12.40	11.40	17.10	10.60
Recreation and culture	86.30	59.20	57.20	44.00	56.40
Education	13.20	5.10	2.10	14.80	5.20
Restaurants and hotels	58.90	38.10	35.50	42.90	35.40
Miscellaneous goods and services	53.30	35.40	30.10	18.20	33.10
Other expenditure items	109.70	69.80	52.70	17.70	58.30
All household expenditure	637.00	447.50	396.10	340.00	406.60
Average household size (number of people)	2.7	2.6	2.7	2.5	2.4

1 See Appendix, Part 6: Household expenditure. Expenditure rounded to the nearest 10 pence.
2 Of the household reference person. Excludes retired households. See Appendix, Part 6: National Statistics Socio-economic Classification, and Retired households.
3 Includes households where the reference person is a student.
4 Includes retired households and others that are not classified.
5 Excludes mortgage interest payments, water charges, council tax and Northern Ireland domestic rates. These are included in 'Other expenditure items'.

Source: Expenditure and Food Survey, Office for National Statistics

Total household expenditure varied greatly across the United Kingdom in 2002/03. Households in the South East and in London spent the most per person, while those in the North East and in Northern Ireland spent the least (Table 6.4). Households in the North East spent 31 per cent less per person than those in the South East. The regional pattern of household expenditure can change over time, as certain areas become more or less affluent. Spending per person by households in the South West rose from 2 per cent below the UK average in 1996/97 to 6 per cent above it in 2002/03. Over the same period, the greatest falls in spending relative to the UK average were by households in Wales and in the West Midlands.

Table **6.4**

Household expenditure[1] per head: by region

Indices (UK=100)

	1996/97	2001/02	2002/03
United Kingdom	100	100	100
England	102	102	102
North East	88	84	83
North West	96	92	95
Yorkshire and the Humber	95	88	92
East Midlands	94	98	94
West Midlands	94	89	86
East	107	104	106
London	108	118	112
South East	116	124	119
South West	98	96	106
Wales	96	86	87
Scotland	93	93	95
Northern Ireland	83	86	83

1 See Appendix, Part 6: Household expenditure.

Source: Family Expenditure Survey and Expenditure and Food Survey, Office for National Statistics

Spending on most categories of goods and services in 2002/03 was highest per person for households in London and in the South East, reflecting the high overall levels of spending by these households. However, expenditure on household goods and services was highest in the South West (21 per cent above the UK average) and on health was highest in the East of England (63 per cent above the UK average).

Spending by children contributes to total household expenditure. However, the pattern of spending varies between boys and girls, and across age groups (Table 6.5). In 2002/03, 7 to 15 year old girls in the United Kingdom spent about 12 per

Table **6.5**

Children's expenditure:[1] by sex and type of purchase, 2002/03

United Kingdom   Percentages

	Males	Females	All aged 7–15
Takeaway and snack food eaten away from home	24	23	24
Clothing and footwear	12	22	17
Games, toys, hobbies and pets	19	6	12
of which computer software and games	11	1	6
Magazines, books and stationery	5	6	6
Music accessories (CDs, DVDs)	7	4	5
Sporting and cultural activities	4	4	4
Mobile phones and charges	3	5	4
Confectionery and snacks	3	4	4
Fares	2	2	2
Other expenditure	20	24	22
All expenditure (=100%) (£ per week)[2]	10.70	12.00	11.40

1 Children aged 7 to 15.
2 Expenditure rounded to the nearest 10 pence.

Source: Expenditure and Food Survey, Office for National Statistics

cent more than boys of the same age. Girls of this age spent a far greater proportion of their money than boys on clothing and footwear (22 per cent compared with 12 per cent). In contrast, boys spent a far greater proportion on games, toys, hobbies and pets. This includes computer software and games, which made up 11 per cent of boys' spending but only 1 per cent of girls' spending.

Spending on takeaway meals and snacks is high among children of all age groups. It accounted for one fifth of spending by 7 to 10 year olds and about one quarter of spending by 11 to 15 year olds. Differences between the age groups were greater for some other types of spending. Games, toys, hobbies and pets comprised 23 per cent of 7 to 8 year olds' expenditure, but just 4 per cent of 15 year olds' spending. Conversely, 5 per cent of 15 year olds' spending was on mobile phones and charges compared with virtually none by 7 to 8 year olds.

The proportion of the UK population over state pension age has been growing steadily for some time. Between 1971 and 2003 the number of people over the state pension age increased by 21 per cent to over 11 million. The pattern of expenditure of a retired household is related to the number of people in the household and whether or not the household is mainly dependent on state pensions and benefits. In 2002/03,

Table 6.6

Expenditure of retired households:[1] by whether or not mainly dependent on state pension and other benefits,[2] 2002/03

United Kingdom   Percentages

	State pension/benefits		Other	
	1 adult	2 adults	1 adult	2 adults
Food and non-alcoholic drink	19	21	13	14
Alcohol and tobacco	3	3	2	3
of which cigarettes and tobacco	2	2	1	1
Clothing and footwear	5	4	3	4
Housing, fuel and power[3]	19	14	16	9
Household goods and services	9	8	10	8
Health	2	2	2	3
Transport	5	9	11	12
Communication	4	3	3	2
Recreation and culture	13	14	12	16
Education	-	0	-	1
Restaurants and hotels	5	5	5	8
Miscellaneous goods and services	8	8	9	9
Other expenditure items	8	8	13	10
All household expenditure (=100%) (£ per week)[4]	103.80	177.10	185.10	326.00

1 See Appendix, Part 6: Retired households.
2 A household is mainly dependent on the state pension or other benefits if at least three quarters of the total household income is derived from these sources.
3 Excludes mortgage interest payments, water charges, council tax and Northern Ireland domestic rates. These are included in 'Other expenditure items'.
4 Expenditure rounded to the nearest 10 pence.

Source: Expenditure and Food Survey, Office for National Statistics

the proportion of spending on housing (which excludes mortgage interest payments, water charges, council tax and Northern Ireland domestic rates), fuel and power was higher among single retired households than couple retired households (Table 6.6). Furthermore, households mainly dependent on state pensions and benefits also spent larger proportions of their total expenditure on housing, fuel and power and other essentials such as food and non-alcoholic drink, reflecting lower income levels.

Traditionally, food and groceries were bought from small independent shops. However, large supermarket chains have gradually increased their share of this market and their range of goods. In 2002/03, over three quarters of UK household expenditure on fresh vegetables, confectionery and snacks, and bread was at large supermarket chains (Table 6.7). The proportion of household expenditure on petrol at large supermarkets increased by 7 percentage points between 1995/96 and 2002/03 to 29 per cent. This reflects the greater number of such petrol outlets and the ability of

Table 6.7

Household expenditure on selected items: by type of outlet, 1995/96 and 2002/03

United Kingdom   Percentages

	Large supermarket chains		All other outlets	
	1995/96	2002/03	1995/96	2002/03
Bread	67	76	33	24
Milk	39	57	61	43
Fresh vegetables	73	84	27	16
Confectionery and snacks	75	79	25	21
Petrol	22	29	78	71

Source: Family Expenditure Survey and Expenditure and Food Survey, Office for National Statistics

Figure **6.8**

Volume of retail sales

Great Britain

Index (2000=100)

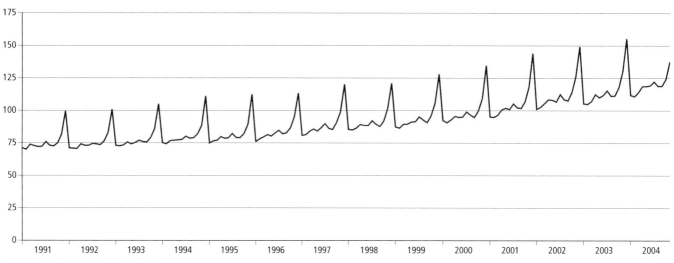

Source: Office for National Statistics

supermarkets to provide petrol at prices lower than the main petrol companies. Over the same period the proportion of expenditure on milk spent at large supermarket chains increased at a faster rate, from 39 per cent to 57 per cent.

In recent years the Internet has provided an alternative to a trip to the shops. About two thirds of all Internet users used it to purchase goods or services during the 12 months up to July 2004, particularly for travel, accommodation or holidays (see Table 13.14).

Transactions and credit

The volume of retail sales in Great Britain has risen over the past 13 years and this continued with a 3.4 per cent rise in the 12 month period to December 2003 (Figure 6.8). This was similar to the year on year increases during much of the 1990s. However, it was less than in each of the three previous years, which ranged from 4.5 per cent in 2000 to 6.2 per cent in 2002. In all years, retail sales follow a strong seasonal pattern, peaking in December.

In 2003, the vast majority (94 per cent) of retail businesses in the United Kingdom had a turnover below £1 million, but their share of the value of retail trade was just 16 per cent, according to data from the Retail Annual Business Inquiry. In contrast, just half a per cent of all retail businesses had a turnover of more than £10 million but accounted in total for 74 per cent of the value of retail trade. This difference in market share has become more extreme since 2000 and is expected to continue, as some large retailers broaden the range of products they sell.

The way in which transactions are undertaken in the United Kingdom changed dramatically between 1991 and 2003 with an increase in the use of plastic cards and a decline in the use of cheques. In 2003, people used debit cards more than any other method of non-cash payment. There were nearly 3.4 billion transactions by debit card, over nine times as many as in 1991. Since 1995 transactions by debit card have exceeded those by credit card, even though both have experienced considerable growth. Total spending on credit and debit cards increased from £209 billion in 2002 to £231 billion in 2003 (see Table 6.10). According to the Association for Payment Clearing Services (APACS), 91 per cent of men and 90 per cent of women in Great Britain had at least one plastic card in 2003 (Table 6.9). This compares with 80 per cent of men and 73 per cent of women in 1993.

Cardholder rates are lowest among young people and older people. In Great Britain in 2003, 87 per cent of both 16 to 24 year olds and those aged 65 and over had a plastic card. In comparison, the proportions for the age groups in between ranged from 91 per cent to 94 per cent.

The growth in the use of plastic cards has been accompanied by a rise in card fraud. This can involve criminals 'skimming' cards to copy the information from the magnetic strips. Card companies have begun issuing 'chip and PIN' cards in an attempt to combat this. At the end of August 2004, there were nearly 48 million 'chip and PIN' cards in circulation out of a total of 132 million. These cards help combat fraud in two ways. Firstly, cardholders' account details are stored on a

Table 6.9

Plastic card holders:[1] by sex

Great Britain

Percentages

	1993		1998		2003	
	Males	Females	Males	Females	Males	Females
Any credit/charge card	41	33	53	46	68	62
Debit card	55	49	75	71	84	83
Store/retailer card[2]	14	19	23	35	27	42
Cheque guarantee card	56	51	68	64	77	75
ATM debit card[3]	65	58	78	75	89	87
Any plastic card	80	73	85	83	91	90

1 Percentage of all adults over 16 holding each type of card.
2 Store/retailer cards converted to Visa or MasterCard are counted as credit cards.
3 Cards used in an ATM for cash withdrawals and other bank services. Includes single function ATM cards and multi-function debit cards, but excludes credit/charge cards, most of which can be used to access ATMs.

Source: Association for Payment Clearing Services

microchip, which is far safer than a magnetic strip. Secondly, the PIN, known only to the cardholder, is used to verify a transaction rather than the cardholder's signature.

Between 1991 and 2003 the growth in debit card use in the United Kingdom has been greater than that of credit cards. The number of debit card transactions increased over eight times during this period compared with just a one and a half times increase in the number of credit card transactions.

Purchases in food and drink outlets accounted for 28 per cent of total spending on debit cards in 2003 (Table 6.10). Credit cards tend to be used in many different stores. The amount spent on credit cards in motoring outlets, travel agents, and household goods stores each accounted for between 11 and 12 per cent of total credit card expenditure.

UK consumer credit rose steadily over the past decade so that in 2004 it was over two and a half times greater than in 1993, after taking account of inflation (Figure 6.11). It also rose as a proportion of annual post-tax income – from less than 46 per

Table 6.10

Debit and credit card spending,[1] 2003

United Kingdom

£ billion

	Debit cards	Credit cards
Food and drink	33.7	13.2
Motoring	17.2	12.2
Household	10.0	12.7
Mixed business	7.6	8.0
Clothing	7.5	5.2
Travel	6.8	12.9
Entertainment	5.6	6.5
Financial	1.7	1.0
Hotels	1.3	4.3
Other services	17.9	15.7
Other retail	13.0	16.8
Total	122.3	108.3

1 By principal business activity of where the purchase was made. Excludes spending outside the United Kingdom by UK cardholders.

Source: Association for Payment Clearing Services

Figure 6.11

Consumer credit

United Kingdom

£ billion at 2003 prices[1]

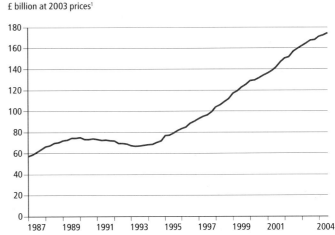

1 Quarterly data, seasonally adjusted. Price deflated using the all items retail prices index deflator.

Source: Bank of England

cent in the first quarter of 1993 to over 88 per cent in the same quarter of 2004. This means that people will find it harder to pay off their debt.

Mortgage equity withdrawal is secured borrowing that is not invested in the housing market, and it can be expressed as a proportion of post-tax income. It grew from around 1 per cent of post-tax income during much of the 1970s and reached a peak in the late 1980s of almost 8 per cent. However, when house prices fell in 1989, many homeowners found their property was worth less than the debt secured on it. Mortgage equity withdrawal then fell during the early 1990s and remained below 1 per cent of post-tax income until 1999. Then between 2001 and the end of 2003 mortgage equity withdrawal rose rapidly again, peaking at 8.4 per cent of total post-tax income. This was caused by a combination of low interest rates and renewed confidence in the housing market. However, during the first three quarters of 2004 it began to fall again; by the third quarter it was 6.2 per cent.

High and continuous levels of borrowing can lead to debts that people cannot pay, known as arrears. Households containing children are more likely to be in arrears than those without, and this likelihood increases with the number of children in the family. One in six households containing one or two children in Great Britain were in some kind of arrears in 2002, compared with nearly one in three households containing four or more children (Table 6.12). Families who rented were over twice as likely as homeowners to be in arrears, and other factors such as low incomes and the head of the family being young also increased the likelihood. Households with children were more likely to be in arrears with mortgage and rent payments than those without children. However, children had little effect on the likelihood of having other types of arrears, such as outstanding mail order payments and loans.

Table **6.12**

Arrears among families with children: by family size, 2002

Great Britain

Percentages

	Behind with any household bills	Any credit arrears	Housing arrears	Any arrears
One or two children	14	4	4	17
Three children	19	5	5	22
Four or more children	25	9	7	31
All families with children	15	4	4	18

Source: Families and Children Study, Department for Work and Pensions

Prices

How people choose to spend their money is affected by the prices of goods and services. An index of prices for a typical 'basket' of goods can be used to measure the 'cost of living'. The retail prices index (RPI), which was introduced in 1947, has been the most familiar UK index. It measures the average change, from month to month, in the prices of goods and services purchased by most households in the United Kingdom. The goods and services in the basket are changed slightly each year to reflect shifting consumer spending patterns. For instance, lard, bottled pale ale and vinyl records were in the basket in 1970 but have since been removed. In contrast, vegetable cooking oil, alcopops and CD albums are some of the items in the basket in 2004, which were not in 1970.

On 10 December 2003, the consumer prices index (CPI) replaced RPI(X) (RPI excluding mortgage interest payments) as the main domestic measure of UK inflation for macroeconomic purposes. Both indices are broadly similar, but there are several differences – the main one being that the CPI basket excludes certain housing costs such as house depreciation, council tax, and buildings insurance, as well as mortgage interest payments. The CPI weights are based on spending by all private households, foreign visitors to the United Kingdom and residents in institutions; the RPI weights are based on spending by private households only, and exclude the highest income households and pensioner households mainly dependent on state benefits. There are also methodological differences in how the two indices combine individual prices. These differences have the effect of lowering the CPI inflation rate relative to the RPI (Figure 6.13). As a result of these changes in December 2003, the Chancellor announced a new inflation target of 2.0 per cent measured by the 12-month change in the CPI. It was previously 2.5 per cent measured by RPI(X).

Levels of UK inflation have varied considerably over the past 30 or so years. Inflation (measured by the RPI) exceeded 20 per cent during some periods in the 1970s, and was above 10 per cent in the early 1980s and again in 1990. However, it has remained below 5 per cent since 1992. The CPI has been consistently below the 2 per cent target since June 1998.

Figure 6.14 shows the percentage change in price of components of the UK CPI between 2002 and 2003. Prices for education increased by 7.5 per cent, more than any other component. However, the CPI weighting for education is less than 2 per cent, so it had little effect on the CPI. In contrast, restaurants and hotels, and transport, had CPI weightings of around 14 to 15 per cent, so their increases of just over 3 per cent had a large impact on the overall index.

Figure **6.13**

Consumer prices index[1] and retail prices index[2]

United Kingdom

Percentage change over 12 months

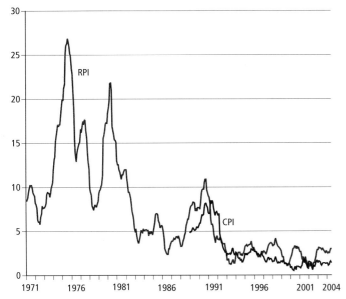

1 Data prior to 1997 are estimates. See Appendix, Part 6: Harmonised index of consumer prices.
2 See Appendix, Part 6: Retail prices index, and Consumer prices index.

Source: Office for National Statistics

Prices fell for three components – clothing and footwear, recreation and culture, and furniture and household goods. Of these, the largest decrease was for clothing and footwear (3.8 per cent).

It is recognised that prices of items vary across the United Kingdom. In response, the Office for National Statistics (ONS) has begun publishing regional consumer price levels. Figure 6.15 shows average regional relative prices for 2004. London prices were nearly 10 per cent higher than the national average, while prices in Wales were nearly 7 per cent below average. The regional difference was greatest for housing costs. They ranged from nearly 29 per cent above the UK average in London to just over 32 per cent below average in Northern Ireland. Price levels were higher in London than in Wales for all goods and services, except fares and other travel costs – these were 1.0 per cent below the UK average in London and 9.5 per cent above it in Wales. Despite Northern Ireland having slightly below average overall prices, the cost of fuel and light was nearly 13 per cent above the UK average.

Although many items are added to, and dropped from, the basket over time, some, such as cigarettes, sliced white bread and granulated sugar, have been included for a considerable period. This allows price comparisons to be made over time. In 2003 the price of cheddar cheese was £1.37 for 250

Figure **6.14**

Percentage change in consumer prices index, 2003[1]

United Kingdom

Percentages

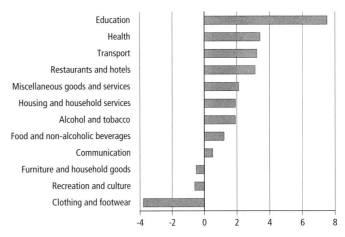

1 Annual average percentage change on the previous year. See Appendix, Part 6: Consumer prices index.

Source: Office for National Statistics

grammes, nearly ten times the price in 1971 (Table 6.16 overleaf). Prices for other goods rose even more. The price of cigarettes in 2003 was nearly 16 times the price in 1971 and has more than doubled since 1991. Prices of beer and unleaded petrol have also risen considerably since 1971 and 1991 respectively. This probably reflects the large increases in duties imposed on them over these periods.

Figure **6.15**

Relative prices: by region,[1] 2004

United Kingdom

Indices (UK=100)

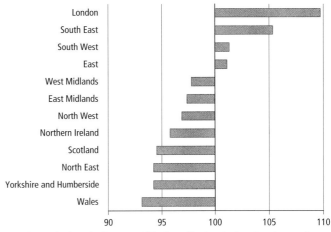

1 Prices calculated using a modified retail prices index. See Appendix, Part 6: Retail prices index.

Source: Office for National Statistics

Table **6.16**

Cost of selected items

United Kingdom

Pence

	1971	1981	1991	1996	2001	2003
250g cheddar cheese	14	58	86	115	128	137
Half dozen eggs (size 2)	11	39	59	79	86	84
1 pint pasteurised milk	6	19	32	36	37	37
1 kg granulated sugar	9	39	66	76	57	69
800g white sliced bread	10	37	53	55	51	58
100g instant coffee	..	..	130	189	181	180
Packet of 20 cigarettes	27	97	186	273	412	425
Pint of beer[1]	15	65	124	154	181	194
Litre of unleaded petrol	..	..	45	57	76	76

1 Bottled in 1971 and 1981, and draught from 1991.

Source: Office for National Statistics

The CPI is used for inflation comparisons between the United Kingdom and other European Union (EU) countries. The United Kingdom continued to experience a low inflation rate in 2003 which, at 1.4 per cent, was below the 2.0 per cent EU-15 average (Table 6.17). On 1 May 2004 the EU was expanded to 25 member states. Within the enlarged EU, the highest rate of inflation occurred in Slovakia (8.5 per cent). Inflation rates of the new member states varied greatly: Lithuania and the Czech Republic had negative rates.

The worldwide spending power of sterling depends on the relative price levels of goods and services and the exchange rates between countries. Comparative price levels are used to indicate whether other countries would have appeared cheaper or more expensive to UK residents. In June 2004 only four of the EU-15 countries (Denmark, Ireland, Finland and Sweden) would have appeared more expensive; Denmark would have appeared the most expensive, with relative prices 20 per cent higher than in the United Kingdom. Figures were also available for four of the new member states (Hungary, Slovakia, the Czech Republic and Poland). A UK visitor to any of these countries would have found prices about half those of the United Kingdom. Although useful indicators of a current situation, these comparative differences are likely to change considerably between years due to fluctuations in exchange rates.

Table **6.17**

Percentage change in consumer prices:[1] EU comparison, 2003

	Percentage change over 12 months		Percentage change over 12 months
EU-15 countries		**Accession states**	
Ireland	4.0	Slovakia	8.5
Greece	3.4	Slovenia	5.7
Portugal	3.3	Hungary	4.7
Spain	3.1	Cyprus	4.0
Italy	2.8	Latvia	2.9
Luxembourg	2.5	Malta	1.9
Sweden	2.3	Estonia	1.4
France	2.2	Poland	0.7
Netherlands	2.2	Czech Republic	-0.1
Denmark	2.0	Lithuania	-1.1
Belgium	1.5		
United Kingdom	1.4		
Austria	1.3		
Finland	1.3		
Germany	1.0		
EU-15 average	2.0		

1 As measured by the harmonised index of consumer prices. See Appendix, Part 6: Harmonised index of consumer prices.

Source: Office for National Statistics; Eurostat

Health

- The proportion of children in the United Kingdom immunised against MMR by their second birthday fell from 90 per cent in the early and mid-1990s to 81 per cent in 2003/04. (Table 7.6)

- The proportion of adults in England who were obese increased between 1993 and 2003: from 13 to 23 per cent of men and from 16 to 23 per cent of women. (Figure 7.8)

- In 2003/04, 40 per cent of men and 23 per cent of women exceeded the recommended daily benchmarks for sensible drinking on at least one day in the previous week. (Table 7.10)

- In 2003/04, smoking was most common among adults in routine and manual households (35 per cent of men and 31 per cent of women) and least prevalent among those in managerial and professional households (20 per cent and 17 per cent respectively). (Page 102)

- The incidence of lung cancer in males has fallen by more than 40 per cent over the past 20 years, mainly as a result of the earlier decline in smoking. (Figure 7.14)

- The suicide rate for men aged 25 to 44 in the United Kingdom doubled between 1971 and 1998 to 27 per 100,000; in 2003 it was 23 per 100,000. (Figure 7.19)

Chapter 7

The patterns of health in the United Kingdom are continually changing, in terms of which diseases people experience, how they act in relation to their own health, and how illness is prevented. Advances in medical science and technology, developments in health services, and improved standards of living have all contributed to gradual improvements in people's health. Current government health strategies place a strong emphasis on reducing ill health through promoting healthy lifestyles.

Key health indicators

A widely used indicator of the nation's health is life expectancy. Life expectancy at birth for males and females born in the United Kingdom has continued to rise. Between 1971 and 2003 it increased from 69.1 to 76.2 years for males and from 75.3 to 80.5 years for females (Table 7.1). While female life expectancy at birth has been consistently higher than that of males throughout this period, the gap has been narrowing, from 6.2 years in 1971 to 4.3 years in 2001.

Despite its use as a general indicator of health, life expectancy takes no account of the quality of life. While males born in the United Kingdom in 2001 could expect to live 4.9 years longer and females 3.6 years longer than those born in 1981, those extra years may not necessarily be spent in good health. Since 1981, data on self-assessed general health have been used to estimate the number of years people can expect to live in good or fairly good health, and this provides an estimate of healthy life expectancy. Between 1981 and 2001 healthy life expectancy in Great Britain rose for both males and females, but the rises were not as great as those in overall life expectancy. In 2001, healthy life expectancy at birth was 67.0 years for males and 68.8 years for females, increases of 2.6 and 2.1 years respectively since 1981. The result is that, as people have been living longer, the number of years spent in

poor health has been increasing. In 1981 the expected time lived in poor health for males was 6.4 years. By 2001 this had risen to 8.7 years. Between 1981 and 2001 the number of years females could expect to live in poor health increased from 10.1 to 11.6 years.

As people get older they are more likely to experience a longstanding illness or disability, including one which limits their daily activities or work in some way. In 2003/04 around 40 per cent of men and women aged 45 to 64 in Great Britain reported having a longstanding illness, rising to over 60 per cent among those aged 75 and over (Table 7.2).

The ageing population has contributed to an increase in the proportion of people reporting a longstanding illness, from 24 per cent in 1975 to 31 per cent in 2003/04. There was a smaller rise in longstanding illness which limited a person's activities from 15 per cent to 18 per cent over the same period. Limiting longstanding illnesses become more apparent at older ages. In 2003/04 limiting longstanding illness was reported by approximately one in ten adults under the age of 45 compared with more than four in ten aged 75 and over.

Among adults, musculoskeletal problems such as arthritis, rheumatism and back problems, and conditions of the heart and circulatory system, are the most commonly reported longstanding conditions. The prevalence of these conditions increases markedly with age. In 2003/04, 29 per cent of adults aged 65 and over in Great Britain were affected by a musculoskeletal condition and 31 per cent by a condition of the heart and circulatory system. The proportions of adults under the age of 45 reporting these conditions were 6 per cent and 2 per cent respectively.

Asthma is a condition which is more likely to be diagnosed in childhood than in later life. It is a disease of the lungs in which the airways are unusually sensitive to a wide range of stimuli,

Table 7.1

Life expectancy and healthy life expectancy[1] at birth: by sex

United Kingdom
Years

	1961	1971	1981	1986	1991	1996	2001	2003
Males								
Life expectancy	67.8	69.1	70.8	71.9	73.2	74.2	75.7	76.2
Healthy life expectancy[1]	..	..	64.4	65.3	66.1	66.6	67.0	..
Females								
Life expectancy	73.6	75.3	76.8	77.7	78.7	79.4	80.4	80.5
Healthy life expectancy[1]	..	..	66.7	67.4	68.5	68.7	68.8	..

1 Data for healthy life expectancy are for Great Britain. See Appendix, Part 7: Expectation of life, and Healthy life expectancy.
Source: Government Actuary's Department; Office for National Statistics

Table 7.2

Self-reported illness:[1] by sex and age, 2003/04

Great Britain   Percentages

	Longstanding illness	Limiting longstanding illness
Males		
0–4	14	4
5–15	18	7
16–44	20	10
45–64	41	24
65–74	62	37
75 and over	61	41
All ages	31	17
Females		
0–4	10	4
5–15	17	7
16–44	22	11
45–64	41	25
65–74	59	37
75 and over	65	46
All ages	32	19

1 See Appendix, Part 7: Self-reported illness.

Source: General Household Survey, Office for National Statistics

Table 7.3

New episodes of asthma:[1] by sex and age

England & Wales   Rates per 100,000 population

	1996	1998	2001	2003
Males				
Under 1	107	75	42	18
1–4	152	114	75	66
5–14	79	71	50	39
15–24	40	33	23	20
25–44	24	26	18	17
45–64	22	21	16	16
65–74	29	26	20	18
75 and over	23	19	21	14
All ages	41	36	26	22
Females				
Under 1	57	37	31	30
1–4	112	94	56	42
5–14	65	59	33	32
15–24	57	53	38	35
25–44	40	35	28	27
45–64	35	33	24	25
65–74	37	35	25	24
75 and over	28	23	21	17
All ages	46	41	29	27

1 Mean weekly incidence. A diagnosis for the first time or a previously
diagnosed asthmatic person having a new attack.

Source: Royal College of General Practitioners

including inhaled irritants and allergens. Among children over the age of one, the condition tends to be more common in boys than girls. In 2003 the diagnosis rate of new episodes in England and Wales among boys aged 1 to 4 years was 66 per 100,000 compared with 42 per 100,000 among girls of the same age (Table 7.3). For both sexes, rates were highest among this age group. In all age groups from 15 years and above incidence rates were higher among females.

Between 1996 and 2003 there was a general decline in the incidence rates of new cases of asthma diagnosed in both sexes and among all age groups. The overall mean weekly incidence rates of new episodes of asthma in England and Wales fell by 46 per cent among males and 41 per cent among females.

Since the early 1970s, circulatory diseases (which include heart disease and stroke) have remained the most common cause of death among males and females in the United Kingdom (Figure 7.4 overleaf). However, these conditions have also declined dramatically during this period. In 1971, age-standardised death rates from circulatory diseases were 6,900 per million males and 4,300 per million females. By 2003 these rates had fallen by over half for both sexes to 3,000 per million

males and 1,900 per million females. Drugs known as statins, which lower blood cholesterol levels, became available in the United Kingdom in 1990. They have since played an important part in reducing the number of deaths from heart disease.

Cancers are the second most common cause of death among both sexes in the United Kingdom. Among males, age-standardised death rates from cancers fell from a peak of around 2,900 per million in the mid-1980s to 2,300 per million in 2003. Cancer death rates among females were lower than those for males, but did not peak until the late 1980s. Since then they have gradually fallen from 1,900 per million in 1989 to 1,600 per million in 2003. The incidence and survival rates from the most common forms of cancer are examined later in this chapter.

The reduction in the infant mortality rate has been one of the major factors contributing to an overall increase in life expectancy, particularly in the first half of the 20th century. In 1921, 84.0 children per 1,000 live births in the United

Figure **7.4**

Mortality:[1] by sex and leading group of causes

United Kingdom[2]

Rates per million population

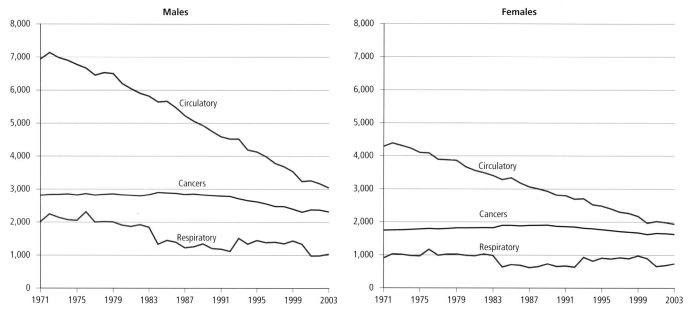

1 Data are for all ages and have been age-standardised using the European standard population. See Appendix, Part 7: Standardised rates, and International Classification of Diseases.
2 Data for 2000 are for England and Wales only.

Source: Office for National Statistics

Kingdom died before the age of one (Figure 7.5). There was a sharp fall in the infant mortality rate following the Second World War, from 48.8 in 1945 to exactly half that only 11 years later in 1956. This decline has continued, so that in 2003 the rate was 5.0. It is expected that the rate will continue to fall gradually with projections indicating that in 2021 it will be 3.9 per 1,000 live births. The fall in infant mortality rates can be linked to improvements in diet and sanitation, better antenatal, postnatal and medical care, and the development of vaccines and immunisation programmes (see Table 7.6).

Nearly all children in the United Kingdom are now immunised against tetanus, diphtheria, poliomyelitis, whooping cough, haemophilus influenzae b, meningitis C and measles, mumps and rubella. Current government immunisation targets are for 95 per cent of children to be immunised against these diseases by the age of two.

A single measles vaccine was introduced in 1968, but had limited effect because coverage was never sufficiently high to have an effect on virus transmission. In 1988 the combined measles/mumps/rubella (MMR) vaccine was introduced in the United Kingdom with coverage levels in excess of 90 per cent being achieved by the early 1990s (Table 7.6). However, in recent years, concerns by some people over the safety of the MMR vaccine have led to a fall in the proportion of children

Figure **7.5**

Infant mortality[1]

United Kingdom

Rate per 1,000 live births

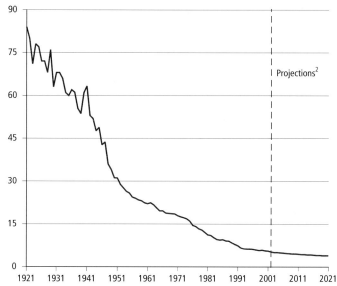

1 Deaths within one year of birth.
2 2002-based projections for 2003 onwards.

Source: Office for National Statistics; General Register Office for Scotland; Northern Ireland Statistics and Research Agency; Government Actuary's Department

Table **7.6**

Immunisation of children by their second birthday[1]

United Kingdom					Percentages
	1981[2]	1991/92	1994/95	1999/00	2003/04
Tetanus	83	94	93	95	94
Diphtheria	83	94	95	95	94
Poliomyelitis	82	94	95	95	94
Whooping cough	45	88	95	94	94
Measles, mumps, rubella[3]	54	90	91	88	81

1 See Appendix, Part 7: Immunisation.
2 Data exclude Scotland.
3 Includes measles-only vaccine for 1981. Combined vaccine was not available prior to 1988.

Source: Department of Health; National Assembly for Wales; National Health Service in Scotland; Department of Health, Social Services and Public Safety, Northern Ireland

immunised against MMR by their second birthday. In 2003/04, 81 per cent of children in the United Kingdom had received the vaccine by their second birthday compared with 90 per cent in 1991/92.

Infectious diseases now account for a very small proportion of deaths each year in the United Kingdom. However, as a result of epidemics, notifications of infectious diseases have fluctuated far more than those for other health conditions. Between 1993 and 1994 a measles epidemic resulted in a doubling of notifications in the United Kingdom from 12,000 to almost 23,500 (Figure 7.7). Notifications then fell progressively each year to 2,700 in 2001. However, between 2001 and 2002 the number increased to 3,700 before falling again to 2,700 notifications in 2003. The number of notifications of whooping cough fell during the late 1990s and in each of the three years up to 2002 there were approximately 1,000 cases. In 2003 the number of notifications halved to around 500.

As with measles and whooping cough, mumps has historically been a disease most commonly experienced in early childhood. However, in 2003, of the 4,200 notifications in England and Wales, just over 60 per cent were diagnosed among those aged 15 and over. Notifications among this age group largely accounted for a doubling in the total number of cases between 2002 and 2003, to the highest recorded number since 1990.

In the second half of the 1990s the number of tuberculosis notifications in the United Kingdom increased steadily to over 7,000 notifications of the disease each year between 2000 and 2002. There was a slight fall in 2003 to 6,700 notifications. Most cases occurred in major cities, particularly in London, where over 40 per cent of notifications were reported in 2003.

Figure **7.7**

Notifications of selected infectious diseases

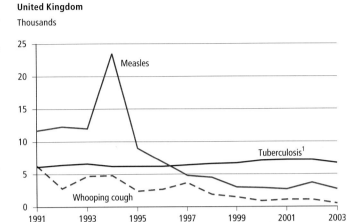

United Kingdom

Thousands

1 Tuberculosis notifications since 2002 should be interpreted with caution since the recent decline in notifications is most likely attributable to changes in surveillance practice at local level.

Source: Health Protection Agency, Centre for Infections; National Health Service in Scotland; Communicable Disease Surveillance Centre (Northern Ireland)

Obesity and diet

Government health strategies seek to reduce deaths and ill-health caused by circulatory diseases (including heart disease and stroke) and diabetes, by promoting healthy lifestyles. The key lifestyle risk factors for circulatory diseases are now well established and include poor nutrition and obesity, as well as smoking and physical inactivity.

Obesity is also related to diabetes and premature death. The body mass index (BMI, see Appendix, Part 7: Body mass index) is a common measure for assessing an individual's weight relative to their height, and a BMI score of over 30 is taken as the definition of obesity for adults aged 16 and over. Over the past decade there has been an increase in the proportion of adults in England who are obese. In 1993, 13 per cent of men and 16 per cent of women aged 16 and over were classified as obese (Figure 7.8 overleaf). By 2003 these proportions had risen to 23 per cent for both men and women. In addition, in 2003 a further 44 per cent of men and 33 per cent of women were classified as overweight.

In recent years there has also been concern over the proportion of children who are obese or overweight. In 2002, 22 per cent of boys and 28 per cent of girls aged 2 to 15 years in England were classified as either overweight or obese, according to the international classification. In 1995 the proportions who were either overweight or obese were 16 and 22 per cent respectively.

Figure **7.8**

Proportion of adults who are obese or overweight:[1] by sex

England
Percentages

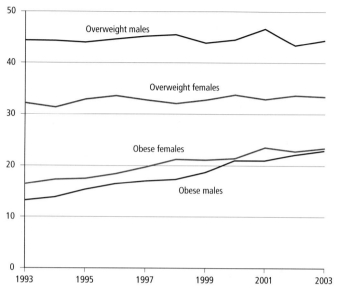

1 Using the body mass index (BMI) for people aged 16 and over. See
   Appendix, Part 7: Body mass index.

Source: Health Survey for England, Department of Health

The level of physical activity and the type of diet consumed have an important influence on weight and general health. A diet which is rich in complex carbohydrates (such as bread, cereals and potatoes), wholegrain cereals, fruit and vegetables, and low in total fat and salt can help to reduce the risk of weight gain, diabetes, cardiovascular disease and some cancers. Evidence from the National Food Survey and the Expenditure and Food Survey reveals that over the past 30 years consumption of some foods eaten at home are increasingly in line with dietary recommendations.

The consumption of red meat in the home has fallen since the mid-1970s. Beef and veal consumption in the United Kingdom fell from 189 grams per person per week in 1974 to 93 grams in 1996, since when it increased to 118 grams in 2002/03 (Figure 7.9). In contrast, the consumption of fish increased over the same period from 123 grams per person per week to 154 grams, while the quantity of poultry eaten increased from 152 grams per person per week in 1978 to 199 grams in 2002/03.

There have been even greater changes in the types of fat consumed. In 2002/03 the amount of butter consumed per person per week was one quarter of that consumed in 1974 and the amount of margarine one sixth. This was linked to a sharp rise in the consumption of low and reduced fat spreads between the mid-1980s and mid-1990s, since when consumption of these products has levelled off at around 70 grams per person per week.

Figure **7.9**

Changing patterns in the consumption of food at home[1]

United Kingdom
Grams per person per week

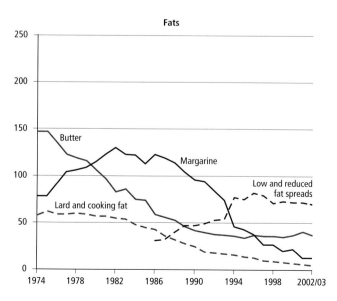

1 Data for 1974 to 2000 are based on adjusted National Food Survey (NFS) results. The NFS ended in March 2001 and was replaced by the Expenditure
   and Food Survey, which merged together the NFS and Family Expenditure Survey. Data are for financial years from 2001/02.

Source: National Food Survey, Department for Environment, Food and Rural Affairs; Expenditure and Food Survey, Office for National Statistics

Alcohol, drugs and smoking

The consumption of alcohol in excessive amounts can lead to ill health, with an increased likelihood of problems such as high blood pressure, cancer and cirrhosis of the liver. Current Department of Health advice on alcohol is that consumption of between three and four units a day for men and between two and three units a day for women should not lead to significant health risks. Consistently drinking more is not advised because of the associated health risks.

In 2003/04, two fifths of men and nearly one quarter of women in Great Britain exceeded the recommended amount of alcohol on at least one day during the previous week (Table 7.10). Young people (aged 16 to 24 years) were more likely to have exceeded the recommended amount than older people.

Heavy drinking, defined as more than eight units a day for men and six units a day for women, on at least one day in the previous week, was also more common among men than women. Between 1998/99 and 2002/03, the proportion of men drinking heavily remained relatively stable (at around 21 to 22 per cent), but rose from 21 per cent in 2002/03 to 23 per cent in 2003/04. Among women, the proportion of heavy drinkers remained at 10 per cent from 2000/01 to 2002/03, following a rise from 8 per cent in 1998/99. In 2003/04, 9 per cent of women were heavy drinkers. Since 1998/99 the gap between the proportion of young men

and women aged 16 to 24 who drink heavily has narrowed from 15 to 11 percentage points. However, in 2003/04, young men were still more likely than young women to drink heavily: 37 per cent compared with 26 per cent.

Alcohol consumption is higher in managerial and professional households than in routine and manual ones. In 2003/04, 76 per cent of adults (82 per cent of men and 71 per cent of women) in managerial and professional households had had a drink in the previous week. This compares with 59 per cent (68 per cent of men and 50 per cent of women) of adults in routine and manual households. The proportion of people in managerial and professional households drinking on five or more days in the previous week was twice that of adults in the routine and manual group (24 per cent compared with 12 per cent).

Young people are more likely to use drugs than older people. In 2002/03, 28 per cent of young people aged 16 to 24 in England and Wales had done so in the previous year in contrast to 5 per cent of those aged 35 to 59.

Cannabis was the most commonly used drug among young people (Table 7.11). In 2002/03, 32 per cent of young men and 21 per cent of young women had used it in the previous year. Ecstasy was the most commonly used Class A drug among young people. In 2002/03, 7 per cent of young men and 4 per cent of young women had used it in the previous year. There was a marked decline in the proportions of young men and

Table **7.10**

Adults exceeding specified levels of alcohol:[1] by sex and age, 2003/04

Great Britain   Percentages

	16–24	25–44	45–64	65 and over	All aged 16 and over
Males					
More than 4 units and up to 8 units	14	17	21	14	17
More than 8 units	37	30	20	6	23
More than 4 units	51	47	41	19	40
Females					
More than 3 units and up to 6 units	14	18	15	4	13
More than 6 units	26	13	5	1	9
More than 3 units	40	30	20	4	23

1 On at least one day in the previous week. Current Department of Health advice is that consumption of between three and four units a day for men and two to three units for women should not lead to significant health risks.

Source: General Household Survey, Office for National Statistics

Table **7.11**

Prevalence of drug misuse by young adults[1] in the previous year: by drug category and sex, 1996 and 2002/03

England & Wales   Percentages

	Males		Females	
	1996	2002/03	1996	2002/03
Cannabis	30	32	22	21
Ecstasy	9	7	4	4
Cocaine	2	7	-	3
Amphetamines	15	4	9	3
Magic mushrooms or LSD	9	3	2	1
All Class A drugs[2]	13	11	6	6
Any drug[3]	34	35	25	23

1 Those aged 16 to 24 years.
2 Include heroin, cocaine (both cocaine powder and 'crack'), ecstasy, magic mushrooms, LSD and unprescribed use of methadone.
3 Includes less commonly used drugs not listed in the table.

Source: British Crime Survey, Home Office

women using amphetamines, magic mushrooms or LSD between 1996 and 2002/03, but cocaine use increased. In 1996, 2 per cent of young men and less than half of one per cent of young women used cocaine with the proportions rising to 7 per cent and 3 per cent respectively in 2002/03.

During the 1990s there was an increase in the number of deaths related to drug poisoning in England and Wales. After peaking at 2,967 deaths in 2000, the number decreased to 2,685 in 2002 (see Appendix, Part 7: Drug-related poisoning deaths). Heroin and morphine accounted for 29 per cent of all drug-related poisoning deaths in 2002, which was more than any other type of drug. However, there were 11 per cent fewer deaths from heroin and morphine poisoning than in the previous year. Cocaine-related poisoning deaths rose from 96 in 2001 to 139 in 2002, and increased more than tenfold between 1993 and 2002. MDMA/Ecstasy-related poisoning deaths increased from 8 in 1993 to 55 in 2002.

Over the past 30 years there has been a substantial decline in the proportion of adults aged 16 and over in Great Britain who smoke cigarettes, from 45 per cent in 1974 to 26 per cent in 2003/04. In 1974, 51 per cent of men and 41 per cent of women smoked (Figure 7.12). Since then the difference between men and women has narrowed, although it has not disappeared completely. In 2003/04, 28 per cent of men and 24 per cent of women were cigarette smokers.

Figure **7.12**

Prevalence of adult[1] cigarette smoking:[2] by sex

Great Britain

Percentages

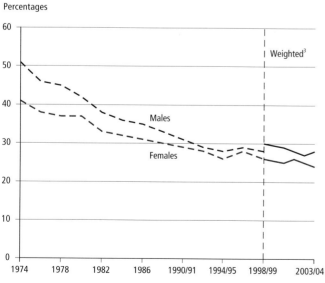

1 People aged 16 and over.
2 From 1988 data are for financial years. Between 1974 and 2000/01 the surveys were run every two years.
3 From 1998/99 data are weighted to compensate for nonresponse and to match known population distributions. Weighted and unweighted data for 1998/99 are shown for comparison.

Source: General Household Survey, Office for National Statistics

Cigarette smoking is more common among people aged 20 to 34 than other age groups. In 2003/04, 36 per cent of 20 to 24 year olds and 34 per cent of 25 to 34 year olds were smokers. This compares with 26 per cent of 16 to 19 year olds and just 15 per cent of those aged 60 and over. There were also marked socio-economic differences. Smoking was most prevalent among adults in routine and manual households (35 per cent for men and 31 per cent for women) and lowest among those in managerial and professional households (20 per cent for men and 17 per cent for women) (see Appendix, Part 6: National Statistics Socio-economic Classification). Since 2001/02 smoking prevalence among routine and manual groups has remained around 31 to 33 per cent. The Government's target is to reduce the overall proportion of cigarette smokers in England to 21 per cent or less by 2010 – with a reduction to 26 per cent or less among routine and manual occupation groups.

In 2003/04, two thirds of adult cigarette smokers in Great Britain said that they would like to stop smoking altogether. Moderate smokers (those smoking 10 to 19 cigarettes per day) were more likely to want to quit than light smokers (less than 10 cigarettes a day) or heavy smokers (20 or more a day). Among moderate smokers, 69 per cent said that they would like to stop smoking altogether compared with 64 per cent of both light and heavy smokers.

According to the ONS Omnibus survey, in 2003, 34 per cent of men and 44 per cent of women who were smokers had sought some help or advice to quit smoking in the previous year Table 7.13). Of the sources of help and advice they used,

Table **7.13**

Sources of help and advice on quitting smoking used in the previous year:[1] by sex, 1999 and 2003

Great Britain

Percentages

	Males		Females	
	1999	2003	1999	2003
Read leaflets/booklets	34	25	40	32
NRT[2] or other prescribed drug	12	14	22	22
Asked doctor or other health professional for help	4	9	6	13
Called a smokers' telephone helpline	2	4	4	5
Been referred/self-referred to a stop smoking group	2	3	1	7
Sought any help or advice	40	34	48	44

1 All smokers aged 16 and over regardless of whether or not they want to quit. Sources used in the 12 months prior to interview.
2 Nicotine replacement therapy.

Source: Omnibus Survey, Office for National Statistics

reading leaflets and booklets was the most popular, followed by the use of Nicotine Replacement Therapy (NRT) products or other prescribed drugs. Around 360,000 people in England set a quit date through the NHS Stop Smoking Services in 2003/04 (see Appendix, Part 7: NHS Stop Smoking Services) and 57 per cent had successfully quit at the four-week follow-up stage.

Cancer

About a third of the population develop cancer at some time in their lives and in its various forms the disease is responsible for around a quarter of all deaths in the United Kingdom. The incidence of some of the most common types of cancer has changed since the early 1980s (Figure 7.14).

The most dramatic fall has been in lung cancer among males, mainly as a result of the decline in smoking (see Figure 7.12). In 1981 the incidence rate in Great Britain was 112 per 100,000 male population. By 2001 the rate had fallen by 41 per cent to 66 per 100,000 males. In contrast, the incidence of both prostate and breast cancer rose considerably over the past 20 years. The incidence rate for prostate cancer rose from 38 per 100,000 males in 1981 to 88 per 100,000 in 2001. In 1999 prostate cancer overtook lung cancer as the most commonly diagnosed cancer among males. Throughout the past 20 years breast cancer has been the most commonly diagnosed form of cancer among females: in 1981 the incidence rate was 78 per 100,000 females and had risen to 114 per 100,000 females in 2001. The increase in the incidence of breast cancer is in part due to the gradual

introduction of the NHS breast cancer screening programme between 1989 and 1993 (see Table 7.16). This resulted in a large number of cases being diagnosed earlier than they would otherwise have been.

In England and Wales survival rates improved for most cancers in both sexes during the 1990s. For the majority of cancers common to both sexes, a slightly higher proportion of females than males aged 15 to 99 diagnosed during 1996 to 1999 survived for at least five years (Figure 7.15 overleaf). Age is an important factor: among adults, the younger the age at diagnosis, the higher the survival rate for most cancers.

Survival rates from lung cancer are very low compared with the other most common cancers. For those diagnosed with lung cancer in England and Wales during 1996 to 1999, the five-year survival rates for both males and females were around 6 per cent, similar to the survival rates of patients diagnosed a decade or so earlier.

For most of the commonly diagnosed cancers there have been notable improvements in survival rates. The five-year survival rate for men diagnosed with prostate cancer during 1996 to 1999 was 65 per cent, around 11 percentage points higher than for men diagnosed during 1991 to 1995. Although currently there is no NHS screening programme available for prostate cancer, the increase in survival is mainly due to the large increase in unorganised screening using the PSA (prostate-specific antigen) test. This has resulted in earlier diagnosis. Although patients may not live longer than they

Figure **7.14**

Standardised incidence rates[1] of selected cancers: by sex

Great Britain

Rates per 100,000 population

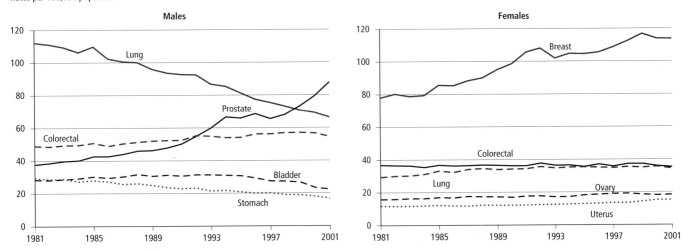

1 Age-standardised to the European standard population. See Appendix, Part 7: Standardised rates.

Source: Office for National Statistics

Figure **7.15**

Five year relative[1] survival rates for major cancers: by sex of patient diagnosed during 1996–99

England & Wales
Percentages

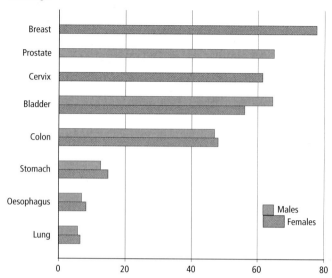

1 People aged 15 to 99. Data have been age-standardised to the European standard population. See Appendix, Part 7: Standardised rates.

Source: Office for National Statistics

would have done without the cancer being diagnosed, this leads to a longer apparent survival time. The breast cancer survival rate at five years among women diagnosed during 1996 to 1999 was 77 per cent, around 5 percentage points higher than for women diagnosed during 1991 to 1995. Again, part of this increase is related to earlier diagnosis by screening, but much of the improvement is real – as confirmed by the sharp downward trend in mortality.

NHS screening programmes aim to prevent deaths from breast cancer and lower the incidence of cervical cancer. Under the UK breast screening programme, every eligible woman aged between 50 and 64 should be invited for a mammogram (breast X-ray) every three years by computerised call-up and recall systems. In England, an extension to the automatic recall system to invite women aged 65 to 70 began on a phased basis in 2001. In Scotland, the extension began on a phased basis in 2003 and will be implemented over a three-year round of screening. In Wales, an extension to women aged 65 to 67 was piloted in certain areas in 2003. Following a review of the pilot, it is intended to extend the screening programme to all women in Wales up to the age of 70.

In 2002/03, three quarters of women invited from the target population in the United Kingdom underwent screening for breast cancer; this proportion is known as 'uptake' (Table 7.16). The uptake in most regions and countries of the United Kingdom varied between 71 and 81 per cent, but in London it was only 61 per cent. Since 1996/97 uptake among the target population has remained at similar levels in most regions and countries of the United Kingdom.

Clinical best practice for cervical screening in England is that women aged 25 to 49 should be screened every three years, and women aged 50 to 64 every five years. In Scotland, the programme invites women aged 20 to 60 for screening every three and a half to five and a half years. The test identifies cervical cells at a pre-cancerous stage which, after a long developmental period, may sometimes proceed to invasive cancer. At end March 2003, just over 80 per cent of the target population had been screened in England and Wales, and almost 90 per cent in Scotland.

Table **7.16**

Breast cancer screening:[1] by region

United Kingdom   Percentages

	1996/97	1998/99	2000/01	2002/03
United Kingdom	75	76	75	75
England	76	76	75	75
North East	79	80	79	79
North West	77	77	75	75
Yorkshire and the Humber	77	77	79	77
East Midlands	80	81	81	81
West Midlands	76	77	77	77
East	79	77	76	77
London	61	63	62	61
South East	78	79	77	77
South West	79	79	78	77
Wales	78	77	77	78
Scotland	72	74	72	75
Northern Ireland	71	71	73	71

1 As a percentage of women aged 50 to 64 invited for screening. See Appendix, Part 7: Breast cancer and cervical screening programmes.

Source: Department of Health; National Assembly for Wales; National Health Service in Scotland; Department of Health, Social Services and Public Safety, Northern Ireland

Mental health

Dealing with mental health problems is one of the main priorities set out in the Government's NHS Plan published in 2000. In 2000, about one in six people aged 16 to 74 living in private households in Great Britain had a neurotic disorder in the seven days prior to interview, such as depression, anxiety or a phobia. A higher proportion of women (19 per cent) than men (14 per cent) experienced such a disorder. Neurotic disorders were most common among those aged between 35 and 44, people who were widowed, divorced or separated, and those who lived alone.

In 2000 around one quarter of both men and women who were widowed, divorced or separated had a neurotic disorder (Table 7.17). In contrast, there were marked differences in the prevalence of neurotic disorder between single men and women. While one fifth of single women had experienced a neurotic disorder only one tenth of single men had. Among women, those who were married or cohabiting were the least likely to experience a neurotic disorder, while married or cohabiting men were slightly more likely than single men to do so.

Many people who experience mental health problems will seek advice from a suitably qualified health professional, who in most cases will be their general practitioner (GP). Treatment will typically be provided through counselling, prescription of an anti-depressant drug, or a combination of these. Since the early 1990s there has been a dramatic increase in the number of NHS prescription items for anti-depressant drugs. Between 1991 and 2003 the number dispensed in the community in England more than trebled from 9 million to 28 million (Figure 7.18 overleaf). In 2003 the net ingredient cost of anti-depressant drugs dispensed in the community in England was £395 million.

Mental illness is an established risk factor associated with suicide. Other risk factors include being male, living alone, unemployment and alcohol or drug misuse. In England, a National Suicide Prevention Strategy was launched in 2002, with a target being set to reduce the death rate from suicide by at least one fifth by 2010, from an age-standardised rate of 9.1 per 100,000 in 1996.

Table 7.17

Prevalence of neurotic disorder:[1] by sex and marital status, 2000

Great Britain   Percentages

	Single	Married/ cohabiting	Widowed, divorced or separated	All
Males				
Mixed anxiety and depressive disorder	4.8	7.2	9.6	6.8
Generalised anxiety disorder	3.2	4.0	10.3	4.3
Depressive episode	2.0	2.0	6.3	2.3
All phobias	2.0	0.9	3.1	1.3
Obsessive compulsive disorder	1.3	0.5	2.6	0.9
Panic disorder	0.7	0.7	0.6	0.7
Any neurotic disorder[2]	11.1	13.1	24.2	13.5
Females				
Mixed anxiety and depressive disorder	13.2	10.1	10.7	10.8
Generalised anxiety disorder	2.7	4.3	8.1	4.6
Depressive episode	3.0	2.3	4.9	2.8
All phobias	2.4	1.6	4.3	2.2
Obsessive compulsive disorder	1.6	1.1	2.0	1.3
Panic disorder	0.6	0.7	1.1	0.7
Any neurotic disorder[2]	20.5	17.9	24.6	19.4

1 Those aged 16 to 74 years living in private households.
2 People may have more than one type of neurotic disorder so the percentage with any disorder is not the sum of those with specific disorders.

Source: Psychiatric Morbidity Survey, Office for National Statistics

Figure **7.18**

Number of prescription items for anti-depressant drugs[1]

England
Millions

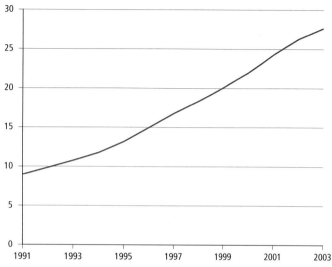

1 Dispensed in the community. See Appendix, Part 7: Prescription Cost Analysis system. Anti-depressants are defined as those drugs within the British National Formulary (BNF) section 4.3, anti-depressant drugs.

Source: Department of Health

Trends in suicide rates by age group and sex have shown marked differences in the United Kingdom over the last 30 years (Figure 7.19). Until the end of the 1980s older men aged 65 and over had the highest suicide rates. In 1986 the suicide rate among men aged 65 and over peaked at 26 per 100,000 population and then fell to 14 per 100,000 in 2003. In contrast, suicide rates for younger men rose. This was most notable among those aged 25 to 44, for whom the suicide rate almost doubled from 14 per 100,000 in 1971 to a peak of 27 per 100,000 in 1998. The suicide rate among men in this age group has since declined, but in 2003 remained the highest at 23 per 100,000.

There is a distinct sex difference in suicide rates. In 2003 the age-standardised rate for all men aged 15 and over was 18 per 100,000, three times that of women at 6 per 100,000. This gap has widened considerably since 1973, when the suicide rate among all men aged 15 and over was around one and a half times that of all women. Among women aged 45 and over, suicide rates have fallen steadily since the early 1980s. However among younger females the rates have remained fairly similar since the mid-1980s.

Figure **7.19**

Suicide rates:[1] by sex and age

United Kingdom
Rates per 100,000 population

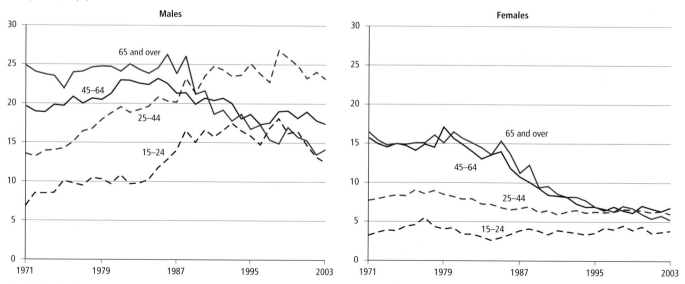

1 Includes deaths with a verdict of undetermined intent (open verdicts). Rates from 2002 are coded to ICD-10. Rates are age-standardised to the European standard population. See Appendix, Part 7: Standardised rates.

Source: Office for National Statistics; General Register Office for Scotland; Northern Ireland Statistics and Research Agency

Sexual health

Since the late 1990s, the increase in the prevalence of diseases that can be sexually transmitted, especially among young people, has become a major public health concern across the United Kingdom. The Government's public health strategy covers the provision of sexual health services, including free contraceptive advice and treatment.

Those who have unprotected sex and multiple sexual partners are at the greatest risk of contracting a sexually transmitted infection in Great Britain. In 2003/04, those below the age of 25 were far more likely than older people to report having had more than one sexual partner in the previous year (Table 7.20). Among each age group, men were more likely than women to have had more than one sexual partner. Among respondents aged 20 to 24, men were almost twice as likely as women to report multiple partners.

People can take action to protect their own health and that of others by using a condom, reducing the risk of contracting sexually transmitted diseases. In 2003/04, 79 per cent of men aged 16 to 49 and 74 per cent of women aged 16 to 49 who had had more than one sexual partner in the previous year had used a condom, compared with 35 per cent of men and 46 per cent of women who had had one partner.

People's reasons for using a condom varied by age and whether or not they had had multiple partners. In 2003/04, around 60 per cent of young men and 80 per cent of young women aged 16 to 19 reported that they had used a condom solely as a means of preventing infection or as well as for contraceptive purposes. In contrast, most people aged 25 and over used condoms only as a form of contraceptive. Among those aged 35 to 44, almost 70 per cent of both men and women used a condom for this reason alone. This reflects the likelihood that older people are in a monogamous relationship rather than having multiple partners.

The estimated number of people living with HIV in the United Kingdom at the end of 2003 was 53,000. Based on notifications received by the end of September 2004, 6,800 new HIV cases were diagnosed in 2003, the highest annual number of new diagnoses recorded to date. Since 1999 sex between men and women has been the most common route of transmission among those diagnosed, overtaking diagnoses in men who have sex with men (Figure 7.21). The increase in the number of cases diagnosed that were transmitted through heterosexual sex has been substantial, rising from 1,400 cases in 1999 to 4,000 in 2003. In 2003 over 80 per cent of infections in heterosexual men and women were acquired in high prevalence areas of the world, particularly Africa. Since 2001, HIV diagnoses each year have

Table **7.20**

Number of sexual partners[1] in the previous year: by sex and age, 2003/04

Great Britain					Percentages
	16–19	20–24	25–34	35–44	45–49
Males					
0 partners	34	16	7	6	7
1 partner	34	51	75	84	86
2 or 3 partners	21	19	11	7	5
4 or more partners	11	13	7	3	2
All aged 16–49	100	100	100	100	100
Females					
0 partners	35	11	8	11	16
1 partner	42	72	82	85	82
2 or 3 partners	18	16	9	4	1
4 or more partners	5	2	2	1	-
All aged 16–49	100	100	100	100	100

1 Self-reported in the 12 months prior to interview.

Source: Omnibus Survey, Office for National Statistics

Figure **7.21**

HIV infections:[1] by year of diagnosis and route of transmission

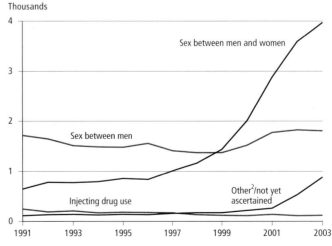

United Kingdom
Thousands

1 Numbers of diagnoses recorded, particularly for recent years, will rise as further reports are received. Those where the probable route of infection was not known, particularly for recent years, will fall as follow-up continues.
2 Other routes of infection include children infected through mother to child transmission and those infected through the receipt of blood or blood products.

Source: Health Protection Agency

Table **7.22**

New episodes of genital chlamydia: by sex and age

England & Wales

Numbers

	1995	1997	1999	2001	2002	2003
Males						
0–15	45	50	74	85	99	128
16–19	1,181	1,866	2,970	4,212	5,285	6,127
20–24	4,462	5,480	7,533	11,132	13,426	15,849
25–34	5,922	7,209	8,741	11,022	11,981	12,673
35–44	1,306	1,694	2,371	3,379	3,757	3,970
45–64	323	369	613	837	960	979
65 and over	32	27	35	39	47	57
All ages[1]	13,276	16,706	22,546	30,728	35,686	39,829
Females						
0–15	394	519	711	954	1,063	1,293
16–19	4,894	7,478	10,261	13,396	15,634	17,254
20–24	6,516	8,306	10,789	14,855	17,267	18,615
25–34	4,382	5,702	6,855	8,810	9,192	9,469
35–44	703	1,005	1,273	1,863	2,038	2,018
45–64	140	210	257	352	376	412
65 and over	19	17	9	26	15	24
All ages[1]	17,083	23,323	30,443	40,292	45,702	49,089

1 Includes those cases where age is unknown.

Source: Health Protection Agency

been higher in heterosexual women than in either heterosexual men or men who have sex with men. In 2003, heterosexual women accounted for 38 per cent of all those diagnosed. It should be noted that numbers for all of these categories for recent years will rise as the Health Protection Agency receives delayed notifications of new cases.

There have also been recent rises in the incidence of other sexually transmitted infections. In 2003 genital chlamydia was the most common sexually transmitted infection diagnosed in

genito-urinary medicine clinics in England and Wales: almost 89,000 cases were diagnosed, 9 per cent more than in 2002 and nearly three times the number in 1995 (Table 7.22).

Between 1995 and 2003 the increase was greatest among those aged under 25. The number of cases diagnosed falls off sharply among females aged 25 and over because of changes in sexual behaviour and decreased susceptibility. Among males aged 25 and over the decrease is not as pronounced as it is for women.

Social protection

- In 2003/04, two thirds of full-time employees in Great Britain were members of an active pension scheme. (Table 8.6)

- The average length of stay of acute patients in UK NHS hospitals fell by nearly three and a half days between 1981 and 2002/03, to 5.1 days. (Table 8.11)

- The proportion of NHS GP consultations in Great Britain that took place in the home in the 14 days before interview fell from 22 per cent in 1971 to just 4 per cent in 2003/04. (Table 8.12)

- In 2002/03 two thirds of 60 to 74 year old men in England, and three fifths of women of the same age, who reported that they had difficulties with daily activities or mobility, said that they received no help from any source, paid or unpaid. (Table 8.17)

- In 2001–02, 64 per cent of parents in the United Kingdom with babies aged 9 to 10 months had used grandparents to look after their babies while the main carer was at work or college. (Figure 8.21)

- Over 26,000 children were on child protection registers in England in March 2003; two fifths were under the age of five. (Table 8.24)

Chapter 8

Social protection describes the help given to those who are in need or are at risk of hardship through, for example, illness, low income, family circumstances or age. Central government, local authorities and private bodies (such as voluntary organisations) can provide help and support. The type of help provided can be direct cash payments such as social security benefits or pensions; payments in kind such as free prescriptions or bus passes; or the provision of services, for example through the National Health Service (NHS). Unpaid care, such as that provided by informal carers, also plays a part in helping people in need.

Expenditure

So that spending on social protection can be compared across the member countries of the European Union (EU), Eurostat has designed a framework for the presentation of information on such expenditure which has been adopted by member states as the European System of integrated Social Protection Statistics (ESSPROS). For this purpose, programmes which are specifically designed to protect people against common sources of hardship are collectively described as expenditure on social protection benefits. Examples include government expenditure on social security (generally excluding tax credits) and personal social services, sick pay paid by employers, and payments made from occupational and personal pension schemes. Protected

people receive a direct benefit from these programmes, whether in terms of cash payments, goods or services.

In 2002/03, £277 billion was spent on social protection benefits in the United Kingdom, using the ESSPROS definitions. Expenditure on benefits for old age and survivors (such as widows) accounted for nearly half of this expenditure, while spending on benefits for sickness, healthcare and disability accounted for nearly two fifths (Figure 8.1). Between 1992/93 and 2002/03 there was a 43 per cent rise in social protection expenditure on old age and survivors in real terms (after allowing for inflation). In part, this reflects an increase in expenditure on state and occupational pensions.

In Figure 8.2, expenditure is expressed in terms of purchasing power parities, to allow direct comparisons between countries. These take account of differences in the general level of prices for goods and services within each country. The differences between countries therefore reflect the differences in the social protection systems, demographic structures, unemployment rates and other social, institutional and economic factors. Measured in this way, UK spending on social protection in 2001 was £3,840 per person, which was close to the EU average of £3,980 for the EU-15 members. Countries such as Luxembourg and Denmark spent considerably more than this, while

Figure **8.1**

Expenditure on social protection benefits in real terms:[1] by function, 1992/93 and 2002/03

United Kingdom

£ billion at 2002/03 prices[1]

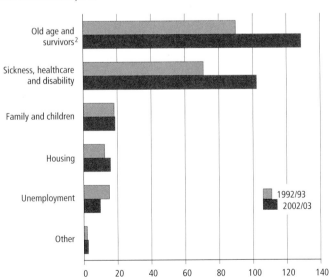

1 Adjusted to 2002/03 prices using the GDP market prices deflator.
2 Survivors are those whose entitlement derives from their relationship to a deceased person (for example, widows, widowers and orphans).

Source: Office for National Statistics

Figure **8.2**

Expenditure[1] on social protection per head: EU comparison, 2001

£ thousand per head

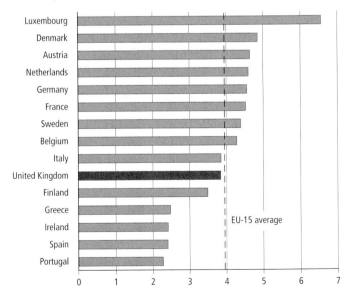

1 Before deduction of tax, where applicable. Tax credits are generally excluded. Figures are Purchasing Power Parities per inhabitant. Includes administrative and other expenditure incurred by social protection schemes.

Source: Eurostat

countries such as Portugal, Spain, Ireland and Greece spent less. However, Luxembourg is a special case as a large proportion of benefits is paid to persons living outside the country.

In real terms, social security benefit expenditure in the United Kingdom rose from £56 billion in 1977/78 to £120 billion in 2003/04 (Figure 8.3). Increases in benefit expenditure are influenced by the economic cycle, demographic changes and government policies on benefits. Spending on social security benefits fell in the late 1980s before rising again in the early 1990s, reflecting changes in the number of people who were unemployed or economically inactive. Since then social security benefit expenditure has generally continued to rise as a result of benefits aimed at pensioners and children rising more rapidly than prices.

Figure **8.3**

Social security benefit expenditure in real terms[1]

United Kingdom
£ billion at 2003/04 prices[1]

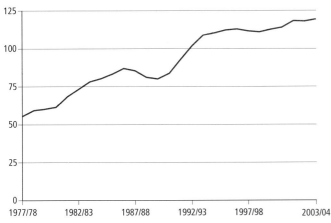

1 Adjusted to 2003/04 prices using the GDP market prices deflator (second quarter 2004).

Source: Department for Work and Pensions; Inland Revenue; Veterans Agency; Department of Health and Social Services, Northern Ireland

Tax credits aim to improve the way that the Government supports families with children and working people on low incomes, including disabled workers. Tax credits for social spending were introduced mid-way through 1999/2000 and since 2000/01 (the first full year of tax credits) spending has increased rapidly from £4.6 billion to £13.6 billion in 2003/04 as the number of families receiving tax credits has increased from 1 million to 5 million.

Hospital and community health service expenditure averaged £708 per head of population in England in 2002/03, but was highest at either end of the life cycle. Those aged 85 and over, received the largest amount of hospital and community health service expenditure per person of any age group (Figure 8.4).

Figure **8.4**

Hospital and community health service expenditure:[1] by age of recipient, 2002/03

England
£ per head of population

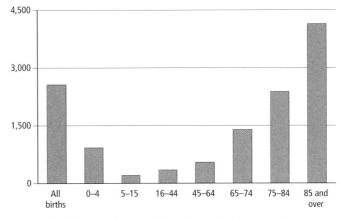

1 Includes administrative expenditure, but excludes expenditure on Joint Finance (NHS and local authority) schemes.

Source: Department of Health

At £4,147 per person it was more than six times the average amount spent on the under 85s (£640). Expenditure per head on the 5 to 15 age group was the lowest at £211, while spending on births was £2,570 per head, similar to that on the 75 to 84 age group (£2,387).

Spending on personal social services by local authorities in England was £15.2 billion in 2002/03. People aged 65 and over accounted for just under half of this expenditure (£6.9 billion) and children and families accounted for almost one quarter (£3.5 billion) (Figure 8.5 overleaf).

There is an increasing emphasis on people making their own provision for retirement, through either an occupational, personal or a stakeholder pension. Many people are members of a pension scheme provided through their employer; this could be the employer's occupational pension, or a group personal pension or a stakeholder pension sponsored by the employer. Personal pension plans and stakeholder pensions are schemes offered by financial service companies into which people who are employed or self-employed make contributions to provide a pension on retirement. Some employers make contributions to personal and stakeholder pensions for their employees.

In 2003/04, 68 per cent of full-time male employees, 65 per cent of full-time female employees and 39 per cent of part-time female employees were active members of a pension scheme in Great Britain (Table 8.6 overleaf). Such employees were more likely to belong to an occupational pension scheme than a personal pension plan.

Figure **8.5**

Local authority personal social services expenditure:[1] by recipient group, 2002/03

England

Percentages

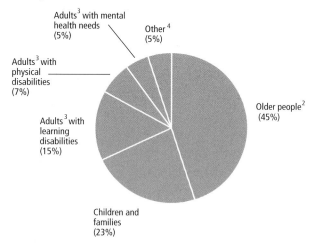

Adults[3] with mental health needs (5%)

Other[4] (5%)

Adults[3] with physical disabilities (7%)

Adults[3] with learning disabilities (15%)

Older people[2] (45%)

Children and families (23%)

Total expenditure: £15.2 billion.

1 All figures include overhead costs.
2 Aged 65 and over.
3 Adults aged under 65.
4 Includes expenditure on asylum seekers and overall service strategy.

Source: Department of Health

Employees aged 25 and over were more likely to be active members of a pension scheme than those aged under 25. For example, 27 per cent of full-time male employees aged 18 to 24 were active members of a scheme, compared with 63 per cent or more of those aged 25 and over. Among employees, the 55 and over age group were less likely to be active members of a pension scheme than both the 35 to 44 and the 45 to 54 age groups. In all age groups women working part time were less likely to be active members of a pension scheme than women working full time.

Help for people in need is also provided by voluntary organisations. The Charities Aid Foundation combines data from the top 500 fundraising charities in the United Kingdom to show their spending on social protection. In 2002/03, children's charities spent the most on social protection (£509 million), followed by charities for people with disabilities (£447 million) and those concerned with cancer (£412 million) (Figure 8.7).

Table **8.6**

Pension scheme membership of employees:[1] by sex and age,[2] 2003/04

Great Britain

Percentages

	18–24	25–34	35–44	45–54	55 and over	All aged 16 and over[2]
Male full-time employees						
Occupational pension[3]	25	51	61	67	57	55
Personal pension[4]	6	19	26	30	28	23
Any pension	27	63	77	83	73	68
Female full-time employees						
Occupational pension[3]	28	56	64	65	59	56
Personal pension[4]	4	16	18	19	22	16
Any pension	30	66	75	75	68	65
Female part-time employees						
Occupational pension[3]	9	37	43	40	28	33
Personal pension[4]	1	11	11	12	12	10
Any pension	9	44	49	47	37	39

1 Active membership of a pension scheme. Excluding those on youth training or employment training.
2 Includes 16 to 17 year olds not shown separately in the table.
3 Includes a small number of people who were not sure if they were in an occupational scheme but thought it possible.
4 Includes stakeholder pensions, a form of personal pension introduced in April 2001.

Source: General Household Survey, Office for National Statistics

Figure **8.7**

Charitable expenditure on social protection by the top 500 charities:[1] by function, 2002/03

United Kingdom
£ million

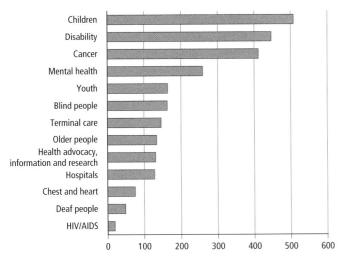

1 Charities Aid Foundation top 500 fundraising charities. Excludes administrative expenditure.

Source: Charities Aid Foundation

Carers and caring

In 2004 there were just under 270,000 available places in care establishments in England (Table 8.8). The majority of all places were provided by the private sector (66 per cent) although the funding may have been provided by the public sector. The voluntary sector provided 20 per cent of places, local

Table **8.8**

Places available in residential care homes:[1] by type of provider, 2004

England   Thousands

	Private sector	Local authority	Voluntary	NHS	Other
Older people[2]	138.5	30.3	30.5	0.2	1.7
People with physical or sensory or learning disabilities	39.2	8.4	20.1	1.1	1.2
People with mental health problems	16.8	1.8	4.4	0.1	-
Other people	1.5	0.4	1.4	0.0	0.1
All places[3]	176.3	35.4	52.5	1.4	2.9

1 Places in staffed residential care homes as at 2 December.
2 Includes residential beds for older mentally infirm people.
3 Figures do not sum to the totals because some places may be dual registered.

Source: Commission for Social Care Inspection

authorities provided 13 per cent and the NHS provided less than 1 per cent. Around 75 per cent of all places were for older people and about 26 per cent were for people with physical or sensory or learning disabilities, although some places were registered for more than one recipient group.

Local authority home care services assist people to continue living in their own home, and to function as independently as possible. During a survey week in September 2003, local authorities in England provided or purchased just over 3 million hours of home care services for around 363,000 households. Between 1993 and 2003 the number of contact hours increased by 75 per cent. The independent sector now provides much of this care. In 2003 around 66 per cent of all contact hours provided or purchased by local authorities were delivered by the independent sector (which includes the private and voluntary sectors) compared with 5 per cent in 1993 (Figure 8.9).

More hours of help are being provided to fewer households. Between September 2000 (the earliest year for which comparable data are available) and September 2003 the number of contact hours provided increased by 12 per cent and the number of households receiving that care fell by 9 per cent. In September 2000, 29 per cent of households

Figure **8.9**

Number of contact hours of home help and home care:[1] by sector

England
Millions

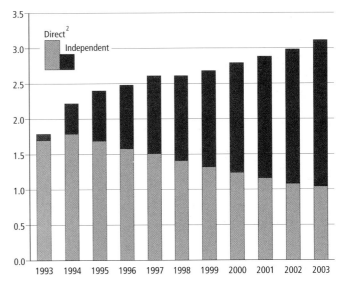

1 During a survey week in September. Contact hours provided or purchased by local authorities. Households receiving home care purchased with a direct payment are excluded.
2 Directly provided by local authorities.

Source: Department of Health

receiving home care received ten or more visits during the survey week and 16 per cent received ten or more hours of help (excluding overnight stays). By September 2003 these figures had increased so that 37 per cent of visited households received ten or more visits and 21 per cent received ten or more hours of help (excluding overnight stays).

Informal carers are people who provide unpaid care for family members, friends, neighbours or others who are sick, disabled or elderly. According to the Census in 2001 there were 5.9 million informal carers living in private households in the United Kingdom providing at least one hour of care a week (Table 8.10).

Table **8.10**

Informal carers[1] who live in households: by sex and age, 2001

United Kingdom				Percentages
	Hours of care per week			All (=100%)
	1–19	20–49	50 and over	(thousands)
Males				
5–15	85	8	7	53
16–24	80	12	8	125
25–34	72	12	15	230
35–44	71	12	17	422
45–54	76	9	15	613
55–64	71	10	19	519
65–74	58	11	31	319
75–84	43	12	44	155
85 and over	34	12	54	24
All males	69	11	20	2,460
Females				
5–15	84	8	8	61
16–24	74	13	13	165
25–34	65	12	23	376
35–44	67	12	21	665
45–54	72	11	17	896
55–64	65	12	23	697
65–74	55	11	34	370
75–84	46	10	44	149
85 and over	41	11	47	20
All females	66	12	22	3,399

1 See Appendix, Part 8: Informal carers.

Source: Census 2001, Office for National Statistics; General Register Office for Scotland; Northern Ireland Statistics and Research Agency

There were 114,000 carers aged 5 to 15 and the numbers increased with each ten-year age band to peak at 1.5 million in the 45 to 54 age group. For subsequent age groups the numbers of carers declined so that there were 304,000 carers aged between 75 and 84 and 44,000 carers aged 85 and over.

The majority of carers were female (3.4 million compared with 2.5 million males) and female carers outnumbered male carers in all except the 75 to 84 and 85 and over age groups. Overall 58 per cent of carers were female, but within the 85 and over age group 54 per cent of carers were men.

Around one in five carers were caring for 50 hours or more a week, but this varied by age. Around 8 per cent of carers aged 5 to 15 were caring for 50 or more hours a week compared with around 50 per cent of carers aged 85 and over. Overall female carers were more likely than male carers to be caring for 50 or more hours a week, but in the 85 and over age groups men were more likely than women to be providing this amount of care.

Sick and disabled people

The NHS offers a range of health and care services for sick and disabled people. It provides primary care through services such as general medical practitioners (GPs), dentists, opticians or through the telephone and Internet service, NHS Direct. NHS hospitals provide acute and specialist services, treating conditions which normally cannot be dealt with by primary care specialists.

Acute finished consultant episodes rose by 47 per cent in the United Kingdom between 1981 and 2002/03 to reach 8.4 million (Table 8.11). The number of finished episodes for the mentally ill was slightly higher in 2002/03 (253,000) than it was in 1981 (244,000), although there has been a reduction of 10 per cent since 1991/92. The number of finished episodes for people with learning disabilities in 2002/03 was 42,000, around 8,000 higher than in 1981.

Between 1981 and 2002/03 the average length of stay for acute patients fell by nearly three and a half days, to just over five days. Data for the duration of stay for the mentally ill and people with learning disabilities are not available for 1981. Between 1991/92 and 2002/03 the average length of stay fell by just over 60 days for the mentally ill. Although the duration of stay for those with learning disabilities was much shorter in 2002/03 than it was in 1991/92, it has fluctuated in recent years from 90 days in 2000/01 to 118 days in 2001/02 and back to 64 days in 2002/03.

People can consult their NHS GP for a number of services including vaccinations and general health advice, as well as the dispensing of prescriptions, the diagnosis of illness and referrals

Table **8.11**

NHS in-patient activity for sick and disabled people[1]

United Kingdom

	1981	1991/92	2000/01	2001/02	2002/03
Acute[2]					
Finished consultant episodes[1] (thousands)	5,693	6,729	8,076	8,204	8,381
In-patient episodes per available bed (numbers)	31.1	45.9	63.7	64.4	65.7
Mean duration of stay (days)	8.4	6.0	5.1	4.9	5.1
Mentally ill					
Finished consultant episodes[1] (thousands)	244	281	265	257	253
In-patient episodes per available bed (numbers)	2.2	4.0	6.4	6.5	6.4
Mean duration of stay (days)	..	114.8	58.4	54.6	54.3
People with learning disabilities					
Finished consultant episodes[1] (thousands)	34	62	43	40	42
In-patient episodes per available bed (numbers)	0.6	2.2	5.3	5.6	6.6
Mean duration of stay (days)	..	544.1	90.4	117.8	64.2

1 See Appendix, Part 8: In-patient activity.
2 General patients on wards, excluding elderly, maternity and neonate cots in maternity units.

Source: Department of Health; National Assembly for Wales; National Health Service in Scotland; Department of Health, Social Services and Public Safety, Northern Ireland

to secondary care services. On average females visit their GP more often than males. In 2003/04 females in the United Kingdom averaged five visits a year compared with three for males. The biggest difference between males and females was in the 16 to 44 age group.

The majority of NHS GP consultations take place in the GPs' surgeries, with smaller numbers taking place over the telephone or in the home (Table 8.12). Proportionally, home consultations by GPs have declined in favour of consultations in the surgery or by telephone. The General Household Survey found that between 1971 and 2003/04 the proportion of GP

consultations in Great Britain which took place in the home in the 14 days before the interview declined from 22 per cent to 4 per cent. Over the same period consultations at the surgery increased from 73 per cent to 86 per cent, and those conducted by telephone increased from 4 per cent to 10 per cent.

In 2002/03, 31 per cent of people in the United Kingdom had received something on prescription in the four weeks prior to their interview in the Family Resources Survey (Table 8.13). Females were more likely than males to have done so, particularly those in their 20s. In 2003, an estimated 2.5 million women in England were receiving contraceptives on prescription.

Table **8.12**

NHS GP consultations:[1] by site of consultation

Great Britain   Percentages

	1971	1981	2001/02	2002/03	2003/04
Surgery[2]	73	79	85	86	86
Telephone	4	7	10	9	10
Home	22	14	5	5	4

1 NHS GP consultations in the 14 days prior to interview. Data for 1971 and 1981 are unweighted.
2 Includes consultations with a GP at a health centre or described as occurring 'elsewhere'.

Source: General Household Survey, Office for National Statistics

Table **8.13**

Receipt of medical treatment:[1] by sex, 2002/03

United Kingdom   Percentages

	Males	Females	All
Received something on prescription	28	35	31
Visited NHS dentist	9	12	11
Had an eyesight test	4	5	5
Purchased glasses or contact lenses	3	4	3

1 Those that had received each type of service in the four weeks prior to interview.

Source: Family Resources Survey, Department for Work and Pensions

In 2002/03, 11 per cent of people in the United Kingdom had visited an NHS dentist in the four weeks prior to the interview. Smaller proportions of people had undergone an eyesight test (5 per cent) or purchased glasses or contact lenses (3 per cent). Females were more likely than males to have received each of these services.

In 2003, the British Social Attitudes survey asked adults aged 18 and over, from their own experience, or from what they had heard, how satisfied or dissatisfied they were with the way in which different parts of the NHS ran. The survey found that 72 per cent of adults in Great Britain were very satisfied or quite satisfied with their local NHS doctors or GPs. Satisfaction with other NHS services was generally lower, with 52 per cent of people saying that they were very satisfied or quite satisfied with the way that dentists' services were run. Among hospital services, more people said that they were very or quite satisfied with out-patient care and in-patient care (54 per cent and 52 per cent respectively), than with accident and emergency care (45 per cent).

Women were generally more likely than men to say that they were satisfied with a range of NHS services (Figure 8.14). In particular, women were more likely to say that they were very or quite satisfied with their dentist and out-patient care. Men were more likely to say that they were very or quite satisfied with accident and emergency services. Some of these differences may be related to use of those services. In 2002 the British Social Attitudes survey found that people who had used a hospital service in the previous year were more likely to say that they were satisfied than those who had not.

Figure **8.14**

Satisfaction with selected NHS services,[1] 2003

Great Britain
Percentages

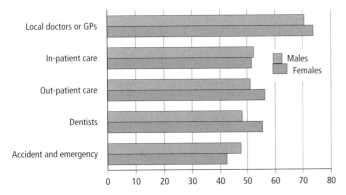

1 Adults aged 18 and over who said that they were 'very satisfied' or 'quite satisfied' when asked 'From your own experience, or from what you have heard, please say how satisfied or dissatisfied you are with the way in which each of these parts of the National Health Service runs nowadays'.

Source: British Social Attitudes Survey, National Centre for Social Research

Primary and secondary healthcare are offered by a variety of health and social services staff. Between 1993 and 2003 the number of NHS hospital and community health medical and dental staff in Great Britain increased by 46 per cent, to 86,000 (Table 8.15). Between 2002 and 2003 the number of NHS medical and dental staff increased by 5 per cent, while the number of nursing, midwifery and health visitor staff increased by 4 per cent to 472,000. There was a similar proportional increase in the number of other non-medical staff, which increased by 6 per cent between 2002 and 2003 to around 551,000.

Table **8.15**

Health and personal social services staff[1]

Great Britain			Thousands
	1993	2002	2003
NHS hospital and community health service staff			
Medical and dental	59	81	86
Nursing, midwifery and health visitors	..	453	472
Other non-medical staff	..	521	551
General medical practitioners	33	34	35
General dental practitioners	18	22	23
Personal social services	..	257	263

1 See Appendix, Part 8: Health and personal social services staff.

Source: Department of Health; National Assembly for Wales; National Health Service in Scotland

In 2003 there were over 35,000 GPs in Great Britain, 8 per cent more than in 1993. Over the same period the population of Great Britain increased by 3 per cent and, according to the General Household Survey, the average number of GP consultations per person fell from five to four. Between 1993 and 2003 the number of NHS dental practitioners rose by 22 per cent to 23,000.

As well as the provision of services such as the NHS, there are a number of cash benefits available to sick and disabled people. Disability Living Allowance (DLA) is a benefit for people who are disabled and have personal care and/or mobility needs. DLA accounted for over half of benefit expenditure on disabled people in Great Britain in 2003/04.

In February 2004 over 2.7 million people were receiving DLA in the United Kingdom. Overall the proportions of male and female recipients were similar, with 47 per 1,000 males and 45 per 1,000 females receiving DLA. The highest rate for both males and females was among the 55 to 64 age group with around one in ten people receiving this benefit (Figure 8.16). The rate for those aged 65 and over is lower than the rate for those aged 55 to 64 because, although those that claimed before their 65th birthday still receive payment, no new claims for DLA can be made by people aged 65 and over. The rate of males receiving DLA was higher than females in the 0 to 15 and the 65 and over age groups, while the rate for females aged 55 to 64 was higher than that for males.

Figure **8.16**

Recipients of disability living allowance (DLA): by sex and age, 2004[1]

United Kingdom

Rate per 1,000 population[2]

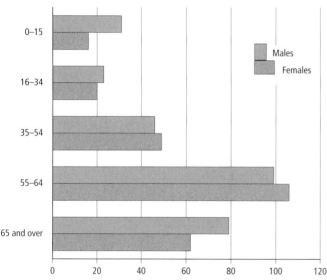

1 At 28 February.
2 Rate calculated using mid-2003 population estimates.

Source: Department for Work and Pensions; Northern Ireland Statistics and Research Agency

Older people

The number of people aged 65 and over in the United Kingdom rose by 28 per cent between 1971 and 2003 (see Figure 1.3 in the Population chapter). There are a number of care services available to older people. Older people occupy the majority of places in residential care homes in England (see Table 8.8), and they have more consultations with GPs per person than other groups within the United Kingdom.

Among people aged 50 and over in England, the proportion who are looking after a parent or parent-in-law falls with increasing age of the carer, and the proportion looking after a spouse increases. For example, 11 per cent of women aged 50 to 54 were caring for a parent or parent-in-law in 2002/03 compared with 1 per cent of women aged 70 to 74. Among people in their 50s and 60s a higher proportion of women than men were caring for their spouse. From the age of

70 onwards this reversed. These differences are associated with differences in life expectancy. Because they live longer, older women are more likely than older men to be widowed and living alone, while older men are more likely to be living with their spouse. Therefore a larger proportion of men are able to both provide care to, and receive care from, their spouse.

In 2002/03, the majority of people aged 60 and over in England who reported that they had difficulties with daily activities or with mobility said that they received no help from any source, paid or unpaid (Table 8.17). Men were more likely than women to say that they received no help. Women aged 75 and over were the most likely to have received some help, though they were less likely than men or younger women to be receiving help from a spouse or partner. One in five women aged 75 and over received help from their daughter; this was almost double the proportion for men of the same age.

Table **8.17**

Reported sources of help[1] for people aged 60 and over who have difficulty with daily activities or mobility:[2] by sex and age, 2002/03

England   Percentages

	Males		Females	
	60–74	75 and over	60–74	75 and over
No help	67.8	52.8	60.4	42.3
Spouse or partner	23.5	23.7	23.3	12.0
Son	5.8	7.6	6.4	12.4
Daughter	5.6	11.5	10.7	20.6
Daughter-in-law or son-in-law	1.8	4.4	3.3	8.0
Grandchild	1.2	3.3	2.1	5.4
Sibling	1.0	0.4	1.8	2.5
Other paid	2.7	10.5	3.8	19.8
Other unpaid	4.7	8.2	6.8	13.1

1 Excludes parents as the proportions receiving such help are negligible.
2 See Appendix, Part 8: Activities of daily living (ADLs) and instrumental activities of daily living (IADLs).

Source: English Longitudinal Study of Ageing, Office for National Statistics

In Great Britain, among people aged 65 and over living in private households in 2001/02, those who lived alone were more likely than those who lived with their spouse to have seen a doctor at home, a social worker or care manager, a chiropodist or an optician in the month before the interview.

In 2001/02, 14 per cent of people aged 65 and over and living in a private household said that they were unable to walk down the road on their own. Women were more likely than men to say this. Those who could not walk down the road without help were far more likely to receive a range of personal social services than those who could manage to do this on their own (Figure 8.18). Of those who needed assistance to walk down the road, 23 per cent received help from a district nurse or health visitor in the month before the interview, and 19 per cent had received private home help. Only 3 per cent of those who were able to walk down the road on their own had used a district nurse or health visitor, while 9 per cent had received private home help. Local authority home help was received by 16 per cent of those who needed help walking outdoors, but by only 2 per cent of those who said that they could manage on their own.

Figure **8.18**

Use of personal social services[1] by people aged 65 and over living in households: by whether they are able to walk outdoors unaided,[2] 2001/02

Great Britain
Percentages

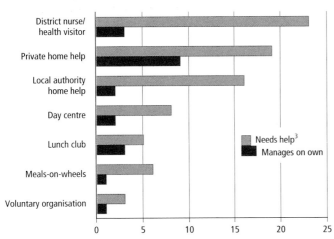

1 Percentage that had used each service in the month prior to interview.
2 Whether they are able to go outdoors and walk down the road unaided.
3 Includes those who cannot go out even with help.

Source: General Household Survey, Office for National Statistics

Older people account for a higher proportion of local authority expenditure (see Figure 8.5) and for more social security benefit expenditure than any other recipient group. Much of central government's expenditure on social protection for older people is through the provision of the state retirement pension. In 2002/03 nearly all people over pension age (women aged 60 and over and men aged 65 and over) received the state retirement pension according to the Family Resources Survey (Table 8.19). In addition, many older people also received other social security benefits, such as council tax benefit or housing benefit, particularly if they were single. Among pensioners living alone, females were more likely than males to be receiving council tax benefit and working families' tax credit, income support or minimum income guarantee.

Table **8.19**

Receipt of selected social security benefits among pensioners: by type of benefit unit,[1] 2002/03

United Kingdom Percentages

	Single		Couple
	Males	Females	
Retirement pension	98	97	98
Incapacity or disablement benefits[2]	20	20	26
Council tax benefit	33	38	17
Housing benefit	25	27	10
Working families' tax credit, income support or minimum income guarantee	14	24	7
Any benefit or tax credit[3]	99	99	99

1 Pensioner benefit units. See Appendix, Part 8: Benefit units.
2 Includes incapacity benefit, disability living allowance (care and mobility components), severe disablement allowance, industrial injuries disability benefit, war disablement pension, attendance allowance and disabled persons tax credit.
3 Includes benefits not listed here. Components do not add up to the total as each benefit unit may receive more than one benefit.

Source: Family Resources Survey, Department for Work and Pensions

Families and children

Child benefit is paid for all children aged under 16 (or under 19 and studying up to A level, NVQ level 3 or equivalent). It is a universal payment, not affected by income or savings or national insurance contributions. In 2002/03 child benefit was received by 97 per cent of families with dependent children in the United Kingdom where the head of the household was below state pension age (Table 8.20). Single parent families were more likely than couple families to be receiving some other benefits such as working families' tax credit or income support, council tax benefit or housing benefit. This reflects the economic activity of lone-parent families: lone mothers, who form the majority of lone-parent families, are generally less likely to be working than mothers with a partner (see Table 4.3 in the Labour market chapter).

A number of changes in society have led to an increased requirement for childcare. Changes in the labour market mean that there are more women in the workplace. In particular, more women with dependent children are working. In March 2004, there were 456,000 registered full day care places in England, an increase of nearly 20 per cent since 2003. Out of school day care rose by 14 per cent over the same period, with 327,000 registered places available in 2004.

Demographic changes mean that the proportion of people who have an elderly parent alive has increased and in 2001–02 grandparents played a large role in the care of babies aged

Table 8.20

Receipt of selected social security benefits among families below pension age: by type of benefit unit,[1] 2002/03

United Kingdom   Percentages

	Single person with dependent children	Couple with dependent children
Child benefit	97	97
Working families' tax credit, income support or minimum income guarantee	76	15
Incapacity or disablement benefits[2]	9	9
Council tax benefit	49	7
Housing benefit	48	6
Any benefit or tax credit[3]	98	98

1 Families below pension age. See Appendix, Part 8: Benefit units.
2 Incapacity benefit, disability living allowance (care and mobility components), severe disablement allowance, industrial injuries disability benefit, war disablement pension, attendance allowance and disabled persons tax credit.
3 Includes all benefits not listed here. Components do not add up to the total as each benefit unit may receive more than one benefit.

Source: Family Resources Survey, Department for Work and Pensions

Figure 8.21

Use of childcare by families with babies,[1] while main carer is employed or a full-time student, 2001–02

United Kingdom
Percentages[2]

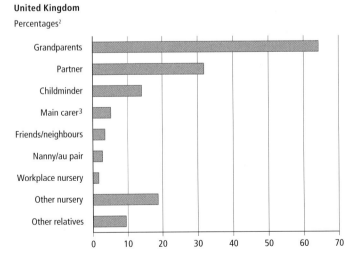

1 Families with babies aged nine to ten months using childcare while main carer is at work or college.
2 Figures do not sum to 100 per cent because the respondents could indicate more than one kind of childcare.
3 The mother herself while at work or college. In seven cases fathers were the main carers but none of these cared for the child themselves while at work.

Source: Millennium Cohort Study, ESRC Centre for Longitudinal Studies

nine to ten months old in the United Kingdom: 64 per cent of parents used grandparents to look after their babies while the main carer was at work or a full-time student (Figure 8.21).

In 2003/04, among those aged four years and under in Great Britain, a higher proportion of boys (14 per cent) than girls (10 per cent) were reported as having a longstanding illness by their parents (See Table 7.2 in the Health chapter). Similarly a higher proportion of boys (17 per cent) than girls (14 per cent) in that age group had seen an NHS GP in the 14 days before the interview. Although the proportion of both boys and girls who were reported as having a longstanding illness was around 18 per cent in the 5 to 15 age group, only 7 per cent of boys and girls in this age group had consulted their GP in the two weeks before the interview.

In 2003/04, small proportions of children in the United Kingdom had seen a health visitor or practice nurse at the GP surgery or had visited a child health or welfare clinic (Table 8.22). Eighty four per cent of children aged 0 to 4 had not used any of these services in the 14 days before interview. Children aged 5 to 15 were even less likely to have used any of these services, with 97 per cent not having done so in the previous 14 days.

Table 8.22

Use of health services[1] by children: by sex and age, 2003/04

United Kingdom   Percentages[2]

	Males		Females	
	0–4	5–15	0–4	5–15
Health visitor at the GP surgery	8	1	7	1
Practice nurse at the GP surgery	5	1	6	1
Child health or welfare clinic	5	1	5	1
None of the above	84	97	84	97

1 Services used in the 14 days prior to interview.
2 Percentages may sum to more than 100 as respondents could give more than one answer.

Source: General Household Survey, Office for National Statistics; Continuous Household Survey, Northern Ireland Statistics and Research Agency

In cases where parents are unable to provide proper care for children, local authorities can take them into care. These children are usually described as being 'looked-after'. As at March 2003 there were 67,400 children being looked after by local authorities in England, Wales and Northern Ireland (Table 8.23 overleaf). The majority of these children, 45,700, were cared for in foster homes. The number of children being looked after in children's homes has remained stable at around 7,200 since 2001. Some children who

Table **8.23**

Children looked after by local authorities:[1] by type of accommodation[2]

England, Wales & Northern Ireland   Thousands

	1993	2001	2003
Foster placements	34.9	42.6	45.7
Placement with parents	6.0	7.8	7.4
Children's homes	8.6	7.3	7.2
Placed for adoption[3]	2.6	3.6	3.6
Other accommodation	2.5	3.7	3.4
All looked after children	54.6	65.1	67.4

1 Excludes children in England and Wales looked after under an agreed series of short-term placements. At 31 March.
2 See Appendix, Part 8: Children looked after by local authorities.
3 Not collected for Northern Ireland.

Source: Department of Health; National Assembly for Wales; Department of Health, Social Services and Public Safety, Northern Ireland

are being looked after by a local authority go on to be adopted. In 2003 around 3,600 looked-after children were placed for adoption, compared with 2,600 in 1993.

Not all children who are referred to local authority social services go on to be looked after. Children may be placed on a local authority child protection register where it is considered that a child is at continuing risk of significant harm and is in need of a child protection plan. Some of these are taken into care, but not all. Likewise, not all children in care are on child protection registers.

As at March 2003, there were 26,300 children on child protection registers in England, with around 900 more boys than girls (Table 8.24). Neglect was the most common reason for both boys and girls to be placed on the register, with around two fifths of children on the register for this reason. Emotional abuse was the second most common reason, accounting for around one fifth of both boys and girls on the register. Girls were more likely than boys to be on the register due to sexual abuse. Sexual abuse accounted for 12 per cent of girls on the register compared with 8 per cent of boys.

Table **8.24**

Children on child protection registers: by sex, age and category of abuse, 2003[1]

England   Percentages

	Under 1	1–4	5–9	10–15	16 and over	All ages
Males						
Neglect	49	45	39	36	30	41
Emotional abuse	8	16	22	22	19	19
Physical abuse	24	18	15	16	15	17
Sexual abuse	6	6	9	11	17	8
Multiple categories/other[2]	13	15	15	16	19	15
All males (=100%) (numbers)[3]	1,400	4,000	4,000	3,900	200	13,600
Females						
Neglect	49	44	37	32	26	38
Emotional abuse	8	17	23	21	15	19
Physical abuse	22	18	12	13	16	15
Sexual abuse	6	8	12	18	28	12
Multiple categories/other[2]	14	13	16	17	15	15
All females (=100%) (numbers)[3]	1,400	3,600	3,700	3,700	310	12,700
All (=100%) (numbers)[3]	2,800	7,600	7,700	7,600	510	26,300

1 As at 31 March, excluding unborn.
2 Contains all cases which do not fall into the four main categories.
3 Figures greater than 1,000 have been rounded to the nearest 100, and figures less than 1,000 to the nearest 10.

Source: Department for Education and Skills

Crime and justice

- Humberside had the highest rate of recorded crime of all the police force areas in England and Wales in 2003/04, at 163 offences per 1,000 population, while Dyfed Powys, at 63 per 1,000, had the lowest. (Map 9.4)

- Crimes involving firearms in England and Wales more than doubled between 1997/98 and 2002/03, to over 10,000. (Table 9.6)

- In 2003/04, women were nearly three times as likely as men in England and Wales to be very worried about physical attack (17 per cent compared with 6 per cent), yet men were more likely than women to be a victim of violent crime (5 per cent compared with 3 per cent). (Tables 9.9 and 9.10)

- Over seven in ten of both men and women previously convicted for theft and handling stolen goods in England and Wales were reconvicted within two years of their discharge from prison in 1999. (Figure 9.13)

- Between 1993 and 2003 the average prison population in England and Wales rose by two thirds, to 73,000. (Figure 9.18)

- Full-time equivalent police officer numbers in England and Wales reached record levels, with 140,600 officers on 31 March 2004. (Table 9.21)

Chapter 9

Many people will be affected by crime in the course of their lives. Crime can affect people's lives directly through loss and suffering, or indirectly, such as through the need for increased security measures. The fear of crime can have a restrictive effect on people's behaviour. Dealing with crime and its associated problems is an ever-present concern for society and the government.

Crime rates

The British Crime Survey (BCS) (see text box opposite) estimated that 11.7 million crimes were committed against adults living in private households in England and Wales in the 12 months before interview in 2003/04, a 5 per cent decrease on the previous year (Figure 9.1). The number of BCS crimes rose steadily through the 1980s and into the 1990s, peaking in 1995 at 19.4 million. It then fell progressively, and was back to the levels of the early 1980s in 2003/04.

In 2003/04, 57 per cent of offences against adults living in private households, as measured by the BCS, involved some type of theft. Vehicle-related theft was the most prevalent type of theft with 2.1 million offences, 18 per cent of all offences. Nevertheless this was only half the number in 1995. Between 1995 and 2003/04 burglary offences also fell, by 47 per cent, to 0.9 million. After theft, the second most common offence group was violent incidents. These accounted for 23 per cent of BCS crime in 2003/04, or 2.7 million offences. This was 36 per cent lower than the 1995 peak.

In 2003/04, 9.1 million BCS crimes, just over three quarters of the total, were comparable with those recorded in police

Table 9.2

Crimes[1] committed within the last 12 months: by outcome, 2003/04

England & Wales

Percentages

	BCS crimes reported to the police	BCS crimes recorded by the police
Burglary	62	46
Comparable property crime[2]	49	40
Vehicle thefts	48	44
Violence[3]	41	25
Theft from the person	38	22
Vandalism	31	23
All comparable crime	42	31

1 BCS crimes that are comparable with those recorded in police statistics.
2 Comprises all acquisitive crime: all burglary, vehicle thefts, bicycle theft and theft from the person.
3 Does not include snatch theft.

Source: British Crime Survey, Home Office

statistics (see text box for details of police statistics). Only 42 per cent of these comparable crimes were reported to the police (Table 9.2). Victims may not have reported a crime for various reasons, such as thinking the crime was too trivial or that it was a private matter. The proportion of crimes reported to the police varied according to the type of offence. Of the comparable crimes shown in Table 9.2, burglary was the most likely to have been reported in 2003/04 (62 per cent).

Figure 9.1

British Crime Survey offences[1]

England & Wales

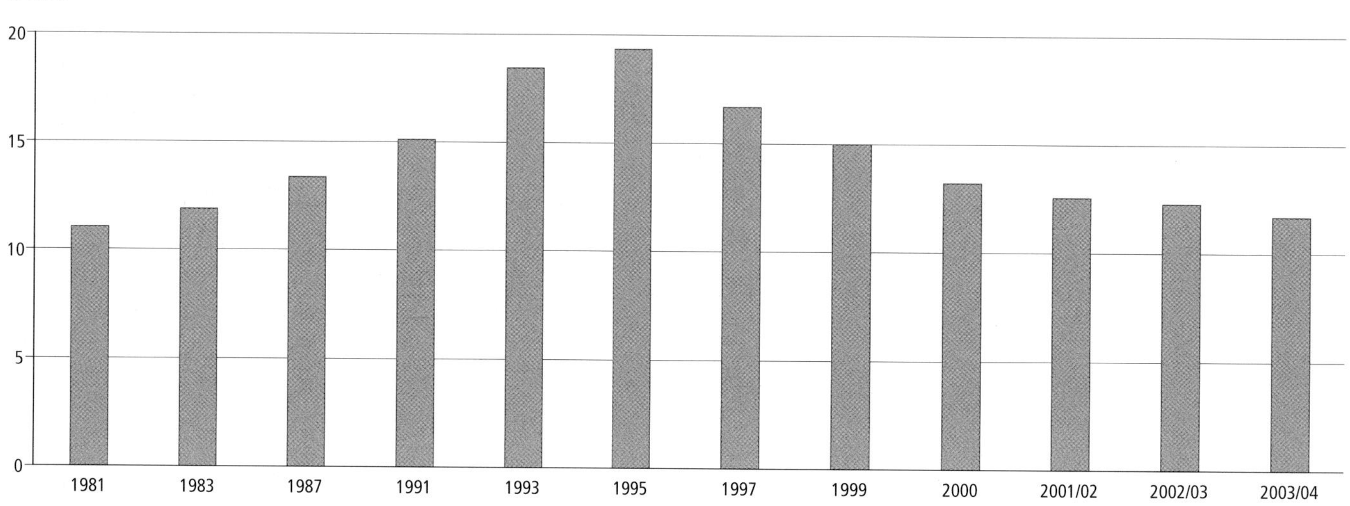

Millions

1 All incidents measured by the survey, whether or not they were recorded by the police.
Source: British Crime Survey, Home Office

Although only around half of all vehicle-related thefts were reported (48 per cent), this rose to 95 per cent when the offence involved the actual theft of a vehicle. This could be because a formal record of such incidents is generally needed for insurance purposes.

Not all crimes that are reported to the police are recorded. As a result, the police only recorded 31 per cent of all comparable BCS crime in 2003/04. Police recording rates also vary according to the type of offence, ranging from 46 per cent of burglaries to 22 per cent of theft from the person. The police may choose not to record a crime for various reasons. They may consider that the report is mistaken, too minor or that there is insufficient evidence. Alternatively, the victim may not want the police to proceed.

The number of crimes recorded by the police in England and Wales increased by 1 per cent between 2002/03 and 2003/04, to 5.9 million. Just under four fifths of these offences were against property (Table 9.3). Theft and handling stolen goods comprised 49 per cent of property crime and 38 per cent of all recorded crime. It includes thefts of, or from, vehicles, which comprised 15 per cent of all recorded crime. Criminal damage, burglary, and fraud and forgery are the other property offences.

Table **9.3**

Recorded crime: by type of offence,[1] 2003/04

Percentages

	England & Wales	Scotland[2]	Northern Ireland
Theft and handling stolen goods	38	38	28
Theft of vehicles	5	4	4
Theft from vehicles	10	9	6
Criminal damage	20	25	25
Violence against the person	16	4	23
Burglary	14	9	13
Fraud and forgery	5	4	5
Drug offences	2	10	2
Robbery	2	1	2
Sexual offences	1	1	2
Other offences[3]	1	8	2
All notifiable offences (=100%) (thousands)	5,935	407	128

1 See Appendix, Part 9: Types of offences in England and Wales, and in Northern Ireland, and Offences and crimes.
2 Figures for Scotland refer to 2003.
3 Northern Ireland includes 'offences against the state'. Scotland excludes 'offending while on bail'.

Source: Home Office; Scottish Executive; Police Service of Northern Ireland

Measures of crime

There are two main measures of the extent of crime in the United Kingdom: surveys of the public, and the recording of crimes by the police. The British Crime Survey (BCS) interviews adult members of households in England and Wales. The BCS, and similar surveys in Scotland and Northern Ireland, are thought to give a better measure of many types of crime than police recorded crime statistics. These surveys are able to find out about the large number of offences that are not reported to the police. They also give a more reliable picture of trends, as they are not affected by changes in levels of reporting to the police or by variations in police recording practice (see Appendix, Part 9: Types of offences in England and Wales).

Recorded crime data collected by the police is a by-product of the administrative procedure of completing a record for crimes that they investigate. A new National Crime Recording Standard (NCRS) was introduced in England and Wales in April 2002 with the aim of taking a more victim-centred approach and providing consistency between forces (see Appendix, Part 9: National Crime Recording Standard).

Police recorded crime and BCS measured crime have different coverage. Unlike crime data recorded by the police, the BCS is restricted to crimes against adults (aged 16 or over) living in private households and their property, and does not include some types of crime (for example, fraud, murder and so-called victimless crimes such as drug use).

In Scotland the term 'crimes' is reserved for the more serious offences (roughly equivalent to 'indictable' and 'triable-either-way' offences in England and Wales), while less serious crimes are called 'offences' (see Appendix, Part 9: Types of offences in England and Wales, and Offences and crimes). Crime in Scotland fell by 5 per cent between 2002 and 2003, when a total of 407,000 crimes were recorded by the police. Theft and handling stolen goods comprised 38 per cent of recorded crime in Scotland, criminal damage 25 per cent and drug offences 10 per cent.

The definitions used in Northern Ireland are broadly comparable with those used in England and Wales. Crime in Northern Ireland decreased by 10 per cent in the year to 2003/04 to 128,000, having reached a peak of 142,000 in 2002/03. Criminal damage comprised one quarter of recorded crime in Northern Ireland and violence against the person accounted for a similar proportion. These proportions were greater than in England and Wales. Conversely, theft and handling stolen goods comprised just 28 per cent of recorded crime in Northern Ireland.

There is considerable variation in the pattern of crime across England and Wales, both geographically and by the type of area. Many of these differences may result from variation in the socio-economic status of these populations. In 2003/04 London had the highest regional rate of recorded crime at 145 offences per 1,000 population, while the South East, at 91 offences per 1,000 population, had the lowest.

Crime rates vary between the police force areas (Map 9.4). In 2003/04 the number of crimes recorded ranged from 63 offences per 1,000 population in Dyfed Powys, to 163 offences per 1,000 in Humberside. Metropolitan police forces, which include the City of London and Greater Manchester, tend to have the highest recorded crime rates. These may be a reflection of the metropolitan police forces being in large cities, with lower resident populations in city centres and large numbers of potential victims visiting these areas for either work or leisure. Together, the eight metropolitan police force areas accounted for 43 per cent of all recorded crime in 2003/04.

Crime tends to be higher in inner city areas than in rural areas. In 2003/04, households in inner city areas in England and Wales were more than twice as likely as those in rural areas to have been a victim of burglary, at 5 per cent and 2 per cent respectively. A similar difference was apparent for vehicle theft: 15 per cent of households in inner city areas were victims compared with 7 per cent in rural areas.

Another way to classify households is by the demographic, employment and housing characteristics of the surrounding

Map **9.4**

Recorded crime: by police force area, 2003/04

England & Wales

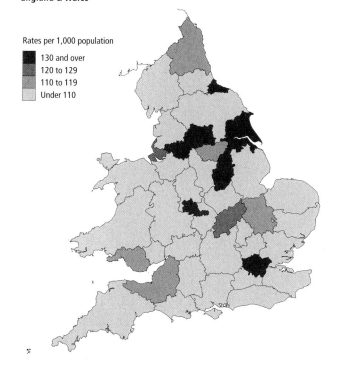

Rates per 1,000 population

- 130 and over
- 120 to 129
- 110 to 119
- Under 110

Source: Home Office

Table **9.5**

Households falling victim to crime:[1] by type of area,[2] 2003/04

England & Wales   Percentages

	All burglary	Vehicle-related theft[3]	Theft from the person	Criminal damage
Wealthy achievers	1.8	6.7	0.9	4.9
Urban prosperity	5.3	13.5	2.9	9.3
Comfortably off	2.4	8.9	1.0	6.6
Moderate means	3.8	12.4	1.4	10.3
Hard pressed	4.5	12.4	1.6	7.2
All households	3.2	9.7	1.4	7.1

1 Proportion of households falling victim once or more to each crime.
2 See Appendix, Part 9: ACORN.
3 Vehicle owning households.

Source: British Crime Survey, Home Office

neighbourhood (see Appendix, Part 9: ACORN). In 2003/04, in England and Wales, households in areas defined as 'wealthy achievers', which included wealthy executives and flourishing families, were less likely to be the victim of crime than households in other areas (Table 9.5). Households in 'hard pressed' areas, which included struggling families and those facing inner city adversity, were more than twice as likely as households in the 'wealthy achievers' areas to have been the victim of burglary – 4.5 per cent, compared with 1.8 per cent.

Offences

The incidence of violent crime is still comparatively rare. Nevertheless, crimes involving firearms more than doubled in England and Wales between 1997/98 and 2002/03, to over 10,000 (Table 9.6). However, there were two changes in counting offences over this period (see Appendix, Part 9: National Crime Recording Standard, and Types of offences in England and Wales). Between 2001/02 and 2002/03 the rise in violent crime involving firearms slowed to 2 per cent. Robbery was the only offence involving firearms to fall in the year to 2002/03, but it still accounted for 45 per cent of all recorded crime involving firearms. Violence against the person was the fastest growing firearms offence in 2002/03, increasing by 22 per cent.

In Northern Ireland there was a 15 per cent drop in firearms crime between 2001/02 and 2003/04 to just over 1,000 firearms offences. Criminal damage involving firearms was the only firearms crime to have increased between 2001/02 and 2003/04 (40 per cent), despite a decrease between 2001/02 and 2002/03.

Table **9.6**

Crimes[1] involving firearms:[2] by offence group

England & Wales   Numbers

	1997/98	1998/99	1999/2000	2000/01	2001/02	2002/03
Robbery	2,836	2,890	3,831	4,011	5,326	4,630
Violence against the person	1,463	1,746	2,264	2,556	3,469	4,238
Burglary	284	238	309	358	461	471
Criminal damage	98	104	135	249	388	460
Other	222	231	304	296	379	449
All crimes	4,903	5,209	6,843	7,470	10,023	10,248

1 Changes in counting offences were made in April 1998 and the National Crime Recording Standard was implemented in April 2002. See Appendix, Part 9: National Crime Recording Standard.
2 Firearms other than air weapons.

Source: Home Office

The BCS definition of vehicle-related theft comprises theft of a vehicle, theft from a vehicle and attempted theft of, and from, a vehicle. An estimated 2.1 million vehicle-related thefts occurred in England and Wales in 2003/04 accounting for 18 per cent of BCS crime. This was a fall from around 4.4 million in 1995 and 10 per cent down on the previous year (Table 9.7). Theft from a vehicle is the most common type of vehicle-related theft and accounted for 63 per cent of vehicle crime in 2003/04. Theft of vehicles decreased the most compared with other types of vehicle-related theft. It fell by 54 per cent between 1991 and 2003/04.

Two thirds of vehicle-related thefts in England and Wales in 2003/04 occurred in areas around the home, and 40 per cent occurred on the street outside the home. Households in 'wealthy achiever' areas are the least likely to be victims of vehicle-related theft (see Table 9.5). This could be due to wealthier households being able to afford newer cars with better security measures such as car alarms, and having off-street parking.

The number of people found guilty of, or cautioned for, drug offences in the United Kingdom rose dramatically from 1981, when the police and courts dealt with 17,900 offences, to peak at 131,200 offences in 1998. After then falling, numbers rose by 10 per cent between 2001 and 2002, to 113,100 (Table 9.8 overleaf). Drug offences can cover a wide range of activities, including unlawful production, supply, and possession of illegal substances. In 2002 nine out of ten drug offences were for unlawful possession.

Drug seizures in the United Kingdom followed a similar trend to drug offences. They too peaked in 1998, at 151,800, and then fell until 2000. They then rose to 131,200 in 2001 and increased a further 5 per cent to 137,300 in 2002. Cannabis seizures accounted for 75 per cent of all drug seizures in 2002; this was 9 per cent up on 2001.

Table **9.7**

Vehicle crime: by type

England & Wales   Thousands

	Theft from vehicles	Theft of vehicles	Attempted theft of and from	All vehicle crime
1991	2,424	522	899	3,845
1995	2,544	510	1,297	4,350
1997	2,200	378	933	3,511
1999	1,849	336	825	3,009
2001/02	1,494	315	682	2,491
2002/03	1,422	278	661	2,361
2003/04	1,337	241	543	2,121

Source: British Crime Survey, Home Office

Victims

People's perception of crime is affected by their fear of being a victim of crime. Women are more worried about a range of crimes than men. The exception is theft of, and from, a car, for which women and men have broadly similar levels of worry (Table 9.9 overleaf). Women are twice as likely as men to be very worried about being mugged, almost three times as likely to be very worried about being physically attacked and more than four times as likely to be very worried about being raped. Men and women in the youngest age group (16 to 29 years old) reported the highest levels of worry for nearly all crimes. Most notably almost one quarter of women aged 16 to 29 were very worried about rape. This worry about crime was lower among men and women aged 60 and over.

Table 9.8

Persons found guilty of, or cautioned for, drug offences:[1] by type of offence

United Kingdom

Thousands

	1981	1991	1996	1998[2]	2001	2002[2]
Unlawful possession	14.9	42.6	84.0	118.1	91.8	102.2
Possession with intent to supply unlawfully	0.7	2.8	7.6	9.6	6.2	6.0
Unlawful supply	1.0	2.1	5.1	7.2	4.9	4.8
Unlawful production[3]	1.6	0.7	4.4	3.5	1.7	2.1
Unlawful import or export	1.4	2.1	1.6	1.2	1.8	1.7
All drug offences[4]	17.9	47.6	95.2	131.2	102.6	113.1

1 Includes persons given a fiscal fine or dealt with by compounding. Fiscal fine implies financial penalty imposed by procurators fiscal in Scotland (included from 1997). Compounding is an administrative sanction involving a financial penalty used by HM Customs and Excise.
2 Court appearance data not available for Northern Ireland for 1998 and 2002.
3 Includes the cultivation of cannabis plants from 1995.
4 Individual components do not sum to the total because each person may appear in more than one category.

Source: Home Office

In 2003/04 the BCS asked respondents whether worry about crime had a minimal, moderate or great effect on their quality of life. Over 60 per cent of respondents said that worry about crime had a minimal impact on their quality of life, and only 6 per cent said it had a great impact.

People's fear of crime does not necessarily reflect their likelihood of being a victim of crime. The risk of becoming a victim of crime once or more fell from 40 per cent in 1995 to 26 per cent in 2003/04 – the lowest recorded level since the BCS began in 1981.

BCS violent incidents include offences such as wounding, robbery and common assault. The BCS estimated that the risk of being a victim of violence once or more in England and Wales in 2003/04 was 4 per cent, with 2.7 million violent incidents experienced. This was a fall of 36 per cent from 1995. Half of the violent incidents experienced in 2003/04 did not result in any injury to the victim.

Despite women being nearly three times as likely as men to be very worried about physical attack (17 per cent compared with 6 per cent), men were nearly twice as likely as women to be a

Table 9.9

Worry about crime:[1] by sex and age, 2003/04

England & Wales

Percentages

	Theft from a car[2]	Theft of a car[2]	Burglary	Mugging	Physical attack	Rape	Insulted or pestered
Males							
16–29	16	18	10	9	8	7	4
30–59	14	14	11	6	5	3	4
60 and over	9	11	10	7	5	2	3
All aged 16 and over	13	14	10	7	6	4	4
Females							
16–29	16	20	16	17	22	24	10
30–59	11	15	15	14	17	19	10
60 and over	8	12	14	15	13	12	7
All aged 16 and over	11	15	15	15	17	18	9

1 Percentages of people who were 'very worried' about selected types of crime.
2 Based on respondents residing in households owning, or with regular use of, a vehicle.

Source: British Crime Survey, Home Office

Table 9.10

Victims of violent crime:[1] by sex and age, 2003/04

England & Wales   Percentages

	Domestic	Mugging	Stranger	Acquaintance[2]	All violence
Males					
16–24	0.8	3.6	7.1	6.1	15.6
25–44	0.6	0.8	3.1	2.0	6.0
45–64	0.2	0.4	1.3	0.8	2.5
65–74	-	0.1	0.4	0.1	0.6
75 and over	-	0.2	-	0.1	0.3
All aged 16 and over	0.4	1.0	2.7	1.9	5.4
Females					
16–24	1.9	2.1	2.1	2.1	7.6
25–44	1.1	0.5	0.9	1.1	3.4
45–64	0.3	0.6	0.4	0.4	1.7
65–74	0.1	0.3	0.2	0.1	0.7
75 and over	-	0.5	-	-	0.5
All aged 16 and over	0.7	0.7	0.8	0.8	2.9

1 Percentage victimised once or more in the previous 12 months.
2 Assaults in which the victim knew one or more of the offenders at least by sight.

Source: British Crime Survey, Home Office

victim of violent crime (5 per cent compared with 3 per cent) (Table 9.10). Men aged 16 to 24 were the most at risk – 16 per cent had experienced a violent crime according to the 2003/04 BCS, compared with 8 per cent of women of the same age. Older men and women were much less likely than younger people to be a victim of violent crime: just over 1 per cent of those aged 65 and over reported they had been victims of some sort of violence. Violence by a stranger was the most common type of crime affecting men while women were equally likely to be victims of violence by an acquaintance or by a stranger.

Domestic violence was the only category of violent crime where the risk for women was higher than that for men. The extent of domestic violence is difficult to quantify due to the sensitive nature of the topic. Overall, it is estimated that domestic violence accounted for 16 per cent of all violent incidents in England and Wales in 2003/04, with 67 per cent of domestic violent incidents being against women. The likelihood of being a victim of domestic violence decreases as people get older.

In an effort to combat crime and the fear of crime, people may implement crime prevention measures such as home security. The proportion of houses fitted with a burglar alarm increased from 18 per cent in 1994 to 28 per cent in 2003/04

(Table 9.11). The security measures people were most likely to have, in 2003/04, were window locks (82 per cent) and double locks or deadlocks on doors (79 per cent). Almost half of BCS respondents who had improved their home security in the year preceding the 2002/03 interview had done so as part of general improvements to their home. Three fifths of households who had not improved their home security felt that their home was already as secure as it could be.

Table 9.11

Home security,[1] 2003/04

England & Wales

	Percentages
Window locks	82
Double/deadlock	79
External light timers/sensors	43
Security chains/bolts	37
Burglar alarm	28
Internal light timers/sensors	27
Window bars/grilles	3

1 See Appendix, Part 9: Home security measures.

Source: British Crime Survey, Home Office

Offenders

In 2003, 1.73 million offenders were found guilty of, or cautioned for, indictable and summary offences in England and Wales, a rise of 5 per cent on the previous year. Most of the offenders were male (81 per cent), of whom around 11 per cent were aged 17 and under. The peak age of known offending for males fell to 18 in 2003, the same as it was from 1988 to 2001 before rising to 19 in 2002. The peak age for females was 15 in 2003. This has fluctuated over the past ten years, mainly between 14 and 15, but rose to 18 in 1997.

In 2003, 484,000 people were found guilty of, or cautioned for, an indictable offence in England and Wales, of whom just over four fifths were men (Table 9.12). Theft and handling stolen goods was the most common offence committed by both male and female offenders. Over half of female

offenders were found guilty of, or cautioned for, theft-related offences compared with almost one third of male offenders. Young people aged 16 to 24 years had the highest offending rates for both males and females.

A relatively small number of offenders are responsible for a disproportionately high number of offences. Often, offending patterns of behaviour are established at an early age. Over seven in ten of both men and women previously convicted for theft and handling stolen goods, and a similar proportion of men convicted for burglary, were reconvicted within two years of their discharge from prison in England and Wales in 1999 (Figure 9.13). For robbery and violence against the person, around half of men were reconvicted in the same period. However, less than one sixth of men convicted for sexual offences were reconvicted within two years of their release from prison.

Table 9.12

Offenders found guilty of, or cautioned for, indictable offences:[1] by sex, type of offence and age, 2003

England & Wales

Rates per 10,000 population

	10–15	16–24	25–34	35 and over	All aged 10 and over (thousands)
Males					
Theft and handling stolen goods	81	162	96	18	124.3
Drug offences	18	156	62	10	86.2
Violence against the person	34	78	34	10	55.7
Burglary	26	45	21	2	29.3
Criminal damage	14	19	7	2	13.2
Robbery	7	13	4	-	6.8
Sexual offences	3	4	3	2	5.6
Other indictable offences[2]	10	101	62	13	72.1
All indictable offences	193	577	288	56	393.2
Females					
Theft and handling stolen goods	52	62	32	6	49.3
Drug offences	3	15	9	2	10.6
Violence against the person	13	13	6	2	11.1
Burglary	3	3	1	-	2.0
Criminal damage	3	2	1	-	1.8
Robbery	2	1	-	-	0.9
Sexual offences	-	-	-	-	0.1
Other indictable offences[2]	3	19	14	3	15.4
All indictable offences	78	116	64	12	91.2

1 See Appendix, Part 9: Types of offences in England and Wales.
2 Other indictable offences includes fraud and forgery and indictable motoring.

Source: Home Office

Figure **9.13**

Prisoners reconvicted within two years of discharge in 1999: by original offence

England & Wales
Percentages

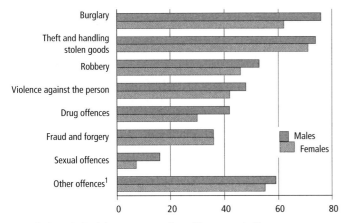

1 Includes criminal damage, motoring offences and other indictable and summary offences.

Source: Home Office

Reconviction rates for those with a first conviction are much lower than for those who had previous convictions. The rate for all first time offenders was 17 per cent compared with 40 per cent for those with one or two previous convictions and 78 per cent for those with 11 or more previous convictions.

Police and courts action

Under the National Crime Recording Standard counting rules, a crime is defined as 'detected' if a suspect has been identified and interviewed, and there is sufficient evidence to bring a charge. There does not have to be a prosecution: for example, the offender may accept a caution or ask for the crime to be taken into consideration by the court, or the victim may not wish to give evidence.

There were just under 1.4 million detected crimes in England and Wales in 2003/04, an increase of less than half a per cent on the previous year. Of these, 19 per cent were detected through an offender being charged or summoned, cautioned, having an offence taken into consideration or receiving a fixed penalty notice ('sanction' detections).

In England and Wales the detection rates for most offences in 2003/04 remained largely unchanged on the previous year at 23 per cent. The main exceptions were sexual offences and violence against the person where both rates fell by 4 per cent. Drug offences were the most likely type of crime to be detected in 2003/04, and theft from vehicles was the least likely (Table 9.14). It should be noted that on occasions there could be a time lapse between an offence being committed and the police clearing it up.

In Scotland detection rates are known as clear-up rates. Scotland had a high detection rate of 47 per cent in 2003, following a similar pattern to England and Wales, with drug offences the crime most likely to be detected. Fraud and forgery also had a high detection rate with nearly nine out of ten offences being detected.

The *Police and Criminal Evidence Act*, which was implemented in January 1986, gave the police certain powers covering stop and searches of people or vehicles, road checks, detention of people and intimate searches of people. Stop and searches in England and Wales rose from 118,000 in 1987 to a peak of nearly 1.1 million searches in 1998/99. In 2002/03 there were 895,000 stop and searches of people and vehicles. This fell by 18 per cent to 734,000 in 2003/04. Stolen property was the most common reason for a stop and search between 1991 and 2001/02. In 2002/03 drugs became the most common reason for stop and searches and this continued in 2003/04, although both categories had an overall decrease in number.

Three quarters of people who were stopped and searched in 2003/04 were White, yet White people comprised just over 90 per cent of the population in England and

Table **9.14**

Recorded crimes detected by the police: by offence group,[1] 2003/04[2]

Percentages

	England & Wales	Scotland	Northern Ireland
Drug offences	93	100	72
Violence against the person	50	79	57
Sexual offences	39	76	51
Rape	31	74	53
Fraud and forgery	26	85	32
Robbery	18	37	14
Theft and handling stolen goods	15	35	16
Theft of vehicles	13	37	16
Theft from vehicles	6	19	5
Criminal damage	13	23	15
Burglary	13	27	12
Other crimes[3]	67	97	50
All recorded crime	23	47	27

1 See Appendix, Part 9: Types of offences in England and Wales, and in Northern Ireland, and Offences and crimes.
2 Some offences cleared up/detected may have been initially recorded in an earlier year. Figures for Scotland are for 2003.
3 The Northern Ireland figure includes offences against the state.

Source: Home Office; Scottish Executive; Police Service of Northern Ireland

Table 9.15

Ethnic[1] composition of stop and searches, 2003/04

England & Wales   Percentages

	White	Black	Asian	Other	Total
Reason for the search					
Drugs	41	53	58	42	44
Stolen property	31	25	19	29	29
Going equipped	13	8	7	10	12
Offensive weapons	7	11	11	10	8
Firearms	1	2	2	2	1
Other reasons	7	2	4	8	6
Total (=100%)					
(thousands)	536.7	106.1	51.8	10.7	721.8

1 Ethnicity of the person stopped and searched as perceived by the police officer concerned. Some searches did not record ethnicity, although these are included in the Total column.

Source: Home Office

Wales (Table 9.15). In 2003/04 the main reason for searching all groups was drugs, followed by stolen property. In previous years White people were more likely to have been searched for stolen property than for drugs. One fifth of people searched for firearms and offensive weapons were Black, yet overall Black people accounted for less than one seventh of those stopped and searched.

In England and Wales a formal caution may be given by a senior police officer when an offender has admitted his or her guilt, there is sufficient evidence for a conviction and it is not in the public interest to institute criminal proceedings. Cautions are more severe than a reprimand. In order for a caution to be given there must be sufficient evidence gathered by the police for the likelihood of a successful prosecution. In 2003, 151,000 cautions for indictable offences in England and Wales were given. This was 52,000 fewer than in the peak year of 1995, but 47,000 more than in 1981 and an increase of almost 8,000 (5 per cent) on 2002 (Table 9.16). The two offence categories receiving the highest number of cautions were theft and handling stolen goods, and drug offences.

The Crown Prosecution Service (CPS) is the government agency that handles the bulk of prosecutions in England and Wales. Most cases in the Crown Court are prosecuted by the CPS. The CPS and other authorities including HM Customs and Excise, the Driver and Vehicle Licensing Agency, and the Environment Agency, also prosecute in magistrates' courts.

Almost 1.3 million defendant cases were prosecuted in magistrates' courts by the CPS in the year ending September 2004 (excluding those committed for trial in the Crown Court), 1 per cent more than in the previous year. The majority of cases at magistrates' courts, in the year ending September 2004, resulted in a conviction (80 per cent), while 19 per cent of cases were terminated early and 2 per cent resulted in dismissal. A further 103,000 were committed or sent for trial in the Crown Court. The CPS completed 99,000 defendant cases in the Crown Court in the year ending September 2004, 3 per cent more than in the previous year, 75 per cent of which resulted in a conviction.

Table 9.16

Offenders cautioned for indictable offences:[1] by type of offence

England & Wales   Thousands

	1981	1991	1995	1998	2001	2002	2003
Theft and handling stolen goods	79.2	108.5	104.9	83.6	63.5	54.2	54.5
Drug offences	0.3	21.2	48.2	58.7	39.4	44.9	45.7
Violence against the person	5.6	19.4	20.4	23.5	19.5	23.6	28.8
Burglary[2]	11.2	13.3	10.5	8.4	6.4	5.8	5.6
Fraud and forgery	1.4	5.6	7.9	7.4	5.8	5.3	5.5
Criminal damage	2.1	3.8	3.8	2.7	3.4	3.1	3.7
Sexual offences	2.8	3.3	2.3	1.7	1.2	1.1	1.4
Robbery	0.1	0.6	0.5	0.5	0.5	0.4	0.4
Other	1.3	4.1	4.0	5.0	4.2	4.4	5.3
All offenders cautioned	103.9	179.9	202.6	191.7	143.9	142.9	150.7

1 Excludes motoring offences.
2 See Appendix, Part 9: Offenders cautioned for burglary.

Source: Home Office

Table **9.17**

Offenders sentenced for indictable offences:[1] by type of offence and type of sentence,[2] 2003

England & Wales   Percentages

	Discharge	Fine	Community sentence	Fully suspended sentence	Immediate custody	Other	All sentenced (=100%) (thousands)
Theft and handling stolen goods	21	19	37	-	22	2	118.6
Drug offences	20	44	19	1	16	1	51.2
Violence against the person	10	10	45	1	30	3	38.0
Burglary	4	2	46	-	47	1	25.4
Fraud and forgery	18	16	41	2	22	2	18.1
Criminal damage	22	15	45	-	11	6	11.1
Motoring	5	37	30	1	27	-	8.9
Robbery	1	-	28	-	70	1	7.3
Sexual offences	6	6	27	2	58	2	4.3
Other offences	10	41	19	1	17	12	51.0
All indictable offences	15	23	33	1	24	4	333.9

1 See Appendix, Part 9: Types of offences in England and Wales.
2 See Appendix, Part 9: Sentences and orders.

Source: Home Office

When an offender has been charged, or summonsed and then found guilty, the court will impose a sentence. Sentences in England, Wales and Northern Ireland can include immediate custody, a community sentence, a fine or, if the court considers that no punishment is necessary, a discharge. In 2003, 334,000 people were sentenced for indictable offences in England and Wales (Table 9.17). The form of sentence varied according to the type of offence committed. In 2003 a community sentence was the most common type of sentence: over two fifths of those sentenced for burglary, violence against the person, criminal damage or fraud and forgery were given a community sentence. Those sentenced for drug offences were the most likely to be fined, with 44 per cent receiving this form of sentence. Of male offenders sentenced for drug offences, 46 per cent received a fine, compared with 26 per cent of female offenders, who were equally likely to be given a discharge for drug offences (26 per cent). A higher proportion of men than women were given an immediate custody sentence for all indictable offences (26 per cent compared with 15 per cent). Offenders who were sentenced for robbery were the most likely to be sentenced to immediate custody.

Courts normally give custodial sentences to the most serious, dangerous and persistent offenders. A defendant may choose in court to either plead guilty or contest the case by pleading not guilty. Appeals against decisions made at magistrates' courts are heard in the Crown Court, while those against Crown Court decisions are made at the Court of Appeal. In 2002,

the Court of Appeal (Criminal Division) received a total of 7,718 applications for leave to appeal in England and Wales.

Prisons and probation

Prison is the usual and eventual destination for offenders given custodial sentences and those who break the terms of their non-custodial sentences. Women prisoners are held in separate prisons or in separate accommodation in mixed prisons. Young offenders receiving custodial sentences have traditionally been separated from adult offenders, enabling them to receive additional educational and rehabilitative treatment.

The prison population in England and Wales was relatively stable in the 1980s and early 1990s. It was in the mid-1990s that the prison population began to increase, rising to an average of over 73,000 by 2003, an increase of 64 per cent since 1993 (Figure 9.18 overleaf). The number of sentenced prisoners increased by 77 per cent while remand prisoners rose by 21 per cent over the same period. In Scotland the prison population also increased between 1993 and 2003, but by only 16 per cent. Northern Ireland's prison population fell by 40 per cent over the same period.

The increased prison population in England and Wales could be a result of the rise in the use of longer prison sentences. Between 1997 and 2002, sentences of four years and over (including life) increased at a faster rate than sentences of under 12 months (29 per cent compared with 4 per cent).

Figure **9.18**

Average prison[1] population

England & Wales

Thousands

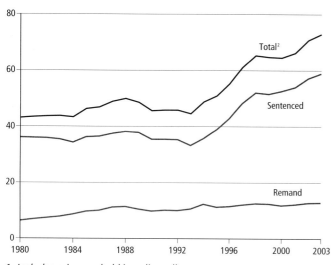

1 Includes prisoners held in police cells.
2 Includes non-criminal prisoners.

Source: Home Office

In November 2003 there were 69,600 male prisoners in England and Wales, compared with 4,400 female prisoners. The number of female prisoners has risen at a faster rate than the number of male prisoners. This has resulted in the proportion of males in the prison population falling from 96 per cent in 1997 to 94 per cent in 2003.

White males and females made up 83 per cent of the prison population of British nationals in England and Wales on 28 February 2003 (Table 9.19). This proportion was slightly lower than in 1996, particularly for males. Within the sentenced British female prison population, there are considerable differences in offence types between White females and those from minority ethnic groups. The proportion of Black British female prisoners sentenced for drug offences (44 per cent) was almost twice that of White British females (25 per cent).

Eligible prisoners who pass a risk assessment may be released overnight on temporary licence for precisely defined activities which cannot be undertaken in the prison. Around 329,000 licences were issued in 2003, 14 per cent more than in 2002. Around 64 per cent of these licences (211,000), were connected with prisoners obtaining additional facilities, such as reparation, training and education and 'working out' (schemes allowing prisoners to experience regular employment in the community).

Table **9.19**

Prison population of British nationals: by ethnic group

England & Wales

Percentages

	1996	1997	1998	1999	2000	2001	2002	2003
Males								
White	86	86	86	86	86	85	84	83
Black	11	10	10	10	10	11	11	12
Asian	2	2	2	2	2	2	3	3
Chinese and other	1	2	2	2	2	2	2	3
Total male population								
(=100%) (thousands)	48.7	54.3	57.8	56.4	56.2	55.7	59.1	59.0
Females								
White	84	84	85	85	85	86	84	83
Black	13	13	12	12	12	12	11	13
Asian	1	1	1	1	1	1	1	1
Chinese and other	2	2	3	2	2	2	3	3
Total female population								
(=100%) (thousands)	2.0	2.3	2.6	2.7	2.8	3.0	3.5	3.4

Source: Home Office

Civil justice

In England and Wales, individuals or companies can bring a case under civil law. The majority of these cases are handled by the county courts and the High Court in England, Wales and Northern Ireland, and by the Sheriff Court and the Court of Session in Scotland. The High Court and Court of Session deal with the more substantial and complex cases. Civil cases may include breach of contract, claims for debt, negligence and recovery of land. Tribunals deal with smaller cases, such as claims for unfair dismissal and disputes over social security benefits. Most tribunals deal with cases that involve the rights of private citizens against decisions of the State in areas such as social security, income tax and mental health. Some tribunals deal with other disputes, such as employment. In all, there are some 80 tribunals in England and Wales, together dealing with over 1 million cases a year.

Once a writ or summons claim has been issued, many cases are settled without the need for a court hearing. The total number of claims issued in county courts in England and Wales rose sharply, from 2.3 million in 1988 to peak at 3.7 million in 1991 (Figure 9.20). This rise may be explained, in part, by the increase in lending as a consequence of financial deregulation. Following this peak, the number of claims issued declined. In

Figure **9.20**

Writs and summonses issued[1]

England & Wales
Millions

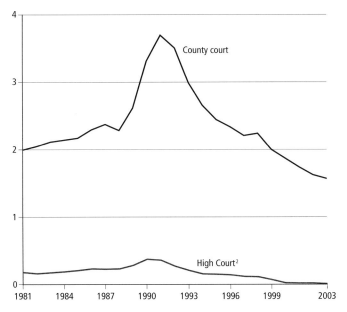

1 See Appendix, Part 9: Civil courts.
2 Queen's Bench Division, see Appendix, Part 9: Civil courts.

Source: Court Service

2003, 1.6 million claims were entered, 3 per cent fewer than in 2002. Money claims represented 86 per cent of the total in 2003. Most of the remainder were actions for the recovery of land (mostly relating to residential premises).

In England and Wales the Legal Services Commission operates the Community Legal Service (CLS), which funds civil legal and advice services and civil representation. The type of practical help offered by the CLS includes legal help, help at court, mediation and representation on tribunals. Immigration, housing and welfare benefits make up about two thirds of the new (non-family) matters handled by the CLS where legal help is offered.

Civil representation certificates are issued for non-family court proceedings. The area where most certificates were issued in 2003/04 was housing, followed by clinical negligence, and immigration and nationality. Three quarters of the certificates issued were for full representation. Where investigative help, rather than full representation was authorised, over three quarters of the cases were for clinical negligence, where extensive research is often necessary to establish whether there is a case to answer.

Resources

A large share of expenditure on the criminal justice system has been traditionally spent on the police force. Full-time equivalent police officer numbers reached record levels, with 140,600 officers in England and Wales on 31 March 2004 (Table 9.21 overleaf). This included 2,100 officers on secondment to the National Crime Squad, National Criminal Intelligence Service and central services. The Metropolitan Police Service is the largest force: it accounted for 21 per cent of all officers on 31 March 2004. The eight Metropolitan forces accounted for 45 per cent of all officers. Scotland had nearly 16,000 police officers at 30 June 2004, and Northern Ireland had over 7,000 police officers on 31 March 2004.

A range of other civilian staff, special constables and traffic wardens augments police resources. There were 11,000 special constables providing a voluntary police resource to police forces and local communities in England and Wales on 31 March 2004. In addition there were 3,400 community support officers, who are civilians employed by a police authority in a highly visible patrolling role.

The government sets employment targets for the recruitment, retention and progression of minority ethnic officers in England and Wales. The targets are intended to ensure that

Table **9.21**

Police officer strength:[1] by rank, sex and ethnic group

England & Wales

Numbers

	Males	Females	All	All minority ethnic officers
ACPO[2] ranks	205	19	224	5
Chief Superintendent	497	43	540	10
Superintendent	857	91	947	22
Chief Inspector	1,732	153	1,885	38
Inspector	5,966	635	6,600	130
Sergeant	16,984	2,397	19,382	422
Constable	86,115	24,871	110,986	4,003
All ranks	112,355	28,209	140,563	4,629
Police staff	26,035	42,662	68,697	3,828
Traffic wardens[3]	972	715	1,688	107
Community support officers	2,102	1,316	3,418	591
Total police strength	141,464	72,901	214,366	9,155
Special constabulary[4]	7,645	3,343	10,988	542

1 At 31 March 2004. Full-time equivalents. Includes staff on secondment to NCS, NCIS and central services. Includes staff on career breaks or maternity/paternity leave.
2 Police officers who hold the rank of Chief Constable, Deputy Chief Constable or Assistant Chief Constable, or their equivalent.
3 Excludes local authority traffic wardens.
4 Headcounts.

Source: Home Office

Figure **9.22**

Students called to the Bar:[1] by sex

England & Wales

Numbers

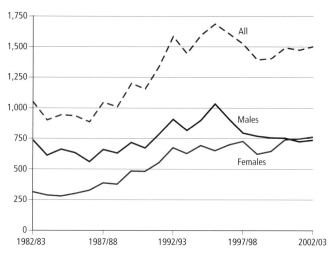

1 Data are for legal years beginning on 1 October. See Appendix, Part 9: Legal professionals.

Source: The Bar Council

by 2009, forces will reflect their minority ethnic population. On 31 March 2004 there were 4,600 minority ethnic officers, representing 3.3 per cent of the total. This compares with 2.9 per cent the previous year. The Metropolitan Police had the largest proportion of minority ethnic officers (6.6 per cent) followed by the West Midlands Police (6.2 per cent) on 31 March 2004.

There were 28,200 female police officers in England and Wales on 31 March 2004, representing 20 per cent of the total. The proportion of women in more senior ranks remained low. Only 9 per cent of officers at the rank of Chief Inspector and above were female compared with 22 per cent of constables.

In 2003 just under 14,000 people practised at the Bar in England and Wales, as either employed or self-employed practitioners: is 27 per cent more than in 1995. The number of both men and women practising at the Bar has risen, but women have increased at a slightly faster rate than men. In 2003, women comprised 32 per cent of those practising at the Bar compared with 26 per cent in 1995. However, in 2002/03, of the 1,500 students called to the Bar, 51 per cent were women (Figure 9.22). This compares with 30 per cent 20 years earlier. Not everyone called to the Bar will practise at the Bar in England and Wales: some may be overseas students, while others may follow an alternative career path.

Housing

- Between 1971 and 2003 the number of dwellings in Great Britain increased by one third, to 25 million. (Figure 10.1)

- The number of owner-occupied dwellings in Great Britain increased by 44 per cent between 1981 and 2003, while the number of rented dwellings fell by 17 per cent. (Figure 10.5)

- In 2003/04, 50 per cent of lone parents with dependent children in the United Kingdom rented their home from the social sector, compared with only 15 per cent of couples with dependent children. (Table 10.8)

- The number of homeless households in England living in temporary accommodation more than doubled between March 1997 and March 2004, from 41,000 to 97,000. (Figure 10.12)

- In 2003 the average price of a dwelling in the United Kingdom was almost £155,500, 16 per cent higher than in 2002. (Table 10.21)

- The average private sector rent (after housing benefit) in England doubled between 1993/94 and 2003/04, while the average local authority rent increased by 47 per cent. (Figure 10.24)

Chapter 10

Over the last 30 years demand for housing in the United Kingdom has been increasing due to population growth and the trend towards smaller households. During the same period there has also been a considerable increase in the number of owner-occupied homes.

Housing stock and housebuilding

In 2003, there were 25 million dwellings in Great Britain, a 32 per cent increase since 1971 (Figure 10.1). This increase has been mirrored across all constituent countries of Great Britain, with the number of dwellings in England and Wales increasing by 32 per cent and the number in Scotland increasing by 29 per cent during this period. The number of dwellings in Northern Ireland has increased more sharply, rising by 48 per cent from 455,000 in 1971 to 673,000 in 2003. In 2003/04, 96 per cent of dwellings in England were occupied, and 3 per cent of housing stock was vacant. The remaining 1 per cent of stock comprised second homes or holiday accommodation.

Figure **10.1**

Dwellings[1]

Great Britain
Millions

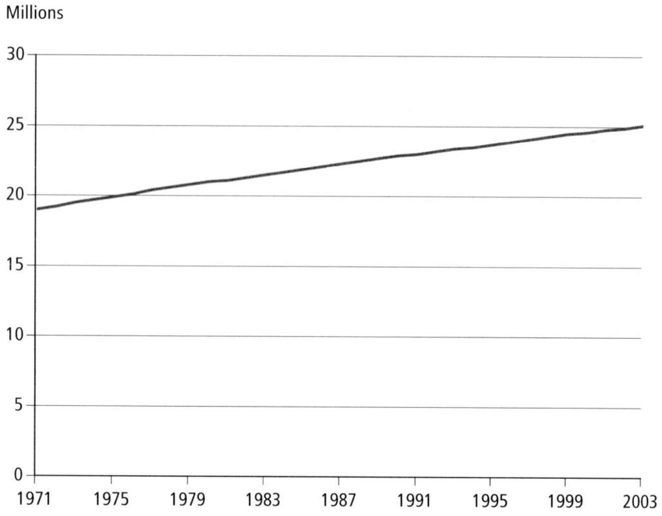

1 See Appendix, Part 10: Dwelling stock.
Source: Office of the Deputy Prime Minster

Much of the current housing stock in the United Kingdom reflects over 100 years of housebuilding, with one fifth having been built before the end of the First World War (Table 10.2). Between the two World Wars there was a shift in the type of home being built, from terraced to semi-detached dwellings. From the mid-1960s there was a further shift towards the building of detached houses and purpose-built flats. Almost six in ten of the current stock of purpose-built flats and maisonettes were built after 1964 and fewer than one in ten was built before 1919. In contrast, over six in ten of the current stock of conversion flats and maisonettes were built before 1919.

Table **10.2**

Type of accommodation: by construction date, 2003/04

United Kingdom   Percentages

	Before 1919	1919– 1944	1945– 1964	1965– 1984	1985 or later	All
House or bungalow						
Detached	14	13	16	31	26	100
Semi-detached	12	28	31	20	9	100
Terraced	35	18	17	20	11	100
Flat or maisonette						
Purpose-built	7	9	25	37	21	100
Conversion	63	25	6	4	2	100
All dwellings[1]	20	19	22	24	15	100

1 Includes other types of accommodation, such as mobile homes.

Source: General Household Survey, Office for National Statistics;
Continuous Household Survey, Northern Ireland Statistics and Research Agency

Following the damage to the nation's housing caused by bombings during the Second World War, the provision of new housing was a government priority. In the early post-war years, local authorities undertook the majority of housing construction. However, since 1959, private enterprise has dominated new housebuilding across the United Kingdom. The peak for housebuilding completions was in 1968 when 426,000 dwellings were completed, 53 per cent by private enterprise and 47 per cent by the social sector, primarily local authorities. In 2003/04 there were 190,000 completions, of which 90 per cent were by the private enterprise sector (Figure 10.3). Since the 1990s registered social landlords (RSLs) – predominantly housing associations – have dominated building in the social sector, accounting for 99 per cent of social sector completions in 2003/04.

In 2003/04, 33 per cent of new dwellings built by private enterprise in England were flats, compared with 21 per cent in 1991/92 and 13 per cent in 1996/97 (Table 10.4). There has also been an increase in the number of bedrooms. In 1991/92 only 9 per cent of all new dwellings completed by private enterprise were two bedroom flats; by 2003/04 this had risen to 24 per cent. Over the same period the proportion of new dwellings that were houses with four or more bedrooms also rose, from 23 per cent to 31 per cent. The rise in the number of bedrooms may reflect an increased expectation that each child should have a separate bedroom, as well as the aspiration to purchase homes with an extra room that could be used as a spare bedroom or office, or for storage.

Figure **10.3**

Housebuilding completions:[1] by sector

United Kingdom

Thousands

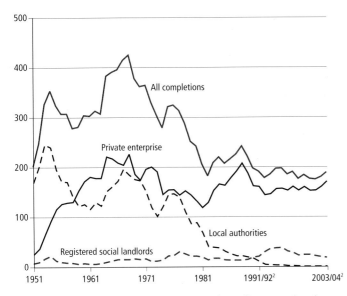

1 See Appendix, Part 10: Dwelling stock, and Dwellings completed.
2 From 1990/91 data are for financial years.

Source: Office of the Deputy Prime Minister; National Assembly for Wales; Scottish Executive; Department of the Environment, Northern Ireland

Table **10.4**

Housebuilding completions:[1] by number of bedrooms

England   Percentages

	1991/92	1996/97	2003/04
Houses			
1 bedroom	4	1	-
2 bedrooms	22	19	8
3 bedrooms	30	37	28
4 or more bedrooms	23	30	31
All houses	79	87	67
Flats			
1 bedroom	11	5	7
2 bedrooms	9	7	24
3 bedrooms	1	1	1
4 or more bedrooms	-	-	-
All flats	21	13	33
All houses and flats			
(=100%)(thousands)	132	121	130

1 By private enterprise.

Source: Office of the Deputy Prime Minister

Compared with new dwellings built by private enterprise, there has been a more equal ratio of houses to flats among those built by RSLs in England since the 1990s. In 2003/04, 54 per cent of new dwellings completed by RSLs were houses and 46 per cent were flats. The trend to include more bedrooms in newly built dwellings has also been evident among RSL constructions. However, in contrast to private enterprise completions, this has been concentrated in a shift from one to two bedroom flats. In 1991/92 one bedroom flats accounted for 35 per cent of all RSL completions and two bedroom flats for 19 per cent. In 2003/04 the proportions were 13 per cent and 31 per cent respectively.

Tenure and accommodation

One of the most notable housing trends since the early 1980s has been the substantial growth in the number of owner-occupied homes. In 2003, 70 per cent of dwellings in Great Britain were owner-occupied (18 million) compared with 58 per cent (12 million) in 1981 (Figure 10.5). Over the same period there was a steady decline in the number of homes rented in the social sector. In 1981 there were nearly 7 million dwellings in this sector; by 2003 the number had fallen by one quarter to just under 5 million.

Figure **10.5**

Stock of dwellings:[1] by tenure

Great Britain

Millions

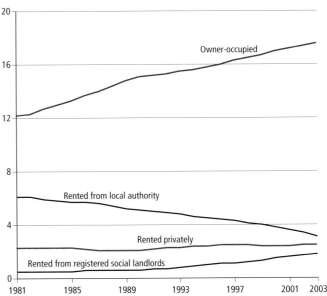

1 See Appendix, Part 10: Dwelling stock. Data for England and Wales are at 31 March, and for Scotland they are at 31 December the previous year, except for 1991, where Census figures are used.

Source: Office of the Deputy Prime Minister

Figure **10.6**

Sales and transfers of local authority dwellings[1]

Great Britain

Thousands

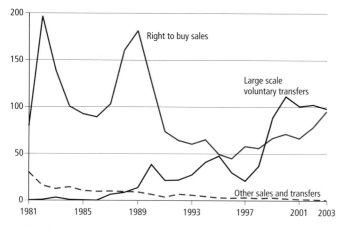

1 Excludes new town and Scottish Homes sales and transfers. See
Appendix, Part 10: Sales and transfers of local authority dwellings.

**Source: Office of the Deputy Prime Minister; National Assembly for
Wales; Scottish Executive**

The growth in owner-occupation since the early 1980s has,
in part, been due to a number of schemes that aim to
increase low-cost home ownership, such as the right to buy
scheme. Since the early 1980s, public tenants with secure
tenancies of at least two years' standing have been entitled
to purchase their own homes. The right to buy scheme was
particularly popular during the 1980s, with peaks of over
180,000 sales in Great Britain in both 1982 and 1989
(Figure 10.6). Another type of scheme which aims to increase
low-cost home ownership is shared ownership, in which
tenants buy a share of their property from an RSL and pay
rent for the remainder.

In 2001 the proportion of people living in households in the
United Kingdom that owned their accommodation, or lived
in it rent-free, was 77 per cent, just above the EU-15 average
of 74 per cent (Table 10.7). Among the EU-15 states, the
proportion tended to be higher in the southern countries than
in the northern countries. In 2001, Spain and Greece had the
highest rates of people in such households at 92 per cent and
90 per cent respectively and Germany the lowest level at
57 per cent. There were particularly high rates among the ten
countries which became EU members in May 2004. In 2001,
at least 90 per cent of people in Lithuania, Cyprus, Hungary,
Slovenia and Estonia lived in households that owned their
own homes or lived in them rent-free.

Tenure varies markedly according to the type of household.
In the United Kingdom in 2003/04, households consisting of
lone-parents with dependent children were much more likely
than any other type of household to rent their property rather

Table **10.7**

People in owner-occupied or rent-free households:[1] EU comparison, 2001[2]

	Percentages		Percentages
EU-15		**Accession countries**	
Spain	92	Lithuania	95
Greece	90	Cyprus	94
Ireland	83	Hungary	94
Italy	83	Slovenia	94
Belgium	81	Estonia	90
Finland	78	Malta	80
Portugal	77	Latvia	78
United Kingdom	77	Poland	70
Luxembourg	75	Czech Republic	..
Austria	71	Slovakia	..
France	71	Accession countries average[3]	77
Netherlands	64		
Germany	57	EU-15 average[3]	74
Denmark	..		
Sweden	..		

1 People living in households that own their accommodation, either
outright or with a mortgage, or live in it rent-free.
2 Data are at 1997 for Cyprus, 2000 for Malta and 2002 for Latvia.
3 Based on the population weighted average of the available individual
national figures.

Source: Eurostat

than own it (Table 10.8). Half of lone-parent households with
dependent children were renting their home from social sector
landlords while over one third were living in owner-occupied
accommodation. In contrast, four fifths of households
containing a couple with dependent children were owner-
occupiers and only one in seven rented from the social sector.
Households consisting of one person under pensionable age
were more likely than any other one person or one family
household to live in privately rented accommodation. Almost
three fifths of one person households over pensionable age
owned their home outright, compared with one in seven of
those under pensionable age. This in part reflects the time it
may take to pay off a mortgage.

Tenure also varies by ethnic group. In the period 2001/02 to
2003/04, 55 per cent of households in England with a
reference person of Bangladeshi origin lived in the social
rented sector, nearly seven times the proportion of
households whose reference person was of Indian origin
(Table 10.9). There were also high proportions of households
with Black African or Black Caribbean reference persons
renting their homes in the social sector. In contrast, the

Table 10.8

Household composition: by tenure, 2003/04

United Kingdom   Percentages

	Owned outright	Owned with mortgage	Rented from social sector	Rented privately[1]	All tenures
One person					
Under pensionable age	15	43	23	19	100
Over pensionable age	58	5	31	6	100
One family households					
Couple[2]					
No children	45	36	10	9	100
Dependent children[3]	9	70	15	7	100
Non-dependent children only	32	55	10	3	100
Lone parent[2]					
Dependent children[3]	7	29	50	15	100
Non-dependent children only	34	31	28	8	100
Other households[4]	20	25	15	40	100
All households[5]	29	40	20	11	100

1 Includes tenants in rent-free accommodation and squatters.
2 Other individuals who were not family members may also be included.
3 See Appendix, Part 2: Families. May also include non-dependent children.
4 Comprising two or more unrelated adults or two or more families.
5 Includes a very small number of same sex couples.

Source: General Household Survey, Office for National Statistics; Continuous Household Survey, Northern Ireland Statistics and Research Agency

Table 10.9

Ethnic group:[1] by tenure, 2001–04[2]

England   Percentages

	Owned outright	Owned with mortgage	Rented from social sector	Rented privately[3]	All tenures (=100%) (millions)
White					
British	30	42	19	9	18.0
Irish	25	35	27	13	0.3
Other White	26	31	17	26	0.8
Mixed	11	39	32	18	0.2
Asian					
Indian	27	53	8	12	0.3
Pakistani	24	48	13	16	0.2
Bangladeshi	9	26	55	10	0.1
Black					
Black Caribbean	13	37	42	8	0.2
Black African	2	21	47	29	0.2
Chinese	14	39	12	34	0.1
Other ethnic groups	17	29	31	23	0.2
All households	29	42	19	10	20.4

1 Ethnic group of household reference person.
2 Combined data for 2001/02, 2002/03 and 2003/04.
3 Includes tenants in rent-free accommodation and squatters.

Source: Survey of English Housing, Office of the Deputy Prime Minister

highest rates of owner-occupation were among households with an Indian reference person, at 80 per cent, but it was households with a White British reference person that were the most likely to own their home outright (30 per cent).

The type of home that people live in is often a reflection of the size and type of their household, and of what they can afford or are provided with. Overall, 81 per cent of households in the United Kingdom lived in a house (or bungalow) in 2003/04 (Table 10.10). Family households were far more likely than one person households to live in a house. Among households with dependent children, couples were more likely than lone parents to live in a house (94 per cent and 80 per cent respectively). The majority of couples with dependent children lived in detached or semi-detached houses (66 per cent). Only 28 per cent of them lived in terraced houses whereas 40 per cent of lone parents with dependent children did so.

Lone parents with dependent children were over three times as likely as couples with dependent children to live in a flat or maisonette (20 per cent compared with 6 per cent respectively). One person households under pensionable age were the most likely to live in a flat or maisonette, (42 per cent).

Homelessness

Homelessness can result from changes in personal circumstances, such as the reluctance or inability of relatives or friends to continue to provide accommodation, the breakdown of relationships (which may also involve violence), and financial hardship leading to rental or mortgage arrears. Local housing authorities have a statutory obligation to ensure that suitable accommodation is available for applicants who are eligible for assistance, have become homeless through no fault of their own, and who fall within a priority need group (this is the 'main homeless duty'). Priority need groups include families with children, and households that include someone who is vulnerable, for example because of pregnancy, domestic violence, old age, or physical or mental disability.

During 2003/04, 137,000 households were accepted as homeless and in priority need in England under the homelessness provisions of the *Housing Act 1996*. This was almost half of all applications. The presence of dependent children in the household was the primary reason why households were accepted as being in priority need (51 per cent).

Table **10.10**

Household composition: by type of dwelling, 2003/04

United Kingdom

Percentages

	House or bungalow			Flat or maisonette		
	Detached	Semi-detached	Terraced	Purpose-built	Other[1]	All dwellings[2]
One person						
Under pensionable age	9	20	29	31	11	100
Over pensionable age	19	30	23	25	3	100
One family households						
Couple[3]						
No children	31	34	24	9	3	100
Dependent children[4]	28	38	28	5	1	100
Non-dependent children only	31	40	26	3	-	100
Lone parent[3]						
Dependent children[4]	7	33	40	18	2	100
Non-dependent children only	14	36	35	13	2	100
Other households[5]	13	27	35	16	8	100
All households[6]	22	32	27	14	4	100

1 Includes converted flats, part of a house and rooms.
2 Includes other types of accommodation, such as mobile homes.
3 Other individuals who were not family members may also be included.
4 See Appendix, Part 2: Families. May also include non-dependent children.
5 Comprising two or more unrelated adults or two or more families.
6 Includes a very small number of same sex couples.

Source: General Household Survey, Office for National Statistics; Continuous Household Survey, Northern Ireland Statistics and Research Agency

Table **10.11**

Homelessness:[1] by household composition, 2002/03

England   Percentages

One person	
Males	18
Females	19
Lone parent with dependent children	
Males	3
Females	35
Couple with dependent children	15
Other households	10
All households	100

1 Households accepted as homeless and in priority need by local
authorities.

Source: Office of the Deputy Prime Minister

Among those households that were accepted as homeless
in 2002/03, there were ten times as many lone mothers with
dependent children as there were lone fathers (35 per cent
compared with 3 per cent) (Table 10.11). This reflects the
higher number of lone mothers than lone fathers in the
population in general. In spring 2004, nine out of ten lone-
parent families were headed by a woman (see Chapter 2).

In relation to the overall population profile there are a
disproportionate number of homeless people from minority
ethnic groups. In 2003/04, 22 per cent of applicants from
households accepted as homeless in England were from a
minority ethnic group. In contrast, 7 per cent of households
in the population as a whole were headed by someone from
a minority ethnic group in 2001.

Most households that are accepted as homeless by local
authorities are provided with temporary accommodation.
Since the mid-1990s there has been a steady rise in these
numbers, increasing from 41,000 in March 1997 to 97,000 in
March 2004 (Figure 10.12). The increase mainly resulted from
a decline in the number of social sector lettings available in
areas of high demand. In March 2004, just over 50 per cent
of these households were living in self-contained properties
leased in the private sector and around 30 per cent in local
authority or housing association stock let on a temporary
basis. A further 11 per cent were accommodated in hostels
or women's refuges and 7 per cent were living in bed and
breakfast (B&B) hotels.

The Homelessness (Suitability of Accommodation) (England)
Order 2003 came into force in April 2004. The Order means

Figure **10.12**

Homeless households[1] in temporary accommodation[2]

England

Thousands

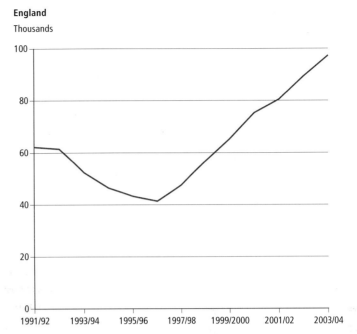

1 Excludes 'homeless at home' cases. See Appendix, Part 10: Homeless at
home.
2 Data are at 31 March and include households awaiting the outcome of
local authority homelessness enquiries.

Source: Office of the Deputy Prime Minister

that local authorities can no longer place families with
children in B&B hotels for longer than six weeks. Between
March 2003 and March 2004 the total number of homeless
households living in B&B hotels fell by 41 per cent to 7,200.

Housing condition and satisfaction with area

Overcrowding is an important indicator of housing conditions.
This is commonly measured by the bedroom standard, which
compares the number of bedrooms actually available to a
household against the number required, given the household's
size and composition (see Appendix, Part 10: Bedroom
standard). Overall, only 2 per cent of households in Great
Britain were below the bedroom standard and hence defined
as overcrowded in 2003/04, compared with 7 per cent in 1971
(Table 10.13 overleaf).

Overcrowding varies according to the tenure of the household.
In 2003/04 it was lowest among owner-occupiers at 1 per
cent. In contrast, 5 per cent of households renting from the
social sector and 4 per cent of private renter households lived
in accommodation below the bedroom standard. Of
households that owned their home outright, 58 per cent had
two or more bedrooms above the bedroom standard and could
therefore be said to be under-occupying. This was a far higher
proportion than in any other tenure group.

Table **10.13**

Overcrowding and under-occupation[1]

Great Britain   Percentages

	1971	1981	1991	2001/02	2003/04
1 or more below standard[2]	7	5	3	2	2
Equal to standard	34	33	29	26	25
1 above standard	38	39	38	38	37
2 or more above standard[3]	21	24	30	34	35
All	100	100	100	100	100

1 See Appendix, Part 10: Bedroom standard.
2 Overcrowded.
3 Under-occupied.

Source: General Household Survey, Office for National Statistics

The majority of homes that are owned outright are owned by older people. Such households are often less likely to be overcrowded than others due to children having grown up and left the family home. While the availability of spare bedrooms facilitates visiting by children and others, such homes can be more expensive to maintain and heat for those with modest retirement income and savings.

To be considered 'decent' a dwelling must meet the statutory minimum standard for housing (that is be fit); be in a reasonable state of repair; have reasonably modern facilities and services; and provide a reasonable degree of thermal comfort.

According to the English House Condition Survey, 7.0 million English dwellings did not meet the standard in 2001, compared with 9.4 million in 1996. The most common reason why dwellings failed to meet the standard in 2001 was that they did not provide a reasonable degree of thermal comfort. This affected 80 per cent of non decent dwellings and most of these (75 per cent) failed through a lack of adequate insulation. Disrepair was the next most frequent reason for not meeting the decent home standard, affecting 27 per cent of non decent dwellings.

Privately rented dwellings and those rented from local authorities are the most likely to fail to meet the decent home standard (49 per cent and 42 per cent were classified as such in 2001 respectively) (Table 10.14). Compared with dwellings in other tenure groups, privately rented dwellings had the highest failure rates on thermal comfort, disrepair and fitness.

Between 1996 and 2001 there were improvements in the condition of housing stock in England across a range of facilities and services. Overall, the proportion of dwellings with central or programmable heating rose from 88 per cent to 94 per cent, those with full or partial double glazing from 59 per cent to 76 per cent, and those with a second WC from 31 per cent to 35 per cent (Table 10.15). Private rented dwellings were the least likely to have central or programmable heating, or full or partial double glazing (85 per cent and 52 per cent of dwellings respectively).

Table **10.14**

Dwellings that fail the decent home standard:[1] by tenure and reason for failure, 2001

England   Percentages

	Reason for failure				All non decent[2]
	Thermal comfort	Disrepair	Fitness	Modernisation	
Owner-occupied					
Owned outright	26	8	3	2	33
Owned with mortgage	21	7	3	1	27
All owner-occupied	23	8	3	1	29
Rented from social sector					
Local authority	33	9	4	6	42
Registered social landlords	22	5	3	2	27
All rented from social sector	30	7	4	5	37
Privately rented	40	17	10	4	49
All tenures	26	9	4	2	33

1 See Appendix, Part 10: Decent home standard.
2 Homes may fail standard for more than one category.

Source: English House Condition Survey, Office of the Deputy Prime Minister

Table **10.15**

Facilities and services: by tenure, 2001

England   Percentages

	Owner-occupied	Rented from social sector	Rented privately	All tenures
Some double glazed windows	29	13	18	25
All windows double glazed	54	52	34	51
Central/programmable heating	95	93	85	94
Garage	55	8	21	42
Smoke detectors[1]	75	70	56	72
Second w/c	42	17	20	35
Secure windows and doors	57	46	36	53
Burglar alarms	31	8	12	25

1 Percentages for smoke detectors are based on households, all other figures are dwelling based.

Source: English House Condition Survey, Office of the Deputy Prime Minister

Owner-occupied dwellings were far more likely than those in any other sector to have a garage. Security features, such as burglar alarms and secure windows and doors, were also more likely to be found in owner-occupied homes.

For many people, a private garden or outside space is an important part of their home. In 2003/04, 85 per cent of households had the use of a garden, a further 5 per cent had

Table **10.16**

Availability of a garden: by accommodation type, 2003/04

England   Percentages

House or bungalow	
Detached	99
Semi-detached	99
Terraced	86
Flat or maisonette	
Purpose-built	37
Conversion	44

Source: Survey of English Housing, Office of the Deputy Prime Minister

a patio or yard, and 1 per cent had a roof terrace or large balcony. Virtually all households (99 per cent) living in detached or semi-detached houses had use of a garden compared with only 37 per cent of those living in purpose-built flats or maisonettes (Table 10.16).

The neighbourhood in which people live can influence how content they are with their homes. In 2002/03, the four aspects of their area that householders in England most commonly wished to see improved were opportunities and facilities for children and young people; crime and vandalism; local amenities, parks and leisure facilities; and public transport services (Table 10.17). These have been the top four aspects

Table **10.17**

Aspects of their area that householders would like to see improved[1]

England   Percentages

	1995/96	1999/2000	2000/01	2001/02	2002/03
Opportunities and facilities for children and young people	39	40	45	38	39
Crime and vandalism	39	26	47	32	32
Local amenities, parks and leisure facilities	27	32	38	31	31
Public transport service	22	29	30	28	29
Shopping and commercial facilities	14	23	26	21	21
Local health services	11	15	20	18	18
Quality of environment	17	18	25	18	18
Availability of jobs	30	21	23	16	17
Amount and quality of housing	12	12	14	12	15
Schools and colleges	8	9	10	9	9
None of these	18	16	8	16	15

1 Respondents were asked to select only from those aspects listed in the table. Percentages do not add up to 100 per cent as respondents could give more than one answer.

Source: Survey of English Housing, Office of the Deputy Prime Minister

each year since 1999/2000 but in the mid-1990s there was greater concern about the availability of jobs.

Satisfaction with the area in which people lived varied by tenure. In 2002/03, 51 per cent of owner-occupiers reported that they were 'very satisfied' compared with 38 per cent of those who were renting in the social sector. Almost twice as many of those living in social rented accommodation (24 per cent) reported crime as a serious problem in their area compared with those who were owner-occupiers (13 per cent).

Housing mobility

The length of time that people remain living at the same address may reflect their stage in life and is associated with tenure. Private renters are the most mobile tenure group. In 2003/04, 44 per cent of those living in privately rented accommodation in the United Kingdom had been at their current address for less than a year (Table 10.18). For people such as students and young professionals who may need to move frequently, private renting offers flexibility and it is the only option for many people who are saving to buy or do not qualify for social rented accommodation. In contrast, the least mobile group are owner-occupiers. In 2003/04, 31 per cent had lived in their home for 20 years or more.

There were, however, marked differences between those who owned outright, 52 per cent of whom had lived in their home for 20 years or more and those who were buying with a mortgage (10 per cent). This partly reflects differences in age. In 2003/04, 69 per cent of those who owned outright were aged 60 and over while 93 per cent of those who were buying with a mortgage were under 60.

People have different reasons for moving. In 2003/04, the most common reasons given for moving in England in the year before interview were the desire for a larger or better home (16 per cent), for work (10 per cent) or to live independently (10 per cent) (Table 10.19). Reasons for moving varied by tenure. Among owner-occupiers, 21 per cent who owned outright moved because they wanted a smaller or cheaper house or flat, reflecting the high proportion of this group who had retired. However, among those buying with a mortgage, 24 per cent had moved because they wanted a larger or better home. Nineteen per cent of private renters gave job-related reasons for their move, a far higher proportion than for any other tenure group.

The mobility of owner-occupiers is also linked to the housing market. Over the past 40 years the housing market and the economy have mirrored one another closely, with booms and

Table **10.18**

Tenure: by length of time at current address,[1] 2003/04

United Kingdom | | | | | | Percentages

	Under 1 year	1–4 years	5–9 years	10–19 years	20 years or more	All
Owner-occupied						
Owned outright	2	10	11	25	52	100
Owned with mortgage	7	32	23	28	10	100
All owner-occupied	5	21	17	27	31	100
Rented from social sector						
Local authority[2]	7	30	19	24	20	100
Registered social landlord	13	32	25	19	11	100
All rented from social sector	10	31	22	22	16	100
Rented privately[3]						
Furnished	59	32	5	2	2	100
Unfurnished[4]	29	42	11	9	9	100
All rented privately	44	37	8	6	6	100
All tenures	9	26	18	24	23	100

1 Of household reference person.
2 Includes council and Scottish Homes.
3 Includes tenants in rent-free accommodation and squatters.
4 Includes 'partly furnished'.

Source: General Household Survey, Office for National Statistics; Continuous Household Survey, Northern Ireland Statistics and Research Agency

Table **10.19**

Main reasons for moving: by post-move tenure,[1] 2003/04

England

Percentages

	Owned outright	Owned with mortgage	Rented from social sector	Rented privately	All tenures
Personal reasons					
Divorce or separation	6	7	8	8	8
Marriage or cohabitation	1	7	2	5	5
Other personal reasons	21	4	16	8	9
Different accommodation					
Wanted larger or better house or flat	9	24	12	12	16
Wanted smaller or cheaper house or flat	21	3	4	3	4
Job-related reasons	3	6	3	19	10
To live independently	1	11	10	10	10
To move to a better area	11	15	5	6	9
Accommodation no longer available	0	0	10	10	6
Wanted to buy	4	15	0	0	6
Couldn't afford mortgage or rent	3	0	2	1	1
Other reasons	20	7	27	18	16
All households (=100%)(thousands)	142	744	412	848	2,146

1 Current tenure of all household reference persons who moved in the year before interview.

Source: Survey of English Housing, Office of the Deputy Prime Minister

slumps in one tending to contribute to the other. The number of residential property transactions that took place rose markedly during the 1980s, mainly as a result of existing owner-occupiers moving home. Home-buying by first-time buyers and public sector tenants (right to buy purchases) (see Figure 10.6) were also factors, but contributed to a lesser extent. The boom was further amplified by the demographic impact of the coming of age of baby boomers and by the liberalisation of the credit market in the early 1980s when more new households opted for ownership rather than renting. In 1989, when interest rates rose and the economic recession set in, the number of transactions fell for several years (Figure 10.20).

In 2003, 1.3 million residential property transactions took place in England and Wales, 16 per cent fewer than in 2002. Much of this decline was due to the fall in the number of first-time buyers, who took out only 29 per cent of loans for house purchases in 2003 compared with 38 per cent in 2002.

Figure **10.20**

Residential property transactions[1]

England & Wales
Millions

1 See Appendix, Part 10: Property transactions.

Source: Inland Revenue

Housing costs and expenditure

In 2003 the average price of a dwelling in the United Kingdom was over £155,000, almost 16 per cent higher than in 2002. Property prices across the United Kingdom varied according to region and the type of accommodation. Although London and the South East remained the most expensive places to purchase a property, prices in many other regions began to catch up. In 2003 year-on-year increases were highest in the North East and East Midlands at 23 per cent (Table 10.21). Annual price increases were lowest, at around 9 per cent, in both Northern Ireland and London.

Table **10.21**

Average dwelling prices:[1] by region, 2003

	All dwellings (£)	Percentage change 2002–03
United Kingdom	155,485	15.7
England	165,834	15.8
North East	94,590	22.5
North West	108,956	18.1
Yorkshire & the Humber	107,325	20.4
East Midlands	133,215	22.5
West Midlands	132,898	18.0
East	181,494	17.8
London	236,476	9.1
South East	213,115	15.1
South West	170,560	18.0
Wales	104,140	20.3
Scotland	92,006	13.8
Northern Ireland	102,348	8.7

1 See Appendix, Part 10: Mix adjusted prices.

Source: Survey of Mortgage Lenders; Office of the Deputy Prime Minister

In recent years the gap between prices paid by first-time buyers and former owner-occupiers in the United Kingdom has grown. In 2003 the average price paid by first-time buyers was £119,000, 8 per cent higher than in 2002. Former owner-occupiers paid £180,000 on average in 2003, 16 per cent higher than in the previous year. The growing difference reflects the impact rising house prices have had on affordability for would-be homeowners.

Although recent UK base interest rates have been at low levels compared with the early 1990s, repaying mortgages still consumes a substantial proportion of people's incomes. In 2003 first-time buyers in the United Kingdom spent 20 per cent of their household income on mortgage repayments while former owner-occupiers who had moved and bought a new home spent 18 per cent (Figure 10.22). This compares with 18 per cent and 17 per cent respectively in 1973. The 2003 proportions were not as high as during the last property boom when mortgage repayments consumed more than one quarter of average household income in 1990, in part due to the higher level of mortgage rates.

Figure **10.22**

New mortgages: average mortgage repayment[1] as a percentage of average household income

United Kingdom

Percentages

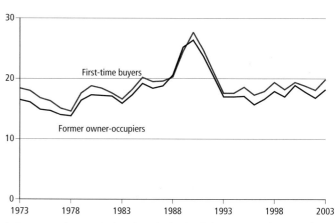

1 Repayments are calculated on the basis of the average advance, after tax relief. Based on a repayment mortgage.

Source: Office of the Deputy Prime Minister

The maximum mortgage advance home buyers are able to obtain is linked to their income. In recent years, the trend for house prices to rise at a far higher rate than income has led to an increase in the multiple of annual income which UK lenders are prepared to advance as a mortgage. In 2004, the median income to mortgage ratios for loans advanced reached their highest recorded levels, at 3.04 for first-time buyers and 2.84 for former owner-occupiers.

Some prospective first-time buyers who are unable to obtain a sufficient mortgage to buy a home may receive financial assistance from their parents. In 2004, the MORI Omnibus Survey conducted among home-owning parents of 18 to 29 year olds in Great Britain, revealed that fewer than half (45 per cent) expected their children to become homeowners without their financial support. Of those parents who anticipated that they would be willing and able to offer financial support, the average sum identified as a likely gift or loan was £17,000.

Table **10.23**

Selected housing costs of owner-occupiers,[1] 2002/03

£ per week

	Mortgage payments	Endowment policies	Structural insurance	Service payments[2]
United Kingdom	60	23	5	..
England	63	24	6	7
North East	41	16	5	3
North West	49	18	5	1
Yorkshire & the Humber	47	19	5	4
East Midlands	48	17	5	5
West Midlands	56	19	5	7
East	69	25	6	9
London	89	29	7	14
South East	78	35	6	10
South West	61	22	5	7
Wales	46	18	5	3
Scotland	47	19	5	4
Northern Ireland	47	17	5	..

1 Relates to both householders with a mortgage and those who own
   their house outright, but excludes part own and part rent properties.
   Those who did not make any payments within each category are
   excluded.
2 Not available for Northern Ireland.

**Source: Family Resources Survey, Department for Work and Pensions;
Northern Ireland Family Resources Survey, Department for Social
Development, Northern Ireland**

Figure **10.24**

Mean rent[1] after housing benefit

England
£ per week

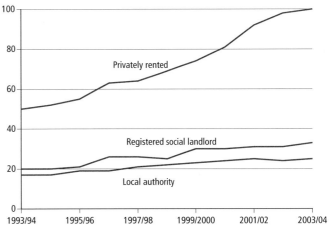

1 The mean rents are based on all tenancies including those where
   housing benefit is not received.

Source: Survey of English Housing, Office of the Deputy Prime Minister

There are large regional variations in mortgage payments reflecting differences in property prices (see Table 10.21) and the related size of mortgages. In 2002/03 owner-occupiers who had a mortgage in London and in the South East had the highest mortgage payments in the United Kingdom at £89 and £78 per week respectively, while those in the North East had the lowest at £41 per week (Table 10.23). While weekly costs for owner-occupiers who have endowment policies followed a similar regional pattern to those for mortgages – being highest in the South East and in London and lowest in the North East – the cost of structural insurance was very similar across all regions.

For those who rent their home, while private sector rents (after housing benefit) have traditionally been higher than those paid in the social sector, the difference has increased sharply over the past 10 years (Figure 10.24). Between 1993/94 and 2003/04 the mean private sector rent in England (after housing benefit) doubled. In contrast, rents in the social sector (after housing benefit) only increased by 65 per cent for RSL accommodation and 47 per cent for local authority accommodation. In 1993/94 the mean weekly private sector rent in England, after housing benefit, was £50, three times that paid by local authority renters. By 2003/04 it had risen to £100 per week, four times that of local authority renters.

Environment

- Carbon monoxide emissions in the United Kingdom fell by 18 per cent between 1971 and 1991, and then by a further 55 per cent between 1991 and 2002. (Figure 11.1)

- Emissions of greenhouse gases in the United Kingdom fell by 15 per cent between 1990 and 2002. (Page 152)

- The United Kingdom produced around 4 per cent of its electricity from renewable sources in 2003, compared with an EU-25 average of 14 per cent. (Table 11.9)

- Between 1996/97 and 2002/03 the amount of household waste collected for recycling in England more than doubled, to 3.7 million tonnes. (Table 11.14)

- In December 2003, 741,000 hectares were under organic production in the United Kingdom compared with just 82,000 in December 1998. (Figure 11.16)

- In 2004 North Sea cod stocks were 82 per cent lower than in 1971. (Figure 11.20)

Chapter 11

The condition of the environment impacts on and is impacted by society locally, nationally and internationally. Phenomena such as industrial pollution and climate change have had, or are likely to have, profound implications both for individuals and the United Kingdom as a whole.

Pollution

Many of the activities we undertake each day produce pollutants which can harm the environment as well as affect human health. However, emissions of the major air pollutants in the United Kingdom have generally been falling since the 1970s, and the rate of decline has accelerated since 1989 (Figure 11.1).

Figure 11.1

Emissions of selected air pollutants

United Kingdom

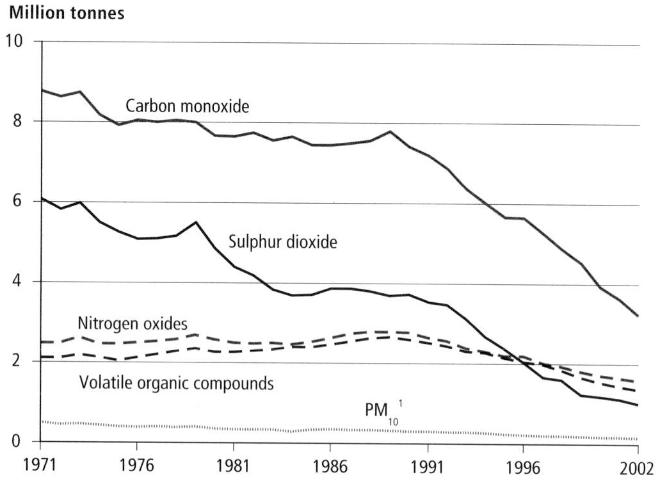

Million tonnes

1 Particulate matter that is less than 10 microns in diameter.

Source: Department for Environment, Food and Rural Affairs; National Environmental Technology Centre

Carbon monoxide (CO) reduces the capacity of the blood to carry and deliver oxygen. Emissions of CO fell by 18 per cent between 1971 and 1991, followed by a 55 per cent reduction between 1991 and 2002, mainly as a result of the introduction of catalytic converters in petrol cars.

Sulphur dioxide (SO_2) is an acid gas which can affect both human health and vegetation. It affects the lining of the nose, throat and lungs, particularly among those with asthma (see Chapter 7, Figure 7.3) and chronic lung disease. SO_2 emissions fell by 72 per cent between 1991 and 2002, largely as a result of a reduction in coal use by power stations and the introduction of the desulphurisation of flue gas at two power stations. However, the rate of decline slowed after 1999. Nitrogen oxides (NOx) are also acid gases and can have similar effects to SO_2. Emissions of NOx pollutants fell by 40 per cent between 1991 and 2002.

Particulate matter that is less than 10 microns in diameter, known as PM_{10}, is generated primarily by combustion processes, as well as from processes such as stone abrasion during construction, mining and quarrying. Particulate matter can be responsible for causing premature deaths among those with pre-existing heart and lung conditions. Emissions fell by 48 per cent between 1991 and 2002. Emissions of carbon dioxide (CO_2), a greenhouse gas that naturally makes up less than 1 per cent of air, are covered in the Global warming and climate change section of this chapter.

Table 11.2

Air pollutants: by source, 2002

United Kingdom   Percentages

	Carbon monoxide	Nitrogen oxides	Volatile organic compounds	Sulphur dioxide	PM_{10}[1]
Road transport	59	45	15	-	24
Power stations	2	24	1	68	6
Production processes	5	-	13	3	7
Power generation within industry[2]	1	6	-	9	5
Solvent use	-	-	29	-	-
Domestic	6	5	2	4	17
Extraction and distribution of fossil fuels	-	-	20	-	-
Refineries	-	2	-	7	1
Other	27	18	19	9	40
All sources (=100%) (million tonnes)	3.2	1.6	1.4	1.0	0.2

1 Particulate matter that is less than 10 microns in diameter.
2 Includes iron and steel and other industrial combustion.

Source: National Environmental Technology Centre

Fossil fuel combustion of one kind or another is the main source of air pollution in the United Kingdom, with road transport and power stations the most important single contributors. Emissions of other pollutants are more evenly spread among different sources, although road transport and electricity supply are, again, important contributors. In 2002 road transport accounted for 59 per cent of CO emissions, and 45 per cent of NOx emissions (Table 11.2). Although the level of road traffic has continued to grow over the last decade (see Chapter 12), changes in vehicle technology have reduced the impact of emissions from this sector. In 1991 road transport accounted for 73 per cent of CO emissions and for 48 per cent of NOx emissions. Power stations produced

68 per cent of SO_2 and 24 per cent of NOx emissions in 2002, compared with 72 per cent and 26 per cent, respectively, in 1991.

Pollution can also affect the fresh water of the United Kingdom. Rivers and canals in the United Kingdom are generally in a favourable condition, and both chemical and biological quality have improved in recent years. In particular, the chemical quality of rivers in England improved markedly between 1990 and 2003, when 93 per cent of river length was classified as being in good or fair condition (Table 11.3). This was, however, still the lowest percentage for any of the constituent countries of the United Kingdom: Wales had the highest proportion of rivers in good or fair condition in 2003, at 98 per cent.

Table **11.3**

Chemical quality[1] of rivers and canals: by country

United Kingdom   Percentage of total river length

	England	Wales	Scotland[2]	Northern Ireland
1990[3]				
Good	43	86	..	44
Fair	40	11	..	51
Poor	14	2	..	4
Bad	3	1	..	1
2001				
Good	66	92	87	58
Fair	28	6	9	37
Poor	5	1	4	4
Bad	-	-	-	0
2003				
Good	62	93	88	58
Fair	31	6	9	35
Poor	6	2	3	7
Bad	1	-	-	-

1 See Appendix, Part 11: Rivers and canals.
2 Data for Scotland are collected on a different basis to the rest of the United Kingdom.
3 Northern Ireland figures are for 1991.

Source: Environment Agency; Scottish Environment Protection Agency; Environment and Heritage Service, Northern Ireland

Improvements in water quality since 1990 are thought to be largely attributable to the investment programme of the water industry and pollution control measures. However, the chemical quality of rivers and canals is not only affected by human activity. Lower than average rainfall and low river flows can also have an adverse effect on river water quality by reducing the dilution of pollutants.

Pollution from the land and rivers can also impact on the seas around the United Kingdom. The microbiological quality of bathing waters can be affected by sewage effluent, storm water overflows and river-borne pollutants which could affect human health. The European Commission's (EC) bathing water directive gives mandatory values for a number of physical, chemical and microbiological parameters at bathing waters, among which total and faecal coliforms are considered to be the most important. Coliforms are bacteria which inhabit the intestines of humans and other vertebrates.

In recent years, there has been an increase in the number of UK bathing waters complying with the EC bathing water directive coliform standards during the bathing season (Table 11.4). In England this amounted to an increase of 19 percentage points between 1993 and 2004, to 98 per cent compliance. Wales achieved 100 per cent compliance in 2004, Scotland 93 per cent and Northern Ireland, 88 per cent.

Table **11.4**

Bathing water – compliance with EC bathing water directive coliform standards:[1] by Environment Agency region[2]

United Kingdom   Percentages

	1993	1998	2002	2003	2004
United Kingdom	80	89	98	98	98
England	79	90	99	99	98
North East	82	84	98	96	96
North West	38	62	97	97	97
Midlands	.	.	.	.	.
Anglian	85	100	100	100	100
Thames	100	100	100	100	100
Southern	87	97	99	100	99
South West	81	91	98	99	98
Wales	84	94	100	99	100
Scotland	78	52	92	95	93
Northern Ireland	94	94	94	100	88

1 During the bathing season. See Appendix, Part 11: Bathing waters.
2 Environment Agency regions for England and Wales only.

Source: Environment Agency; Scottish Environment Protection Agency; Environment and Heritage Service, Northern Ireland

Noise pollution is an environmental issue which affects many people. It is often a local problem, being caused directly by neighbours – nearly three quarters of noise complaints received by Environmental Health Officers (EHOs) in England and Wales had domestic premises as their source in

Table **11.5**

Noise complaints received by Environmental Health Officers:[1] by source

England & Wales			Rates per million population	
	1990/91	2000/01	2001/02	2002/03
Domestic premises	2,264	5,001	5,540	5,573
Commercial/leisure/industrial	913	1,381	1,273	1,315
Vehicles, machinery and equipment in streets[2]	..	365	372	377
Construction/demolition sites[2]	252	325	347	325
Aircraft[3]	34	26	101	104
Road traffic[3]	46	44	37	36
Railway[3]	..	16	12	18
Total[3]	3,644	7,158	7,682	7,748

1 Figures relate to those authorities making returns.
2 1990/91 complaints about road works and 'noise in the street' were included with 'Construction/demolition sites'.
3 Figures for 1990/91 include noise in the streets controlled by the Control and Pollution Act 1974 and other complaints not controlled by the Environment Protection Act 1990. See Appendix, Part 11: Noise complaints.

Source: The Chartered Institute of Environmental Health

2002/03 (Table 11.5). The number of noise complaints to EHOs has more than doubled since the early 1990s. This may reflect an increase in the incidence of nuisance noise and/or an increased tendency to complain among the public.

Global warming and climate change

Both global and local (as measured in central England) average temperatures rose during the 20th century (Figure 11.6). Global temperatures rose during the first half of the 20th century and, after a period of levelling off, rose again steeply from 1975. The ten hottest years on record have been since 1990, with 1998 being the warmest year since global records began in 1860. Temperatures in central England also rose in the first half of the 20th century and, after a period with little change, mirrored the global pattern and rose steeply from the early 1980s. Four of the five warmest years in central England since the earliest records in 1772 occurred after 1990. The highest temperature ever recorded in the United Kingdom, 38.5 degrees centigrade, was measured on 10 August 2003 at Brogdale (near Faversham). The Intergovernmental Panel on Climate Change (IPCC) reported in 2001 that there is new and stronger evidence that most of the warming over the last 50 years is attributable to human activities – chief among these is the emission of 'greenhouse gases', such as carbon dioxide, methane and nitrous oxide.

Figure **11.6**

Difference in average surface temperature: deviation from 1961–90 average

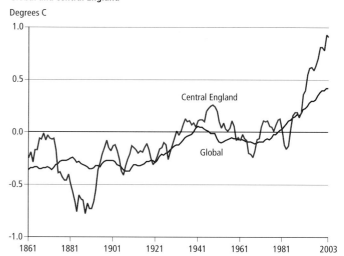

Global and central England

Degrees C

Source: Hadley Centre for Climate Prediction and Research

Under the Kyoto Protocol, the EU as a unit is committed to reducing emissions of six greenhouse gases by 8 per cent below the 1990 level over the 'commitment period' of 2008 to 2012. This target only refers to the 15 member states that formed the EU when the protocol was ratified in May 2002. However, the ten accession countries, which joined the EU in May 2004, have all since ratified the Kyoto Protocol and have their own Kyoto targets of between 6 and 8 per cent.

The United Kingdom has a legally binding target to reduce emissions by 12.5 per cent relative to 1990 over the period 2008 to 2012. The Government intends to move beyond that target towards a goal of reducing its carbon dioxide emissions to 20 per cent below 1990 levels by 2010. Emissions of greenhouse gases are one of the Government's headline indicators of sustainable development, and fell by 15 per cent between 1990 and 2002.

Carbon dioxide (CO_2) is the most significant greenhouse gas, and contributed 85 per cent of the potential warming effect of man-made emissions in the United Kingdom in 2002, when 9.1 tonnes of CO_2 per person were emitted (Table 11.7). The United Kingdom was one of six EU countries that has succeeded in reducing its emissions of CO_2 per person, with a fall of 11 per cent between 1990 and 2002, although this fall was not continuous. Other greenhouse gases, such as hydrochlorofluorocarbons (HFCs), have much higher warming potentials but are produced in much lower quantities.

Table **11.7**

Emissions of carbon dioxide: EU comparison

Tonnes per capita

	1990	2002	Percentage change 1990–2002
Luxembourg	31.3	23.0	-26
Finland	12.5	13.4	7
Belgium	11.8	12.3	4
Ireland	9.0	11.7	30
Netherlands	10.7	11.0	3
Germany	12.8	10.7	-17
Denmark	10.2	10.1	-1
Greece	8.4	9.8	17
United Kingdom	10.3	9.1	-11
Austria	7.8	8.7	11
Italy	7.6	8.2	8
Spain	5.8	8.0	38
France	7.0	6.8	-2
Portugal	5.0	6.5	30
Sweden	6.5	6.1	-5
EU-15 average	9.1	8.9	-2

Source: European Environment Agency

Use of resources

Fossil fuels accounted for 90 per cent of fuels used in the production of energy in the United Kingdom in 2003. The use of coal and petroleum for the production of energy fell between 1971 and 2003, by 54 per cent and 21 per cent respectively, although consumption of petroleum has remained relatively stable since 1990 (Figure 11.8). As total consumption of fuels for energy use has increased steadily since 1983 by around one fifth, natural gas and primary electricity production from nuclear energy, hydroelectric and other renewables have become increasingly important. Natural gas consumption rose by 419 per cent between 1971 and 2003. However, between 2000 and 2003, total consumption of all sources of energy has remained steady overall.

Renewable electricity can be generated from wind (both offshore and onshore), water (hydro, wave and tidal power), sunlight (the direct conversion of solar radiation into electricity, called photovoltaics or PV), biomass (energy from forestry, crops or biodegradable waste) and from the earth's heat (geothermal energy). None of these forms of generation, except biomass, involves the production of carbon dioxide, and biomass generation produces only the carbon that the material has absorbed from the atmosphere while growing.

Figure **11.8**

Consumption of fuels[1] for energy use

United Kingdom

Million tonnes of oil equivalent

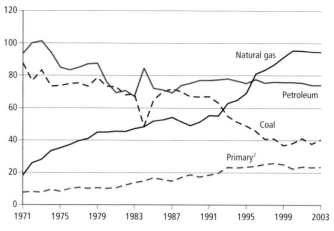

1 See Appendix, Part 11: Fuels for energy use.
2 Includes nuclear, hydroelectric and renewable energy.

Source: Department of Trade and Industry

The United Kingdom produced around 4 per cent of its electricity from renewable sources in 2003. This was far less than many other countries in the EU, and compares with an EU-25 average of 14 per cent (Table 11.9 overleaf). This figure reflects the absence of both high mountains in the United Kingdom, which would facilitate large scale hydro generation, and extensive forests that would prompt biomass generation, although there is scope to develop extensive wind and wave power. It also reflects the United Kingdom's historically abundant indigenous coal and gas resources. Under its own Renewables Obligation, the Government is committed to increase the contribution of electricity from renewable sources in the United Kingdom so that by 2010, 10 per cent of licensed electricity sales should be from eligible renewable sources. The EU-wide target is 22 per cent of electricity from renewable sources by 2010.

The amount of electricity generated from renewable sources in the United Kingdom almost doubled between 1990 and 2003 (Table 11.10 overleaf). The biggest increases in production, among those renewable resources used widely in both 1990 and 2003, came from exploiting landfill gas, and wind power. Hydro sources have traditionally accounted for the bulk of electricity generated from renewable resources, but in 2003 dry weather led to a substantial fall in output of 33 per cent. Very little energy was generated from wind and wave power in 1990, but it accounted for 12 per cent of the electricity generated from renewable resources in 2003. This was driven in part by the Renewables Obligation targets, which windfarms are currently best placed to meet.

Table 11.9

Proportion of electricity produced by renewable sources: EU comparison, 2003

Percentages and terawatt hours

	Hydro and wind	Biomass and geothermal	All renewable sources	All fuels (=100%) (terawatt hours)		Hydro and wind	Biomass and geothermal	All renewable sources	All fuels (=100%) (terawatt hours)
EU-15					**Accession countries**				
Germany	8	1	9	572	Poland	3	-	3	144
France	12	1	13	559	Czech Republic	4	1	4	76
United Kingdom	2	1	4	387	Hungary	1	-	1	36
Italy	17	2	20	284	Slovakia	17	0	17	32
Spain	14	2	16	246	Lithuania	4	-	4	18
Sweden	46	3	49	146	Slovenia	23	1	24	15
Netherlands	1	3	4	96	Estonia	-	-	-	9
Belgium	2	2	4	82	Cyprus	0	0	0	4
Finland	14	13	27	75	Latvia	62	-	63	4
Austria	68	3	70	62	Malta	0	0	0	2
Greece	8	0	8	55	EU-25 average	12	2	14	3,018
Portugal	19	4	23	46					
Denmark	13	6	19	39					
Ireland	7	-	7	25					
Luxembourg	28	2	29	4					

Source: Eurostat

Table 11.10

Electricity generated from renewable resources

United Kingdom

Gigawatt hours

	1990	1995	2000	2002	2003
Landfill gas	139	562	2,188	2,679	3,276
Hydro	5,207	4,838	5,085	4,788	3,228
Wind and wave	9	392	946	1,256	1,286
Municipal solid waste combustion[1]	140	471	840	907	965
Other biofuels[2]	-	199	401	807	947
Co-firing with fossil fuels	-	-	-	286	602
Sewage sludge digestion	316	410	367	368	343
Solar photovoltaics	-	-	1	3	3
Total	5,811	6,871	9,828	11,093	10,649

1 Biodegradable part only.
2 Includes electricity from farm waste digestion, poultry litter combustion, meat and bone combustion, straw and short rotation coppice.

Source: Department of Trade and Industry

Figure **11.11**

Environmental impact of households

United Kingdom
Indices (1973=100)

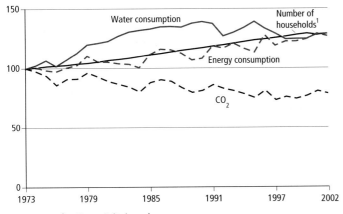

1 Data are for Great Britain only.

*Source: Department for Environment, Food and Rural Affairs;
Department of Trade and Industry; Office for National Statistics;
National Environmental Technology Centre.*

The number of households in Great Britain increased by 29 per cent between 1973 and 2002 (Figure 11.11). Household energy consumption in the United Kingdom has increased roughly in line with household numbers, at 27 per cent over the same period. Water consumption grew faster, peaking in the mid-1990s, when there were droughts (households tend to use more water during droughts, for example to water gardens). Water

consumption fell somewhat in the second half of the 1990s as rainfall rose, and has since begun to increase again. In 2002, water consumption was 29 per cent higher than it was in 1973.

In terms of energy use, changes such as increased efficiency of appliances and improved thermal insulation of houses have been counterbalanced by an increased use of appliances and a tendency for people to heat their homes to higher temperatures than previously. The increase in water consumption can be linked to greater ownership of appliances such as washing machines, washer-dryers and dishwashers, the increased use of those appliances within the home, and also the greater number of smaller households (see Chapter 2). Sixty five per cent of households had a washing machine in 1970, compared with 94 per cent in 2002/03, when 29 per cent of households had a dishwasher.

Land is a finite resource and, in an attempt to minimise the effect of housebuilding on the countryside, the Government has set targets for the amount of new housing which is to be built on 'brownfield', or previously developed sites in England. In 2003, 33 per cent of land changing to residential use in England was previously used for agriculture, compared with 55 per cent which was previously developed land (Table 11.12). In 1993 these figures were 37 per cent and 46 per cent respectively. The area of land changing to residential use has fallen since 1995 – which could in part be a reflection of the fact that fewer houses were being built (see Chapter 10).

Table **11.12**

Land changing to residential use:[1] by previous use

England   Percentages

	1993	1995	1997	1999[2]	2001	2003
Agriculture	37	39	42	40	35	33
Urban not previously developed uses	11	11	10	9	9	8
Other rural uses	5	5	6	5	5	4
All not previously developed uses	54	55	57	55	49	45
Minerals, landfill and defence[3]	1	1	1	1	2	1
Residential[4]	16	14	12	14	15	17
Vacant and derelict land	23	21	20	19	22	25
Other urban uses	7	8	9	12	12	12
All previously developed uses	46	45	43	45	51	55
All land changing to residential uses (=100%) (hectares)[5]	5,956	6,402	6,371	..	5,779	..

1 Information relates to map changes recorded by Ordnance Survey as at June 2004 for which the year of change has been estimated by surveyors
   from available information. See Appendix, Part 11: Land use change.
2 1999 estimates are subject to some uncertainty due to incomplete data.
3 Some mineral and landfill sites may be classified as not previously developed land.
4 Includes only changes between residential uses that involve new dwellings or demolitions.
5 Aggregate figures for the most recent years are subject to upward revision due to the lag between the change occurring and it being recorded.

Source: Office of the Deputy Prime Minister

Table 11.13

Management of municipal waste: by method

England

Thousand tonnes

	1996/97	1998/99	2000/01	2002/03
Landfill	20,635	21,517	22,039	21,969
Recycled/composted[1]	1,751	2,523	3,446	4,577
Incineration with energy from waste	1,435	2,139	2,391	2,607
Other[2]	767	158	182	156
Total	24,588	26,337	28,057	29,309

1 Includes household and non-household sources collected for recycling or for centralised composting; home composting estimates are not included in this total.
2 Includes incineration without energy from waste and refuse derived fuel manufacture. Excludes any processing prior to landfilling and materials sent to materials reclamation facilities.

Source: Department for Environment, Food and Rural Affairs

Waste management

The collection and disposal of domestic waste, and litter and rubbish from public areas (as well as some commercial waste) is the responsibility of local authorities throughout the United Kingdom. In England, nearly 90 per cent of this municipal waste is generated by households, and most of it has traditionally been disposed to landfill, a method which makes little use of the waste and produces greenhouse gases (mainly CO_2 and methane). In 2002/03, 75 per cent of municipal waste was disposed to landfill, while 16 per cent was recycled or composted (Table 11.13).

Between 2001/02 and 2002/03, municipal waste disposed in landfill sites fell by 1 per cent, while the amount recycled increased by 17 per cent. However, the amount of municipal waste produced continues to grow year on year. Between 1996/97 and 2002/03 the amount produced in England increased by 19 per cent.

The Government has set a target to recycle 25 per cent of waste produced by households by 2005/06. In 2002/03, 14 per cent (3.7 million tonnes) of household waste was collected for recycling in England (Table 11.14). This was more than double the amount collected in 1996/97.

Table 11.14

Materials collected from households for recycling[1]

England

Thousand tonnes

	1996/97	1998/99	2000/01	2001/02	2002/03
Compost[2]	279	668	798	954	1,187
Paper and card	600	863	934	981	1,125
Glass	311	384	397	426	471
Scrap metal and white goods	199	265	310	369	422
Co-mingled[3]	77	182	206	221	267
Textiles	32	44	45	46	54
Cans[4]	18	32	26	26	27
Plastics	6	13	13	8	13
Other[5]	2	93	84	155	176
Total	1,678	2,543	2,812	3,191	3,742

1 Includes data from different types of recycling schemes collecting waste from household sources, including private/voluntary schemes such as kerbside and 'bring' systems.
2 Includes organic materials (kitchen and garden waste) collected for centralised composting. Home composting is not included.
3 Co-mingled materials are separated after collection.
4 Includes ferrous and aluminium cans.
5 Includes oils, batteries, aluminium foil, books and shoes.

Source: Department for Environment, Food and Rural Affairs

Compost, and paper and card constitute a large proportion of household waste collected for recycling, accounting for 32 per cent and 30 per cent, respectively, of the total amount by weight in 2002/03. The amount of paper and card collected has grown steadily in recent years, in line with most types of waste. The amount of compost has increased more rapidly, quadrupling between 1996/97 and 2002/03. Kerbside collection by local authorities is one way in which households can recycle their waste. This accounted for 30 per cent of waste collected for recycling in 2002/03. The amount of household waste recycled varies considerably across the country. In 2002/03 the South East and East had the highest rates, at 20 per cent and 19 per cent, respectively.

Countryside, farming and wildlife

Three quarters of land in the United Kingdom is used for agriculture (Table 11.15), and much of what many people consider 'natural' landscape is a product of many centuries of human intervention. Northern Ireland has the largest proportion of agricultural land, 81 per cent, while England has the smallest, 71 per cent. There is also considerable variability in the use to which agricultural land is put. Almost 30 per cent of the total area of England is covered by crops and bare fallow, compared with only 3 per cent of Wales, 7 per cent of Scotland and 4 per cent of Northern Ireland.

Many people are concerned about the quality of the food they eat and its possible impact on their health and the

Figure **11.16**

Land under organic crop production[1]

United Kingdom
Thousand hectares

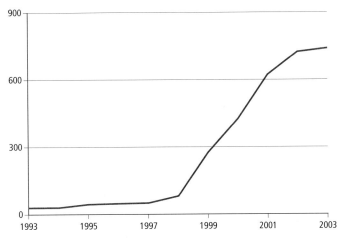

1 As at December each year.

Source: Department for Environment, Food and Rural Affairs

environment. The use of pesticides, BSE in cattle, animal husbandry practices and the development of genetically modified (GM) crops, among other things, have led to an increased interest in organic farming over the past ten years. There has been a dramatic increase in the area of land under organic production in the United Kingdom since 1998, and at December 2003, 741,000 hectares were under organic production (Figure 11.16). As at March 2004, Scotland had the

Table **11.15**

Land: by agricultural and other uses, 2003

United Kingdom

Percentages

	England	Wales	Scotland	Northern Ireland	United Kingdom
Agricultural land					
Crops and bare fallow	29	3	7	4	19
Grasses and rough grazing	36	73	66	76	51
Other[1]	6	1	2	1	4
Forest and woodland[2]	9	14	17	6	12
Urban land not otherwise specified[3]	20	9	8	13	14
Total land[4,5] (=100%) (thousand hectares)	13,028	2,073	7,793	1,358	24,251
Inland water[4] (thousand hectares)	76	13	169	64	325

1 Set aside and other land on agricultural holdings, eg farm roads, yards, buildings, gardens, ponds. Excludes woodland on agricultural holdings which is in 'Forests and woodland'.
2 See Appendix, Part 11: Forest and woodland.
3 Figures are derived by subtracting land used for agricultural and forestry purposes from the land area. Figures include: land used for urban and other purposes, eg transport and recreation; non-agricultural, semi-natural environments such as sand dunes, grouse moors and non-agricultural grasslands; and inland waters.
4 As at January 2001.
5 Because data come from a number of sources the components do not always add to the total.

Source: Department for Environment, Food and Rural Affairs

largest proportion of organic land, at 8 per cent of its total area, Wales had 4 per cent, England 3 per cent, and Northern Ireland less than 1 per cent.

Most land that is organically farmed (or is in the process of being converted to organic farming) in the United Kingdom is used for permanent or temporary pasture – 88 per cent in March 2003. In contrast, 67 per cent of all agricultural land in 2003 was grassland or used for rough grazing. Just 8 per cent of organic land was used for growing cereals and other crops in March 2003, and 2 per cent for fruit and vegetables.

The British public are, in general, reluctant to accept GM food, and women tend to show more concern than men. In 2003, the British Social Attitudes survey found that only 16 per cent of men and 12 per cent of women aged 18 or over agreed or strongly agreed with the statement that 'On balance, the advantages of genetically modified foods outweigh any dangers' (Table 11.17). A higher proportion of men disagreed to some extent than agreed with the statement that 'Genetically modified foods should be banned, even if food prices suffer as a result'. For women, it was the reverse. When considering the question 'In general, do you think that growing genetically modified foods poses a danger to other plants and wildlife?', more than half of those asked thought that it definitely or probably did.

There were indications that younger age groups were more accepting of genetically modified foods than older age groups.

When asked whether 'It is important for me to check whether or not foods contain genetically modified ingredients', 24 per cent of 18 to 24 year olds agreed, compared with 46 per cent of those aged 65 and over.

Bird populations are thought to be good indicators of the condition of UK wildlife and the countryside, as birds have a wide range of habitats and tend to be at or near the top of the food chain. Since the 1970s, breeding populations of some common farmland and woodland birds have fallen. Between 1994 and 2003, using the most recent consistent measure, breeding populations of farmland birds such as the skylark, yellowhammer and starling declined, by 14 per cent, 17 per cent and 28 per cent respectively (Table 11.18). However, other species, particularly woodland species, have increased over the same period. Changes in farming practices may have contributed to the decline in certain species, particularly those whose principal breeding habitat is farmland. Increased use of chemicals and loss of hedgerows have led to a decline and deterioration in suitable breeding and feeding areas. The Government has set a target to reverse the long-term decline in the number of farmland birds by 2020.

The area of forested land in the United Kingdom fell to a low of around 1.1 million hectares at the beginning of the 20th century but has been increasing since then, reaching 2.8 million hectares in 2004. Ancient woodland, which has existed since the earliest reliable records began (over 400 years ago in

Table **11.17**

Attitudes towards genetically modified (GM) foods, 2003

Great Britain

Percentages

	Males					Females				
	Agree/ Agree strongly	Neither agree nor disagree	Disagree/ Disagree strongly	Other[1]	All	Agree/ Agree strongly	Neither agree nor disagree	Disagree/ Disagree strongly	Other[1]	All
In order to compete with the rest of the world, Britain should grow genetically modified foods	18	32	40	12	100	11	28	49	11	100
Genetically modified foods should be banned, even if food prices suffer as a result	25	32	32	13	100	33	33	21	12	100
On balance, the advantages of genetically modified foods outweigh any dangers	16	41	29	16	100	12	35	37	15	100
It is important for me to check whether or not foods contain genetically modified ingredients	40	30	20	12	100	46	27	15	11	100

1 Includes 'Can't choose' and not answered.

Source: British Social Attitudes Survey, National Centre for Social Research

Table **11.18**

Breeding populations of selected birds

United Kingdom   Indices (1994=100)

	1994	1997	2000	2003
Pheasant (Woodland)	100	100	113	133
Great tit (Woodland)	100	112	118	126
Dunnock (Woodland)	100	94	108	121
Blue tit (Woodland)	100	119	102	118
Blackbird (Woodland)	100	95	114	118
Song thrush (Woodland)	100	83	112	118
Robin (Woodland)	100	89	119	117
Wren (Woodland)	100	81	123	117
Woodpigeon (Farmland)	100	95	104	112
Chaffinch (Woodland)	100	100	107	107
Skylark (Farmland)	100	93	92	86
Yellowhammer (Farmland)	100	89	88	83
Starling (Farmland)	100	100	96	72

Source: British Trust for Ornithology; Joint Nature Conservation Committee; Royal Society for the Protection of Birds

England and Wales) and which may contain complex and fragile ecosystems, and preserve historical features, covers only around 2 per cent of the United Kingdom.

Although there are more conifers in Great Britain than broadleaved trees, broadleaved new woodland creation has exceeded that of conifers since 1993/94 (Figure 11.19). Prior to

the 1990s timber production remained the key priority, resulting in the planting of conifers, which were suitable for timber, but mainly not native to Britain. Since then, additional incentives for planting broadleaved trees and native pinewood, and for planting on former agricultural land, have led to a growth in the number of broadleaved trees planted.

Fish have traditionally formed an important food resource for many people in the United Kingdom, and they are vital elements of ocean ecosystems. Stocks of herring, after declining to very low levels in the 1970s, have recovered strongly (Figure 11.20). Haddock stocks have fluctuated dramatically since the 1960s, and continue to do so: they more than quadrupled between 2000 and 2004.

Stocks of cod in the North Sea and elsewhere are causing particular concern to the Government and other interested parties. After increasing in the 1960s, and fluctuating somewhat in the 1970s, North Sea stocks have declined steadily since the early 1980s, and in 2004 were 68 per cent lower than in 1983. There was, however, an increase between 2001 and 2004. The depletion in numbers is thought to have occurred through a combination of overfishing, small numbers of fish surviving to a size where they are taken commercially, and possible environmental factors. Measures have been put in place that aim to halt and ultimately reverse the decline in cod stocks. These have included restrictions on cod fishing during the key spring spawning periods, cuts in the numbers that can be caught, and a limit to the number of days each month fishermen can spend at sea catching cod.

Figure **11.19**

New woodland creation[1]

Great Britain

Thousand hectares

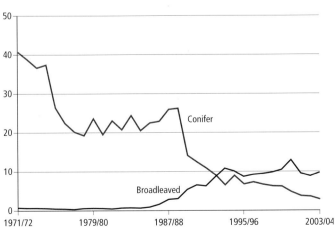

1 Figures exclude areas of new private woodland created without grant aid. See Appendix, Part 11: New woodland creation.

Source: Forestry Commission

Figure **11.20**

North Sea fish stocks[1]

Indices (1963=100)

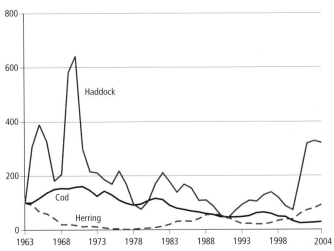

1 Spawning stock biomass.

Source: Centre for Environment, Fisheries and Aquaculture Science; International Council for the Exploration of the Sea

Transport

- The total distance travelled by people within Great Britain increased by 90 per cent between 1971 and 2003, to 794 billion passenger kilometres. (Table 12.1)

- The volume of goods transported by road in Great Britain grew by 86 per cent between 1971 and the peak year of 1998, then stabilised; 159 billion tonne kilometres were transported in 2003. (Figure 12.5)

- Between 1981 and 2002/03, UK household expenditure on motoring increased by 71 per cent in real terms, while spending on fares and other travel costs rose by 22 per cent. (Table 12.6)

- The number of licensed cars on Britain's roads continued to increase to nearly 28 million in 2003, over four times the number in 1961. (Table 12.9)

- Over 4.5 billion journeys in Great Britain were made by local bus in 2003/04, more than twice the number made by rail. (Page 168)

- UK residents made 61 million visits abroad in 2003, over three times as many as in 1981. (Table 12.16)

Chapter 12

The last ten years have seen the continuation of long-term trends in many areas of transport and travel, for example the increase in the distance each person travels in a year, the rising number of cars on the roads, and the ever-increasing reliance on those cars. Travel overseas, and particularly air travel, has increased substantially over the same period.

Table 12.1

Passenger transport: by mode[1]

Great Britain — Billion passenger kilometres

	1961	1971	1981	1991	2001	2003
Road						
Car and van[2]	157	313	394	582	654	678
Bus and coach	76	60	48	44	47	47
Motorcycle	11	4	10	6	5	6
Bicycle	11	4	5	5	4	5
All road	255	381	458	637	710	736
Rail[3]	39	35	34	39	47	49
Air[4]	1	2	3	5	8	9
All modes	295	419	495	681	765	794

1 Road transport data from 1993 are not directly comparable with earlier years. See Appendix, Part 12: Road traffic.
2 Includes taxis.
3 Data relate to financial years.
4 Includes Northern Ireland, Channel Islands and Isle of Man.

Source: Department for Transport

Travel patterns

The total distance travelled by people within Great Britain grew dramatically between 1961 and 2003, from 295 billion to 794 billion passenger kilometres (Table 12.1). Air travel grew fastest, but from a very low base, and only comprised about 1 per cent of distance travelled in 2003. Travel by car, van and taxi contributed most to the overall increase in distance travelled. Since the early 1960s the car has been the dominant means of transport, accounting for 85 per cent of all passenger kilometres travelled in 2003. The rapid rates of increase that occurred particularly in the 1960s and 1980s were replaced by more gradual growth from 1989. The total distance travelled by car rose by an average of nearly 5 per cent a year in the 1980s, compared with an annual average of 1 per cent between 1991 and 2003.

Overall, travel by rail grew from 39 billion to 49 billion passenger kilometres between 1961/62 and 2003/04. There was a decline in the number of passenger kilometres travelled for much of the early part of this period, with a low point of 31 billion in 1982. Passenger kilometres then rose for much of the 1980s, before declining again in the early 1990s. Between 1994 and 2003, passenger kilometres travelled rose by an average of nearly 4 per cent a year.

Table 12.2

Trips per person per year: by sex, main mode and trip purpose,[1] 2002–03

Great Britain — Percentages

	Males						Females					
	Car	Walk	Bus and coach	Rail[2]	Other	All modes	Car	Walk	Bus and coach	Rail[2]	Other	All modes
Social/entertainment	24	21	20	17	25	23	26	17	18	21	29	23
Other escort and personal business	22	15	13	6	9	19	24	17	13	8	13	21
Commuting	20	5	20	51	31	18	13	7	18	39	16	12
Shopping	17	21	22	5	10	18	21	21	32	10	15	22
Education	3	14	20	6	13	7	3	10	14	10	14	6
Business	6	1	1	11	3	5	2	1	1	5	3	2
Holiday/day trip	4	1	3	5	8	4	4	1	2	6	8	3
Escort education	3	4	1	-	-	3	6	11	2	1	2	7
Other, including just walk	-	18	-	-	-	4	-	15	-	-	-	4
All purposes (=100%) (numbers)	654	223	48	21	47	994	622	263	70	15	33	1,003

1 See Appendix, Part 12: National Travel Survey.
2 Includes London Underground.

Source: National Travel Survey, Department for Transport

Table **12.3**

Travel to work trips: by sex, age and mode, 2003

Great Britain   Percentages

	Walk	Bicycle	Car/Van	Bus/Coach	Rail	Other[1]	All trips (=100%) (millions)
Males							
18–24	15	4	59	12	7	3	1.6
25–44	6	4	75	5	7	3	6.6
45–64	5	3	81	3	5	2	4.8
65 and over	9	2	79	3	6	1	0.3
All males aged 18 and over	7	4	75	5	6	3	13.3
Females							
18–24	18	1	52	20	7	1	1.5
25–44	12	2	71	8	6	1	5.6
45–64	15	2	70	9	3	1	4.0
65 and over	21	3	61	11	3	1	0.2
All females aged 18 and over	14	2	68	10	5	1	11.2

1 Includes taxis and motorcycles.

Source: Labour Force Survey, Office for National Statistics

Travel on buses and coaches fell steadily from 76 billion passenger kilometres in 1961 to around 43 billion in 1992. After remaining broadly steady for much of the 1990s, the distance travelled by bus and coach rose slowly to 47 billion passenger kilometres in 2000, where it has remained. Buses and coaches and the railways each accounted for just 6 per cent of all passenger kilometres in 2003.

The National Travel Survey (NTS) found that British residents travelled an average of nearly 11,000 kilometres within Great Britain in 2003, over 600 kilometres a year more than in 1992–94. In contrast, the average number of trips made per person in a year fell by 6 per cent between 1992–94 and 2003, to 990. Consequently, the average trip length rose to over 11 kilometres in 2003, while the average trip time was nearly 22 minutes.

Overall, males were more likely to travel by car, using it for 66 per cent of their trips, compared with 62 per cent of trips made by females in 2002–03 (Table 12.2). Females were more likely than males to walk, making 26 per cent of their trips on foot, compared with 22 per cent of trips made by males. Compared with males, a higher proportion of females' trips were for shopping and escorting people to education, and fewer were for commuting and business.

The majority of trips made to work in Great Britain for both men and women are made by car, 75 per cent and 68 per cent respectively in 2003 (Table 12.3). Walking is the next most common mode of travel to work for both sexes, although a higher proportion of women than men walk to work. Young people aged 18 to 24 are the least likely to travel to work by car and the most likely to travel by bus or coach.

The ways in which children travel to school have changed over the last ten years. In general, fewer are walking and more are travelling in cars (Table 12.4 overleaf). For example, in 1992–94, 30 per cent of trips to school by 5 to 10 year olds were in a car or van; by 2003 this figure had risen to 39 per cent. For 11 to 16 year olds the proportion rose from 16 per cent to 23 per cent. The average length of trips to school also increased over the same period – from 1.9 to 2.3 kilometres for children aged 5 to 10, and from 4.8 to 5.2 kilometres for those aged 11 to 16. Since trips to school usually take place at the same time each morning and evening, they have a major impact on levels of congestion in residential areas. In 2003, at 8.50 am on weekdays in term time (the peak time for school traffic) an estimated 18 per cent of all cars on the road in urban areas were taking children to school.

Table **12.4**

Trips to and from school:[1] by age of child and mode

Great Britain

Percentages

	Age 5–10			Age 11–16		
	1992–94	1998–2000	2003	1992–94	1998–2000	2003
Walk[2]	61	56	53	44	43	41
Bicycle	1	-	1	4	2	2
Car/Van	30	36	39	16	19	23
Private bus	4	3	3	8	8	9
Local bus	4	4	3	24	24	23
Rail	-	-	-	1	1	1
Other	2	1	1	2	3	2
All modes	100	100	100	100	100	100
Average length (kilometres)	1.9	2.2	2.3	4.8	4.6	5.2

1 Trips of under 80 kilometres (50 miles) only.
2 Short walks are believed to be under-recorded in 2003 compared with earlier years.

Source: National Travel Survey, Department for Transport

The volume of goods transported within Great Britain has grown markedly over the last 30 years, although it has remained broadly stable since 2000 (Figure 12.5). Much of this increase can be attributed to the movement of goods by road, which grew from 86 billion tonne kilometres in 1971 to

Figure **12.5**

Goods moved by domestic freight transport: by mode

Great Britain

Billion tonne kilometres

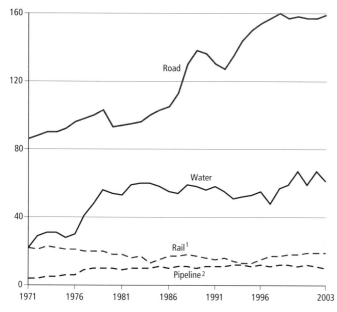

1 Data are for financial years from 1991.
2 Carrying petroleum products.

Source: Department for Transport

159 billion in 2003. The volume of freight carried by water also rose over the period, although much of this growth occurred between the mid 1970s and early 1980s. In 2003, only 19 billion tonne kilometres of goods were moved by rail. This was 14 per cent lower than in 1971, although it represents an increase on the low of 13 billion in 1984, 1994 and 1995.

The rise in the volume of goods moved by road has been driven by increases in both the weight of goods lifted and the average length of haul. Between 1993 and 2003 the weight of freight rose by 7 per cent to 1,725 million tonnes, and the average length of haul rose by 10 per cent, to 92 kilometres.

Prices and expenditure

In 2002/03, transport and travel accounted for 17 per cent of all household expenditure (Table 12.6). After taking into account the effect of inflation, UK household expenditure on transport and travel increased by 63 per cent between 1981 and 2002/03. This compares with a 36 per cent increase in household spending on all goods and services.

Between 1981 and 2002/03, household expenditure on motoring increased by 71 per cent in real terms, while expenditure on fares and other travel costs increased by 22 per cent. In 2002/03, household expenditure on motoring was nearly seven times the expenditure on fares and other travel costs.

UK transport prices rose substantially during the 1980s and 1990s (Table 12.7). Between 1981 and 1991 there were rises of 64 per cent in the 'All motoring' index of the retail prices index

Table **12.6**

Household expenditure on transport in real terms[1]

United Kingdom					£ per week

	1981	1986	1991	1996/97	2001/02	2002/03
Motoring						
Cars, vans and motorcycle purchase	12.75	15.52	20.97	18.36	25.91	25.57
Repairs, servicing, spares and accessories	5.38	4.89	5.68	6.71	6.84	6.79
Motor vehicle insurance and taxation	4.31	5.14	6.29	6.94	9.27	10.78
Petrol, diesels and other oils	11.70	11.30	11.25	13.60	15.09	14.83
Other motoring costs	0.93	0.91	1.17	1.97	1.98	2.03
All motoring expenditure	35.08	37.76	45.37	47.58	59.09	60.00
Fares and other travel costs						
Rail and tube fares	1.82	1.30	1.28	1.49	1.66	1.57
Bus and coach fares	2.54	1.89	1.66	1.59	1.37	1.28
Taxi, air and other travel costs[2]	2.59	3.56	3.49	3.92	4.78	4.86
All fares and other travel costs[3]	7.25	7.49	7.42	8.61	8.88	8.81
All transport and travel	42.33	45.25	52.79	56.18	67.97	68.81
All expenditure groups	292.33	316.90	344.47	358.67	401.43	396.83

1 At 2002/03 prices deflated by the 'All items' retail prices index.
2 Includes combined fares.
3 Includes expenditure on bicycles and boats – purchases and repairs.

Source: Family Expenditure Survey and Expenditure and Food Survey, Office for National Statistics

Table **12.7**

Passenger transport prices[1]

United Kingdom					Indices (1991=100)

	1981	1986	1991	1996	2001	2003	2004
Motoring costs							
Vehicle tax and insurance	45	66	100	136	195	203	211
Maintenance[2]	51	71	100	129	160	179	189
Petrol and oil	64	93	100	137	188	183	186
Purchase of vehicles	70	81	100	114	106	103	102
All motoring expenditure	61	81	100	125	146	147	149
Fares and other travel costs							
Bus and coach fares	51	70	100	132	158	169	178
Rail fares	50	68	100	130	151	158	161
Other	74	79	100	115	133	141	147
All fares and other travel	54	72	100	123	144	152	158
Retail prices index	54	74	100	115	131	137	141

1 At January each year based on the retail prices index. See Appendix, Part 6: Retail prices index.
2 Includes spares and accessories, repairs and motoring organisation membership fees.

Source: Office for National Statistics

and 85 per cent in the 'All fares and other travel' index. These were greater than the increases between 1991 and 2004 (49 per cent and 58 per cent, respectively). However, the increases in motoring costs in the later period outpaced general inflation, which was not the case between 1981 and 1991. Prices on public transport rose even more: bus and coach fares increased by 78 per cent between 1991 and 2004, compared with an increase of 61 per cent for rail fares.

Since 2000, the increases in motoring prices have almost levelled off, and between 2001 and 2004 there was little overall increase in the 'All motoring' index. This was largely due to a fall in the prices for purchase of vehicles, and by 2004 such prices were only 2 per cent above 1991 levels. Petrol and oil prices fell between 2002 and 2003 but then rose again, by nearly 2 per cent, between 2003 and 2004.

In June 2004, the United Kingdom was the second most expensive place in the EU-15 in which to buy premium unleaded petrol (Table 12.8). The most expensive place was the Netherlands. The cheapest price was in Greece, where a litre cost one third less on average than it did in the United Kingdom. The average price of unleaded petrol in the United Kingdom in June 2004 was 81.7 pence a litre. This was higher

(at current prices) than in June 2002 and June 2003 – but cheaper than it was in June 2000, when it was 84.3 pence a litre.

Taxes and duties form a major component of petrol prices across the EU-15 – 66 per cent on average in mid-June 2004. The tax component in the United Kingdom was the largest in the EU-15, at 73 per cent. France and Germany had the next highest tax components, 72 per cent each, whereas Greece had the lowest, at 53 per cent.

The roads

The number of licensed cars on Britain's roads has continued to increase, reaching over 27.7 million in 2003 (Table 12.9). This was over four times the number in 1961, when there were only 6.2 million licensed cars. The number of licensed motorcycles declined from 1980 up to the mid-1990s reaching a low of 594,000 in 1995. There has been a recovery in recent years and in 2003, the number of licensed motorcycles exceeded 1 million for the first time since 1986. However, new motorcycle registrations have been declining since 2000.

Table **12.8**

Premium unleaded petrol[1] prices: EU comparison, mid-June 2004

			Pence per litre[2]
	Price excluding tax and duty	Pump price	Tax component (percentages)
Netherlands	25.5	82.9	69
United Kingdom	22.3	81.7	73
Italy	26.2	75.9	65
Finland	22.1	75.3	71
Germany	21.3	75.1	72
Denmark	22.1	73.0	70
Portugal	25.8	71.9	64
Belgium	22.8	71.4	68
Sweden	22.2	71.1	69
France	19.9	70.6	72
Austria	25.6	64.6	60
Ireland	22.1	62.3	65
Luxembourg	26.1	62.1	58
Spain	24.4	59.0	59
Greece	25.3	53.5	53

1 Premium unleaded petrol, 95RON.
2 Prices converted to pounds sterling using mid-month exchange rates.

Source: Department of Trade and Industry

Table **12.9**

Cars[1] and motorcycles[2] currently licensed,[3] and new registrations[4]

Great Britain

Thousands

	Currently licensed		New registrations	
	Cars	Motorcycles	Cars	Motorcycles
1961	6,240	1,577	743	212
1971	11,895	899	1,462	128
1981	16,490	1,371	1,644	272
1991	21,952	750	1,709	77
2001	26,443	882	2,710	177
2002	27,165	941	2,816	162
2003	27,715	1,005	2,821	157

1 Includes light goods vehicles.
2 Includes scooters and mopeds.
3 At 31 December each year.
4 New methods of estimating vehicle stock were introduced in 1992, and changes to the vehicle taxation system were introduced from 1 July 1995.

Source: Department for Transport

The increase in licensed cars is reflected in the growth in the number of households with two or more cars. Since the early 1970s the percentage of households with one car only has been stable at around 45 per cent (Figure 12.10). However, the percentage with no car fell from 48 per cent in 1971 to 26 per cent in 2002. The percentage of households with two or more cars increased from 8 per cent to 29 per cent over the same

Figure **12.10**

Households with regular use of a car[1]

Great Britain

Percentages

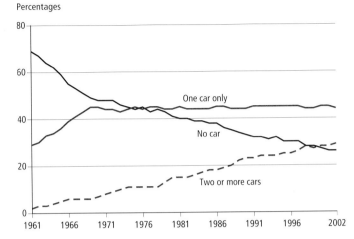

1 See Appendix, Part 12: Car ownership.

Source: Family Expenditure Survey and General Household Survey, Office for National Statistics; National Travel Survey, Department for Transport

Table **12.11**

Average daily flow[1] of motor vehicles: by class of road[2]

Great Britain   Thousands

	1993	1998	2001	2002	2003
Motorways[3]	58.2	68.7	71.6	73.0	73.2
Urban major roads	19.2	20.2	20.1	20.2	20.1
Trunk	32.4	34.6	27.5	28.5	31.0
Principal	17.6	18.6	19.6	19.6	19.5
Rural major roads	8.9	10.0	10.3	10.5	10.8
Trunk	14.3	16.4	17.0	17.7	18.7
Principal	6.5	7.2	7.4	7.7	8.1
All major roads	11.3	12.4	12.6	12.8	13.0
All minor roads	1.3	1.3	1.4	1.4	1.4
All roads	2.9	3.2	3.3	3.4	3.4

1 Flow at an average point on each class of road.
2 See Appendix, Part 12: Road traffic.
3 Includes motorways owned by local authorities.

Source: National Road Traffic Survey, Department for Transport

period. The higher a household's income, the more likely it is to have access to a car. Only 42 per cent of households in the lowest equivalised income quintile had access to at least one car in 2002/03. This proportion rose to 60 per cent for those in the next quintile and reached 92 per cent for households in the highest income quintile. For an explanation of equivalised income and what quintiles represent, see the analysing income distribution box in Chapter 5.

Historically, men have been much more likely than women to hold a full car driving licence. In 1975–76, 69 per cent of men in Great Britain held such a licence compared with only 29 per cent of women. However, women are catching up. The proportion of men with a driving licence was 81 per cent (17.9 million) in 2003, while among women the proportion was 61 per cent (14.4 million). The gap between the sexes is smallest in the youngest age groups and largest in the oldest. Thirty one per cent of men and 24 per cent of women aged 17 to 20 held licences in 2003, whereas among those aged 70 and over, 69 per cent of men held a licence compared with only 27 per cent of women. However, the proportion of younger (17 to 20 year old) men and women holding a licence has decreased since the early 1990s.

Growth in the number of motor vehicles and the greater distances travelled by individuals have led to an increase in the average daily flow of vehicles on Great Britain's roads. Between 1993 and 2003 average traffic flows rose by 17 per cent, to 3,400 vehicles per day (Table 12.11). Motorways had the highest flow of any type of road, 73,200 vehicles a day in 2003. This was an increase of 26 per cent since 1993, with

nearly half of this increase occurring between 1993 and 1996. Rural trunk roads saw the greatest increase (31 per cent), and urban trunk roads saw the only decrease (4 per cent), in traffic flows between 1993 and 2003.

One consequence of increased traffic can be lower average speeds, especially in urban areas. Transport for London found that the average traffic speed for all areas of London during 2000–03 was 15.7 miles per hour in the evening peak period, lower than at any time since 1968–70.

The average speed of vehicles passing a particular point is measured using spot speeds, which tend to be taken where traffic is relatively free flowing. In 2003 cars averaged 71 miles an hour on motorways, and 48 miles an hour on single carriageways (Table 12.12 overleaf). Buses and coaches, in comparison, averaged 59 miles an hour on motorways and 45 miles an hour on single carriageways. In 2003, over half of motorcycles and cars on motorways and dual carriageways exceeded the speed limit. A greater proportion of buses and coaches than cars exceeded the speed limit on non-urban single carriageways, although the speed limits for these two categories of vehicle are different. In urban areas, more than one quarter of all motorcycles, cars and light goods vehicles exceeded 35 miles per hour on roads where the speed limit was 30 miles per hour, compared with fewer than one in ten buses and coaches.

Table **12.12**

Traffic speeds: by class of road and type of vehicle, 2003

Great Britain

Miles per hour

	Motorcycles	Cars	Light goods vehicles[1]	Buses and coaches
Motorways				
Average speed	72	71	70	59
Speed limit	70	70	70	70
Percentage exceeding limit[2]	*59*	*57*	*51*	*4*
Dual carriageways				
Average speed	69	69	68	58
Speed limit	70	70	70	60
Percentage exceeding limit[2]	*50*	*50*	*43*	*39*
Single carriageways				
Average speed	50	48	48	45
Speed limit	60	60	60	50
Percentage exceeding limit[2]	*22*	*9*	*10*	*23*

1 Goods vehicles under 3.5 tonnes gross weight.
2 See Appendix, Part 12: Traffic speeds.

Source: Department for Transport

Buses and coaches are the most widely used form of public transport, and accounted for 1 per cent of motor vehicle traffic in 2003. Over 4.5 billion journeys were made by local bus in Great Britain in 2003/04, more than twice the number of journeys made by rail. Just over one third of all journeys on local buses in Great Britain took place in London. After a long period of post-war decline, which continued into the 1990s, local bus use in terms of passenger journeys stabilised towards the end of the decade and started to increase from 1999/2000 (Figure 12.13). The overall distance travelled by buses recovered from a low point in the mid-1980s until the mid-1990s, before it too stabilised.

The availability of bus services in Great Britain is fairly good overall, with nine in ten households living within 13 minutes' walk of a bus stop with a service at least once an hour in 2003 (Table 12.14). This does, however, depend on the type of area in which people live. Ninety nine per cent of households in metropolitan built up areas, and 98 per cent of households in London boroughs, lived within 13 minutes' walk of a bus stop with a service at least once an hour. This compares with 88 per cent in small urban areas and 55 per cent in rural areas. Nevertheless, this was an improvement on 1992–94, when the proportions in small urban areas and rural areas were 82 per cent and 40 per cent, respectively.

Figure **12.13**

Bus travel[1]

Great Britain

Indices (1981/82=100)

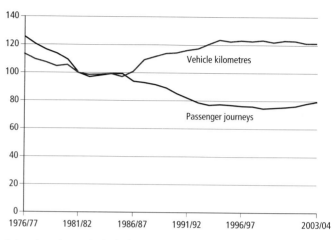

1 Local services only. Includes street-running trams but excludes modern 'supertram' systems. Financial years from 1985/86.

Source: Department for Transport

Table **12.14**

Time taken to walk to nearest bus stop: by type of area, 2003

Great Britain

Percentages

	6 minutes or less	7 to 13 minutes	14 minutes or more	Bus availability indicator[1]
London borough	*89*	*9*	*1*	*98*
Metropolitan built-up area	*91*	*8*	*1*	*99*
Large urban	*89*	*8*	*3*	*96*
Medium urban	*89*	*9*	*2*	*95*
Small urban	*83*	*13*	*5*	*88*
Rural	*76*	*11*	*12*	*55*
All areas	*87*	*10*	*4*	*90*

1 Proportion of households within 13 minutes' walk of a bus stop with a service at least once an hour.

Source: National Travel Survey, Department for Transport

Table **12.15**

Rail journeys:[1] by operator

Great Britain   Millions

	1981	1991/92	1995/96	2001/02	2002/03	2003/04
Main line/underground						
National rail	719	792	761	960	976	1,014
London Underground	541	751	784	953	942	948
Glasgow Underground	11	14	14	14	13	13
All national rail and underground	1,271	1,557	1,559	1,927	1,931	1,975
Light railways and trams						
Docklands Light Railway	.	8	14	41	46	49
Tyne and Wear Metro	14	41	36	33	37	38
Manchester Metrolink	.	.	13	18	19	19
Croydon Tramlink	.	.	.	18	19	20
South Yorkshire Supertram	.	.	5	11	12	12
West Midlands Metro	.	.	.	5	5	5
Blackpool Corporation Tram	6	5	5	5	5	4
All light railways and trams	20	54	73	132	141	147
All journeys by rail	1,291	1,611	1,632	2,059	2,072	2,122

1 Excludes railways and tramways operated principally as tourist attractions.

Source: Department for Transport

The railways

The number of journeys made on Great Britain's railways rose by 50 million between 2002/03 and 2003/04, to 2.1 billion (Table 12.15). The annual number of passenger journeys was around 1.3 billion in the early 1980s and, apart from a period in the early 1990s, it has generally increased since then, growing by 30 per cent between 1995/96 and 2003/04. In 2003/04, more than 1 billion passenger journeys were made on national rail, the first time this number has been reached since 1961. This represented 41 billion passenger kilometres, the most since 1946. National rail and London Underground accounted for 48 and 45 per cent, respectively, of all rail journeys in 2003/04.

Several new light railways and tram lines were built during the 1990s, and more are planned over the next decade in metropolitan areas across the country. Passenger numbers rose by 4 per cent between 2002/03 and 2003/04, and have more than doubled between 1995/96 and 2003/04.

International travel

UK residents are making more trips abroad each year than ever before, with over three times as many in 2003 as in 1981 (Table 12.16 overleaf). The use of air travel has grown consistently over the period. In 1981, it accounted for 60 per cent of all trips taken abroad. By 2003, this had risen to 77 per cent. Conversely, the relative importance of sea travel has declined, from 40 per cent of all trips in 1981 to just 15 per cent in 2003.

The number of trips to the United Kingdom by overseas residents also grew over the period, increasing by 125 per cent between 1981 and 1998, to a high of 25.7 million. However, in subsequent years numbers fell back slightly, and in 2001 were severely affected by both the outbreak of foot-and-mouth disease and the terrorist attacks of September 11. Although the number of visitors from overseas increased in 2003 to 24.7 million, they did not reach the levels of the late 1990s.

Table **12.16**

International travel: by mode[1]

United Kingdom
Millions

	1981	1986	1991	1996	2001	2002	2003
Visits abroad by UK residents							
Air	11.4	16.4	20.4	27.9	43.0	44.0	47.1
Sea	7.7	8.6	10.4	10.7	9.7	10.0	9.2
Channel Tunnel	.	.	.	3.5	5.6	5.3	5.1
All visits abroad	19.0	24.9	30.8	42.1	58.3	59.4	61.4
Visits to the United Kingdom by overseas residents							
Air	6.9	8.9	11.6	16.3	16.1	17.1	17.6
Sea	4.6	5.0	5.5	6.2	4.0	4.4	4.4
Channel Tunnel	.	.	.	2.7	2.8	2.7	2.7
All visits to the United Kingdom	11.5	13.9	17.1	25.2	22.8	24.2	24.7

1 Mode of travel from, and into, the United Kingdom.

Source: International Passenger Survey, Office for National Statistics

There has been a continued and substantial rise in the number of air passengers at UK airports. There was a 79 per cent increase in the number of domestic passengers at UK airports between 1993 and 2003 (Table 12.17). All the major airports, except London Heathrow and Aberdeen, experienced growth in domestic air passengers between these years. The largest percentage increases in domestic air passengers occurred at Luton and Stansted airports, at over 800 per cent and 700 per cent, respectively. These airports are both satellite airports for London.

There are more than three times as many passengers for international flights as there are for domestic flights at UK airports. Between 1993 and 2003 the largest increases in numbers of international passengers occurred at Heathrow (15.8 million), Stansted (13.7 million) and Gatwick (7.3 million). These include passengers in transit to other countries who do not stop overnight in the United Kingdom. However, regional airports have also expanded. Liverpool for example, experienced an increase of more than 900 per cent in the numbers of international passengers.

The Department for Transport forecasts that demand for air travel is set to continue. Mid-range estimates suggest that between 2005 and 2020 the number of passengers at UK airports will grow from 229 million to 401 million. The growth in international passengers is forecast to outstrip that in domestic passengers, with growth of nearly 80 per cent compared with nearly 70 per cent.

Table **12.17**

Air passengers:[1] by airport

United Kingdom
Millions

	1993[2]		2003	
	Domestic	International	Domestic	International
Heathrow	6.8	40.8	6.7	56.6
Gatwick	1.4	18.7	3.9	26.0
Manchester	2.0	10.8	3.1	16.4
Stansted	0.3	2.3	2.7	16.0
Birmingham	0.8	3.3	1.4	7.5
Luton	0.2	1.7	1.7	5.1
Glasgow	2.4	2.6	4.6	3.5
East Midlands	0.3	1.1	0.8	3.4
Bristol	0.2	0.9	1.1	2.8
Newcastle	0.6	1.4	1.5	2.5
Liverpool	0.2	0.2	0.7	2.4
Edinburgh	2.2	0.6	5.5	2.0
Cardiff	0.1	0.7	0.4	1.6
Leeds/Bradford	0.3	0.4	0.5	1.5
Belfast International	1.6	0.6	3.0	1.0
Aberdeen	1.5	0.8	1.5	1.0
London City	-	0.2	0.4	1.0
Belfast City	0.8	-	2.0	-
Other UK airports	4.0	2.5	4.4	3.9
All UK airports	25.7	89.7	45.8	154.1

1 Passengers are recorded at both airport of departure and arrival.
2 Excludes air taxi operations.

Source: Civil Aviation Authority

Table **12.18**

International travel: by mode of travel and purpose of visit, 2003

United Kingdom   Percentages

	UK residents[1]				Overseas residents[2]			
	Air	Sea	Channel Tunnel	All modes	Air	Sea	Channel Tunnel	All modes
Holiday	69	65	51	67	29	43	38	32
Visiting friends and relatives	15	12	10	14	31	20	21	28
Business	13	8	17	13	29	22	33	28
Other	3	15	23	6	11	15	8	11
All purposes (=100%) (millions)	47.1	9.2	5.1	61.4	17.6	4.4	2.7	24.7

1 Visits abroad by UK residents.
2 Visits to the United Kingdom by overseas residents.

Source: International Passenger Survey, Office for National Statistics

In 2003, holidays accounted for two thirds of the 61 million trips made abroad by UK residents (Table 12.18). The EU-15 was the destination for 67 per cent of trips by air and 95 per cent of visits by sea or the Channel Tunnel. Business trips accounted for a greater proportion of trips made by the Channel Tunnel than other routes, 17 per cent in 2003. The number of trips made abroad by UK residents was two and a half times the number overseas residents made to the United Kingdom. Additionally, greater proportions of overseas residents visiting the United Kingdom than UK residents visiting overseas were doing so either for business or to visit relatives. Only around one third of overseas residents' journeys to the United Kingdom were for a holiday.

Transport safety

The safety levels of most major forms of transport are much improved over those of the early 1980s (Table 12.19). Despite improvements in road safety, other forms of transport, such as rail, air and sea transport continue to have much lower death rates from accidents. Conversely, motorcycling, walking and cycling are by some margin the most dangerous forms of transport. Death rates per passenger kilometre among motorcyclists were over 40 times greater than those among car users in 2002.

Almost all passenger deaths in transport accidents in Great Britain occur on the roads. In 2003 there were 3,508 deaths

Table **12.19**

Passenger death rates:[1] by mode of transport

Great Britain   Rate per billion passenger kilometres

	1981	1986	1991	1996	2001	2002
Motorcycle	115.8	100.3	94.4	108.0	112.3	111.3
Walk	76.9	77.6	74.6	56.0	47.5	44.1
Bicycle	56.9	49.6	46.8	49.9	32.6	29.4
Car	6.1	5.1	3.7	3.0	2.8	2.7
Van	3.7	3.6	2.1	1.0	0.9	1.0
Bus or coach	0.3	0.5	0.6	0.2	0.2	0.4
Rail[2]	1.0	0.9	0.8	0.4	0.2	0.3
Water[3]	0.4	0.5	0.0	0.8	0.4	0.0
Air[3]	0.2	0.5	0.0	0.0	0.0	0.0

1 See Appendix, Part 12: Passenger death rates.
2 Financial years. Includes train accidents and accidents occurring through movement of railway vehicles.
3 Data are for the United Kingdom.

Source: Department for Transport

caused by road accidents, compared with an annual average of 3,578 in 1994–98, and 5,846 in 1981. In 2003, 50 per cent of deaths from road accidents were occupants of cars, 22 per cent of those killed were pedestrians, 20 per cent riders or passengers of two-wheeled motor vehicles, and 3 per cent were pedal cyclists. Occupants of buses, coaches and goods vehicles accounted for the remaining 4 per cent of deaths.

The number of pedestrians killed each year has fallen steadily since the mid-1990s. There were 774 pedestrian fatalities in 2003, 23 per cent lower than the yearly average for the period 1994–98. Conversely, the number of car users killed in 2003 was little changed from the annual average in 1994–98, 1,769 compared with 1,762, although this figure fell to a low of 1,665 in 2000.

Excessive speed and alcohol are major contributors to road accidents. Over the years there have been many campaigns to discourage drink-driving. The numbers of casualties from road accidents involving illegal alcohol levels in the United Kingdom fell sharply between the mid-1980s and mid-1990s. After a period when the number of casualties stabilised, they rose steadily between 1999 and 2002, with a slight fall to 19,750 in 2003 (Figure 12.20). In 2003, around 600 people died as a result of road accidents involving illegal alcohol levels, compared with over 1,000 people in 1986. In 2003, around half of the 300,000 car drivers involved in accidents resulting in injury in Great Britain were breath tested for alcohol levels. Five per cent of these failed or refused to take a breath test.

Table **12.21**

Road deaths: EU comparison, 2002

EU-15	Rate per 100,000 population	Accession Countries	Rate per 100,000 population
Sweden	6.0	Slovakia	11.3
United Kingdom	6.1	Slovenia	13.7
Netherlands	6.1	Hungary	14.0
Finland	8.0	Czech Republic	14.0
Germany	8.3	Poland	15.3
Denmark	8.6	Cyprus	..
Ireland	9.6	Estonia	..
Italy	11.7	Latvia	..
Austria	11.9	Lithuania	..
France	12.9	Malta	..
Spain	13.2		
Luxembourg	14.0		
Belgium	14.5		
Portugal	16.1		
Greece	..		

Source: Organisation for Economic Co-operation and Development

There is also concern over the role illegal drug use may play in causing road accidents. In the most recent study for the Department for Transport, completed in 2000, nearly one quarter of all road users killed in road accidents had at least one medicinal or illicit drug in their system.

The United Kingdom has a good record for road safety compared with most other EU countries. According to the Organisation for Economic Co-operation and Development, the United Kingdom had one of the lowest road death rates in the EU-25, at 6.1 per 100,000 population in 2002 (Table 12.21). Portugal had the highest recorded road death rate in the EU, at 16.1 per 100,000 population, although this figure was 21.0 in 2000. The UK rate was also substantially lower than those for other industrialised nations such as Japan (7.5 per 100,000 population), Australia (8.8) and the United States (14.9).

The United Kingdom also has a relatively good record in terms of road accidents involving children and older people. In 2002 the UK road accident death rate for children aged 0 to 14, at 1.5 per 100,000 of population, was the fifth lowest in the EU-15. Sweden had the lowest rate, at 1.1 per 100,000 population, while Portugal had the highest, at 4.5 per 100,000. The UK road accident death rate for those aged 65 and over was 7.0 per 100,000, the lowest rate in the EU-15.

Figure **12.20**

Casualties from road accidents involving illegal alcohol levels

United Kingdom
Thousands

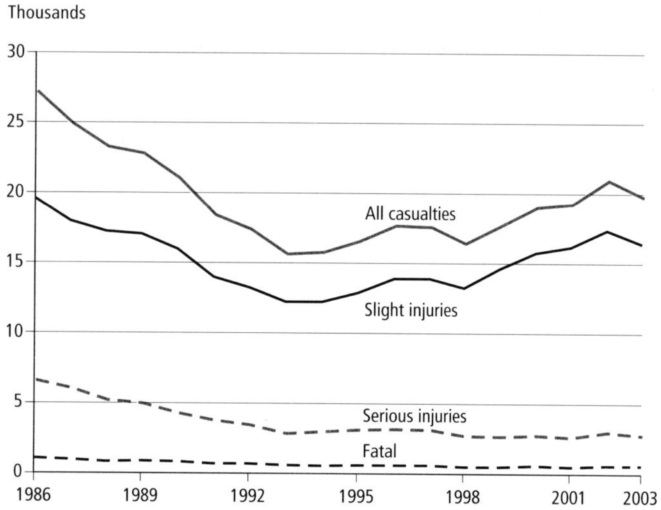

Source: Department for Transport; Police Service of Northern Ireland

Lifestyles and social participation

- There were 171 million cinema admissions in 2004, the second highest number for over 30 years. (Page 175)

- In 2002/03, 59 per cent of adults in Great Britain had participated in a sport, game or physical activity in the four weeks before interview, 6 percentage points lower than in 1990/91. (Table 13.8)

- The Internet could be accessed at home by 45 per cent of UK households (10.9 million) in 2002/03, more than four times the proportion in 1998/99. (Figure 13.10)

- In 2003/04, 37 per cent of adults in Great Britain had never used the Internet, and this proportion rose to 69 per cent of those aged 55 and over. (Page 178)

- UK residents took 41.2 million holidays abroad in 2003, six times the number in 1971; Spain was the most popular destination in both years. (Table 13.16)

- Thirty nine per cent of the UK electorate voted in the 2004 European Parliament elections, an increase of 15 percentage points on the previous election in 1999. (Figure 13.18)

Chapter 13

The ways in which people spend their time outside work have altered considerably over the past few decades. Changes in working patterns, technological advances and income all influence the time people spend on different activities.

Time use

Details of how people spend their time each day were recorded in the UK 2000 Time Use Survey. Adults aged 16 and over were asked to keep a detailed diary of how they spent their time on a selected day during the week and a selected day at the weekend. The survey found that there were substantial differences between men and women in the amount of time they spent on various activities. Women still do the majority of the household chores: on average women spent 4 hours 3 minutes a day on housework and childcare compared with 2 hours 17 minutes for men (Table 13.1). Men, on the other hand, worked or studied 1 hour 35 minutes a day more than women. Men also spent more time than women on leisure activities (5 hours 17 minutes compared with 4 hours 52 minutes). Men and women spent a similar amount of time sleeping, travelling, and on personal care.

Table 13.1

Time spent on main activities:[1] by sex, 2000–01

United Kingdom   Hours and minutes per day

	Males	Females
Sleep	8:23	8:33
Leisure		
Watching TV and Video/DVD	2:41	2:17
Social life and entertainment	1:16	1:33
Reading and listening to radio and music	0:36	0:35
Hobbies and games	0:26	0:16
Sport	0:18	0:11
All leisure	5:17	4:52
Employment and study[2]	4:17	2:42
Housework and childcare	2:17	4:03
Personal care[3]	2:07	2:19
Travel	1:28	1:21
Other	0:09	0:10

1 Adults aged 16 and over.
2 Includes voluntary work and meetings.
3 Includes eating, drinking, washing and dressing.

Source: Time Use Survey, Office for National Statistics

Differences between men and women were generally smaller for those in full-time work. Nevertheless, men spent 53 minutes a day more than women in paid or voluntary work (including study), and women spent 56 minutes a day more

than men on households tasks. People in full-time employment spent less time on leisure activities than adults overall – an average of 4 hours 16 minutes a day for men and 3 hours 50 minutes for women.

Leisure activities

Around half of all leisure time in the United Kingdom is spent watching television. On average, men spent 2 hours 35 minutes watching television each day as a main activity in 2000–01, while women watched 2 hours 12 minutes a day. In 2002/03, watching television was the most widespread leisure activity, with 99 per cent of adults in Great Britain, regardless of their age, watching at least once in the four weeks prior to the interview (Table 13.2).

Table 13.2

Adult participation[1] in selected leisure activities: by age, 2002/03

Great Britain   Percentages

	Watching TV	Listening to radio	Listening to records/tapes	Reading books
16–19	100	92	98	63
20–24	99	93	97	67
25–29	99	93	95	66
30–44	99	92	91	65
45–59	99	89	83	67
60–69	99	82	71	64
70 and over	99	76	57	64
All aged 16 and over	99	88	83	65

1 Participating in the four weeks before interview.

Source: General Household Survey, Office for National Statistics

Analogue terrestrial television is planned to be phased out by 2012. Although both analogue and digital television signals are available, viewers are rapidly acquiring digital television. Despite the increase in choice of channels, in 2003, 36 per cent of viewers aged 16 and over said that they would choose BBC One if they could only choose one channel (Table 13.3). This was the most common choice among all age groups, although for 25 to 44 year olds ITV was almost equally popular. Compared with other age groups, BBC One and BBC Two were more popular among those aged 65 and over, whereas Channel 4 and Sky Sports were more popular among the 16 to 24 age group.

Listening to the radio continues to be a popular pastime. Around 89 per cent of males and 87 per cent of females aged 16 and over listened at least once in the four weeks prior to

Table **13.3**

TV channel of choice:[1] by age, 2003

United Kingdom   Percentages

	16–24	25–44	45–64	65 and over	All aged 16 and over
BBC One	26	31	40	47	36
ITV1	20	29	26	25	26
Channel 4 (S4C in Wales)	12	7	6	5	7
BBC Two	6	4	6	10	6
Sky Sports	12	3	2	2	4
Five	2	4	3	3	3
Sky One	5	4	1	1	3

1 'Other', 'None of these' and 'Don't know' not shown.

Source: Ofcom

Figure **13.4**

Adults who have read books:[1] by sex and socio-economic classification,[2] 2002/03

Great Britain

Percentages

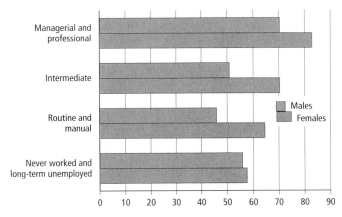

1 In the four weeks before interview.
2 Of the household reference person.

Source: General Household Survey, Office for National Statistics

interview in Great Britain in 2002/03. This has remained stable over the last 15 years. Radio listening declines with age: over 90 per cent of adults aged under 45 listened to it in the four-week period compared with 76 per cent of those aged 70 and over (see Table 13.2).

Digital radio and television offer audiences a greater choice of channels. According to RAJAR (Radio Joint Audience Research Limited), 29 per cent of adults in the United Kingdom listened to radio via their television in September 2004. Listening in this way has increased steadily, from 13 per cent in September 2001 and 20 per cent in September 2003. Radio listening via the Internet is also on the increase: 15 per cent of adults said they had listened online in June 2004 compared with 9 per cent in June 2001.

Many people enjoy reading in their spare time. Around 58 per cent of males and 72 per cent of females aged 16 and over had read a book in the four weeks prior to interview in Great Britain in 2002/03. Reading rates have risen over the last 25 years, from 54 per cent of adults in 1977 to 65 per cent in 2002/03.

Book reading rates vary according to socio-economic group. In 2002/03, 77 per cent of adults in the managerial and professional group reported reading books in the four weeks before interview compared with 56 per cent of those in routine or manual households and 57 per cent of those with a household reference person who had never worked or was long-term unemployed. The difference in the proportions of men and women who read books was widest among those in intermediate households (19 percentage points) and smallest for the never worked and long-term unemployed group (Figure 13.4). The June 2002 Omnibus Survey found that

44 per cent of adults had read at least five books for pleasure in the previous 12 months, with 19 per cent having read 20 or more books.

Reading material varies by age. Magazines are more popular among younger than older adults: in June 2002, 70 per cent of 16 to 24 year olds in Great Britain had read a magazine in the seven days prior to interview, compared with 59 per cent of those aged 55 to 64. In contrast, 55 to 64 year olds were more likely than 16 to 24 year olds to read fiction: 43 per cent compared with 33 per cent.

More than 34 million people in the United Kingdom (58 per cent of the population) were registered members of their local library in 2002/03, a figure which has remained fairly constant over the last five years. Reasons for visiting the library have changed little since 1998, with the exception of new activities related to the use of computers and the Internet, and borrowing or returning DVDs (Table 13.5 overleaf). Borrowing or returning books remains the most common activity, although this has fallen from 77 per cent of library visitors in 1998 to 73 per cent in 2003.

Cinema admissions in the United Kingdom in 2004 stood at 171 million, the second highest for over 30 years. This is despite the increased availability of DVDs and home channels dedicated to films. Young people aged 15 to 24 are the most likely age group to go to the cinema (Figure 13.6 overleaf). In 2003, 52 per cent of those in this age group reported that they went to the cinema at least once a month.

Table **13.5**

Activities undertaken by library visitors

United Kingdom   Percentages[1]

	1998	2000	2003
Borrow or return book(s)	77	75	73
Browse	30	30	28
Seek information	22	22	21
Use the Internet	..	..	13
Read newspaper or magazine	15	13	12
Use a computer	..	..	12
Sit to study or work	7	7	9
Borrow or return video(s)	7	8	8
Use photocopier	6	6	7
Borrow or return cassette(s)	7	6	6
Borrow or return CD(s)	4	5	5
Borrow or return DVD(s)	..	..	3
See exhibition or event	3	3	2
Borrow or return CD-rom(s)	..	..	1
Other reason	7	10	8

1 Percentages do not add up to 100 as respondents could give more than one answer.

Source: Institute of Public Finance Limited

Figure **13.6**

Cinema attendance:[1] by age

Great Britain

Percentages

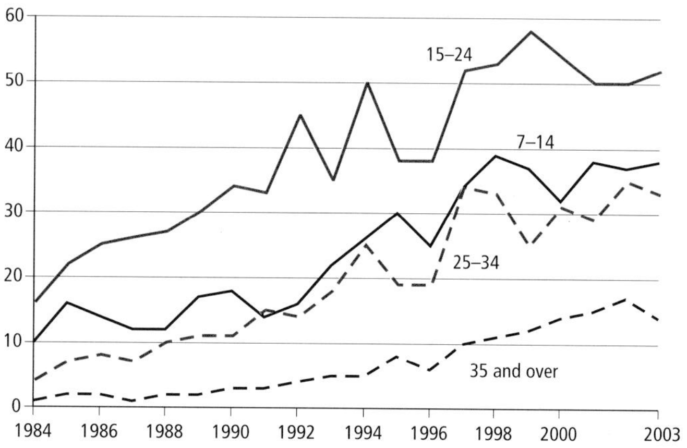

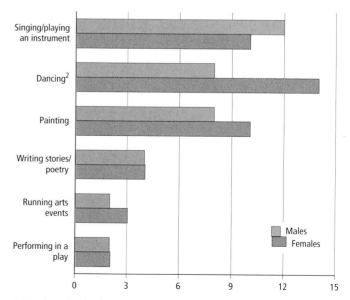

1 Respondents who said that they attend the cinema once a month or more.

Source: Cinema Advertising Association/Cinema and Video Industry Audience Research

Since 2000, the top grossing films at the UK box office have been aimed at the younger audience. In 2003 the top grossing film was *Finding Nemo* (£37 million), in 2002 it was *Harry Potter and the Chamber of Secrets* (£51 million), while in 2001 and 2000 the top films were *Harry Potter and the Philosopher's Stone* (£57 million) and *Toy Story 2* (£44 million) respectively.

In 2002/03 the General Household Survey asked adults in Great Britain about selected activities in the arts in which they had taken part in the four weeks prior to interview. Of those selected activities, the most common activity for men was singing or playing a musical instrument (12 per cent) while for women it was dancing (Figure 13.7). Women were nearly twice as likely as men to have been dancing in the previous four weeks (14 per cent compared with 8 per cent). Dancing was particularly common among young women: 33 per cent of 16 to 19 year olds had been dancing in the previous four weeks. Young people aged 16 to 19 were also more likely than older people to have performed in a play, painted, written a story or poetry, or sung or played a musical instrument.

Use of leisure time for sport and other physical activities is important for a healthy lifestyle. In 2002/03, the overall rate of adult participation in any sport, game or physical activity over a four-week period was 59 per cent (Table 13.8). This was 6 percentage points lower than in 1990/91, but only 2 percentage points lower than in 1987. The biggest

Figure **13.7**

Adult participation[1] in selected arts activities: by sex, 2002/03

Great Britain

Percentages

1 Participating in the four weeks before interview.
2 Excludes fitness classes and aerobics.

Source: General Household Survey, Office for National Statistics

Table **13.8**

Adult participation[1] in a sport, game or physical activity:[2] by age

Great Britain   Percentages

	1987	1990/91	1996/97	2002/03[3]
16–19	86	87	86	77
20–24	77	81	81	69
25–29	74	78	77	70
30–44	71	73	73	67
45–59	56	63	63	59
60–69	47	54	55	50
70 and over	26	31	31	30
All aged 16 and over	61	65	64	59

1 Participating in the four weeks before interview.
2 Includes walking two miles or more for recreational purposes.
3 Data for 2002/03 are weighted.

Source: General Household Survey, Office for National Statistics

decreases in participation between 1990/91 and 2002/03 were among the under 25s, in particular among 20 to 24 year olds. Despite this, 16 to 19 year olds were the most likely of all age groups to participate in any such activity (77 per cent in 2002/03). However, participation rates for those aged 45 and over were higher in 2002/03 than in 1987.

Overall, participation rates in sports, games and other physical activities for men are higher than for women, although the gap between the two has narrowed over the last 15 years. In 1987 there was an 18 percentage point difference, compared with 12 percentage points in 2002/03. Male participation was higher than female participation across all age groups in 2002/03, with the greatest difference in the 25 to 29 age group (79 per cent of males compared with 62 per cent of females).

Walking is the most common physical activity among adults. Over a third of men and women walked two miles or more for recreational purposes at least once in the four weeks before interview in 2002/03 (Table 13.9). This was followed by keep fit or yoga for women and snooker, pool or billiards for men. Swimming and cycling were among the top five activities for both men and women. Compared with other activities, keep fit or yoga and swimming were the most likely to have been done on a regular basis: 8 per cent of adults had done keep fit or yoga approximately once a week and 7 per cent had been swimming once a week. Swimming and keep fit or yoga were the most commonly mentioned activities among those who said they were interested in doing a sport they did not already do.

Table **13.9**

Top ten sports, games and physical activities[1] among adults: by sex, 2002/03

Great Britain   Percentages

	Males		Females
Walking[2]	36	Walking[2]	34
Snooker/pool/billiards	15	Keep fit/yoga	16
Cycling	12	Swimming	15
Swimming	12	Cycling	6
Soccer	10	Snooker/pool/billiards	4
Golf	9	Weight training	3
Weight training	9	Running	3
Keep fit/yoga	7	Tenpin bowling	3
Running	7	Horse riding	2
Tenpin bowling	4	Tennis	2

1 Participation in the four weeks before interview.
2 Walking two miles or more for recreational purposes.

Source: General Household Survey, Office for National Statistics

Use of technology and the Internet

We are living through a historic period of technological change, brought about by the development and the widening application of information and communications technology (ICT). ICT is already an integral part of our daily lives, providing us with useful tools and services in our homes, our workplaces, and elsewhere in the community. Figure 13.10 (overleaf) shows that household ownership of mobile phones in the United Kingdom more than quadrupled between 1996/97 and 2002/03 to 70 per cent. In 2002/03, 45 per cent of households (10.9 million) could access the Internet from home. This was more than four times the proportion in 1998/99. Ownership of other technological goods has also increased. By 2002/03, 55 per cent of households had a home computer and 83 per cent had a CD player. Ownership of DVD players was recorded for the first time in 2002/03 when 31 per cent of households owned one.

Household Internet access varies across the United Kingdom. The highest levels of access in 2002/03 were in London, the South East and the East of England where around 50 per cent of households could connect to the Internet at home, while only around 35 per cent of households in Northern Ireland and Wales could do so (Figure 13.11 overleaf). This partly reflects regional differences in computer ownership. In 2002/03, around 45 per cent of households in Northern Ireland and Wales had a computer compared with around 60 per cent in London, the South East and the East of England.

Figure **13.10**

Households with selected durable goods[1]

United Kingdom
Percentages

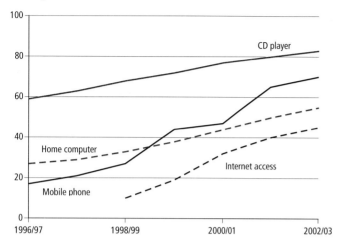

1 Based on weighted data.

Source: Family Expenditure Survey and Expenditure and Food Survey, Office for National Statistics

Levels of Internet access are also related strongly to household income. In 2002/03 only 12 per cent of households in the United Kingdom with gross household income below £123 a week (the lowest income decile group) had access to the Internet. In contrast, 85 per cent of households with gross income of over £1,085 (the highest income decile group) had access. (See analysing income distribution box in Chapter 5 for an explanation of decile groups.)

Figure **13.11**

Households with home access to the Internet: by region, 2002/03

Percentages

Source: Expenditure and Food Survey, Office for National Statistics

According to the ONS Omnibus Survey, 58 per cent of adults in Great Britain had used the Internet in the three months prior to interview in 2003/04. This was a rise of 10 percentage points since 2001/02. Internet usage varies considerably by age, with older people using it less frequently than younger people. However, there has been strong growth in Internet use among those aged 55 and over. Between 2001/02 and 2003/04, the proportion of people in this age group who had used the Internet in the three months prior to interview rose from 18 per cent to 27 per cent. This compares with an increase from 63 per cent to 73 per cent among people aged under 55. In 2003/04, among people aged 55 and over who used the Internet, a considerable proportion used it every day or almost every day (38 per cent), while 10 per cent used it less than once a month.

The most popular Internet activities across all age groups who had used the Internet in the three months prior to interview in 2003/04 were the use of email (84 per cent) and searching for information about goods and services (80 per cent) (Table 13.12). People aged 55 and over were less likely than 16 to 34 year olds to have 'surfed' the Internet, downloaded music or software, read or downloaded online news or purchased over the Internet.

Overall, 37 per cent of all adults, and 69 per cent of those aged 55 and over, had never used the Internet. The majority of people in the 55 and over age group who had not used the Internet said that they did not want or need the Internet, or had no interest in it (57 per cent).

Use of the Internet in the United Kingdom is far higher among children than among adults. According to the UK Children Go Online study, which surveyed 9 to 15 year olds between January and March 2004, 74 per cent of children have ever accessed the Internet via a computer from home and 93 per cent have accessed it at school. Information gathering and school work were their main reasons for use.

Households with children are more likely than those without children to own a computer or have Internet access. In 2004, 87 per cent of children aged 9 to 15 lived in a household with a computer. Of these, 62 per cent lived in a household with one computer, and 38 per cent lived in a household with more than one computer. Twenty three per cent of children had broadband access at home.

There has been much concern about the suitability of some of the material available online for young people and the possible danger of contact with others, both online and in person. Among 9 to 15 year olds in the United Kingdom who went online at least once a week, 72 per cent had visited a chat room, 47 per cent had seen pornography online and

Table **13.12**

Purpose of Internet use: by age,[1] 2003/04

Great Britain   Percentages

	16–34	35–54	55 and over	All adults
Using email	83	84	85	84
Searching for information about goods or services	80	84	74	80
Searching for information about travel and accommodation	63	74	70	69
General browsing or surfing	76	66	49	67
Buying goods, tickets or services	51	52	42	50
Internet banking	34	39	33	36
Activities related specifically to employment	39	37	17	35
Reading or downloading online news	37	34	25	34
Activities related to an education course	38	23	11	28
Playing or downloading music	37	18	12	25
Other educational activities	26	26	18	25
Downloading other software	27	22	18	23
Listening to web radios	20	13	9	15
Other financial services	7	9	9	8

1 Adults who have used the Internet in the last three months.

Source: Omnibus Survey, Office for National Statistics

Figure **13.13**

What 9 to 15 year olds[1] have done on the Internet and their parents' perceptions, January to March 2004

United Kingdom
Percentages

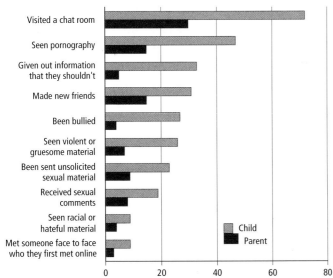

1 All 9 to 15 year olds who use the Internet at least once a week and their parents who were asked 'have you/has your child done these things on the Internet?'

Source: UK Children Go Online, Economic and Social Research Council

33 per cent felt that they had given out information online that they should not have done (Figure 13.13). Parents' perceptions of what their children did online were somewhat different. Only 30 per cent thought that their children had visited chat rooms, 15 per cent thought that their children had seen pornography online and only 5 per cent thought that their children had given out information online that they should not have done. Almost one in three children who used the Internet at least once a week had made new friends online (31 per cent). Nine per cent of children had met someone face to face that they had first met online but only 3 per cent of parents thought their children had done so.

Internet shopping is increasingly popular. In 2003/04 nearly three in ten of all adults in Great Britain had bought or ordered goods and services over the Internet in the three months prior to interview. This was a rise of 9 percentage points since 2001/02. The most popular purchases made by adults in the 12 months prior to interview in 2003/04 were travel, accommodation or holidays (Table 13.14 overleaf). The types of goods and services bought or ordered over the Internet varies between men and women. In general, a higher proportion of men than women use the Internet to purchase goods and services associated with leisure, such as music or CDs, computer software, and videos or DVDs.

Table **13.14**

Types of goods and services adults bought over the Internet,[1] 2003/04

Great Britain   Percentages

	Males	Females	All
Travel, accommodation or holidays	20	15	18
Tickets for events	14	12	13
Books or magazines/e-learning/ training material	14	11	13
Music or CDs	16	10	13
Videos or DVDs	13	9	11
Clothes or sports goods	9	10	10
Household goods	8	7	7
Computer software	10	4	7
Food or groceries	6	7	7
Insurance	8	5	6
Electronic equipment	8	4	6
Computer hardware	9	3	6
Shares or financial services	4	1	3
Subscriptions, access to databases	4	1	2
Other goods and services	5	3	4

1 Adults who had bought goods and services in the 12 months prior to interview for personal and private use as a percentage of all adults aged 16 and over.

Source: Omnibus Survey, Office for National Statistics

Among people who had used the Internet at some time, 39 per cent had never bought anything online. The main reasons for not doing so were preferring to shop in person (29 per cent), or feeling there was no need (26 per cent). In addition, 21 per cent of people who did not buy or order goods and services online said that they had security concerns.

In October 2003 adults in Great Britain who had used the Internet were asked how they felt about giving payment details out over the Internet and telephone. Two fifths (40 per cent) said that they would disclose their payment details over both media, while 26 per cent would only give out their details over the phone rather than the Internet, and 16 per cent would give out their details over the Internet rather than the phone. Thirteen per cent stated they would not give out their details over either medium. The remaining 5 per cent did not have a credit or debit card.

Security on the Internet is becoming a great concern to people who use it. Receiving too many junk emails was the most common security problem reported by 42 per cent of adults who had used the Internet in the 12 months prior to interview in 2003/04. Twenty nine per cent had experienced a computer virus and 19 per cent had received inappropriate or offensive emails.

Holidays and leisure visits

The 2002/03 Great Britain Day Visits Survey collected information on day trips made for leisure purposes from home to locations anywhere in Great Britain. Adults took an estimated 5.2 billion leisure day visits from home in 2002/03, 12 per cent fewer than in 1998 and 9 per cent fewer than in 1996. In 2002/03 the most common activities were to go out for a meal or a drink; walking, hill-walking and rambling; visiting friends and relatives; and shopping (Table 13.15). These have been the four most popular activities since the first survey in 1994. While men were more likely than women to go out for a meal or drink, the reverse was true for visiting friends or relatives. Women were almost twice as likely as men to go on a shopping trip.

There are around 6,500 visitor attractions in the United Kingdom including leisure and theme parks, museums and art galleries, historic houses and castles, and gardens. Among the top tourist attractions in 2003 were Blackpool Pleasure Beach with 6.2 million visitors, the British Museum (4.6 million) and the National Gallery (4.4 million). However, all these attractions were free. The top tourist attraction that charged admission was the British Airways London Eye (3.7 million visitors).

Table **13.15**

Day visits[1] from home: by sex and main activity, 2002/03

Great Britain   Percentages

	Males	Females	All
Eating or drinking out	21	15	18
Walking, hill-walking, rambling	14	16	15
Visiting friends or relatives at their home	12	16	14
Shopping (not food or other essentials)	8	15	11
Taking part in sports or active pursuits	12	6	9
A hobby or special interest	7	8	8
For entertainment	5	5	5
Taking part in informal sports, games, relaxation and wellbeing	4	3	4
Visiting a leisure attraction, place of interest or special event/exhibition	3	4	3
Swimming	2	3	3
Visiting a park or garden	3	3	3
Other[2]	8	5	7
All visits	100	100	100

1 Main activity on a day visit made by adults aged 16 and over.
2 Includes watching live sport, driving, sightseeing, picnicking, pleasure boating, cycling, mountain biking, visiting the beach, sunbathing and paddling in the sea.

Source: Great Britain Day Visits Survey, The Countryside Agency

UK residents took an estimated 91.0 million holidays of one night or more within the United Kingdom in 2003. They also took 41.2 million holidays abroad (Table 13.16), 3 per cent more than in 2002. This continued an unabated rise in overseas holidays over the last three decades from 6.7 million in 1971. UK residents' favourite destinations in 2003 continued to be Spain, which hosted 30 per cent of holidays taken abroad, followed by France (18 per cent). After two years of decline in the number of holidays, the United States experienced a small increase in 2003. It continued to be the most popular non-European holiday destination, accounting for 5 per cent of all holidays.

Social participation

People participate in communities in different ways. High levels of participation are considered to be indicators of healthy and well-functioning communities. Volunteering, either formally or informally, is one way that people can contribute. Formal volunteering involves giving unpaid help to a group, club or organisation. In 2003 the Home Office Citizenship Survey found that 28 per cent of adults in

England volunteered formally at least once a month in the 12 months before interview (around 11.1 million people).

Of those who volunteered formally in 2003, 57 per cent had organised or helped to run an activity or event (Table 13.17). The next most common activity among volunteers was raising or handling money (54 per cent), followed by leading a group or being a member of a committee (40 per cent). The pattern of activities was broadly similar to that found in 2001, though proportions generally fell over the period. Formal volunteers in 2003 were most likely to have been working in sport or exercise (43 per cent). Other common areas were hobbies, recreation, arts and social clubs (40 per cent), and activities relating to children's education and school, and religion (both 37 per cent).

Voting is something that many people consider as their civic duty and, as such, is a way of contributing towards their community. Although there are concerns that some sections of the community, such as young people, are not voting, the majority of people in the United Kingdom use their right to vote in general elections. In the last general election, in 2001, the official turnout was 59 per cent.

Table **13.16**

Holidays[1] abroad: by destination

United Kingdom					Percentages
	1971	1981	1991	2001	2003
Spain[2]	34	22	21	28	30
France	16	27	26	18	18
Greece	5	7	8	8	7
United States	1	6	7	6	5
Italy	9	6	4	4	5
Portugal	3	3	5	4	4
Ireland	..	4	3	4	4
Cyprus	1	1	2	4	3
Netherlands	4	2	4	3	3
Turkey	..	-	1	2	2
Belgium	..	2	2	2	2
Germany	3	3	3	1	1
Austria	6	3	2	1	1
Malta	..	3	2	1	1
Other countries	19	14	12	14	14
All destinations (=100%) (millions)	6.7	13.1	20.8	38.7	41.2

1 A visit made by a UK resident for holiday purposes. Business trips, visits to friends or relatives and other miscellaneous visits are excluded.
2 Excludes the Canary Islands prior to 1981.

Source: International Passenger Survey, Office for National Statistics

Table **13.17**

Type of help given by formal volunteers,[1] 2001 and 2003

England & Wales		Percentages
	2001	2003
Organising or helping to run an activity or event	61	57
Raising or handling money	56	54
Leading a group/being a member of a committee	44	40
Giving other practical help	40	32
Provide transport/driving	31	29
Giving advice/information/counselling	34	28
Secretarial, administrative or clerical work	24	24
Befriending/mentoring people	..	19
Representing	20	16
Campaigning	14	9
Any other help	8	9

1 Adults aged 16 and over who volunteered formally at least once a month in the last 12 months before interview.

Source: Citizenship Survey, Home Office

Since 1979 elections have also been held for the European Parliament. Thirty nine per cent of the UK electorate voted in the 2004 EU election, an increase of 15 percentage points on the previous election in 1999 (Figure 13.18). The large increase is believed to be partly due to combining the local and European elections in many areas of the United Kingdom, and partly due to the low turnout in 1999. This was attributed to the Scottish Parliament, the Welsh Assembly and the local elections being held a short period before the EU election, which led to election fatigue. While the United Kingdom recorded its biggest ever turnout for EU elections in 2004, the EU average reached its lowest point of 46 per cent, having decreased steadily from 63 per cent in 1979. Belgium and Luxembourg had the highest turnout figures in 2004, at 91 and 89 per cent respectively, although voting is mandatory for these countries; Slovakia had the lowest at 17 per cent.

Figure **13.18**

Participation in elections[1] to the EU Parliament

Percentages

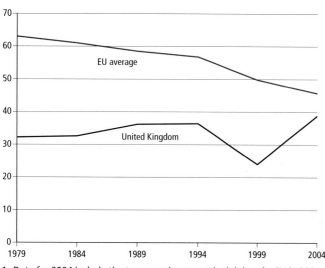

1 Data for 2004 include the ten accession countries joining the EU in 2004.

Source: European Parliament

Religion

Affiliation with a religion is an important part of many people's lives. Many people derive their values and ethical and charitable motivation from faith. In the 2001 Census, 77 per cent of people in Great Britain stated that they had a religion (Table 13.19). Christianity is the main religion with 41 million Christians making up almost three quarters (72 per cent) of the population. Muslims (1.6 million) were the next largest religious group. They made up 3 per cent of the total population of Great Britain and constituted over half (52 per cent) of the non-Christian religious population. Hindus were the second largest non-Christian religious group followed by Sikhs, Jews and Buddhists.

Muslims have the youngest age profile of all the religions in Great Britain. About one third of Muslims were under 16 years of age in 2001, as were one quarter of Sikhs and a fifth of Hindus. Jewish and Christian groups have the oldest age profiles with about one in five being aged 65 years or over.

Table **13.19**

Religion,[1] 2001

Great Britain

	Percentages	Thousands
Christian	71.8	41,015
Muslim	2.8	1,589
Hindu	1.0	558
Sikh	0.6	336
Jewish	0.5	267
Buddhist	0.3	149
Other	0.3	159
Any religion	77.2	44,074
No religion	15.1	8,596
Religion not stated	7.8	4,434

1 The question was voluntary, with tick box options, and asked 'What is your religion?' in the England and Wales Census and 'What religion, religious denomination or body were you brought up in?' in the Scotland Census.

Source: Census, Office for National Statistics; Census, General Register Office for Scotland

Websites and contacts

Chapter 1: Population

Websites

National Statistics
www.statistics.gov.uk

Eurostat
www.europa.eu.int/comm/eurostat

General Register Office for Northern Ireland
www.groni.gov.uk

General Register Office for Scotland
www.gro-scotland.gov.uk

Government Actuary's Department
www.gad.gov.uk

Home Office Immigration and Asylum Statistics
www.homeoffice.gov.uk/rds/immigration1.html

National Assembly for Wales
www.wales.gov.uk/keypubstatisticsforwales

Northern Ireland Statistics and Research Agency
www.nisra.gov.uk

Scottish Executive
www.scotland.gov.uk

The Commonwealth
www.thecommonwealth.org

United Nations
www.unfpa.org

Contacts

Office for National Statistics

Chapter author
020 7533 5778

Internal Migration
01329 813872

International Migration
01329 813255

Labour Market Statistics Helpline
020 7533 6094

Population Estimates General Enquiries
01329 813318

Other organisations

Eurostat
00352 4301 34296

General Register Office for Scotland
0131 314 4254

Government Actuary's Department
020 7211 2622

Home Office
020 8760 8274

Northern Ireland Statistics and Research Agency – General Register Office
028 9025 2020

United Nations Information Centre
020 7630 1981

Welsh Assembly Government
029 2082 5058

Chapter 2: Households and families

Websites

National Statistics
www.statistics.gov.uk

Department of Health
www.dh.gov.uk

ESRC Research Centre for Analysis of Social Exclusion
http://sticerd.lse.ac.uk/case

Eurostat
www.europa.eu.int/comm/eurostat

General Register Office for Northern Ireland
www.groni.gov.uk

General Register Office for Scotland
www.gro-scotland.gov.uk

Home Office
www.homeoffice.gov.uk

Institute for Social and Economic Research
www.iser.essex.ac.uk

National Assembly for Wales
www.wales.gov.uk/keypubstatisticsforwales

National Centre for Social Research
www.natcen.ac.uk

Northern Ireland Statistics and Research Agency
www.nisra.gov.uk

Office of the Deputy Prime Minister
www.odpm.gov.uk

Scottish Executive
www.scotland.gov.uk

Teenage Pregnancy Unit
www.teenagepregnancyunit.gov.uk

Contacts

Office for National Statistics

Chapter author
020 7533 5778

Fertility and Birth Statistics
01329 813758

General Household Survey
020 7533 5444

Labour Market Statistics Helpline
020 7533 6094

Marriages and Divorces
01329 813758

Other organisations

Department of Health – Abortion Statistics
020 7972 5533

ESRC Research Centre for Analysis of Social Exclusion
020 7955 6679

Eurostat
00352 4301 35427

General Register Office for Scotland
0131 314 4243

Home Office – Family Policy Unit
020 7217 8393

Institute for Social and Economic Research
01206 872957

National Centre for Social Research
020 7549 8520

Northern Ireland Statistics and Research Agency – General Register Office
028 9025 2020

Office of the Deputy Prime Minister
020 7944 3303

Welsh Assembly Government
029 2082 5058

Chapter 3: Education and training

Websites

National Statistics
www.statistics.gov.uk

Department for Education and Skills (DfES)
www.dfes.gov.uk

DfES: Research and Statistics Gateway
www.dfes.gov.uk/rsgateway

DfES: Trends in Education and Skills
www.dfes.gov.uk/trends

Higher Education Statistics Agency
www.hesa.ac.uk

Learning and Skills Council
www.lsc.gov.uk

National Assembly for Wales
www.wales.gov.uk/keypubstatisticsforwales

National Centre for Social Research
www.natcen.ac.uk

National Foundation for Educational Research
www.nfer.ac.uk

Northern Ireland Department of Education
www.deni.gov.uk

Northern Ireland Department for Employment and Learning
www.delni.gov.uk

Office for Standards in Education
www.ofsted.gov.uk

Organisation for Economic Co-operation and Development
www.oecd.org

Scottish Executive
www.scotland.gov.uk

Contacts

Office for National Statistics

Chapter author
020 7533 6174

Other organisations

Department for Education and Skills
01325 392754

Northern Ireland Department of Education
028 9127 9279

Northern Ireland Department for Employment and Learning
028 9025 7400

Scottish Executive
0131 244 0442

Welsh Assembly Government
029 2082 3507

Chapter 4: Labour market

Websites

National Statistics
www.statistics.gov.uk

Department of Trade and Industry
www.dti.gov.uk

Department for Work and Pensions
www.dwp.gov.uk

Eurostat
www.europa.eu.int/comm/eurostat

Jobcentre Plus
www.jobcentreplus.gov.uk

Learning and Skills Council
www.lsc.gov.uk

Contacts

Office for National Statistics

Chapter author
020 7533 6174

Labour Market Statistics Helpline
020 7533 6094

Other organisations

Eurostat
00352 4301 33209

Jobcentre Plus (Jobseekers direct)
0845 6060 234

Learning and Skills Council
0870 900 6800

New Deal
0114 209 8227

Chapter 5: Income and wealth

Websites

National Statistics
www.statistics.gov.uk

Department for Education and Skills
www.dfes.gov.uk

Department for International Development
www.dfid.gov.uk

Department for Work and Pensions
www.dwp.gov.uk

EU Statistics UK
www.eustatistics.gov.uk

Eurostat
www.europa.eu.int/comm/eurostat

HM Treasury
www.hm-treasury.gov.uk

Inland Revenue
www.inlandrevenue.gov.uk

Institute for Fiscal Studies
www.ifs.org.uk

Institute for Social and Economic Research
www.iser.essex.ac.uk

National Centre for Social Research
www.natcen.ac.uk

Women and Equality Unit
www.womenandequalityunit.gov.uk

Contacts

Office for National Statistics

Chapter author
020 7533 5757

Annual Survey of Hours and Earnings
01633 819024

Effects of taxes and benefits
020 7533 5770

General Household Survey
020 7533 5444

National accounts
020 7533 5938

New Earnings Survey
01633 819024

Public sector accounts
020 7533 5989

Regional accounts
020 7533 5809

Retail prices index
020 7533 5874

Department for Work and Pensions

Families and Children Study
020 7712 2090

Family Resources Survey
020 7962 8092

Households Below Average Income
020 7962 8232

Individual Income
020 7712 2258

Pensioners' Incomes
020 7962 8975

Other organisations

Department for Education and Skills – Student Income and Expenditure
  Survey (SIES)
020 7925 5057

Department for International Development
01355 843329

Eurostat
00352 4301 35129

EU Statistics UK
01633 813369

Inland Revenue
020 7147 3082

Institute for Fiscal Studies
020 7291 4800

Institute for Social and Economic Research
01206 872957

National Centre for Social Research
020 7250 1866

Chapter 6: Expenditure

Websites

National Statistics
www.statistics.gov.uk

Association for Payment Clearing Services
www.apacs.org.uk

Bank of England
www.bankofengland.co.uk

Department for Work and Pensions
www.dwp.gov.uk

Eurostat
www.europa.eu.int/comm/eurostat

Organisation for Economic Co-operation and Development
www.oecd.org

Contacts

Office for National Statistics

Chapter author
020 7533 5130

Comparative price levels
020 7533 5818

Expenditure and Food Survey
020 7533 5752

Harmonised index of consumer prices
020 7533 5818

Household expenditure
020 7533 5999

Retail prices index
020 7533 5853

Volume of retail sales/retail sales index
01633 812713

Other organisations

Association for Payment Clearing Services
020 7711 6265

Bank of England
020 7601 4878

Department for Trade and Industry
020 7215 3305

Chapter 7: Health

Websites

National Statistics
www.statistics.gov.uk

Department for Environment, Food and Rural Affairs
www.defra.gov.uk

Department of Health
www.dh.gov.uk

Department of Health, Social Services and Public Safety,
  Northern Ireland
www.dhsspsni.gov.uk

Eurostat
www.europa.eu.int/comm/eurostat

General Register Office for Northern Ireland
www.groni.gov.uk

General Register Office for Scotland
www.gro-scotland.gov.uk

Government Actuary's Department
www.gad.gov.uk

Health Protection Agency
www.hpa.org.uk

Information Services Division (NHS Scotland)
www.isdscotland.org

National Assembly for Wales
www.wales.gov.uk/keypubstatisticsforwales

National Centre for Social Research
www.natcen.ac.uk

Northern Ireland Cancer Registry
www.qub.ac.uk/nicr

Northern Ireland Statistics and Research Agency
www.nisra.gov.uk

Scottish Executive
www.scotland.gov.uk

Welsh Cancer Intelligence and Surveillance Unit
www.velindre-tr.wales.nhs.uk/wcisu

Contacts

Office for National Statistics

Chapter author
020 7533 5081

Cancer statistics
020 7533 5230

Condom use
020 7533 5391

General Household Survey
020 7533 5444

General Practice Research Database
020 7533 5240

Life expectancy by social class
020 7533 5186

Mortality statistics
01329 813758

Psychiatric Morbidity Survey
020 7533 5305

Sudden Infant Death Syndrome
020 7533 5198

Department of Health

Health Survey for England
020 7972 5718/5660

Immunisation and cancer screening
020 7972 5533

Prescription Cost Analysis
020 7972 5515

Smoking, misuse of alcohol and drugs
020 7972 1724

Other organisations

Department for Environment, Food and Rural Affairs – Expenditure and Food Survey
01904 455077

Department of Health, Social Services and Public Safety, Northern Ireland
028 9052 2800

Eurostat
00352 4301 32056

General Register Office for Northern Ireland
028 9025 2031

General Register Office for Scotland
0131 314 4227

Government Actuary's Department
020 7211 2635

Health Protection Agency
020 8200 6868

Home Office
020 7273 2084

National Centre for Social Research
020 7250 1866

NHS National Services Scotland, Information Services Division
0131 275 7777

Northern Ireland Cancer Registry
028 9026 3136

Northern Ireland Statistics and Research Agency – Continuous Household Survey
028 9034 8243

Welsh Assembly Government
029 2082 5080

Welsh Cancer Intelligence and Surveillance Unit
029 2037 3500

Chapter 8: Social protection

Websites

National Statistics
www.statistics.gov.uk

Charities Aid Foundation
www.cafonline.org

Department of Health
www.dh.gov.uk/publicationsandstatistics/statistics

Department of Health, Social Services and Public Safety, Northern Ireland
www.dhsspsni.gov.uk/stats&research

Department for Education and Skills
www.dfes.gov.uk

Department for Social Development, Northern Ireland
www.dsdni.gov.uk

Department for Work and Pensions
www.dwp.gov.uk/asd/statistics.asp

ESRC Centre for Longitudinal Studies
www.cls.ioe.ac.uk/Cohort/MCS/mcsmain

Eurostat
www.europa.eu.int/comm/eurostat

Government Actuary's Department
www.gad.gov.uk

Local Government Data Unit – Wales
www.dataunitwales.gov.uk

National Assembly for Wales
www.wales.gov.uk/keypubstatisticsforwales

NHS in Scotland
www.show.scot.nhs.uk/isd

Northern Ireland Statistics and Research Agency
www.nisra.gov.uk

Scottish Executive
www.scotland.gov.uk

The National Centre for Social Research
www.natcen.ac.uk

Contacts

Office for National Statistics

Chapter author
020 7533 5778

General Household Survey
020 7533 5444

Labour Force Survey
020 7533 6094

Department for Education and Skills

Children's social services
020 7925 3804

Day care for children
01325 392827

Department for Work and Pensions

Family Resources Survey
020 7962 8092

Number of benefit recipients
0191 225 7373

Department of Health

Acute services activity
0113 254 5522

Adult social services
020 7972 5582

Community and cross-sector services
020 7972 5524

General dental and community dental service
020 7972 5398

General medical services statistics
0113 254 6411

Hospital Episode Statistics
020 7972 5529

Mental illness/handicap
020 7972 5546

NHS expenditure
0113 254 6012

NHS medical staff
0113 254 5892

NHS non-medical manpower
0113 254 5744

Non-psychiatric hospital activity
020 7972 5529

Personal social services expenditure
020 7972 5595

Residential care and home help
020 7972 5582

Social services staffing and finance data
020 7972 5595

Department of Health, Social Services and Public Safety, Northern Ireland

Health and personal social services activity
028 9052 2800

Health and personal social services manpower
028 9052 2468

Scottish Executive

Adult community care
0131 244 3777

Children's social services
0131 244 3551

Social work staffing
0131 244 3740

Other organisations

Charities Aid Foundation
01732 520000

Department for Social Development, Northern Ireland
028 9052 2280

ESRC Centre for Longitudinal Studies – Millennium Cohort Study
020 7612 6874

Eurostat
00352 4301 34122

Local Government Data Unit – Wales
029 2090 9500

National Health Service in Scotland
0131 551 8899

Northern Ireland Statistics and Research Agency
028 9034 8246

Welsh Assembly Government
029 2082 5080

Chapter 9: Crime and justice

Websites

National Statistics
www.statistics.gov.uk

Community Legal Service
www.clsdirect.org.uk

Court Service
www.courtservice.gov.uk

Crime Statistics for England and Wales
www.crimestatistics.org.uk

Crown Office and Procurator Fiscal
www.crownoffice.gov.uk

Crown Prosecution Service
www.cps.gov.uk

Department for Constitutional Affairs
www.dca.gov.uk

Home Office
www.homeoffice.gov.uk

Home Office (Criminal Justice System)
www.cjsonline.org

Legal Services Commission
www.legalservices.gov.uk

National Assembly for Wales
www.wales.gov.uk/keypubstatisticsforwales

Northern Ireland Court Service
www.courtsni.gov.uk

Northern Ireland Office
www.nio.gov.uk

Northern Ireland Prison Service
www.niprisonservice.gov.uk

Police Service of Northern Ireland
www.psni.police.uk

Police Services of the United Kingdom
www.police.uk

Prison Service for England and Wales
www.hmprisonservice.gov.uk

Scottish Executive
www.scotland.gov.uk

Scottish Prison Service
www.sps.gov.uk

The Bar Council
www.barcouncil.org.uk

Contacts

Office for National Statistics

Chapter author
020 7533 5776

Other organisations

Department for Constitutional Affairs
020 7210 8500

Home Office
0870 000 1585

Northern Ireland Office
028 9052 7538

Police Service of Northern Ireland
028 9065 0222 ext. 24865

Scottish Executive Justice Department
0131 244 2228

Welsh Assembly Government
029 2080 1388

Chapter 10: Housing

Websites

National Statistics
www.statistics.gov.uk

Council of Mortgage Lenders
www.cml.org.uk

Court Service
www.courtservice.gov.uk

Department for Social Development, Northern Ireland
www.dsdni.gov.uk

Department for Work and Pensions
www.dwp.gov.uk

Eurostat
www.europa.eu.int/comm/eurostat

Land Registry
www.landreg.gov.uk

National Assembly for Wales
www.wales.gov.uk/keypubstatisticsforwales

Northern Ireland Statistics and Research Agency
www.nisra.gov.uk

Office of the Deputy Prime Minister
www.odpm.gov.uk

Scottish Executive
www.scotland.gov.uk

Social Exclusion Unit
www.socialexclusionunit.gov.uk

Contacts

Office for National Statistics

Chapter author
020 7533 5081

Expenditure and Food Survey
020 7533 5754

General Household Survey
020 7533 5444

Office of the Deputy Prime Minister

Housing Data and Statistics
020 7944 3317

Planning and Land Use Statistics
020 7944 5533

Other organisations

Council of Mortgage Lenders
020 7440 2251

Court Service
020 7210 1773

Department for Social Development, Northern Ireland
028 9052 2762

Department for Work and Pensions – Family Resources Survey
020 7962 8092

Eurostat
00352 4301 32056

Land Registry
0151 473 6008

Northern Ireland Statistics and Research Agency
028 9034 8243

Scottish Executive
0131 244 7236

Welsh Assembly Government
029 2082 5063

Chapter 11: Environment

Websites

National Statistics
www.statistics.gov.uk

Centre for Ecology and Hydrology, Wallingford
www.ceh-nerc.ac.uk

Department for Environment, Food and Rural Affairs
www.defra.gov.uk/environment/index.htm

Department of the Environment Northern Ireland (DOE NI)
www.doeni.gov.uk

Department of Trade and Industry
www.dti.gov.uk/energy/index.htm

Environment Agency
www.environment-agency.gov.uk

Environment and Heritage Service (DOE NI)
www.ehsni.gov.uk

European Environment Agency
www.eea.eu.int

Eurostat
www.europa.eu.int/comm/eurostat

Forestry Commission
www.forestry.gov.uk/statistics

Joint Nature Conservation Committee
www.jncc.gov.uk

National Assembly for Wales
www.wales.gov.uk/keypubstatisticsforwales

Northern Ireland Statistics and Research Agency
www.nisra.gov.uk

Office of the Deputy Prime Minister
www.odpm.gov.uk/planning/statistics

Scottish Environment Protection Agency
www.sepa.org.uk

Scottish Executive
www.scotland.gov.uk

Contacts

Office for National Statistics

Chapter author
020 7533 5283

Other organisations

Centre for Ecology and Hydrology
01491 838800

Department for Environment, Food and Rural Affairs
020 7082 8608

Department of the Environment Northern Ireland
028 9054 0540

Department of the Environment Northern Ireland – Environment and Heritage Service
028 9023 5000

Department of Trade and Industry
020 7215 2697

Environment Agency
0845 9333 111

European Environment Agency
0045 3336 7100

Eurostat
00352 4301 33023

Forestry Commission
0131 314 6337

Joint Nature Conservation Committee
01733 562626

Office of the Deputy Prime Minister
020 7944 5534

Scottish Environment Protection Agency
01786 457700

Scottish Executive
0131 244 0445

Welsh Assembly Government
029 2082 5111

Chapter 12: Transport

Websites

National Statistics
www.statistics.gov.uk

Civil Aviation Authority Economic Regulation Group
www.caaerg.co.uk

Department for Transport
www.dft.gov.uk/transtat

Department of the Environment Northern Ireland
www.doeni.gov.uk

Department of Trade and Industry
www.dti.gov.uk

European Commission Directorate-General for Energy and Transport
http://europa.eu.int/comm/dgs/energy_transport/index_en.html

National Centre for Social Research
www.natcen.ac.uk

Scottish Executive
www.scotland.gov.uk

Strategic Rail Authority
www.sra.gov.uk

Contacts

Office for National Statistics

Chapter author
020 7533 5283

Census Customer Services
01329 813800

Expenditure and Food Survey
020 7533 5755

Household expenditure
020 7533 6001

International Passenger Survey
020 7533 5765

Retail prices index
020 7533 5874

Department for Transport

General Enquiries
020 7944 8300

National Travel Survey
020 7944 3097

Civil Aviation Authority Economic Regulation Group
020 7453 6213

Other organisations

Department of Trade and Industry
020 7215 5000

Department of the Environment Northern Ireland
028 9054 0540

Driving Standards Agency
0115 901 2852

National Centre for Social Research
020 7250 1866

Police Service of Northern Ireland
028 9065 0222 ext. 24135

Scottish Executive
0131 244 7255/7256

Strategic Rail Authority
020 7654 6072

Chapter 13: Lifestyles and social participation

Websites

National Statistics
www.statistics.gov.uk

British Market Research Bureau
www.bmrb.co.uk

Cinema Advertising Association
www.carltonscreen.com

Department for Culture, Media and Sport
www.culture.gov.uk

European Parliament (UK Office)
www.europarl.org.uk

Home Office
www.homeoffice.gov.uk

IPF Market Research Unit
www.ipfmarketresearch.net

National Reading Campaign
www.readon.org.uk

Ofcom
www.ofcom.org.uk

Pearl and Dean
www.pearlanddean.com

RAJAR
www.rajar.co.uk

Sport England
www.sportengland.org

StarUK (statistics from the National Tourist Boards)
www.staruk.org.uk

The Countryside Agency
www.countryside.gov.uk

UK Children Go Online
www.children-go-online.net

VisitBritain
www.visitbritain.com

Contacts

Office for National Statistics

Chapter author
020 7533 5776

Expenditure and Food Survey
020 7533 5755

General Household Survey
020 7533 5444

International Passenger Survey
020 7533 5765

Omnibus Survey
020 7533 5329

UK 2000 Time Use Survey
020 7533 5468

Other organisations

British Broadcasting Corporation
020 7765 1064

Cinema Advertising Association
020 7534 6363

Department for Culture, Media and Sport
020 7211 6200

European Parliament (UK Office)
020 7227 4300

Home Office
0870 000 1585

National Centre for Social Research
020 7250 1866

Northern Ireland Statistics and Research Agency
028 9034 8246

The Countryside Agency
01242 521381

VisitBritain
020 8846 9000

References and further reading

From January 2005 Office for National Statistics (ONS) products published by TSO are now available from Palgrave Macmillan. Many can also be found on the National Statistics website: www.statistics.gov.uk

General

Regional Trends, (ONS), TSO

Focus on Ethnicity and Identity, Internet only publication, ONS: www.statistics.gov.uk/focuson/ethnicity

Focus on Gender, Internet only publication, ONS: www.statistics.gov.uk/focuson/gender

Focus on Health, Internet only publication, ONS: www.statistics.gov.uk/focuson/health

Focus on Older People, Internet only publication, ONS: www.statistics.gov.uk/focuson/olderpeople

Focus on People and Migration, Internet only publication, ONS: www.statistics.gov.uk/focuson/migration

Focus on Religion, Internet only publication, ONS: www.statistics.gov.uk/focuson/religion

Focus on Social Inequalities, (ONS), TSO, also available at: www.statistics.gov.uk/focuson/social inequalities

Focus on Wales: Its People, Internet only publication, ONS: www.statistics.gov.uk/focuson/wales

Ffocws ar Gymru: Ei Phobl, Internet only publication, ONS: www.statistics.gov.uk/focuson/cymru

UK 2005: The Official Yearbook of the United Kingdom of Great Britain and Northern Ireland, Palgrave Macmillan

Chapter 1: Population

Annual Abstract of Statistics, Palgrave Macmillan

Annual Report of the Registrar General for Northern Ireland, Palgrave Macmillan

Annual Report of the Registrar General for Scotland, General Register Office for Scotland

Asylum Statistics – United Kingdom, Home Office

Birth Statistics, England and Wales (Series FM1), Internet only publication, ONS: www.statistics.gov.uk/statbase/Product.asp?vlnk=5768

Census 2001: First results on population for England and Wales, (ONS), TSO

Control of Immigration: Statistics, United Kingdom, TSO

European Social Statistics – Population, Eurostat

Health Statistics Quarterly, Palgrave Macmillan

International Migration Statistics (Series MN), Internet only publication, ONS: www.statistics.gov.uk/statbase/Product.asp?vlnk=507

Key Population and Vital Statistics (Series VS/PP1), (ONS), TSO

Mid-year Population Estimates, Northern Ireland, Northern Ireland Statistics and Research Agency

Mid-year Population Estimates, Scotland, General Register Office for Scotland

Mid-year Population Estimates for England and Wales, Internet only publication, ONS: www.statistics.gov.uk/statbase/product.asp?vlnk=601

Migration Statistics, Eurostat

Mortality Statistics for England and Wales (Series DH1 2,3,4), Internet only publications, ONS: www.statistics.gov.uk/statbase/Product.asp?vlnk=620 www.statistics.gov.uk/statbase/Product.asp?vlnk=618 www.statistics.gov.uk/statbase/Product.asp?vlnk=6305 www.statistics.gov.uk/statbase/Product.asp?vlnk=621

National Population Projections, UK (Series PP2), TSO

Patterns and Trends in International Migration in Western Europe, Eurostat

Persons Granted British Citizenship – United Kingdom, Home Office

Population and Projections for areas within Northern Ireland, Northern Ireland Statistics and Research Agency

Population Projections, Scotland (for Administrative Areas), General Register Office for Scotland

Population Projections for Wales (sub-national), National Assembly for Wales/Welsh Office

Population Trends, Palgrave Macmillan

Chapter 2: Households and families

Abortion Statistics (Series AB), TSO (to 2001)

Abortion Statistics Statistical Bulletin, Department of Health (from 2002)

Annual Report of the Registrar General for Northern Ireland, TSO

Annual Report of the Registrar General for Scotland, General Register Office for Scotland

Attitudes towards ideal family size of different ethnic/nationality groups in Great Britain, France and Germany, *Population Trends* 108, Penn R and Lambert P, Palgrave Macmillan

Birth Statistics, England and Wales, (Series FM1), Internet only publication, ONS: www.statistics.gov.uk/statbase/Product.asp?vlnk=5768

Birth Statistics: Historical Series, 1837–1983 (Series FM1), TSO

British Social Attitudes, National Centre for Social Research

Choosing Childlessness, Family Policy Studies Centre

European Social Statistics – Population, Eurostat

General Household Survey 2003/04, Internet only publication, ONS: www.statistics.gov.uk/ghs/

Health Statistics Quarterly, Palgrave Macmillan

Key Population and Vital Statistics (Series VS/PP1), (ONS), TSO

Marriage and Divorce Statistics 1837–1983 (Series FM2), (ONS), TSO

Marriage, Divorce and Adoption Statistics, England and Wales, (Series FM2), Internet only publication, ONS: www.statistics.gov.uk/statbase/Product.asp?vlnk=581

Population Trends, Palgrave Macmillan

Projections of Households in England to 2021, Office of the Deputy Prime Minister

Recent Demographic Developments in Europe, Council of Europe

Survey of English Housing: Housing in England 2000/01, TSO

Teenage Pregnancy, Report by the Social Exclusion Unit, TSO

The British Population, Oxford University Press

Chapter 3: Education and training

Education at a Glance, OECD Indicators 2004, Organisation for Economic Co-operation and Development, 2004

Knowledge and Skills for Life, Organisation for Economic Co-operation and Development, 2001

Learning and Training at Work 2002, IFF Research Ltd, for the Department for Education and Skills, Research Report 399, 2003, TSO

National Adult Learning Survey 2002, National Centre for Social Research, for the Department for Education and Skills, Research Report 415, 2003, TSO

National Employers Skills Survey 2003, Learning and Skills Council, 2004

Reading All Over the World: PIRLS National Report for England, National Foundation for Educational Research, 2003

Statistical Volume: Education and Training Statistics for the United Kingdom, Department for Education and Skills, 2004, TSO

Statistical Volume: Statistics of Education: Schools in England, Department for Education and Skills, 2004, TSO

Chapter 4: Labour market

British Social Attitudes, National Centre for Social Research

European Social Statistics – Labour Force Survey Results, Eurostat

Factors affecting the labour market participation of older workers, Department for Work and Pensions

How Exactly is Unemployment Measured?, ONS: www.statistics.gov.uk/statbase/Product.asp?vlnk=2054

Labour Force Survey Historical Supplement, ONS: www.statistics.gov.uk/statbase/Product.asp?vlnk=11771

Labour Force Survey Quarterly Supplement, ONS: www.statistics.gov.uk/statbase/Product.asp?vlnk=545

Labour Market Trends, Palgrave Macmillan

National Employers Skills Survey 2003, Learning and Skills Council

Northern Ireland Labour Force Survey, Department of Enterprise, Trade and Investment, Northern Ireland

Results of the first flexible working employee survey, Department of Trade and Industry

The State of the Labour Market, ONS

Trade Union Membership 2003, Department of Trade and Industry

What exactly is the Labour Force Survey?, ONS: www.statistics.gov.uk/statbase/Product.asp?vlnk=4756

Chapter 5: Income and wealth

British Social Attitudes, National Centre for Social Research

Changing Households: The British Household Panel Survey, Institute for Social and Economic Research

Distribution of Income and Wealth 1975; report by Royal Commission, quoted in book by Atkinson A B and Harrison A J, *Distribution of Personal Wealth in Britain*, Cambridge University Press 1978, Table 6.1

Economic Trends, Palgrave Macmillan

European Community Finances: Statement on the 2004 EC Budget and Measures to Counter Fraud and Financial Mismanagement, TSO

Eurostat National Accounts ESA, Eurostat

Family Resources Survey, Department for Work and Pensions

Fiscal Studies, Institute for Fiscal Studies

For Richer, For Poorer, Institute for Fiscal Studies

Households Below Average Income, 1994/95–2002/03, Department for Work and Pensions

Income and Wealth. The Latest Evidence, Joseph Rowntree Foundation

Individual Incomes 1996/97–2002/03, Women and Equality Unit

Inequality and two decades of British tax and benefit reforms (2004), Fiscal Studies, vol. 25, pp. 129–58, by Clark T and Leicester A

Inland Revenue Statistics, Inland Revenue

Labour Market Trends, Palgrave Macmillan

Low/moderate-income Families in Britain: Changes in 1999 and 2000, Marsh A and Rowlingson K, Research Report, Department for Work and Pensions

Monitoring Poverty and Social Exclusion, Joseph Rowntree Foundation

New Earnings Survey, Internet only publication, ONS: www.statistics.gov.uk/statbase/Product.asp?vlnk=5750

Poverty and Inequality in Britain: 2004, Commentary no. 96, by Brewer M, Goodman A, Myck M, Shaw J and Shephard A, London: Institute for Fiscal Studies

Poverty and Social Exclusion in Britain, 2000, Joseph Rowntree Foundation

Savings and life events, Department for Work and Pensions, Research Report 194 (2003) by McKay S and Kempson E

Social Security, Departmental Report, TSO

Social Security Statistics, TSO

The Distribution of Wealth in the UK, Institute for Fiscal Studies

The Pensioners' Incomes Series, Department for Work and Pensions

United Kingdom National Accounts (The Blue Book), (ONS), TSO

Chapter 6: Expenditure

Characteristics of Families in Debt and the Nature of Indebtedness, Department for Work and Pensions

Consumer Price Indices – A Brief Guide, Internet only publication, ONS: www.statistics.gov.uk/statbase/product.asp?vlnk=62

Consumer Trends, Internet only publication, ONS: www.statistics.gov.uk/consumertrends

Economic Trends, Palgrave Macmillan

Family Spending, (ONS), TSO

Financial Statistics, Palgrave Macmillan

Focus on Consumer Price Indices, Internet only publication, ONS: www.statistics.gov.uk/statbase/Product.asp?vlnk=867

Harmonised Index of Consumer Prices: Historical Estimates, *Economic Trends*, No. 541

In Brief 2003, Payment Markets Briefing, Association for Payment Clearing Services

The new inflation target: the statistical perspective, *Economic Trends*, No. 602

United Kingdom National Accounts (The Blue Book), (ONS), TSO

Chapter 7: Health

Alcohol Harm Reduction Strategy for England, The Cabinet Office

Annual Report of the Registrar General for Northern Ireland, Northern Ireland Statistics and Research Agency

Annual Report of the Registrar General for Scotland, General Register Office for Scotland

Annual Review of the Registrar General on deaths in England and Wales, TSO

Cancer Trends in England and Wales 1950–1999, (ONS), TSO

Community Statistics, Department of Health, Social Services and Public Safety, Northern Ireland

General Household Survey 2003/04, Internet only publication, ONS: www.statistics.gov.uk/ghs/

Geographic Variations in Health, (ONS), TSO

Health in Scotland. The Annual Report of the Chief Medical Officer on the State of Scotland's Health, Scottish Executive

Health Statistics Quarterly, Palgrave Macmillan

Health Statistics Wales, National Assembly for Wales

Health Survey for England, TSO

Key Health Statistics from General Practice 1998, ONS

Mortality Statistics for England and Wales (Series DH1 2,3,4) Internet only publications, ONS:
www.statistics.gov.uk/statbase/Product.asp?vlnk=620
www.statistics.gov.uk/statbase/Product.asp?vlnk=618
www.statistics.gov.uk/statbase/Product.asp?vlnk=6305
www.statistics.gov.uk/statbase/Product.asp?vlnk=621

On the State of the Public Health – The Annual Report of the Chief Medical Officer of the Department of Health, TSO

Population Trends, Palgrave Macmillan

Psychiatric Morbidity Survey Among Adults Living in Private Households 2000, (ONS), TSO

Report of the Chief Medical Officer, Department of Health, Social Services and Public Safety, Northern Ireland

Results of the ICD-10 bridge coding study, England and Wales, 1999, *Health Statistics Quarterly* 14, Palgrave Macmillan

Scottish Health Statistics, Information Services Division, NHS Scotland

Smoking, Drinking and Drug Use among Young People in 2003, Department of Health

Smoking Kills – A White Paper on Tobacco, TSO

Statistical Publications on Aspects of Health and Personal Social Services Activity in England (various), Department of Health

Welsh Health: Annual Report of the Chief Medical Officer, National Assembly for Wales

World Health Statistics, World Health Organisation

Chapter 8: Social protection

Annual News Releases (various), Scottish Executive

British Social Attitudes, National Centre for Social Research

Charity Trends, Charities Aid Foundation

Chief Executive's Report to the NHS, Department of Health

Children's social service statistics, Department for Education and Skills

Community Statistics for Northern Ireland, Department of Health, Social Services and Public Safety, Northern Ireland

Continuous Household Survey, Northern Ireland Statistics and Research Agency

ESSPROS Manual 1996, Eurostat

Family Resources Survey, Department for Work and Pensions

General Household Survey 2003/04, Internet only publication, ONS: www.statistics.gov.uk/ghs/

Health, wealth and lifestyles of the older population in England: The 2002 English Longitudinal Study of Ageing, Lessof C and Nazroo J, The Institute of Fiscal Studies

Health and Personal Social Services Statistics, Department of Health

Health Statistics Wales, National Assembly for Wales

Hospital Activity Statistics, Department of Health

Hospital Episode Statistics for England, Department of Health

Hospital Statistics for Northern Ireland, Department of Health, Social Services and Public Safety, Northern Ireland

Millennium Cohort Study First Survey: A User's Guide to Initial Findings, ESRC Centre for Longitudinal Studies

Occupational Pension Schemes 2000, Government Actuary's Department

Scottish Community Care Statistics, Scottish Executive

Scottish Health Statistics, National Health Service in Scotland, Common Services Agency

Social Protection Expenditure and Receipts, Eurostat

Social Security Departmental Report, TSO

Social Services Statistics Wales, Local Government Data Unit – Wales

Statistical Publications on Aspects of Community Care in Scotland (various), Scottish Executive Health Department

Statistical Publications on Aspects of Health and Personal Social Services Activity in England (various), Department of Health

Work and Pension Statistics, Department for Work and Pensions

Chapter 9: Crime and justice

A Commentary on Northern Ireland Crime Statistics, TSO

Civil Judicial Statistics Scotland (2001), TSO

Costs, Sentencing Profiles and the Scottish Criminal Justice System, Scottish Executive

Crime and the Quality of Life: Public Perceptions and Experiences of Crime in Scotland, Scottish Executive

Crime in England and Wales 2003/04, Home Office

Criminal Statistics, England and Wales 2003, TSO

Crown Prosecution Service, Annual Report 2003/04, TSO

Digest 4: Information on the Criminal Justice System in England and Wales, Home Office

Digest of Information on the Northern Ireland Criminal Justice System 3, TSO

HM Prison Service Annual Report and Accounts, TSO

Home Office Departmental Report 2004, TSO

Home Office Research Findings, Home Office

Home Office Statistical Bulletins, Home Office

Judicial Statistics, England and Wales, TSO

Legal Services Commission Annual Report 2003/04, TSO

Northern Ireland Judicial Statistics, Northern Ireland Court Service

Police Statistics, England and Wales, CIPFA

Prison Statistics, England and Wales 2002, TSO

Prison Statistics Scotland 2003, Scottish Executive

Prisons in Scotland Report, TSO

Race and the Criminal Justice System, Home Office

Record crime in Scotland 2003, Scottish Executive

Report of the Chief Constable 2003–04, Police Service of Northern Ireland

Report of the Parole Board for England and Wales, TSO

Report on the work of the Northern Ireland Prison Service, TSO

Review of Crime Statistics: a Discussion Document, Home Office

Review of Police Forces' Crime Recording Practices, Home Office

Scottish Crime Survey, Scottish Executive

Scottish Executive Statistical Bulletins: Criminal Justice Series, Scottish Executive

Statistical Report 2003/04, Police Service of Northern Ireland

Statistics on Women and the Criminal Justice System, Home Office

The Criminal Justice System in England and Wales, Home Office

The Work of the Prison Service, TSO

Chapter 10: Housing

A Review of Flexible Mortgages, Council of Mortgage Lenders

Becoming a Home-owner in Britain in the 1990s – The British Household Panel Survey, ESRC Institute for Social and Economic Research

Bringing Britain Together: A National Strategy for Neighbourhood Renewal, Social Exclusion Unit, Cabinet Office

Changing Households: The British Household Panel Survey, Institute for Social and Economic Research

Divorce, Remarriage and Housing: The Effects of Divorce, Remarriage, Separation and the Formation of New Couple Households on the Number of Separate Households and Housing Demand Conditions, Department of the Environment, Transport and the Regions

English House Condition Survey 2001, TSO

General Household Survey 2003/04, Internet only publication, ONS: www.statistics.gov.uk/ghs/

Housing Finance, Council of Mortgage Lenders

Housing in England: Survey of English Housing, TSO Housing Statistics, TSO

Living conditions in Europe – Statistical Pocketbook, Eurostat

Local Housing Statistics, TSO

My Home Was My Castle: Evictions and Repossessions in Britain, ESRC Institute of Social and Economic Research and Institute Local Research

Northern Ireland House Condition Survey, Northern Ireland Housing Executive

Northern Ireland Housing Statistics, 2003/04, Department for Social Development, Northern Ireland

Office of the Deputy Prime Minister, Annual Report 2004, TSO

On the Move: The Housing Consequences Migration, YPS

Private Renting in England, TSO

Private Renting in Five Localities, TSO

Projections of Households in England to 2021, TSO

Scotland's People: Results from the 1999 Scottish Household Survey, TSO

Scottish House Condition Survey 2002, Communities Scotland

Statistical Bulletins on Housing, Scottish Executive

Statistics on Housing in the European Community, Eurostat

The Social Situation in the European Union, Eurostat

Welsh House Condition Survey 1998, National Assembly for Wales

Welsh Housing Statistics, National Assembly for Wales

Chapter 11: Environment

Accounting for Nature: Assessing Habitats in the UK Countryside, Department for Environment, Food and Rural Affairs

Achieving a Better Quality of Life, 2003, Department for Environment, Food and Rural Affairs

Agriculture in the United Kingdom 2003, TSO

Air Quality Strategy for England, Scotland, Wales and Northern Ireland, TSO

Air Quality Strategy for England, Scotland, Wales and Northern Ireland: Addendum, Department for Environment, Food and Rural Affairs

Bathing Water Quality in England and Wales, TSO

Biodiversity: The UK Action Plan, TSO

Digest of United Kingdom Energy Statistics, TSO

e-Digest of Environmental Statistics, Internet only publication, Department for Environment, Food and Rural Affairs: www.defra.gov.uk/environment/statistics/index.htm

Forestry Facts and Figures 2004, Forestry Commission

Forestry Statistics 2004, Forestry Commission

GM Nation. The Findings of the Public Debate, Department for Environment, Food and Rural Affairs

General Quality Assessment, Environment Agency

Hydrological Summaries for the United Kingdom, Centre for Hydrology and British Geological Survey

Land Use Change Statistics, Office of the Deputy Prime Minister

Municipal Waste Management Survey, Department for Environment, Food and Rural Affairs

OECD Environmental Data Compendium, OECD

Organic Statistics, Department for Environment, Food and Rural Affairs

Planning Public Water Supplies, Environment Agency

Pollution Incidents in England and Wales, 2002, Environment Agency

Quality of life counts – indicators for a strategy for sustainable development for the United Kingdom: a baseline assessment, Department of the Environment, Transport and the Regions

Scottish Environment Protection Agency Annual Report 2001–2002, SEPA

Survey of Public Attitudes to Quality of Life and to the Environment - 2001, Department for Environment, Food and Rural Affairs

Sustainable Development Indicators in your Pocket 2004, Department for Environment, Food and Rural Affairs

The Environment in your Pocket, Department for Environment, Food and Rural Affairs

Chapter 12: Transport

A New Deal for Transport: Better for Everyone, TSO

A Strategy for Sustainable Development for the United Kingdom, TSO

Annual Report, Central Rail Users Consultative Committee

British Social Attitudes, National Centre for Social Research

Driving Standards Agency Annual Report and Accounts, TSO

European Union Energy and Transport in Figures, 2002, European Commission

Focus on Personal Travel, TSO

Focus on Public Transport, TSO

International Passenger Transport, TSO

National Rail Trends, Strategic Rail Authority

National Travel Survey Bulletins, Department for Transport

Rail Complaints, Office of the Rail Regulator

Road Casualties Great Britain – Annual Report, TSO

Road Accidents, Scotland, Scottish Executive

Road Accidents: Wales, National Assembly for Wales

Road Traffic Accident Statistics Annual Report, Police Service of Northern Ireland

Road Traffic Statistics Great Britain, Department for Transport

Scottish Transport Statistics, Scottish Executive

Transport Statistical Bulletins, Scottish Executive

Transport Statistics Bulletins and Reports, Department for Transport

Transport Statistics Great Britain, TSO

Transport Trends, TSO

Travel Trends, (ONS), TSO

Vehicle Licensing Statistics, Department for Transport

Vehicle Speeds in Great Britain, Department for Transport

Welsh Transport Statistics, National Assembly for Wales

Chapter 13: Lifestyles and social participation

2003 Home Office Citizenship Survey: people families and communities, Home Office

Annual Report of Department for Culture, Media and Sport, TSO

Arts in England and Wales: Attendance, Participation and Attitudes in 2001, Arts Council of England

BBC Annual Reports and Accounts, BBC

British Social Attitudes, National Centre for Social Research

Cinema and Video Industry Audience Research, CAA

GB Leisure Day Visits 2002/03, The Countryside Agency

General Household Survey 2003/04, Internet only publication, ONS: www.statistics.gov.uk/ghs/

Public Library User Surveys, The Institute of Public Finance (IPF) Limited, Market Research Unit

Sport and leisure – Results from the sport and leisure module of the 2002 General Household Survey, (ONS), TSO, also available at: www.statistics.gov.uk/lib2002/

The 2004 European Parliamentary Elections in the United Kingdom, Electoral Commmision

The UK Tourist: Statistics, English Tourism Council, VisitScotland, Wales Tourist Board and Northern Ireland Tourist Board

Travel Trends, (ONS), TSO

UK 2000 Time Use Survey, ONS

Visits to Visitor Attractions, English Tourism Council, VisitScotland, Wales Tourist Board and Northern Ireland Tourist Board

Young People and ICT, Department for Education and Skills

Young People and Sport in England, Sport England

Geographical areas

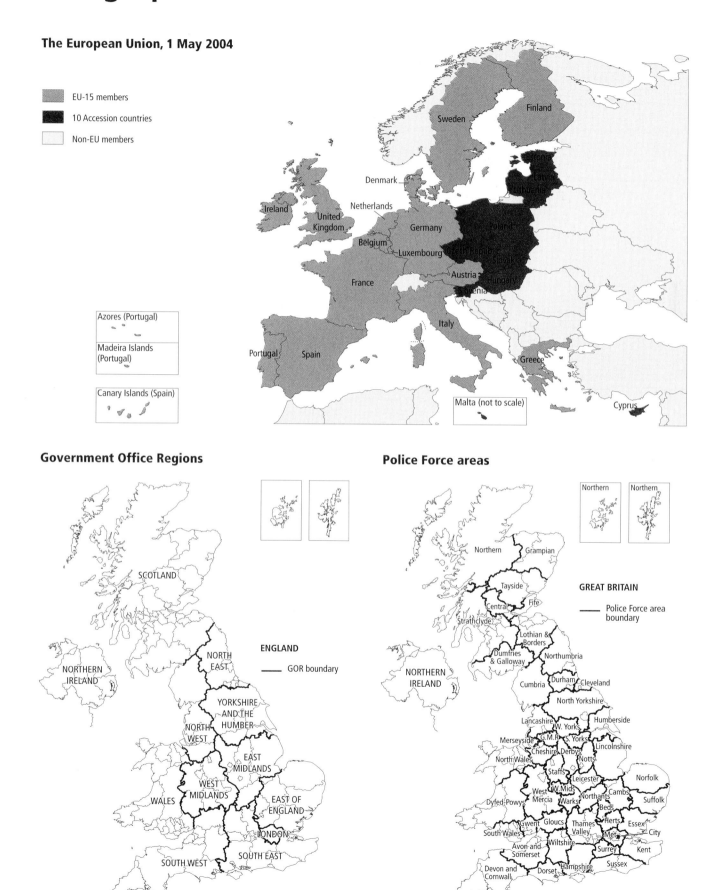

The European Union, 1 May 2004

- EU-15 members
- 10 Accession countries
- Non-EU members

Sweden
Finland
Denmark
Estonia
Latvia
Lithuania
Ireland
Netherlands
United Kingdom
Germany
Poland
Belgium
Luxembourg
Czech Republic
France
Slovakia
Austria
Hungary
Slovenia
Italy
Greece
Portugal
Spain
Cyprus

Azores (Portugal)

Madeira Islands (Portugal)

Canary Islands (Spain)

Malta (not to scale)

Government Office Regions

SCOTLAND

NORTHERN IRELAND

NORTH EAST

ENGLAND
—— GOR boundary

YORKSHIRE AND THE HUMBER

NORTH WEST

EAST MIDLANDS

WEST MIDLANDS

WALES

EAST OF ENGLAND

LONDON

SOUTH EAST

SOUTH WEST

Police Force areas

Northern
Grampian
Tayside
Central
Fife

GREAT BRITAIN
—— Police Force area boundary

Strathclyde

Lothian & Borders

Dumfries & Galloway

Northumbria

NORTHERN IRELAND

Cumbria
Durham
Cleveland

North Yorkshire

Lancashire
W. Yorks
Humberside

Merseyside
G.M.R.
S. Yorks
Lincolnshire

Cheshire
Derbys
Notts

North Wales
Staffs
Leicester
Norfolk

West Mids
Northants
Cambs
Suffolk

Dyfed-Powys
Mercia
Warks
Beds
Herts
Essex

Gwent
Gloucs
Thames Valley
Met
City

South Wales
Avon and Somerset
Wiltshire
Surrey
Kent

Devon and Cornwall
Dorset
Hampshire
Sussex

Northern
Northern

Health areas (from July 2003)

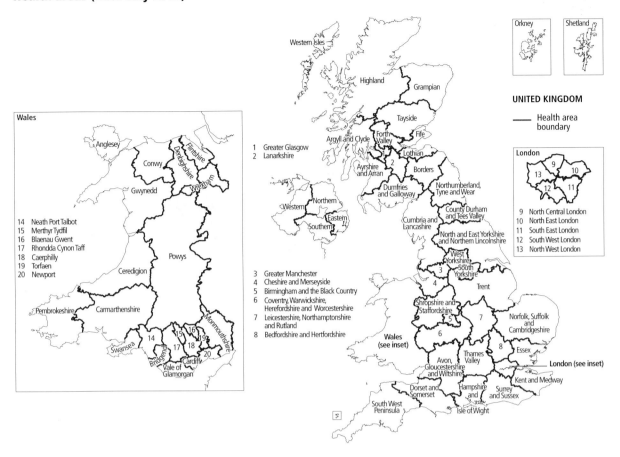

Wales

14 Neath Port Talbot
15 Merthyr Tydfil
16 Blaenau Gwent
17 Rhondda Cynon Taff
18 Caerphilly
19 Torfaen
20 Newport

1 Greater Glasgow
2 Lanarkshire

3 Greater Manchester
4 Cheshire and Merseyside
5 Birmingham and the Black Country
6 Coventry, Warwickshire, Herefordshire and Worcestershire
7 Leicestershire, Northamptonshire and Rutland
8 Bedfordshire and Hertfordshire

UNITED KINGDOM

—— Health area boundary

London

9 North Central London
10 North East London
11 South East London
12 South West London
13 North West London

Environment Agency regions

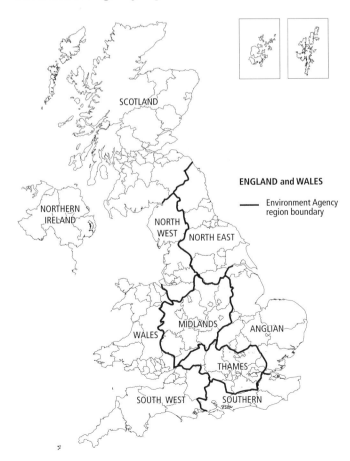

ENGLAND and WALES

—— Environment Agency region boundary

Major surveys

	Frequency	Sampling frame	Type of respondent	Coverage	Effective sample size[1] (most recent survey included in *Social Trends*)	Response rate (percentages)
Annual Survey of Hours and Earnings	Annual	Inland Revenue PAYE records	Employee	UK	240,000	85
British Crime Survey	Annual	Postcode Address File	Adult in household	EW	38,000 addresses	75
British Household Panel Survey	Annual	Postal addresses in 1991, members of initial wave households followed in subsequent waves	All adults in households	GB	5,798 households	88.5[2]
British Social Attitudes Survey	Annual	Postcode Address File	One adult per household	GB	7,493 addresses	59[3]
Census of Population	Decennial	Detailed local	Adult in household	UK	Full count	98
Continuous Household Survey	Continuous	Valuation and Lands Agency Property	All adults in household	NI	3,942 addresses	69
Day Visits Survey	Continuous	Postcode Address File	Adults aged 16 and over	GB	6,600 interviews achieved	43
English House Condition Survey	Annual[4]	Postcode Address File	Any one householder	E	32,863 addresses	51[5]
English Longitudinal Study of Ageing	Biennial	1998 and 1999 core sample and 2001 Health Survey for England	People aged 50 and over living in private households	E	12,100 individuals	67
European Community Household Panel Survey	Annual	Various	All household members aged 16 and over	UK	60,000 households	90[6]
Expenditure and Food Survey	Continuous	Postcode Address File in GB, Rating and Valuation lists in Northern Ireland	All adults in households aged 16 or over[7]	UK	11,019 addresses[8]	58[9]
Families and Children Study	Annual	Child benefit records[10]	Mothers	GB	7,883 families	80[10]
Family Resources Survey	Continuous	Postcode Address File	All adults in household	UK	50,162 households	63
General Household Survey	Continuous	Postcode Address File	All adults in household	GB	14,302 households	70
Health Survey for England	Continuous	Postcode Address File	All household members	E	13,680 addresses	73[11]
Home Office Citizenship Survey	Continuous	Postcode Address File	One adult per household	EW	14,057 interviews	64[12]
International Passenger Survey	Continuous	International passengers	Individual traveller	UK[13]	251,000 individuals	80
Labour Force Survey	Continuous	Postcode Address File	All adults in household	UK	57,000 households	74[14]
Millennium Cohort Study	Biennial	Electoral wards	Parents of living babies born between specific dates[15]	UK	18,553 families	72
National Employers Skills Survey	Annual	Yell's Business Database	Employers	E	72,100 interviews achieved	42
National Travel Survey	Continuous	Postcode Address File	All household members	GB	13,765 households per year	60[16]
New Earnings Survey	Annual	Inland Revenue PAYE records	Employee	GB	[17]	[17]
National Statistics Omnibus Survey	Continuous	Postcode Address File	Adults aged 16 or over living in private households	GB	Approximately 12,000[18]	66
Psychiatric Morbidity Survey	Ad hoc	Postcode Address File	Adults aged 16 to 74 years living in private households	GB	15,804 addresses	69
Survey of English Housing	Continuous	Postcode Address File	Household	E	29,400 households	72
UK 2000 Time Use Survey	Ad hoc	Postcode Address File	Adults and children 8 years and over (aged 16 to 19)	UK	10,579 individuals	61[19]

1 Effective sample size includes non-respondents but excludes ineligible households.
2 Wave on wave response rate at wave twelve. Around 57 per cent of eligible wave one sample members were respondents in wave twelve.
3 Response rate refers to 2003 survey.
4 Although the EHCS runs on a continuous annual basis, its reporting is based on a rolling two year sample.
5 The EHCS response combines successful outcomes from two linked surveys where information is separately gathered about the household and the dwelling for each address.
6 Response rates vary between EU countries.
7 There is an optional diary for children aged 7 to 15 in Great Britain.
8 Basic sample for Great Britain only.
9 Response rate refers to Great Britain.
10 Sampled in selected postal sectors. Panel sample boosted each year with new births and movers to the area. Response rate for the annual survey.
11 Response rate for fully and partially responding households.
12 Response rate refers to the core sample of the 2003 survey.
13 Includes UK and overseas residents.
14 Response rate to first wave interviews of the quarterly LFS averages over the period November 2003 to October 2004.
15 Between 1 September 2000 and 31 August 2001 in England & Wales and between 22 November 2000 and 11 January 2002 in Scotland and Northern Ireland.
16 Data are for 2003.
17 In the New Earnings Survey employers supply data on a 1 per cent sample of employees who are members of PAYE schemes. For the 2003 sample approximately 239,000 were selected and there was an 88 per cent response, but some 48,000 returned questionnaires were not taken onto the results file for various reasons.
18 Achieved sample size per Omnibus cycle. The Omnibus interviews at one household per sampled address and one adult per household. Data are weighted to account for the fact that respondents living in smaller households would have a greater chance of selection.
19 Response rate for the household questionnaire.

Symbols and conventions

Reference years	Where, because of space constraints, a choice of years has to be made, the most recent year or a run of recent years is shown together with the past population census years (2001, 1991, 1981, 1971, etc) and sometimes the mid-points between census years (1986, etc). Other years may be added if they represent a peak or trough in the series.
Rounding of figures	In tables where figures have been rounded to the nearest final digit, there may be an apparent discrepancy between the sum of the constituent items and the total as shown.
Billion	This term is used to represent a thousand million.
Provisional and estimated data	Some data for the latest year (and occasionally for earlier years) are provisional or estimated. To keep footnotes to a minimum, these have not been indicated; source departments will be able to advise if revised data are available.
Seasonal adjustment	Unless otherwise stated, unadjusted data have been used.
Financial year	– eg 1 April 2002 to 31 March 2003 would be shown as 2002/03.
Academic year	– eg September 2002 to July 2003 would be shown as 2002/03.
Combined years	– eg 2000–03 shows data for more than one year that have been combined.
Units on tables	Where one unit predominates it is shown at the top of the table. All other units are shown against the relevant row or column. Figures are shown in italics when they represent percentages.
Household reference person	Sometimes it is necessary to select one person in a household to indicate the general characteristics of the household. For this purpose the household reference person has replaced the head of household in all government-sponsored household surveys after 2000–01. The household reference person is identified during the interview and is: a. the householder (in whose name the accommodation is owned or rented) or b. in households with joint householders, the person with the highest income or, if both householders have the same income, the oldest householder.
Dependent children	Those aged under 16, or single people aged 16 to 18 and in full-time education unless otherwise indicated.
EU	Unless otherwise stated, data relate to the enlarged European Union of 25 countries (EU-25) as constituted since 1 May 2004. EU-15 refers to the 15 members of the EU before enlargement.
Germany	Unless otherwise stated, data relate to Germany as constituted since 3 October 1990.
Ireland	Refers to the State of Ireland and does not include Northern Ireland.
Symbols	The following symbols have been used throughout *Social Trends:* .. not available . not applicable - negligible (less than half the final digit shown) 0 nil

Appendix

Part 1: Population

Population estimates and projections

The estimated and projected populations are of the resident population of an area, i.e. all those usually resident there, whatever their nationality. Members of HM Forces stationed outside the United Kingdom are excluded; members of foreign forces stationed in the United Kingdom are included. Students are taken to be resident at their term-time addresses. Figures for the United Kingdom do not include the population of the Channel Islands or the Isle of Man.

The population estimates for mid-2001 are based on results from the 2001 Census and the Local Authority Population Studies. The Local Authority Population Studies were designed to improve population estimates in the areas that proved hardest to count in the 2001 Census. A full report can be found on the ONS website: www.statistics.gov.uk/about/ Methodology_by_theme/LAStudies.asp.

The most recent set of national population projections published for the United Kingdom are based on the populations of England, Wales, Scotland and Northern Ireland at mid-2003. Further details of these can be found on the Government Actuary's Department's website (www.gad.gov.uk).

Classification of ethnic groups

The recommended classification of ethnic groups for National Statistics data sources was changed in 2001 to bring it broadly in line with the 2001 Census.

There are two levels to this classification. Level 1 is a coarse classification into five main ethnic groups. Level 2 provides a finer classification of Level 1. The preference is for the Level 2 (detailed) categories to be adopted wherever possible. The two levels and the categories are in the box below.

Direct comparisons should not be made between the figures produced using this new classification and those based on the previous classification.

Further details can be found on the National Statistics website: www.statistics.gov.uk/ about/classifications/downloads/ ns_ethnicity_statement.doc

Internal migration estimates

The estimates of internal migration presented in this volume are based on data provided by the NHS Central Register (NHSCR), which records movements of patients between former Health Authority areas (HAs). Using this data source, the definition of a migrant is therefore someone who changes their doctor and moves from one former HA to another. Historically, internal migration estimates were only available at the former HA level; these were equivalent to shire counties, metropolitan districts and groupings of London boroughs. HA-level migration estimates are available from 1975 on a quarterly rolling year basis.

Internal migration estimates by age and gender became available for all local authority areas in 1999. By obtaining a download from each patient register and by combining all the patient register extracts together, ONS creates a total register for the whole of England and Wales. Comparing records in one year with those of the previous year enables identification of people who have changed their postcode. A migrant in the Patient Register Data System is therefore defined as a person who, between one year and the next, changes their area of residence. Estimates at local authority level are made by constraining the migration estimates from the patient registers with the NHSCR estimates at the former HA level.

It has been established that internal migration data under-report the migration of males aged between 16 and 36. Currently, however, there are no suitable sources of data available to enable adjustments or revisions to be made to the estimates. Further research is planned on this topic and new data sources may become available in the future. However, for the present time, historical estimates will not be revised and future estimates will not be adjusted.

International migration estimates

An international migrant is defined as someone who changes his or her country of usual residence for a period of at least a year, so that the country of destination becomes the country of usual residence. The richest source of information on international migrants comes from the International Passenger Survey (IPS), which is a sample survey of passengers arriving at, and departing from, the main UK air and sea ports and the Channel Tunnel. This survey provides migration estimates based on respondents' intended length of stay in the United Kingdom or abroad.

Adjustments are made to account for people who do not realise their intended length of stay. First, an estimate is made for the number of people who initially come to or leave the United Kingdom for a short period but subsequently stay for a year or longer ('visitor switchers'). Second, the number of people who intend to be migrants, but who in reality stay in the United Kingdom or abroad for less than a year ('migrant switchers') are also estimated.

Classification of ethnic groups

Level 1	Level 2
White	White
	British
	Irish
	Other White background
	All White groups
Mixed	White and Black Caribbean
	White and Black African
	White and Asian
	Other Mixed background
	All Mixed groups
Asian or Asian British	Indian
	Pakistani
	Bangladeshi
	Other Asian background
	All Asian groups
Black or Black British	Caribbean
	African
	Other Black background
	All Black groups
Chinese or other ethnic Group	Chinese
	Other ethnic group
	All Chinese or other groups
All ethnic groups	All ethnic groups
Not stated	Not stated

Data from other sources are used to supplement the IPS migration estimates. First, Home Office asylum seeker data are used to estimate the number of asylum seekers and their dependants who enter or leave the country without being counted in the IPS. Second, estimates of migration between the United Kingdom and Ireland are made using information from the Irish Central Statistics Office.

Part 2: Households and families

Although definitions differ slightly across surveys and the Census, they are broadly similar.

Households

A household: is a person living alone or a group of people who have the address as their only or main residence and who either share one meal a day or share the living accommodation.

Students: those living in halls of residence are recorded under their parents' household and included in the parents' family type in the Labour Force Survey (LFS), although some surveys/projections include such students in the institutional population.

In the General Household Survey (GHS), children aged 16 or over who live away from home for purposes of either work or study and come home only for holidays are not included at the parental address.

Families

Children: are never-married people of any age who live with one or both parent(s). They include stepchildren and adopted children (but not foster children) and also grandchildren (where the parents are absent).

Dependent children: in the 1971 and 1981 Census, dependent children were defined as never-married children in families who were either under 15 years of age, or aged 15 to 24 and in full-time education. In the 1991 Census, the LFS and the General Household Survey (GHS), dependent children are childless never-married children in families who are aged under 16, or aged 16 to 18 and in full-time education and living in the household (and, in the 1991 Census, economically inactive). In the 2001 Census a dependent child is a person aged under 16 in a household (whether or not in a family) or aged 16 to 18, in full-time education and living in a family with their parent or parents.

A family: is a married or cohabiting couple, either with or without their never-married child or children (of any age), including couples with no children or a lone parent together with his or her never-married child or children provided they have no children of their own. A family could also consist of a grandparent or grandparents with their grandchild or grandchildren if the parents of the grandchild or grandchildren are not usually resident in the household. In the LFS, a family unit can also comprise a single person. LFS family units include non-dependent children (who can in fact be adult) those aged 16 or over and not in full-time education provided they are never married and have no children of their own in the household.

One family and no others: A household comprises one family and no others if there is only one family in the household and there are no non-family people.

Multi family household: A household containing two or more people who cannot be allocated to a single family as defined in 'a family' above. This includes households with two or more unrelated adults and can also include a grandparent or grandparents with their child or children and grandchild or grandchildren in one household.

A lone parent family in the Census is a father or mother together with his or her never-married child or children.

A lone parent family in the LFS consists of a lone parent, living with his or her never-married children, provided these children have no children of their own living with them.

A lone parent family in the GHS consists of a lone parent, living with his or her never-married dependent children, provided these children have no children of their own. Married lone mothers whose husbands are not defined as resident in the household are not classified as lone parents. Evidence suggests the majority are separated from their husband either because he usually works away from home or for some other reason that does not imply the breakdown of the marriage.

Conceptions

Conception statistics used in Table 2.16 include pregnancies that result in one or more live or still births, or a legal abortion under the 1967 Act. Conception statistics do not include miscarriages or illegal abortions. Dates of conception are estimated using recorded gestation for abortions and still births, and assuming 38 weeks gestation for live births.

True birth order

At registration, the question on previous live births is not asked where the birth occurred outside marriage. At the registration of births occurring within marriage, previous live births occurring outside marriage and where the woman had never been married to the father are not counted. The information collected on birth order, therefore, has been supplemented to give estimates of overall true birth order, which includes births both within and outside marriage. These estimates are obtained from details provided by the General Household Survey.

Part 3: Education and training

Stages of education

Education takes place in several stages: nursery (now part of the foundation stage in England), primary, secondary, further and higher education, and is compulsory for all children between the ages of 5 (4 in Northern Ireland) and 16. The non-compulsory fourth stage, further education, covers non-advanced education, which can be taken at both further (including tertiary) education colleges, higher education institutions and increasingly in secondary schools. The fifth stage, higher education, is study beyond GCE A levels and their equivalent, which, for most full-time students, takes place in universities and other higher education institutions.

Nursery education

In recent years there has been a major expansion of pre-school education. Many children under five attend state nursery schools or nursery classes within primary schools. Others may attend playgroups in the voluntary sector or in privately run nurseries. In England and Wales many primary schools also operate an early admissions policy where they admit children under five into what are called 'reception classes'. The *Education Act 2002* extended the National Curriculum for England to include the foundation stage. The foundation stage was introduced in September 2000 and covers children's education from the age of three to the end of the reception year, when most are just five and some almost six years old. The 'Curriculum guidance for the foundation stage' supports practitioners in their delivery of the foundation stage.

Figure 3.1 reflects those children in early years education in maintained nursery and primary schools. Other provision also takes place in independent and special schools and in non-school education settings in the private and voluntary sector, such as nurseries (which usually provide care, education and play for children up to the age of five), playgroups and pre-schools (which provide childcare, play and early years education usually for children aged between two and five), and combined/family centres.

Primary education

The primary stage covers three age ranges: nursery (under 5), infant (5 to 7 or 8) and junior (up to 11 or 12) but in Scotland and Northern Ireland there is generally no distinction between infant and junior schools. Most public sector primary schools take both boys and girls in mixed classes. It is usual to transfer straight to secondary school at age 11 (in England, Wales and Northern Ireland) or 12 (in Scotland), but in England some children make the transition via middle schools catering for various age ranges between 8 and 14. Depending on their individual age ranges middle schools are classified as either primary or secondary.

Secondary education

Public provision of secondary education in an area may consist of a combination of different types of school, the pattern reflecting historical circumstances and the policy adopted by the LEA. Comprehensive schools largely admit pupils without reference to ability or aptitude and cater for all the children in a neighbourhood, but in some areas they co-exist with grammar, secondary modern or technical schools. In Northern Ireland, post primary education is provided by secondary intermediate and grammar schools. In England, the Specialist Schools Programme helps schools, in partnership with private sector sponsors and supported by additional government funding, to establish distinctive identities through their chosen specialisms. Specialist schools have a focus on their chosen subject area but must meet the National Curriculum requirements and deliver a broad and balanced education to all pupils. Any maintained secondary school in England can apply to be designated as a specialist school in one of ten specialist areas: arts, business & enterprise, engineering, humanities, language, mathematics & computing, music, science, sports, and technology. Schools can also combine any two specialisms.

Special schools

Special schools (day or boarding) provide education for children who require specialist support to complete their education, for example because they have physical or other difficulties. Many pupils with special educational needs are educated in mainstream schools. All children attending special schools are offered a curriculum designed to overcome their learning difficulties and to enable them to become self-reliant.

Pupil referral units

Pupil referral units (PRUs) are legally a type of school established and maintained by a LEA to provide education for children of compulsory school age who may otherwise not receive suitable education. The aim of such units is to provide suitable alternative education on a temporary basis for pupils who may not be able to attend a mainstream school. The focus of the units should be to get pupils back into a mainstream school. Pupils in the units may include: teenage mothers, pupils excluded from school, school phobics and pupils in the assessment phase of a statement of special educational needs (SEN).

Further education

The term further education may be used in a general sense to cover all non-advanced courses taken after the period of compulsory education, but more commonly it excludes those staying on at secondary school and those in higher education, i.e. courses in universities and colleges leading to qualifications above GCE A level, Higher Grade (in Scotland), GNVQ/NVQ level 3, and their equivalents. Since 1 April 1993 sixth form colleges in England and Wales have been included in the further education sector.

Higher education

Higher education is defined as courses that are of a standard that is higher than GCE A level, the Higher Grade of the Scottish Certificate of Education/National Qualification, GNVQ/NVQ level 3 or the Edexcel (formerly BTEC) or SQA National Certificate/Diploma. There are three main levels of HE course:

1. Postgraduate courses leading to higher degrees, diplomas and certificates (including postgraduate certificates of education and professional qualifications) which usually require a first degree as entry qualification.

2. Undergraduate courses, which include first degrees, first degrees with qualified teacher status, enhanced first degrees, first degrees obtained concurrently with a diploma, and intercalated first degrees.

3. Other undergraduate courses, which includes all other higher education courses, for example HNDs and Diplomas in HE.

As a result of the 1992 *Further and Higher Education Act*, former polytechnics and some other higher education institutions were designated as universities in 1992/93. Students normally attend HE courses at higher

education institutions, but some attend at further education colleges. Some also attend institutions that do not receive public grants (such as the University of Buckingham) and these numbers are excluded from the tables.

Up to 2000/01, figures for higher education students in Table 3.9 are annual snapshots taken around November or December each year, depending on the type of institution, except for Scotland further education colleges from 1998/99, for which counts are based on the whole year. From 2001/02, figures for higher education institutions are based on the Higher Education Statistics Agency (HESA) July 'standard registration' count, and are not directly comparable with previous years. The Open University is included in these estimates.

Main categories of educational establishments

Educational establishments in the United Kingdom are administered and financed in several ways. Most schools are controlled by local education authorities (LEAs), which are part of the structure of local government, but some are 'assisted', receiving grants direct from central government sources and being controlled by governing bodies that have a substantial degree of autonomy. Outside the public sector completely are non-maintained schools run by individuals, companies or charitable institutions.

Up to March 2001, further education (FE) courses in FE sector colleges in England and in Wales were largely funded through grants from the respective Further Education Funding Councils. In April 2001, however, the Learning and Skills Council (LSC) took over the responsibility for funding the FE sector in England, and the National Council for Education and Training for Wales (part of Education and Learning Wales – ELWa) did so for Wales. The LSC in England is also responsible for funding provision for FE and some non-prescribed higher education in FE sector colleges; it also funds some FE provided by LEA maintained and other institutions referred to as 'external institutions'. In Wales, the National Council – ELWa, funds FE provision made by FE institutions via a third party or sponsored arrangements. The Scottish FEFC (SFEFC) funds FE colleges in Scotland, while the Department for Employment and Learning funds FE colleges in Northern Ireland.

Higher education (HE) courses in HE establishments are largely publicly funded through block grants from the HE funding councils in England and Scotland, the Higher Education Council – ELWa in Wales, and the Department for Employment and Learning in Northern Ireland. In addition, some designated HE (mainly HND/HNC Diplomas and Certificates of HE) is also funded by these sources. The FE sources mentioned above fund the remainder.

Numbers of school pupils are shown in Table 3.2. Nursery schools figures for Scotland prior to 1998/99 only include data for local authority pre-schools. Data thereafter include partnership pre-schools. Secondary 'Other' schools largely consist of middle schools in England, and secondary intermediate schools in Northern Ireland. Special schools include maintained and non-maintained sectors, while public sector

and non-maintained schools totals exclude special schools. The 'All schools' total includes pupil referral units, which accounted for around 13,000 pupils in 2003/04.

Qualifications

In England, Wales and Northern Ireland the main examination for school pupils at the minimum school leaving age is the General Certificate of Secondary Education (GCSE), which can be taken in a wide range of subjects. This replaced the GCE O Level and CSE examinations in 1987 (1988 in Northern Ireland). In England, Wales and Northern Ireland the GCSE is awarded in eight grades, A* to G, the highest four (A* to C) being regarded as equivalent to O level grades A to C or CSE grade 1.

GCSE (or equivalent) entries and achievements by selected subject are shown in Table 3.13. Where a candidate attempted an examination in the same subject more than once, only the highest value pass has been counted. In the same table, data for mathematics include related subjects such as statistics whereas data for design and technology include craft and design, graphic communications, and technological studies in Scotland. Data for information technology include computer studies, information systems, and any combined syllabus where information technology is a major part. The single science award is equivalent to a standard grade in general science in Scotland.

GCE A level is usually taken after a further two years of study in a sixth form or equivalent, passes being graded from A (the highest) to E (the lowest).

Following the Qualifying for Success consultation in 1997, a number of reforms were introduced to the 16 to 19 qualifications structure in September 2000. Under these reforms, students were encouraged to follow a wide range of subjects in their first year of post-16 study, with students expected to study four Advanced Subsidiaries before progressing three of them on to full A levels in their second year. In addition, students are encouraged to study a combination of both general and vocational advanced level examinations.

The Advanced Subsidiary (AS) qualification covers the first half of the full A level. New specifications introduced in 2001 are now in place and A levels now comprise units, normally six for a full A level (now A2) and three for the AS level, which is half a full A level. The full A level is normally taken either over two years (modular) or as a set of exams at the end of the two years (linear). The AS is a qualification in its own right, whereas A2 modules do not make up a qualification in their own right.

From 1999/2000, National Qualifications (NQ) were introduced in Scotland. NQs include Standard Grades, Intermediate 1 and 2 and Higher Grades. Pupils study for the Scottish Certificate of Education (SCE)/NQ Standard Grade, approximately equivalent to GCSE, in their third and fourth years of secondary schooling (roughly ages 14 and 15). Each subject has several elements, some of which are internally assessed in school, and an award is only made (on a scale of 1 to 6) if the whole course has been completed and examined. The Higher Grade requires one further year of study and for the more able candidates the range of subjects taken may be as wide as at Standard Grade with as many as five or six subjects spanning both arts and science. Three or more Highers are regarded as being approximately the equivalent of two or more GCE A levels.

After leaving school, people can study towards higher academic qualifications such as degrees. However, a large number of people choose to study towards qualifications aimed at a particular occupation or group of occupations – these qualifications are called vocational qualifications.

Vocational qualifications can be split into three groups, namely National Vocational Qualifications (NVQs), General National Vocational Qualifications (GNVQs) and vocationally related qualifications.

NVQs are based on an explicit statement of competence derived from an analysis of employment requirements. They are awarded at five levels. Scottish Vocational Qualifications (SVQs) are the Scottish equivalent.

GNVQs are a vocational alternative to GCSEs and GCE A levels. They are awarded at three levels: Foundation, Intermediate and Advanced. Advanced GNVQs were redesigned and relaunched as Vocational A levels or, more formally, Advanced Vocational Certificates of Education (VCEs) and, as well as being available at AS level and A level, there are also double awards (counting as 12 units). General Scottish Vocational Qualifications (GSVQs) are the Scottish equivalent.

There are also a large number of other vocational qualifications, which are not NVQs, SVQs, GNVQs or GSVQs, for example, a BTEC Higher National Diploma or a City and Guilds Craft award.

Other qualifications (including academic qualifications) are often expressed as being equivalent to a particular NVQ level so that comparisons can be made more easily.

An NVQ level 5 is equivalent to a Higher Degree.

An NVQ level 4 is equivalent to a First Degree, a HND or HNC, a BTEC Higher Diploma, an RSA Higher Diploma, a nursing qualification or other Higher Education.

An NVQ level 3 is equivalent to two A levels, an advanced GNVQ, an RSA advanced diploma, a City & Guilds advanced craft, an OND or ONC or a BTEC National Diploma.

An NVQ level 2 is equivalent to five GCSEs at grades A* to C, an Intermediate GNVQ, an RSA diploma, a City and Guilds craft or a BTEC first or general diploma.

For achievement at GCE A level shown in Figure 3.14, data are for pupils in schools and students in further education institutions generally aged 16 to 18 at the start of the academic year as a percentage of the 17 year old population. Data prior to 1995/96, and for Wales and Northern Ireland for 2002/03, are for school pupils only. In Scotland pupils generally sit Highers one year earlier than the rest of the United Kingdom sit A levels. The figures for Scotland relate to the results of pupils in year Secondary 5/6.

Social class

Social class is based on occupation and is a classification system that has grown out of the original Registrar-General's social class classification. These are defined in the Classification of Occupations 1990 (SOC90), which was revised and updated in SOC2000, prepared by the Office for National Statistics. The five categories are:

I. Professional, etc. occupations

II. Managerial and technical occupations

III. Skilled occupations

   (N) non-manual

   (M) manual

IV. Partly skilled occupations

V. Unskilled occupations.

From 2001, the National Statistics Socio-economic Classification (NS-SEC) was adopted for all official surveys, in place of social class based on occupation, see Appendix, Part 6: National Statistics Socio-economic Classification.

The National Curriculum

Under the *Education Reform Act 1988* a National Curriculum has been progressively introduced into primary and secondary schools in England and Wales. This consists of English (or the option of Welsh as a first language in Wales), mathematics and science. The second level of curriculum additionally comprises the so-called 'foundation' subjects, such as history, geography, art, music, information technology, design and technology and physical education (and Welsh as a second language in Wales). The *Education Act 2002* extended the National Curriculum for England to include the foundation stage. It has six areas of learning namely, personal, social and emotional development; communication, language and literacy; mathematical development; knowledge and understanding of the world; physical development; and creative development.

Measurable targets have been defined for four key stages, corresponding to ages 7, 11, 14 and 16. Pupils are assessed formally at the ages of 7, 11 and 14 by a mixture of teacher assessments and by national tests in the core subjects of English, mathematics and science (and in Welsh speaking schools in Wales, Welsh), though the method varies between subjects and countries. Sixteen year olds are assessed by means of the GCSE examination. Statutory authorities have been set up for England and for Wales to advise the Government on the National Curriculum and promote curriculum development generally. Statutory assessment at the end of Key Stage 1 in Wales from 2002, is by means of teacher assessment only, as the National Curriculum Tests/Tasks were discontinued in 2002, following the outcome of the public consultation on proposed changes to the assessment arrangements contained in *The Learning Country – A Comprehensive Education and Lifelong Learning Programme to 2010 in Wales*. Northern Ireland has its own common curriculum that is similar but not identical to the National Curriculum in England and Wales. Assessment arrangements in Northern Ireland

became statutory from September 1996 and Key Stage 1 pupils are assessed at the age of 8. Pupils in Northern Ireland are not assessed in science at Key Stages 1 and 2.

In Scotland there is no statutory national curriculum. Pupils aged 5 to 14 study a broad curriculum based on national guidelines, which set out the aims of study, the ground to be covered and the way the pupils' learning should be assessed and reported. Progress is measured by attainment of six levels based on the expectation of the performance of the majority of pupils on completion of certain stages between the ages of 5 and 14: Primary 3 (age 7/8), Primary 4 (age 8/9), Primary 7 (age 11/12) and Secondary 2 (age 13/14). It is recognised that pupils learn at different rates and some will reach the various levels before others. The curriculum areas are language; mathematics; environmental studies; expressive arts; and religious and moral education with personal and social development and health education. Though school curricula are the responsibility of education authorities and individual head teachers, in practice almost all 14 to 16 year olds study mathematics, English, science, a modern foreign language, a social subject, physical education, religious and moral education, technology and a creative and aesthetic subject.

England	Attainment expected
Key Stage 1	Level 2 or above
Key Stage 2	Level 4 or above
Key Stage 3	Level 5/6 or above
Key Stage 4	GCSE

National Employers Skills Survey

National Employers Skills Survey (NESS) 2003 is the latest in an annual series of employer surveys that investigate the provision of learning and training at work.

Learning and training information had previously been collected in the Learning and Training at Work (LTW) surveys between 1999 and 2002, and prior to that, along with information on recruitment difficulties, skill shortages and skill gaps, in the annual Skill Needs in Britain (SNIB) surveys, which were carried out between 1990 and 1998.

The aim of the NESS 2003 study was to provide the Learning and Skills Council (LSC) and its partners with information on the current and future skill needs of employers in England, and how these needs vary by size of industry, by region and also by local LSC.

Adult education

Local Education Authorities (LEAs) provide a range of learning opportunities for adults. In November 2002 opportunities fell into two categories – those that did not lead to academic or vocational qualifications and those that did. LEAs offered the former provision in response to their statutory duty to secure adequate provision for further education. Although not leading to a qualification, these courses could cover a wide range of topics including vocational, social, physical and recreational training, as well as organised leisure-time occupation provided in association with such activities. They were normally designated non-Schedule 2 courses to distinguish them from those courses set out in Schedule 2 to the *Further and Higher Education Act 1992*, for which the Further Education Funding Council (FEFC) had statutory responsibility for securing provision. LEAs also had the power, although not the duty, to provide courses that fell within Schedule 2 and many authorities chose to do so. The *Learning and Skills Act* transferred LEAs' duties to the Learning and Skills Council (LSC) and removed from the legislation the distinction between learning opportunities that lead to qualifications and those that do not.

The establishment of the LSC in March 2001 led to changes in the arrangements for planning and funding learning opportunities for adults as well as data collection. From 2003/04, adult education data will be collected by the LSC and incorporated into the Individualised Learner Record (ILR). The ILR already covers learners in further education and on work based learning for young people.

Part 4: Labour market

Labour Force Survey (LFS) reweighting

The results from the 2001 Census, published in September 2002, showed that previous estimates of the total UK population were around 1 million too high. As a result, the Office for National Statistics (ONS) published interim revised estimates of the population for the years 1982 to 2001, which were consistent with the 2001 Census population findings.

The interim mid-year population estimates (MYEs) and projections are available by age and sex and these have been used to produce interim revised LFS estimates of employment, unemployment and inactivity by age and sex. Other LFS analyses, eg full/part-time, have been produced by scaling to these age/sex adjusted data. This scaling has been applied to the existing LFS data and summed to obtain new aggregate LFS totals.

In spring (February and March) 2003 slightly revised population estimates were published and these were incorporated into the April 2003 LFS national and regional interim estimates and, later, the LFS microdata (see below).

In autumn (September and October) 2004, ONS published the 2003 MYEs along with revised MYEs for 2001 and 2002. These revised population estimates took into account the census matching studies for Manchester and Westminster; population studies in 15 local authorities; and refinements to the method for allocating migration estimates. MYEs for 1992 to 2000, consistent with these revised estimates were also published. Also in autumn 2004, the Government Actuary's Department (GAD) published revised population projections for 2004 and later years, based on the revised population estimates. These latest population revisions were incorporated into LFS estimates published on 13 October 2004.

LFS data in this edition of *Social Trends* that have been adjusted in line with population estimates published in spring 2003 are calculated using the LFS microdata, whereas data that have been adjusted in line with

population estimates published in autumn 2004 are taken from published ONS sources such as the Labour Market Statistics First Release.

It is planned that the revised LFS time series, taking account of the 2004 MYE, to be released in September 2005 should be produced entirely consistently with the LFS microdata, without the need for any interim adjustment procedure. ONS does not plan to make any more revisions to the population estimates following the census.

For more information, see:
www.statistics.gov.uk/cci/
nugget.asp?id=207 and 'Labour Force Survey reweighting and seasonal adjustment review', pp 167–72, *Labour Market Trends*, April 2004
www.statistics.gov.uk/cci/article.asp?id=887

Historical LFS-consistent time series

The Office for National Statistics (ONS) has produced a set of historical estimates covering the period 1971–91, which are fully consistent with post-1992 Labour Force Survey (LFS) data. The data cover headline measures of employment, unemployment, economic activity, economic inactivity and hours worked. These estimates were published on an experimental basis in 2003, but following further user consultation and quality assurance, these estimates have now been made National Statistics. As such, they represent ONS' best estimate of the headline labour market series over this period. The overview article at the beginning of *Social Trends 35* uses these headline historical estimates. The labour market chapter uses data from these estimates only where headline data are reported (Figures 4.1, 4.7 and 4.17) since the historical estimates are not yet available for subgroups of the population, other than by sex and for key age groups. Therefore, tables and figures showing further breakdowns of headline data are not fully consistent with the historical estimates. As such, the headline levels reported in Table 4.2 are not fully consistent with the historical estimates.

For more information, see:
www.statistics.gov.uk/cci/nugget.asp?id=419

Unemployment

The UK definition of unemployment is based on International Labour Organisation (ILO) guidelines and refers to people without a job who were available to start work within two weeks and had either looked for work in the previous four weeks or were waiting to start a job they had already obtained.

The former GB/UK Labour Force definition of unemployment, the only one available for estimates up to 1984, counted people not in employment and seeking work in a reference week (or prevented from seeking work by a temporary sickness or holiday, or waiting for the results of a job application, or waiting to start a job they had already obtained), whether or not they were available to start (except students not able to start because they had to complete their education).

Following a quality review of its labour market statistics, the ONS has re-labelled 'ILO unemployment' as 'unemployment'. This emphasises that the Labour Force Survey figures

provide the official, and only internationally comparable, measure of unemployment in the United Kingdom. Claimant count data will continue to be published monthly to provide further information about the labour market, but these will not be presented as an alternative measure of UK unemployment.

Annual local area Labour Force Survey

Estimates from the annual local area Labour Force Survey (LFS) use data compiled annually from the main LFS together with additional interviews in England, Wales and, in 2003/04, for the first time, Scotland.

For more information see:
www.statistics.gov.uk/statbase/
Product.asp?vlnk=11711

The annual local area LFS data presented here have been weighted to be consistent with the population estimates published in February and March 2003.

Jobs densities for local areas

Jobs density is the total number of filled jobs in an area divided by the resident population of working age in that area. The total number of jobs is a workplace-based measure of jobs and comprises employees, self-employment jobs, government-supported trainees and HM Forces. The number of jobs in an area is composed of jobs done by residents (of any age) and jobs done by workers (of any age) who commute into the area. The working-age population comprises residents of working age who work in the area plus workers of working age who commute out of the area to work in other areas and those who are unemployed or economically inactive of working age.

For more information, see:
www.statistics.gov.uk/articles/
labour_market_trends/jobs_densities.pdf

Labour disputes

Statistics of stoppages of work caused by labour disputes in the United Kingdom relate to disputes connected with terms and conditions of employment. Small stoppages involving fewer than ten workers or lasting less than one day are excluded from the statistics unless the aggregate number of working days lost in the dispute is 100 or more. Disputes not resulting in a stoppage of work are not included in the statistics.

Workers involved and working days lost relate to persons both directly and indirectly involved (unable to work although not parties to the dispute) at the establishments where the disputes occurred. People laid off and working days lost at establishments not in dispute, due for example to resulting shortages of supplies, are excluded.

There are difficulties in ensuring complete recording of stoppages, in particular near the margins of the definition; for example short disputes lasting only a day or so, or involving only a few workers. Any under-recording would affect the total number of stoppages much more than the number of working days lost.

Part 5: Income and wealth

Household sector

The data for the household sector as derived from the National Accounts have been compiled according to the definitions and conventions set out in the European System of Accounts 1995 (ESA95). At present, estimates for the household sector cannot be separated from the sector for non-profit institutions serving households and so the data in *Social Trends* cover both sectors. The most obvious example of a non-profit institution is a charity: this sector also includes many other organisations of which universities, trade unions and clubs and societies are the most important. The household sector differs from the personal sector, as defined in the National Accounts prior to the introduction of ESA95, in that it excludes unincorporated private businesses apart from sole traders. More information is given in *United Kingdom National Accounts Concepts, Sources and Methods* published by The Stationery Office.

In ESA95, household income includes the value of national insurance contributions and pension contributions made by employers on behalf of their employees. It also shows property income (that is, income from investments) net of payments of interest on loans. In both these respects, National Accounts conventions diverge from those normally used when collecting data on household income from household surveys. Employees are usually unaware of value of the national insurance contributions and pension contributions made on their behalf by their employer, and so such data are rarely collected. Payments of interest are usually regarded as items of expenditure rather than reductions of income. Thus from *Social Trends 33* onwards, the National Accounts data for household sector income have been adjusted to omit employers' national insurance contributions and to express property income gross of any payments of interest on loans, in order to increase comparability with the data on income derived from household surveys used elsewhere in the chapter.

Individual income

Net individual income refers to the weekly personal income of women and men after deduction of income tax and national insurance contributions as reported in the Family Resources Survey. Income is from all sources received by an individual, including earnings, income from self-employment, investments and occupational pensions/annuities, benefit income, and tax credits. Income that accrues at household level, such as council tax benefit, is excluded. Income from couples' joint investment accounts is assumed to be received equally. Benefit income paid in respect of dependants, such as Child Benefit, is included in the individual income of the person nominated for the receipt of payments. Full details of the concepts and definitions used may be found in *Individual Income 1996/97 to 2002/03* available on the Women and Equality Unit website: **www.womenandequalityunit.gov.uk/ indiv_incomes/index/htm** or from the Information and Analysis Division, Department for Work and Pensions.

Equivalisation scales

The Department for Work and Pensions (DWP), the Office for National Statistics (ONS), the Institute for Fiscal Studies (IFS) and the Institute for Social and Economic Research (ISER) all use McClements equivalence scales in their analysis of the income distribution, to take into account variations in the size and composition of households. This reflects the common sense notion that a household of five adults will need a higher income than will a single person living alone to enjoy a comparable standard of living. An overall equivalence value is calculated for each household by summing the appropriate scale values for each household member. Equivalised household income is then calculated by dividing household income by the household's equivalence value. The scales conventionally take a married couple as the reference point with an equivalence value of 1; equivalisation therefore tends to increase relatively the incomes of single person households (since their incomes are divided by a value of less than 1) and to reduce incomes of households with three or more persons. For further information see *Households Below Average Income*, Corporate Document Services, DWP. There are two McClements equivalence scales, one for adjusting incomes before housing costs and one for adjusting income after housing costs, see box.

The DWP and IFS both use different scales for adjustment of income before and after the deduction of housing costs.

McClements equivalence scales:

Household member	Before housing costs	After housing costs
First adult (head)	0.61	0.55
Spouse of head	0.39	0.45
Other second adult	0.46	0.45
Third adult	0.42	0.45
Subsequent adults	0.36	0.40
Each dependant aged:		
0–1	0.09	0.07
2–4	0.18	0.18
5–7	0.21	0.21
8–10	0.23	0.23
11–12	0.25	0.26
13–15	0.27	0.28
16 or over	0.36	0.38

Earnings surveys

The Annual Survey of Hours and Earnings (ASHE) replaced the New Earnings Survey (NES) from October 2004. ASHE improves on the NES by extending the coverage of the survey sample, introducing weighting and publishing estimates of quality for all survey outputs. The new survey methodology produces weighted estimates of earnings, using weights calculated by calibrating the survey responses to totals from the Labour Force Survey by occupation, gender, region and age. The survey sample

has been increased to include employees in businesses outside the PAYE system and those changing jobs between the survey sample identification and the survey reference date. The new survey design also produces outputs that focus on median rather than mean levels of pay. Full details of the methodology of ASHE can be found on the ONS website at: **www.statistics.gov.uk/articles/nojournal/ ASHEMethod_article.pdf**

Back series using the ASHE methodology applied to the NES data sets are available for 1998 to 2003 at: **www.statistics.gov.uk/ STATBASE/Product.asp?vlnk=13101** Estimates for the years for 1992 to 1997 will be released in due course. However, in this edition of *Social Trends* the NES is retained for time series data.

Households Below Average Income (HBAI)

Information on the distribution of income based on the Family Resources Survey is provided in the Department for Work and Pensions publication *Households Below Average Income: 1994/95–2002/03*, available both in hard copy and on the DWP website. This publication provides estimates of patterns of personal disposable income in Great Britain, and of changes in income over time. It attempts to measure people's potential living standards as determined by disposable income. Although as the title would suggest, HBAI concentrates on the lower part of the income distribution, it also provides estimates covering the whole of the income distribution.

In 2002/03, the Family Resources Survey was extended to cover Northern Ireland. However, because inclusion of these data into the main HBAI might introduce discontinuities in some results, results on a UK basis are presented separately in *Households Below Average Income: 1994/95–2002/03* (Appendix 3).

Disposable household income includes all flows of income into the household, principally earnings, benefits, occupational and private pensions, and investments. It is net of tax, employees' national insurance contributions, council tax, contributions to occupational pension schemes (including additional voluntary contributions), maintenance and child support payments, and parental contributions to students living away from home.

Two different measures of disposable income are used in HBAI: before and after housing costs are deducted. Housing costs consist of rent, water rates, community charges, mortgage interest payments, structural insurance, ground rent and service charges.

Redistribution of Income

Estimates of the incidence of taxes and benefits on household income based on the Expenditure and Food Survey (EFS), formerly the Family Expenditure Survey (FES), are published by the Office for National Statistics on the NS website: **www.statistics.gov.uk** and in *Economic Trends*. The article covering 2001–02 was published on the NS website in October 2003 and contains details of the definitions and methods used.

Difference between Households Below Average Income and Redistribution of Income series

These are two separate and distinct income series produced by two different government departments. Each series has been developed to serve the specific needs of that department. The DWP series, Households Below Average Income (HBAI), provides estimates of patterns of disposable income and of changes over time and shows disposable income before and after housing costs (where disposable income is as defined in the section on HBAI above). The ONS series, Redistribution of Income (ROI), shows how government intervention through the tax and benefit system affects the income of households; it covers the whole income distribution and includes the effects of indirect taxes like VAT and duty on beer, as well as estimating the cash value of benefits in kind (eg from state spending on education and health care). The ROI results are designed to show the position in a particular year rather than trends in income levels over time, although trends in the distribution of income are given. An important difference between the two series is that HBAI counts individuals and ROI counts households. Also, whereas ROI provides estimates for the United Kingdom, from 1994/95 onwards HBAI provides estimates for Great Britain only (but see above).

Families and Children Study

The DWP's Families and Children Study (FACS) examines the living standards of families with children according to their material deprivation – measured as the ability to purchase essential goods and to participate in leisure activities. Families were asked whether they possessed or took part in each of the following 34 items or activities, and if not, whether this was because it could not afford to or because it did not want or need the item:

Food and meal items
Main meal every day
Meat/fish every other day
Roast meat every week
Vegetables most days
Fruit most days
Cakes/biscuits most days
Brand name food most days

Clothing and shoes items
Waterproof coat for each adult
Waterproof coat for each child
Two pairs of shoes for each adult
Two pairs of shoes for each child
New clothes when needed
Best outfit for each child
Brand clothing/shoes for each child

Consumer durable items
Colour TV
Cable/satellite/digital TV
Refrigerator
Separate deep freeze
Washing machine
Tumble drier
Telephone (incl mobile)
Dishwasher
Video recorder
Central heating
Microwave
Car or van
Music system
Home computer

Leisure activities
Celebrations with presents at special occasions
Toys/sports gear for each child
Money for trips/outings/gifts to parties
One-week holidays (not staying with relatives)
Night out once a month
Friends/relatives for a meal once a month

For more information see *DWP Research Report no 206*, Chapter 16.

Net wealth of the household sector

Revised balance sheet estimates of the net wealth of the household (and non-profit institutions) sector were published in an article in *Economic Trends* November 1999. These figures are based on the new international system of national accounting and incorporate data from new sources. Quarterly estimates of net financial wealth (excluding tangible and intangible assets) are published in *Financial Statistics*.

Distribution of personal wealth

The estimates of the distribution of the marketable wealth of individuals relate to all adults in the United Kingdom. They are produced by combining Inland Revenue (IR) estimates of the distribution of wealth identified by the estate multiplier method with independent estimates of total personal wealth derived from the Office for National Statisitcs (ONS) National Accounts balance sheets. Estimates for 1995 onwards have been compiled on the basis of the new System of National Accounts, but estimates for earlier years are on the old basis. The methods used were described in an article in *Economic Trends* (October 1990) entitled 'Estimates of the Distribution of Personal Wealth'. Net wealth of the personal sector differs from marketable wealth for the following reasons:

Difference in coverage: the ONS balance sheet of the personal sector includes the wealth of non-profit making bodies and unincorporated businesses, while the IR estimates exclude non-profit making bodies and treat the bank deposits and debts of unincorporated businesses differently from ONS;

Differences in timing: the ONS balance sheet gives values at the end of the year, whereas IR figures are adjusted to mid-year;

IR figures: exclude the wealth of those under 18;

Funded pensions: are included in ONS figures (including personal pensions) but not in the IR marketable wealth. Also the ONS balance sheet excludes consumer durables and includes non-marketable tenancy rights, whereas the IR figures include consumer durables and exclude non-marketable tenancy rights.

Part 6: Expenditure

Household expenditure

The National Accounts definition of household expenditure, within household final consumption expenditure, consists of: personal expenditure on goods (durable, semi-durable and non-durable) and services, including the value of income in kind; imputed rent for owner-occupied dwellings; and the purchase of second-hand goods less the proceeds of sales of used goods. Excluded are interest and other transfer payments; all business expenditure; and the purchase of land and buildings (and associated costs).

In principle, expenditure is measured at the time of acquisition rather than actual disbursement of cash. The categories of expenditure include that of non-resident as well as resident households and individuals in the United Kingdom.

From September 2003, UK economic growth has been calculated in a different way. Previously the detailed estimates for growth for different parts of the economy were summed to a total by weighting each component according to its share of total expenditure in 1995. The year from which this information was drawn was updated at five-yearly intervals. This is described as 'fixed base aggregation'.

The new method, 'annual chain-linking', uses information updated every year to give each component the most relevant weight that can be estimated. The new method has been used for estimating change in household expenditure since 1971.

For further details see *Consumer Trends* at: **www.statistics.gov.uk/consumertrends**

From April 2001, the Family Expenditure Survey (FES) was replaced by the Expenditure and Food Survey (EFS). This was formed by merging the FES with the National Food Survey (NFS). It continues to produce the information previously provided by the FES.

The EFS definition of household expenditure represents current expenditure on goods and services. This excludes those recorded payments that are savings or investments (for example, life assurance premiums). Similarly, income tax payments, national insurance contributions, mortgage capital repayments and other payments for major additions to dwellings are excluded. For further details see *Family Spending* at: **www.statistics.gov.uk/familyspending**

Classification of Individual Consumption by Purpose

From 2001/02, the **C**lassification **O**f **I**ndividual **CO**nsumption by **P**urpose (COICOP) was introduced as a new coding frame for expenditure items in the Expenditure and Food Survey. COICOP has been adapted to the needs of Household Budget Surveys (HBS) across the European Union and, as a consequence, is compatible with similar classifications used in National Accounts and consumer price indices. This allows the production of indicators that are comparable Europe-wide, such as the Harmonised Indices of Consumer Prices.

Twelve categories are used and in this edition of *Social Trends*, labelled as food and non-alcoholic drink; alcohol and tobacco; clothing and footwear; housing, water and fuel; household goods and services; health; transport; communication; recreation and culture; education; restaurants and hotels; and miscellaneous goods and services.

A major difference also exists in the treatment of rent and mortgages that were included as part of 'housing' expenditure in the previous editions of *Social Trends* in the FES coding frame. Rent and mortgages are now excluded from the COICOP 'housing, water and fuel' category and are recorded under 'other expenditure items'.

National Statistics Socio-economic Classification (NS-SEC)

From 2001, the National Statistics Socio-economic Classification (NS-SEC) was adopted for all official surveys, in place of Social Class based on Occupation and Socio-economic Group. NS-SEC is itself based on the Standard Occupational Classification 2000 (SOC2000) and details of employment status.

The NS-SEC is an occupationally-based classification designed to provide coverage of the whole adult population. The version of the classification, which will be used for most analyses, has eight classes, the first of which can be subdivided. These are:

1. Higher managerial and professional occupations, sub-divided into:

    1.1 Large employers and higher managerial occupations

    1.2 Higher professional occupations

2. Lower managerial and professional occupations

3. Intermediate occupations

4. Small employers and own account workers

5. Lower supervisory and technical occupations

6. Semi-routine occupations

7. Routine occupations

8. Never worked and long-term unemployed

The classes can be further grouped into:

i. Managerial and professional occupations 1,2

ii. Intermediate occupations 3,4

iii. Routine and manual occupations 5,6,7

Never worked and long-term unemployed 8

The 'Never worked and long-term unemployed' have no class number. Users have the option to include them in the overall analysis or keep them separate. The long-term unemployed are defined as those unemployed and seeking work for 12 months or more. Members of the armed forces, who were shown separately in tables of Social Class, are included within the NS-SEC classification. Residual groups that remain unclassified include students and those with inadequately described occupations. For the purposes of Family Spending, retired individuals are not assigned an NS-SEC category.

Further details can be found on the National Statistics website: **www.statistics.gov.uk/ methods_quality/ns_sec/default.asp**

Retired households

Retired households are those where the household reference person is over state pension age (65 years old for men and 60 years old for women) and economically inactive. Hence if, for example, a male household reference person is over 65 years of age, but working part time or waiting to take up a part-time job, this household would not be classified as a retired household. For analysis purposes two categories are used:

a. 'A retired household mainly dependent upon state pensions' is one in which at least three quarters of the total income of the household is derived from national insurance retirement and similar pensions, including housing and other benefits paid in supplement to or instead of such pensions. The term 'national insurance retirement and similar pensions' includes national insurance disablement and war disability pensions, and income support in conjunction with these disability payments.

b. 'Other retired households' are retired households that do not fulfil the income conditions of 'retired household mainly dependent upon state pensions' because more than a quarter of the household's income derives from occupational retirement pensions and/or income from investments, annuities, etc.

Harmonised index of consumer prices

The harmonised index of consumer prices (HICP) has been known as the consumer prices index in the United Kingdom since 10 December 2003. HICPs are calculated in each member state of the European Union for the purposes of European comparisons, as required by the Maastricht Treaty. From January 1999 the HICP has been used by the European Central Bank (ECB) as the measure for its definition of price stability across the euro area. Further details are contained in an ECB Press Notice released on 13 October 1998: 'A stability oriented monetary policy strategy for the ESCB'.

A guide to the HICP can be found on the National Statistics website: **www.statistics.gov.uk/hicp**

Before 1995 the HICP had to be estimated using available data sources. For 1988 to 1995 the HICP was estimated from archived RPI price quotes and historical weights data, and aggregated up to the published COICOP weights. Therefore, the estimated HICP is based on the RPI household population and not all private households, and it does not account for all items included in the official HICP. Between 1975 and 1987 the estimated HICP was based on published RPI section indices and weights, and unpublished item indices and weights for items excluded from the HICP. This estimated HICP can only be considered as a broad indicator of the official HICP.

For more information about how the HICP was estimated see the 'Harmonised Index of Consumer Prices: Historical Estimates' paper in Economic Trends, no. 541.

Retail prices index

The retail prices index (RPI) is the most familiar general purpose measure of inflation in the United Kingdom. It measures the average change from month to month in the prices of goods and services purchased by most households in the United Kingdom. The spending pattern on which the index is based is revised each year, mainly using information from the Expenditure and Food Survey (EFS). The RPI comprises all private households (i.e. not those living in institutions such as prisons, retirement homes or in student accommodation) excluding:

a. high income households, defined as those households with a total income within the top

4 per cent of all households, as measured by each quarter's EFS; and

b. 'pensioner' households which derive at least three quarters of their total income from state pensions and benefits.

It is considered that such households are likely to spend their money on atypical things and including them in the scope of the RPI would distort the overall average. Expenditure patterns of one-person and two-person 'pensioner' households differ from those of the households upon which the RPI is based. Separate indices have been compiled for such pensioner households since 1969, and quarterly averages are published on the National Statistics website, Focus on Consumer Price Indices (formerly known as the Consumer Price Indices (CPI) Business Monitor MM23). They are chained indices constructed in the same way as the RPI. It should, however, be noted that the pensioner indices exclude housing costs.

A guide to the RPI can be found on the National Statistics website: **www.statistics.gov.uk/rpi**

Consumer prices index

The consumer prices index (CPI) is the main UK domestic measure of inflation for macro-economic purposes. Prior to 10 December 2003 this index in the United Kingdom was published as the harmonised index of consumer prices and the two shall remain one and the same index.

The methodology of the CPI is similar to that of the RPI but differs in the following ways:

1. in the CPI, the geometric mean is used to aggregate the prices at the most basic level whereas the RPI uses arithmetic means;

2. a number of RPI series are excluded from the CPI, most particularly, those mainly relating to owner occupiers' housing costs (eg mortgage interest payments, house depreciation, council tax and buildings insurance);

3. the coverage of the CPI indices is based on the international classification system, COICOP (Classification of Individual Consumption by Purpose), whereas the RPI uses its own bespoke classification;

4. the CPI includes series for university accommodation fees, foreign students' university tuition fees, unit trust and stockbrokers charges, none of which are included in the RPI;

5. the index for new car prices in the RPI is imputed from movements in second hand car prices, whereas the CPI uses a quality adjusted index based on published prices of new cars;

6. the CPI weights are based on expenditure by all private households, foreign visitors to the UK and residents of institutional households. In the RPI, weights are based on expenditure by private households only, excluding the highest income households, and pensioner households mainly dependent on state benefits; and

7. in the construction of the RPI weights, expenditure on insurance is assigned to the relevant insurance heading. For the CPI weights, the amount paid out in insurance claims is distributed amongst the COICOP headings according to the nature of the claims expenditure with the residual (i.e. the

service charge) being allocated to the relevant insurance heading.

A guide to the CPI can be found on the National Statistics website: www.statistics.gov.uk/cpi

Part 7: Health

Expectation of life

The expectation of life is the average total number of years that a person of that age could be expected to live, if the rates of mortality at each age were those experienced in that year. The mortality rates that underlie the expectation of life figures are based, up to 2003, on total deaths occurring in each year for England and Wales and the total deaths registered in each year in Scotland and Northern Ireland.

Healthy life expectancy

Healthy life expectancy, defined as expected years of life in good or fairly good self-assessed general health, is one example of health expectancy. ONS calculates this measure using life tables from the Government Actuary's Department and morbidity data from the ONS General Household Survey (GHS), specifically responses to the question 'Over the last 12 months would you say your health has on the whole been good, fairly good, or not good?' 'Good' and 'Fairly good' responses are taken as a positive measure of health. The GHS was not conducted in either 1997 or 1999. The resulting modifications to the annual series of healthy life expectancy data are:

a. no data points are calculated for the years 1996, 1998 and 2000;

b. the data points for 1997 and 1999 are each calculated on just two years of GHS health data, 1997 on 1996 and 1998 data, and 1999 on 1998 and 2000 data.

Self-reported illness

The General Household Survey includes two measures of self-reported illness:

a. *Chronic illness*. Respondents aged 16 and over are asked whether they have any longstanding illness or disability that has troubled them for some time. Information about children is collected from a responsible adult, usually the mother. Those who report a longstanding condition, either on their own behalf or that of their children, are asked whether it limits their activities in any way (this is shown in Table 7.2 as 'limiting longstanding illness').

b. *Acute sickness*. Respondents are asked whether they had to cut down on their normal activities in the two weeks before interview as a result of illness or injury (this is known as 'restricted activity').

Standardised rates

Directly age-standardised incidence rates enable comparisons to be made between geographical areas, over time, and between the sexes, which are independent of changes in the age structure of the population. In each year, the crude rates in each five-year age group are multiplied by the European standard population for that age group. These are then summed and divided by the total standard population for these age groups to give an overall standardised rate.

International Classification of Diseases

The International Classification of Diseases (ICD) is a coding scheme for diseases and causes of death. The Tenth Revision of the ICD (ICD10) was introduced for coding the underlying cause of death in Scotland from 2000 and in the rest of the United Kingdom from 2001. The causes of death included in Figure 7.4 correspond to the following ICD10 codes: circulatory diseases I00–I99: cancer C00–D48: respiratory diseases J00–J99 and infectious diseases A00–B99. Rates for 2000 are for England and Wales only.

The data presented in Figure 7.4 cover three different revisions of the ICD. Although they have been selected according to codes that are comparable, there may still be differences between years that are due to changes in the rules used to select the underlying cause of death. This can be seen in deaths from respiratory diseases where different interpretation of these rules were used to code the underlying cause of death from 1983 to 1992, and from 2001 onwards in England and Wales, and 2000 onwards in Scotland.

Immunisation

Data shown in Table 7.6 relate to children reaching their second birthday and immunised by their second birthday.

Body mass index

The body mass index (BMI) shown in Figure 7.8, is the most widely used index of obesity among adults aged 16 and over. The BMI standardises weight for height and is calculated as weight $(kg)/height (m)^2$. Underweight is defined as a BMI of 20 or less, desirable over 20 to 25, overweight over 25 to 30 and obese over 30. There is no generally agreed BMI criterion for classifying overweight and obesity in children, but two widely favoured indicators are based respectively on percentiles of UK reference curves (85th percentile for overweight, 95th percentile for obesity) and on reference points derived from an international (six country) survey.

Drug-related poisoning deaths

These figures represent the number of deaths where the underlying cause of death is regarded as resulting from drug-related poisoning, according to the current National Statistics definition. This includes all drug-related poisoning deaths, including those from prescription drugs such as paracetamol. The data on drug-related poisoning deaths do not include deaths from other causes that may have been related to drug taking (eg road traffic accidents or HIV/AIDS).

NHS Stop Smoking Services

The establishment and development of NHS Stop Smoking Services (or Smoking Cessation Services) is an important element of the Government's strategy, in recognition that many smokers want to stop but find it hard to do so. Stop Smoking Services provide a new approach to helping people to quit smoking through advice from healthcare professionals and the use of pharmacological products, such as Nicotine Replacement Therapy products and bupropion (Zyban). General Practitioners are also encouraged to provide brief advice to smokers to stop, in the course of their normal duties.

Breast cancer and cervical screening programmes

Screening programmes are in operation in the United Kingdom for breast and cervical cancer. Under the breast screening programme, every women aged between 50 and 64 is invited for mammography (breast X-ray) every three years by computerised call-up and recall systems. In addition, all women over the age of 64 can refer themselves for screening. In England, an extension to the automatic recall system to invite women aged 65 to 70 began on a phased basis in 2001. In Scotland, the extension began on a phased basis in 2003 and will be implemented over a three-year round of screening. In Wales, an extension to women aged 65 to 67 was piloted in certain areas in 2003. Following a review of the pilot, it is intended to extend the screening programme to all women in Wales up to the age of 70.

Prescription Cost Analysis system

Data from the Prescription Cost Analysis system cover all prescriptions dispensed by community pharmacists and dispensing doctors in England. The system covers prescriptions originating from general practices and also those written by nurses, dentists and hospital doctors provided they are dispensed in the community. Also included are prescriptions written in Wales, Scotland, Northern Ireland and the Isle of Man but dispensed in England. Information on items dispensed in hospitals is not available.

Part 8: Social protection

Informal carers

Within the Census 2001, the term 'unpaid care' covers any unpaid help, looking after or supporting family members, friends, neighbours or others because of long-term physical or mental ill-health or disability or problems related to old age.

In-patient activity

In Table 8.11 in-patient data for England and later years for Northern Ireland are based on finished consultant episodes (FCEs). Data for Wales, Scotland and Northern Ireland are based on deaths and discharges and transfers between specialities (between hospitals in Northern Ireland). An FCE is a completed period of care of a patient using a bed, under one consultant, in a particular NHS Trust or directly managed unit. If a patient is transferred from one consultant to another within the same hospital, this counts as an FCE but not a hospital discharge. Conversely if a patient is transferred from one hospital to another provider, this counts as an FCE and a hospital discharge.

Data for England, Wales and Northern Ireland exclude NHS beds and activity in joint-user and contractual hospitals. For Scotland, data for joint-user and contractual hospitals are included.

Health and personal social services staff

In Table 8.15, general medical practitioners (GMPs) include general medical services (GMS) unrestricted principals, personal medical services (PMS) contracted GPs, PMS salaried GPs, restricted principals, assistants, GP registrars, salaried doctors and other PMS, but excludes GP retainers. GP whole time equivalent data have been estimated using the results from the 1992–93 GMP Workload Survey where full time equalled 1.00; three quarter time equalled 0.69; job share equalled 0.65; and half time equalled 0.60. Data are at 30 September except for England in 1993, which are for 1 October, and for Scotland, which are at 1 October every year.

The number of general dental practitioners is a headcount of dentists on Primary Care Trust /Health Authority/Family Health Services Authority lists and their assistants and vocational dental practitioners at 30 September.

Personal social services staff includes staff employed only at local authority social services departments (whole time equivalent) at 30 September. The figures for Scotland relate to the first Monday in October.

Activities of daily living (ADLs) and instrumental activities of daily living (IADLs)

Within Table 8.17, to assess mobility, ADLs and IADLs, respondents were asked whether they had any problem doing any of the activities on a showcard. For the mobility question subjects were asked to exclude any difficulties which they expected to last less than three months.

Mobility (leg) and arm function showcard
1 Walking 100 yards
2 Sitting for about two hours
3 Getting up from a chair after sitting for long periods
4 Climbing several flights of stairs without resting
5 Climbing one flight of stairs without resting
6 Stooping, kneeling, or crouching
7 Reaching or extending your arms above shoulder level
8 Pulling or pushing large objects like a living room chair
9 Lifting or carrying weights over 10 pounds, like a heavy bag of groceries
10 Picking up a 5p coin from a table
96 None of these.

ADLs and IADLs showcard
1 Dressing, including putting on shoes and socks
2 Walking across a room
3 Bathing or showering
4 Eating, such as cutting up food
5 Getting in or out of bed
6 Using the toilet, including getting up or down
7 Using a map to figure out how to get around in a strange place
8 Preparing a hot meal
9 Shopping for groceries
10 Making telephone calls
11 Taking medications
12 Doing work around the house or garden
13 Managing money such as paying bills and keeping track of expenses
96 None of these.

Benefit units

A benefit unit is a single adult or couple living as married and any dependent children, where the head is below state pension age (60 and over for females and 65 and over for males). A pensioner benefit unit is where the head is over state pension age. The head of the benefit unit is either the household reference person where he or she belongs to the benefit unit, otherwise it is the first person listed at interview in the benefit unit – for couples it is usually the male.

Children looked after by local authorities

In England and Wales children's homes include homes, hostels and secure units. In Northern Ireland this category includes homes and secure units but excludes hostels, which are included in the other accommodation category.

In Northern Ireland, the category placement with parents is collected as 'placed with family'.

Part 9: Crime and justice

Types of offences in England and Wales

The figures are compiled from police returns to the Home Office or directly from court computer systems.

In England and Wales, indictable only offences cover those offences that can only be tried at the Crown Court and include the more serious offences. Summary offences are those for which a defendant would normally be tried at a magistrates' court and are generally less serious – the majority of motoring offences fall into this category. Triable-either-way offences are triable either on indictment or summarily.

Recorded crime statistics broadly cover the more serious offences. Up to March 1998 most indictable and triable-either-way offences were included, as well as some summary ones; from April 1998, all indictable and triable-either-way offences were included, plus a few closely related summary ones.

Recorded offences are the most readily available measures of the incidence of crime, but do not necessarily indicate the true level of crime. Many less serious offences are not reported to the police and cannot, therefore, be recorded. Moreover, the propensity of the public to report offences to the police is influenced by a number of factors and may change over time.

From 2000, some police forces have changed their systems to record the allegations of victims unless there is credible evidence that a crime has *not* taken place. In April 2002, the new National Crime Recording Standard (NCRS) formalised these changes across England and Wales.

There have been changes to the methodology of the British Crime Survey. Between 1982 and 2001 the survey was carried out every two years, and reported on victimisation in the previous calendar year. The 2002/03 and 2003/04 surveys cover the financial year of interviews and report on victimisation in the 12 months before the interview.

This change makes the survey's estimates more comparable with figures collected by the police. Because of these significant changes

taking place in both measures of crime, direct comparisons with figures for previous years cannot be made.

Types of offences in Northern Ireland

In recording crime, the Police Service of Northern Ireland broadly follows the Home Office rules for counting crime. As from 1 April 1998 notifiable offences are recorded on the same basis as those in England and Wales. Prior to the revision of the rules, criminal damage offences in Northern Ireland excluded those where the value of the property damaged was less than £200.

Offences and crimes

There are a number of reasons why recorded crime statistics in England and Wales, Northern Ireland and Scotland cannot be directly compared:

Different legal systems: The legal system operating in Scotland differs from that in England and Wales, and Northern Ireland. For example, in Scotland children aged under 16 are normally dealt with for offending by the Children's Hearings system rather than the courts.

Differences in classification: There are significant differences in the offences included within the recorded crime categories used in Scotland and the categories of notifiable offences used in England, Wales and Northern Ireland. Scottish figures of 'crime' have therefore been grouped in an attempt to approximate to the classification of notifiable offences in England, Wales and Northern Ireland.

Counting rules: In Scotland each individual offence occurring within an incident is recorded whereas in England, Wales and Northern Ireland only the main offence is counted.

Burglary: This term is not applicable to Scotland where the term used is 'housebreaking'.

Theft from vehicles: In Scotland data have only been separately identified from January 1992. The figures include theft by opening lockfast places of a motor vehicle and other theft from a motor vehicle.

National Crime Recording Standard

Changes in the counting rules for recorded crime on 1 April 1998 affected both the methods of counting and the coverage for recorded crime, and had the effect of inflating the number of crimes recorded. For some offence groups – homicide, violence against the person and burglary – there was likely to be little effect on numbers recorded. However the changes will have had more effect on figures for minor violence and criminal damage. In April 2002 a new National Crime Recording Standard (NCRS) was introduced in England and Wales with the aim of taking a more victim centred approach and providing more consistency between police forces. Prior to 2002, police forces in England and Wales did not necessarily record a crime that was reported if there was no evidence to support the claim of the victim. Therefore recorded crime rates have been adjusted to allow comparison between recent years and pre-2002 statistics.

It is not possible to assess the effect of NCRS on recorded firearms crimes. NCRS inflated the overall number of offences of violence against the person and criminal damage, but has less effect on the number of robberies. Many firearms offences are among the less serious categories, and these types of offences are among those most affected by NCRS.

The introduction of the NCRS may have had an effect on the recorded crime detection rate, but this is difficult to quantify.

ACORN

A Classification Of Residential Neighbourhoods (ACORN), developed by CACI Ltd, classifies households according to the demographic, employment and housing characteristics of the surrounding neighbourhood. ACORN is most useful in determining the social environment in which households are located. The new 2001 ACORN has been used in the 2003/04 British Crime Survey. The main ACORN groups are characterised as follows:

Wealthy Achievers: Wealthy executive, affluent older people and well-off families.

Urban Prosperity: Prosperous professionals, young urban professionals and students living in town and city areas.

Comfortably Off: Young couples, secure families, older couples living in the suburbs and pensioners.

Moderate Means: Asian communities, post-industrial families and skilled manual workers.

Hard Pressed: Low-income families, residents in council areas, people living in high-rise, inner-city estates.

Home security measures

The British Crime Survey (BCS) included a module about crime prevention and security measures in homes that covered the following:

Police Security Survey: Respondents were asked if they had had a security survey done since moving to the house currently occupied.

Burglar/dummy alarms: The 1994 and 1996 surveys asked if the house had a burglar alarm. From 1998 it asked about both real and dummy alarm boxes. From 2000 the question on real burglar alarms specified that the alarm must be real and not a dummy, whereas in 1998 this was not the case.

Security chains/bolts: Results are not directly comparable. From 2001/02 respondents were asked if there were chains on the inside of at least some doors. Previously the question had specified chains and bolts on at least some doors and windows, and in the 2000 BCS the question specified external doors.

Window locks and Window bars/grilles: On at least some windows/doors.

Internal and External light timers/sensors: From 1998 there were separate questions for internal and external security lights. In previous BCS surveys this distinction was not made.

Offenders cautioned for burglary

In England and Wales offenders cautioned for going equipped for stealing, etc were counted

against burglary offences until 1986 and against other offences from 1987. Historical data provided in Table 9.16 have been amended to take account of this change. Drug offences were included under other offences for 1971.

Sentences and orders

The following are the main sentences and orders that can be imposed upon those persons found guilty. Some types of sentence or order can only be given to offenders in England and Wales in certain age groups. Under the framework for sentencing contained in the *Criminal Justice Acts 1991, 1993* and the *Powers of Criminal Courts (Sentencing) Act 2000*, the sentence must reflect the seriousness of the offence. The following sentences are available for adults (a similar range of sentences is available to juveniles aged 10 to 17):

Absolute and conditional discharge: A court may make an order discharging a person absolutely or (except in Scotland) conditionally where it is inexpedient to inflict punishment and, before 1 October 1992, where a probation order was not appropriate. An order for conditional discharge runs for such period of not more than three years as the court specifies, the condition being that the offender does not commit another offence within the period so specified. In Scotland a court may also discharge a person with an admonition.

Attendance Centre Order: Available in England, Wales and Northern Ireland for young offenders and involves deprivation of free time.

Reparation Order: Introduced under the *Powers of Criminal Courts (Sentencing) Act 2000*. This requires the offender to make an apology to the victim or apologise in person. Maximum duration of the order is 24 hours and is only available to youngsters aged 10 to 18 in England and Wales.

Action Plan Order: An order imposed for a maximum of three months in England, Wales and Northern Ireland to address certain behavioural problems. This is again available for the younger age groups and is considered as early intervention to stop serious offending.

Drug Treatment and Testing Order: This is imposed as a treatment order to reduce the person's dependence on drugs and to test if the offender is complying with treatment. Length of order can run from six months to three years in England, Wales and Northern Ireland. This was introduced under the *Powers of Criminal Courts (Sentencing) Act 2000* for persons aged 16 years and over.

Community sentence: The term 'community sentence' refers to community rehabilitation orders, supervision orders, community punishment orders, attendance centre orders, community punishment and rehabilitation orders, reparation orders, action plan orders, drug treatment and testing orders, curfew orders and referral orders. Under the *Criminal Justice and Courts Services Act 2000*, certain community orders current at 1 April 2001 were renamed. Probation orders were renamed community rehabilitation orders, community service orders were renamed community punishment orders and combination orders were renamed community punishment and rehabilitation orders.

Community Rehabilitation Order: An offender sentenced to a probation order is under the supervision of a probation officer (social worker in Scotland), whose duty it is (in England and Wales and Northern Ireland) to advise, assist and befriend him or her. The court has the power to include any other requirement it considers appropriate. A cardinal feature of the order is that it relies on the co-operation of the offender. Community rehabilitation orders may be given for any period between six months and three years inclusive.

Community Punishment Order: An offender who is convicted of an offence punishable with imprisonment may be sentenced to perform unpaid work for not more than 240 hours (300 hours in Scotland), and not less than 40 hours. Twenty hours minimum community service is given for persistent petty offending or fine default. In Scotland the *Law Reform (Miscellaneous Provisions) (Scotland) Act 1990* requires that community service can only be ordered where the court would otherwise have imposed imprisonment or detention. Probation and community service may be combined in a single order in Scotland. Community Punishment Order came into effect under the *Powers of Criminal Courts (Sentencing) Act 2000* when it replaced the Supervision Order.

Community Punishment and Rehabilitation Order: The *Criminal Justice Act 1991* introduced the combination order in England and Wales only, which combines elements of both probation supervision and community service. Meanwhile, Article 15 of the Criminal Justice (NI) Order 1996 introduced the combination order to Northern Ireland. The *Powers of Criminal Courts (Sentencing) Act 2000* brought into effect the Community Punishment and Rehabilitation Order, known as the Combination Order, which requires an offender to be under a probation officer and to take on unpaid work.

Detention and Training Order: This was introduced for youths aged 10 to 18 under the *Powers of Criminal Courts (Sentencing) Act.* It is for youths who have committed a serious crime. They can serve the sentence at a young offender institution or at a local authority establishment, or local authority secure training centre. The sentence is given from 4 to 24 months, but sentences can run consecutively.

Imprisonment: The custodial sentence for adult offenders. In the case of mentally disordered offenders, hospital orders, which may include a restriction order, may be considered appropriate.

Home Office or Scottish Executive consent is needed for release or transfer. A new disposal, the 'hospital direction', was introduced in 1997. The court, when imposing a period of imprisonment, can direct that the offender be sent directly to hospital. On recovering from the mental disorder, the offender is returned to prison to serve the balance of their sentence. The *Criminal Justice Act 1991* abolished remission and substantially changed the parole scheme in England and Wales. Those serving sentences of under four years, imposed on or after 1 October 1992, are subject to Automatic Conditional Release and are released, subject to certain criteria, halfway through their sentence.

Home Detention Curfews result in selected prisoners being released up to two months early with a tag that monitors their presence during curfew hours. Those serving sentences of four years or longer are considered for Discretionary Conditional Release after having served half their sentence, but are automatically released at the two thirds point of sentence. The *Crime (Sentences) Act 1997*, implemented on 1 October 1997, included, for persons aged 18 or over, an automatic life sentence for a second serious violent or sexual offence unless there are exceptional circumstances. All offenders serving a sentence of 12 months or more are supervised in the community until the three quarter point of sentence. A life sentence prisoner may be released on licence subject to supervision and is always liable to recall. In Scotland the *Prisoners and Criminal Proceedings (Scotland) Act 1993* changed the system of remission and parole for prisoners sentenced on or after 1 October 1993. Those serving sentences of less than four years are released unconditionally after having served half of their sentence, unless the court specifically imposes a Supervised Release Order that subjects them to social work supervision after release. Those serving sentences of four years or more are eligible for parole at half sentence. If parole is not granted then they will automatically be released on licence at two thirds of sentence subject to days added for breaches of prison rules. All such prisoners are liable to be 'recalled on conviction' or for breach of conditions of licence, i.e. if between the date of release and the date on which the full sentence ends a person commits another offence that is punishable by imprisonment, or breaches his/her licence conditions, then the offender may be returned to prison for the remainder of that sentence whether or not a sentence of imprisonment is also imposed for the new offence.

Fully suspended sentences: These may only be passed in exceptional circumstances. In England, Wales and Northern Ireland, sentences of imprisonment of two years or less may be fully suspended. A court should not pass a suspended sentence unless a sentence of imprisonment would be appropriate in the absence of a power to suspend. The result of suspending a sentence is that it will not take effect unless during the period specified the offender is convicted of another offence punishable with imprisonment. Suspended sentences are not available in Scotland.

Fines: The *Criminal Justice Act 1993* introduced new arrangements on 20 September 1993 whereby courts are now required to fit an amount for the fine that reflects the seriousness of the offence and takes account of an offender's means. This system replaced the more formal unit fines scheme included in the *Criminal Justice Act 1991*. The Act also introduced the power for courts to arrange deduction of fines from income benefit for those offenders receiving such benefits. The *Law Reform (Miscellaneous Provision) (Scotland) Act 1990* as amended by the *Criminal Procedure (Scotland) Act 1995* provides for the use of supervised attendance orders by selected courts in Scotland. The *Criminal Procedure (Scotland) Act 1995* also makes it easier for

courts to impose a supervised attendance order in the event of a default and enables the court to impose a supervised attendance order in the first instance for 16 and 17 year olds.

Custody Probation Order: An order unique to Northern Ireland reflecting the different regime there that applies in respect of remission and the general absence of release on licence. The custodial sentence is followed by a period of supervision for a period of between 12 months and 3 years.

Civil courts

England and Wales: The main civil courts are the High Court and the county courts. The High court is divided into three divisions:

1. The *Queen's Bench Division* deals with disputes relating to contracts, general commercial matters and breaches of duty – known as 'liability in tort' – covering claims of negligence, nuisance or defamation.

2. The *Chancery Division* deals with disputes relating to land, wills, companies and insolvency.

3. The *Family Division* deals with matrimonial matters, including divorce, and the welfare of children.

Magistrates' courts also have some civil jurisdiction, mainly in family proceedings. Most appeals in civil cases go to the Court of Appeal (Civil Division) and may go from there to the House of Lords. Since July 1991, county courts have been able to deal with all contract and tort cases and actions for recovery of land, regardless of value. Cases are presided over by a judge who almost always sits without a jury. Jury trials are limited to specified cases, for example, actions for libel.

Scotland: The Court of Session is the supreme civil court. Any cause, apart from causes excluded by statute, may be initiated in, and any judgment of an inferior court may be appealed to, the Court of Session. The Sheriff Court is the principal local court of civil jurisdiction in Scotland. It also has jurisdiction in criminal proceedings. Apart from certain actions the civil jurisdiction of the Sheriff Court is generally similar to that of the Court of Session.

Legal professionals

To qualify as a barrister, it is necessary to complete three stages of training:

1. *Academic:* To fulfill this stage prospective barristers must achieve one of the following: pass an approved law degree (minimum grade 2:2) or pass a non-law degree (minimum grade 2:2) followed by a law conversion course, known as the Common Professional Examination (CPE) or a Graduate Diploma in Law (GDL), or a Senior Status Law degree. Exceptionally, mature people with a professional qualification considered equivalent to a degree may be granted a certificate of academic standing that allows them to take the CPE or GDL.

2. *Vocational:* When the academic stage has been completed, the vocational stage is undertaken – this involves joining one of the four Inns of Court. Once the Bar Vocational Course (BVC) is completed students are 'called to the Bar' by their Inn of Court. They remain a member of their Inn for the rest of their career.

3. *On the job training:* Pupilage is the final stage of training in which the students carry out a funded full-time 12-month period of on the job training, under the guidance of an approved pupil supervisor.

In the first three years of practice, barristers must obtain a tenancy in a set of chambers, or work with another barrister who has at least five years' experience. Barristers may then set up their own practice. Once qualified, barristers are subject to certain requirements to keep their practising certificates. This is called Continuing Professional Development (CPD) and is usually in the form of courses or lectures.

Part 10: Housing

Dwelling stock

The definition of a dwelling used follows the census definition applicable at that time. Currently the 2001 Census is used. This defined a dwelling as 'structurally separate accommodation'. This was determined primarily by considering the type of accommodation, as well as separate and shared access to multi-occupied properties.

In all stock figures, vacant dwellings are included but non-permanent dwellings are generally excluded. For housebuilding statistics, only data on permanent dwellings are collected.

Estimates of the total dwelling stock, stock changes and the tenure distribution for each country are made by the Office of the Deputy Prime Minister (ODPM), the Scottish Executive, the National Assembly for Wales, and the Northern Ireland Department for Social Development. These are primarily based on census output data for the number of dwellings (or households converted to dwellings) from the censuses of population for Great Britain. Adjustments were carried out if there were specific reasons to do so. Census years' figures are based on outputs from the censuses. For years between censuses, the total figures are obtained by projecting the base census year's figure forward yearly. The increment is based on the annual total number of completions plus the annual total net gain due to other housing flows statistics, i.e. conversions, demolitions and changes of use.

Estimates of dwelling stock by tenure category are primarily based on the census except in the situation where it is considered that for some specific tenure information, there are other more accurate sources. In this situation, it is assumed that the other data sources contain vacant dwellings also, but it is not certain and it is not expected that these data are very precise. Thus the allocation of vacant dwellings to tenure categories may not be completely accurate. This means that the margin of error for tenure categories are wider than for estimates of total stock.

For the 2001 Census, a comparison with other available sources indicated that for local authorities' stock, figures supplied by local authorities are more reliable. Similarly, it was found that Housing Corporation's own data are more accurate than those from the census for the registered social landlords' (RSLs) stock. Hence only the rented privately or with a job or business tenure data were used directly from the census. The owner-occupied data were taken as the residual of the total from the census. For non-census years, the same approach was adopted except for the privately rented or with a job or business for which Labour Force Survey results were considered to be appropriated for use.

In the Survey of English Housing, data for privately rented unfurnished accommodation include accommodation that is partly furnished.

For further information on the methodology used to calculate stock by tenure and tenure definitions, see Appendix B Notes and Definitions in the ODPM annual volume *Housing Statistics* or the housing statistics page of the ODPM website at: **www.odpm.gov.uk**

Dwellings completed

In principle, a dwelling is regarded as completed when it becomes ready for occupation whether it is in fact occupied or not. In practice, there are instances where the timing could be delayed and some completions are missed, for example, because no completion certificates were requested by the owner.

Tenure definition for housebuilding is only slightly different from that used for stock figures. For further information on the methodology used to calculate stock by tenure and tenure definitions, see Appendix B Notes and Definitions in the ODPM annual volume *Housing Statistics* or the housing statistics page of the ODPM website.

Sales and transfers of local authority dwellings

Right to buy was established by the *Housing Act 1980* and was introduced across Great Britain in October 1980.

In England, large scale voluntary transfers (LSVTs) of stock have been principally to housing associations/registered social landlords; figures include transfers supported by estate renewal challenge funding (ERCF). The figures for 1993 include 949 dwellings transferred under Tenants' Choice.

In Scotland large scale voluntary transfers to registered social landlords and trickle transfers to housing associations are included.

Homeless at home

Homeless at home refers to any arrangement where a household for whom a duty has been accepted (i.e. eligible for assistance, unintentionally homeless and in priority need) is able to remain in, or return to the accommodation from which they are being made homeless, or temporarily stay in other accommodation found by the applicant. Such schemes may locally be referred to as: Direct Rehousing, Prevention of Homelessness; Concealed Household Schemes; Prevention of Imminent Homelessness Schemes; Impending Homeless Schemes or Pre-eviction Schemes.

Bedroom standard

The concept is used to estimate occupation density by allocating a standard number of bedrooms to each household in accordance with its age/sex/marital status composition and the relationship of the members to one another. A separate bedroom is allocated to each married or cohabiting couple, any other person aged 21 or over, each pair of adolescents aged 10 to 20 of the same sex, and each pair of children under 10. Any unpaired person aged 10 to 20 is paired if possible with a child under 10 of the same sex, or, if that is not possible, is given a separate bedroom, as is any unpaired child under 10. This standard is then compared with the actual number of bedrooms (including bedsitters) available for the sole use of the household, and deficiencies or excesses are tabulated. Bedrooms converted to other uses are not counted as available unless they have been denoted as bedrooms by the informants; bedrooms not actually in use are counted unless uninhabitable.

Decent home standard

The Government's key housing target is for all housing rented from social landlords in England to meet the decent home standard by 2010. A decent home is one that:

a. meets the current statutory minimum for housing, which at present is the 'fitness standard';

b. is in a reasonable state of repair;

c. has reasonably modern facilities and services; and

d. provides a reasonable degree of thermal comfort.

Property transactions

The figures are based on the number of particular delivered (PD) forms processed by the Stamp Office or District Land Registry. They relate to the transfer or sale of any freehold interest in land or property, or the grant or transfer of a lease of at least 21 years and one day. In practice there is an average lag of about one month between the transaction and the date on which the PD form is processed.

Mix adjusted prices

Information on dwelling prices at national and regional levels are collected and published by the Office of the Deputy Prime Minister (ODPM) on a monthly basis from a sample survey of mortgage completions, the Survey of Mortgage Lenders (SML). The Survey covers about 50 banks and building societies that are members of the Council of Mortgage Lenders.

Data prior to the first quarter of 2002 were derived from a 5 per cent sample of completions data and were calculated on an old mix adjusted methodology. As a consequence of a significantly increased sample (to an average 25,000 cases per month), the ODPM has recently been able to introduce a new monthly series. The mix adjusted methodology has also been enhanced. The monthly series are available back to February 2002 and the prices for the calendar year 2003 have been derived as an average of these monthly prices. The annual change in price is shown as the average percentage change over the year and is calculated from the house price index.

A simple average price will be influenced by changes in the mix of properties bought in each period. This effect is removed by applying fixed weights to the process at the start of each year, based on the average mix of properties purchased during the previous three years, and these weights are applied to prices during the year.

The mix adjusted average price excludes sitting tenant (right to buy) purchases, cash purchases, remortgages and further loans.

Part 11: Environment

Rivers and canals

The chemical quality of rivers and canal waters in the United Kingdom are monitored in a series of separate national surveys in England and Wales, Scotland and Northern Ireland. In England, Wales and Northern Ireland the General Quality Assessment (GQA) Scheme provides a rigorous and objective method for assessing the basic chemical quality of rivers and canals based on three determinands: dissolved oxygen, biochemical oxygen demand (BOD) and ammoniacal nitrogen). The GQA grades river stretches into six categories (A–F) of chemical quality. Table 11.3 uses two broader groups – good (classes A and B) and fair (classes C and D). Classification of biological quality is based on the River Invertebrate Prediction and Classification System (RIVPACS).

The length of rivers chemically classified in Northern Ireland increased by more than 40 per cent between 1991 and 2001.

In Scotland water quality is based upon the Scottish River Classification Scheme of 20 June 1997, which combines chemical, biological, nutrient and aesthetic quality using the following classes: excellent (A1), good (A2), fair (B), poor (C) and seriously polluted (D). In 1999 a new Digitised River Network was introduced.

Bathing waters

Directive 76/160/EEC concerning the quality of bathing waters sets the following mandatory standards for the coliform parameters:

1. for total coliforms, 10,000 per 100 millilitres; and

2. for faecal coliforms 2,000 per 100 millilitres.

The directive requires that at least 95 per cent of samples taken for each of these parameters over the bathing season must meet the mandatory values. In practice this has been interpreted in the following manner: where 20 samples are taken only one sample for each parameter may exceed the mandatory values for the water to pass the coliform standards; where less than 20 samples are taken, none may exceed the mandatory values for the water to pass the coliform standards.

The bathing season is from mid-May to end-September in England and Wales, but is shorter in Scotland and Northern Ireland. Bathing waters that are closed for a season are excluded for that year.

The boundaries of the Environment Agency regions are based on river catchment areas and not county borders. In particular, the figures shown for Wales are for the Environment Agency Welsh Region, the boundary of which does not correspond to the boundary of Wales.

Noise complaints

Complaints about road traffic, aircraft and other noise, which fall outside the responsibilities of the Environmental Health Officers (EHOs), are likely to be considerably understated in this data. Complaints about road traffic noise are more likely to be addressed to highway authorities or the Department for Transport (DfT) and complaints about aircraft noise would be more likely to be reported to aircraft operators, airports, DfT or the Civil Aviation Authority so would not be included in Table 11.5. Consequently, the information reported to the EHOs is considered to give an approximate indication of the trend in noise complaints from these sources.

Fuels for energy use

Energy use of fuel mainly comprises use for lighting, heating or cooling, motive power and power for appliances. Non-energy uses of fuel include chemical feedstock, solvents, lubricants, and road making material.

Coal includes other solid fuels. Petroleum excludes marine bunkers. Natural gas includes colliery methane and non-energy use of natural gas up to 1998. Primary includes nuclear, hydroelectric and renewable energy.

Land use change

The uses of land given are as defined in *Land Use Change Statistics*, published by the Office of the Deputy Prime Minister.

Land use change data have been obtained from Ordnance Survey (OS) since 1985. A land use change is recorded as part of OS's map revision process, when the current land use category of a parcel of land differs from that depicted on the existing OS map. A change is also recorded where there is no change in the appropriate land use category, but new features are added, such as a house being demolished and one or more built in its place, or an additional house being built within the grounds of an existing house. Change is not recorded, however, if it does not affect the OS map, generally where there is no physical change. This would include in particular, conversions within existing buildings.

The majority of changes are recorded within five years of the change occurring. However, changes involving physical development (eg new houses or industrial buildings) tend to be recorded more quickly than changes between other uses (eg between agriculture and forestry).

Forest and woodland

The forestry data shown in Table 11.15 for Great Britain are compiled by the Forestry Commission and cover both private and state-owned land. Estimates are based on the results of the National Inventory of Woodland and Trees for 1995–99 and extrapolated forward using information about new planting and other changes. Data for Northern Ireland are compiled separately by the Forest Service, an agency of the Northern Ireland Department of Agriculture and Rural Development, and also cover both private and state-owned land.

New woodland creation

For Figure 11.19, areas receiving grant aid are allocated to years by date of payment, except

for England in 2003–04, which are by date of claim. A further 1,478 hectares of new planting, claimed in 2002–03 and paid in 2003–04, is excluded.

Part 12: Transport

Road traffic

The figures from 1993 to 2002 have been produced on a new basis and are not directly comparable with earlier figures. In 2001/02, steps were taken to improve the quality of Department for Transport's major road network database. The net result of these improvements has been little change to the estimates of total motor vehicle traffic for Great Britain for after 1993, but some changes to the composition of the overall figure. In general, from 1993 to 1999 the new motorway traffic estimates are now higher than before, while those for other major roads are lower, with the reverse being true for 2000 and 2001.

National Travel Survey

The National Travel Survey (NTS) has been conducted on a small scale continuous basis since July 1988. The last of the previous ad hoc surveys was carried out in 1985–86.

Information was collected from about 3,000 households in Great Britain each year up to 2001, 7,400 households in 2002 and over 8,000 in 2003. Each member of the household provides personal information (for example, age, sex, working status, driving licence, season ticket) and details of trips carried out in a sample week, including the purpose of the trip, method of travel, time of day, length, duration, and cost of any tickets bought.

Travel included in the NTS covers all trips by British residents within Great Britain for personal reasons, including travel in the course of work.

A trip is defined as a one-way course of travel having a single main purpose. It is the basic unit of personal travel defined in the survey. A round trip is split into two trips, with the first ending at a convenient point about half-way round as a notional stopping point for the outward destination and return origin. A stage is that portion of a trip defined by the use of a specific method of transport or of a specific ticket (a new stage being defined if either the mode or ticket changes).

Cars are regarded as household cars if they are either owned by a member of the household, or available for the private use of household members. Company cars provided by an employer for the use of a particular employee (or director) are included, but cars borrowed temporarily from a company pool are not.

The main driver of a household car is the household member that drives the furthest in that car in the course of a year.

The purpose of a trip is normally taken to be the activity at the destination, unless that destination is 'home' in which case the purpose is defined by the origin of the trip. The classification of trips to 'work' is also dependent on the origin of the trip. The following purposes are distinguished:

Commuting: trips to a usual place of work from home, or from work to home.

Business: personal trips in the course of work, including a trip in the course of work back to work. This includes all work trips by people with no usual place of work (eg, site workers) and those who work at or from home.

Education: trips to school or college, etc by full-time students, students on day-release and part-time students following vocational courses.

Escort: used when the traveller has no purpose of his or her own, other than to escort or accompany another person; eg, taking a child to school. Escort commuting is escorting or accompanying someone from home to work or from work to home.

Shopping: all trips to shops or from shops to home, even if there was no intention to buy.

Personal business: visits to services, eg hairdressers, launderettes, dry-cleaners, betting shops, solicitors, banks, estate agents, libraries, churches; or for medical consultations or treatment, or for eating and drinking, unless the main purpose was entertainment or social.

Social or entertainment: visits to meet friends, relatives, or acquaintances, both at someone's home or at a pub, restaurant, etc; all types of entertainment or sport, clubs, and voluntary work, non-vocational evening classes, political meetings, etc.

Holidays or day trips: trips (within Great Britain) to or from any holiday (including stays of four nights or more with friends or relatives) or trips for pleasure (not otherwise classified as social or entertainment) within a single day.

Just walk: walking pleasure trips along public highways including taking the dog for a walk and jogging.

Car ownership

The figures for household ownership include four wheeled and three wheeled cars, off-road vehicles, minibuses, motorcaravans, dormobiles, and light vans. Company cars normally available for household use are also included.

Traffic speeds

The speed limits given in Table 12.12 are the national speed limits for each type of road. Data in the table are for non-urban roads, and are average traffic speeds from 27 motorway sites, 7 dual carriageway sites and 26 single carriageway sites. Urban roads are major and minor roads within an urban area with a population of 10,000 or more, based on the 2001 Office of the Deputy Prime Minister definition of Urban Settlements. Speed measurements for urban roads with speed limits of 30 miles per hour were taken from 26 sites.

Passenger death rates

Passenger fatality rates given in Table 12.19 can be interpreted as the risk a traveller runs of being killed, per billion kilometres travelled. The coverage varies for each mode of travel and care should be exercised in drawing comparisons between the rates for different modes.

The table provides information on passenger fatalities and where possible travel by drivers and other crew in the course of their work has been excluded. Exceptions are for private journeys and those in company owned cars and vans where drivers are included.

Figures for all modes of transport exclude confirmed suicides and deaths through natural causes. Figures for air, rail and water exclude trespassers and rail excludes attempted suicides. Accidents occurring in airports, seaports and railway stations that do not directly involve the mode of transport concerned are also excluded, eg, deaths sustained on escalators or falling over packages on platforms.

The figures are compiled by the Department for Transport. Further information is available in the annual publications *Road Casualties Great Britain: Annual Report* and *Transport Statistics Great Britain*. Both are published by The Stationery Office and are available at: **www.dft.gov.uk/transtat**

The following definitions are used:

Air: accidents involving UK registered airline aircraft in UK and foreign airspace. Fixed wing and rotary wing aircraft are included but air taxis are excluded. Accidents cover UK airline aircraft around the world not just in the United Kingdom.

Rail: train accidents and accidents occurring through movement of railway vehicles in Great Britain. As well as national rail the figures include accidents on underground and tram systems, Eurotunnel and minor railways.

Water: figures for travel by water include both domestic and international passenger carrying services of UK registered merchant vessels.

Road: figures refer to Great Britain and include accidents occurring on the public highway (including footways) in which at least one road vehicle or a vehicle in collision with a pedestrian is involved and which becomes known to the police within 30 days of its occurrence. Figures include both public and private transport.

Bus or coach: figures for work buses are included. From 1 January 1994, the casualty definition was revised to include only those vehicles equipped to carry 17 or more passengers regardless of use. Prior to 1994 these vehicles were coded according to construction, whether or not they were being used for carrying passengers. Vehicles constructed as buses that were privately licensed were included under 'bus and coach' but PSV licensed minibuses were included under cars.

Car: includes taxis, invalid tricycles, three and four wheel cars and minibuses. Prior to 1999 motor caravans were also included.

Van: vans mainly include vehicles of the van type constructed on a car chassis. From 1 January 1994 these are defined as those vehicles not over 3.5 tonnes maximum permissible gross vehicle weight. Prior to 1994 the weight definition was not over 1.524 tonnes unladen.

Two-wheeled motor vehicle: mopeds, motor scooters and motor cycles (including motor cycle combinations).

Pedal cycle: includes tandems, tricycles and toy cycles ridden on the carriageway.

Pedestrian: includes persons riding toy cycles on the footway, persons pushing bicycles, pushing or pulling other vehicles or operating pedestrian controlled vehicles, those leading or herding animals, occupants of prams or wheelchairs, and people who alight safely from vehicles and are subsequently injured.

Articles published in previous editions

No.1 1970

Some general developments in social statistics Professor C A Moser, CSO

Public expenditure on the social services Professor B Abel-Smith, London School of Economics and Political Science

The growth of the population to the end of the century Jean Thompson, OPCS

A forecast of effective demand for housing in Great Britain in the 1970s A E Holmans, MHLG

No.2 1971

Social services manpower Dr S Rosenbaum, CSO

Trends in certificated sickness absence F E Whitehead, DHSS

Some aspects of model building in the social and environmental fields B Benjamin, CSC

Social indicators – health A J Culyer, R J Lavers and A Williams, University of York

No.3 1972

Social commentary: change in social conditions CSO

Statistics about immigrants: objectives, methods, sources and problems Professor C A Moser, CSO

Central manpower planning in Scottish secondary education A W Brodie, SED

Social malaise research: a study in Liverpool M Flynn, P Flynn and N Mellor, Liverpool City Planning Department

Crimes of violence against the person in England and Wales S Klein, HO

No.4 1973

Social commentary: certain aspects of the life cycle CSO

The elderly D C L Wroe, CSO

Subjective social indicators M Abrams, SSRC

Mental illness and the psychiatric services E R Bransby, DHSS

Cultural accounting A Peacock and C Godfrey, University of York

Road accidents and casualties in Great Britain J A Rushbrook, DOE

No.5 1974

Social commentary: men and women CSO

Social security: the European experiment E James and A Laurent, EC Commission

Time budgets B M Hedges, SCPR

Time budgets and models of urban activity patterns N Bullock, P Dickens, M Shapcott and P Steadman, Cambridge University of Architecture

Road traffic and the environment F D Sando and V Batty, DOE

No.6 1975

Social commentary: social class CSO

Areas of urban deprivation in Great Britain: an analysis of 1971 Census data S Holtermann, DOE

Note: Subjective social indicators M Abrams, SSRC

No.7 1976

Social commentary: social change in Britain 1970–1975 CSO

Crime in England and Wales Dr C Glennie, HO

Crime in Scotland Dr Bruce, SHHD

Subjective measures of quality of life in Britain: 1971 to 1975 J Hall, SSRC

No.8 1977

Social commentary: fifteen to twenty-five: a decade of transition CSO

The characteristics of low income households R Van Slooten and A G Coverdale, DHSS

No.9 1979

Housing tenure in England and Wales: the present situation and recent trends A E Holmans, DOE

Social forecasting in Lucas B R Jones, Lucas Industries

No.10 1980

Social commentary: changes in living standards since the 1950s CSO

Inner cities in England D Allnutt and A Gelardi, DOE

Scotland's schools D Wishart, SED

No.14 1984

Changes in the life-styles of the elderly 1959–1982 M Abrams

No.15 1985

British social attitudes R Jowell and C Airey, SCPR

No.16 1986

Income after retirement G C Fiegehen, DHSS

No.17 1987

Social Trends since World War II Professor A H Halsey, University of Oxford

Household formation and dissolution and housing tenure: a longitudinal perspective A E Holmans and S Nandy, DOE; A C Brown, OPCS

No.18 1988

Major epidemics of the 20th century: from coronary thrombosis to AIDS Sir Richard Doll, University of Oxford

No.19 1989

Recent trends in social attitudes L Brook, R Jowell and S Witherspoon, SCPR

No.20 1990

Social Trends, the next 20 years T Griffin, CSO

No.21 1991

The 1991 Census of Great Britain: plans for content and output B Mahon and D Pearce, OPCS

No.22 1992

Crime statistics: their use and misuse C Lewis, HO

No.24 1994

Characteristics of the bottom 20 per cent of the income distribution N Adkin, DSS

No.26 1996

The OPCS Longitudinal Study J Smith, OPCS

British Household Panel Survey J Gershuny, N Buck, O Coker, S Dex, J Ermish, S Jenkins and A McCulloch, ESRC Research Centre on Micro-social Change

No.27 1997

Projections: a look into the future T Harris, ONS

No.28 1998

French and British societies: a comparison P Lee and P Midy, INSEE and A Smith and C Summerfield, ONS

No.29 1999

Drugs in the United Kingdom – a jigsaw with missing pieces A Bradley and O Baker, Institute for the Study of Drug Dependence

No.30 2000

A hundred years of social change A H Halsey, Emeritus Fellow, Nuffield College, Oxford

No.31 2001

200 hundred years of the census of population M Nissel

No.32 2002

Children B Botting, ONS

No.33 2003

Investing in each other and the community: the role of social capital P Haezewindt, ONS

No.34 2004

Ageing and gender: diversity and change S Arber and J Ginn, University of Surrey

215

Index